CAMBODIAN PRIVATE INTERNATIONAL LAW

This book is the leading reference on Cambodian private international law in English.

The chapters systematically cover the whole of Cambodian private international law, including commercial matters, family law, succession, intellectual property, competition (antitrust), and environmental disputes.

The chapters do not merely cover the traditional conflict of law areas of jurisdiction, applicable law (choice of law) and enforcement. They also look into conflict of law questions arising in arbitration and assess Cambodia's involvement in the harmonisation of private international law globally and regionally within the Association of Southeast Asian Nations (ASEAN).

Similarly to the other volumes in the Studies in Private International Law – Asia series, this book presents the Cambodian conflict of laws through a combination of common and civil law analytical techniques and perspectives, providing readers worldwide with a more profound and comprehensive understanding of the subject.

Volume 14 in the series Studies in Private International Law - Asia

Studies in Private International Law – Asia

Editor: Anselmo Reyes
Advisory Editor: Paul Beaumont
Assistant Editors: Kazuaki Nishioka and Wilson Lui

Much has been written about private international law in the EU and the US. Less is known about the conflict of laws in Asia. Thus, little attention has been paid so far to the modernisation of private international law codes and rules that has been taking place over the last decade all over Asia. That trend continues. Now is the time to take stock of those reforms that have already taken place and suggest further improvements for the future.

Published under the celebrated series *Studies in Private International Law*, this monograph sub-series provides a forum for discussion and analysis of private international law in Asia. The series is not solely a survey of jurisdictions for practitioners. Comprising both in-depth thematic and country-specific studies, each volume considers the private international law of Asian countries from a variety of perspectives. An underlying assumption is that private international law in different jurisdictions follows broadly discernible patterns. Each volume in this sub-series highlights those patterns and discusses how rules in different Asian jurisdictions are either converging with, or diverging from, the patterns identified. Such an analytical framework will assist academics, judges, lawyers and legislators to envisage ways in which laws affecting cross-border relationships can be harmonised across jurisdictions and be made more responsive to the needs of citizens in Asia and elsewhere.

Volume 1: Recognition and Enforcement of Judgments in Civil and Commercial Matters
Edited by Anselmo Reyes

Volume 2: Indonesian Private International Law
Afifah Kusumadara

Volume 3: Chinese Private International Law
Edited by Xiaohong Liu and Zhengyi Zhang

Volume 4: Direct Jurisdiction: Asian Perspectives
Edited by Anselmo Reyes and Wilson Lui

Volume 5: Japanese Private International Law
Kazuaki Nishioka and Yuko Nishitani

Volume 6: Indian Private International Law
Stellina Jolly and Saloni Khanderia

Volume 7: Treatment of Foreign Law in Asia
Edited by Kazuaki Nishioka

Volume 8: Choice of Law and Recognition in Asian Family Law
Edited by Anselmo Reyes, Wilson Lui and Kazuaki Nishioka

Volume 9: Private International Law in East Asia: From Imitation to Innovation and Exportation
Edited by Olivier Gaillard and Krista Nadakavukaren Schefer

Volume 10: Overriding Mandatory Rules in International Commercial Disputes: Korean and Comparative Law
Min Kyung KIM

Volume 11: Privacy and Personal Data Protection Law in Asia
Edited by Adrian Mak, Ching Him Ho and Anselmo Reyes

Volume 12: Hong Kong Private International Law
Wilson Lui and Anselmo Reyes

Volume 13: Choice of Forum Clauses in Asia
Lemuel D Lopez

Volume 14: Cambodian Private International Law
Nobumichi Teramura

Cambodian Private International Law

Nobumichi Teramura

•HART•
OXFORD • LONDON • NEW YORK • NEW DELHI • SYDNEY

HART PUBLISHING

Bloomsbury Publishing Plc

Kemp House, Chawley Park, Cumnor Hill, Oxford, OX2 9PH, UK

1385 Broadway, New York, NY 10018, USA

Bloomsbury Publishing Ireland Limited, 29 Earlsfort Terrace, Dublin 2, D02 AY28, Ireland

First published in Great Britain 2025

1

A catalogue record for this book is available from the British Library.

A catalogue record for this book is available from the Library of Congress.

Library of Congress Control Number: 2025936931

ISBN: HB: 978-1-50995-404-9
ePDF: 978-1-50995-406-3
ePub: 978-1-50995-405-6

Typeset by Compuscript Ltd, Shannon
Printed and bound in Great Britain by CPI Group (UK) Ltd, Croydon CR0 4YY

FSC www.fsc.org MIX Paper | Supporting responsible forestry FSC® C013604

For product safety related questions contact productsafety@bloomsbury.com

To find out more about our authors and books visit www.hartpublishing.co.uk. Here you will find extracts, author information, details of forthcoming events and the option to sign up for our newsletters.

SERIES EDITORS' PREFACE

Dr Nobumichi Teramura's *Cambodian Private International Law* is the sixth work in the country sub-series of Hart's *Studies in Private International Law: Asia*. Previous volumes in the sub-series have covered Indonesian, Chinese, Japanese, Indian and Hong Kong private international law. Of those six volumes, this is possibly the most challenging.

As Dr Teramura summarises in Chapter 2, between 1976 and 1979, the Khmer Rouge 'abolished virtually all social systems and institutions existing under previous Cambodian regimes, including the judicial courts'. The Khmer Rouge were ousted in 1979 by a combination of Vietnamese troops and the Vietnamese-backed Cambodian rebel army. Negotiations among various stakeholders then took place. But the negotiations only culminated in 1991 with the Paris Peace Agreements and the departure of the Vietnamese from Cambodia. A Constituent Assembly having been established in 1993, a National Programme to Rehabilitate and Develop Cambodia was implemented in the following year to restore (among other matters) the Cambodian legal and judicial systems. In the circumstances, one might ask whether it is too early to speak of, much less write about, a coherent body of Cambodian private international law (PIL).

Dr Teramura answers that question resoundingly in the affirmative. The restoration of the rule of law in Cambodia and the establishment of a transparent judicial system are urgent commitments of the present Cambodian government. If Cambodia is to attract much needed foreign direct investment (FDI), it needs to establish PIL codes quickly. There is no luxury of time. Unfortunately, much of the pre-existing domestic legal expertise was eradicated by the Khmer Rouge and the present government has had to seek foreign technical assistance for the daunting task of promulgating new legislation.

Among the international contributors to the revitalisation of Cambodia laws, Dr Teramura has focused on the help provided by the Japan International Cooperation Agency (JICA) in the drafting of key principles of Cambodian PIL, especially as found in the 2007 Civil Code and the 2006 Code of Civil Procedure, both of which "were perceived by the Cambodian government as crucial for building the foundation of a sustainable market economy". The two Codes borrow heavily from Japanese law, albeit always bearing Cambodian usages, customs and culture firmly in mind. Dr Teramura is of the view that guidance on the development of Cambodia's PIL may be obtained by examining Japanese legal practice in like cases. However, the exercise of referring to Japanese law must be conducted with care and sensitivity to Cambodian circumstances. It cannot be assumed that Japanese legal principles may readily be imported into Cambodia, with or without adaptation. Time and time again throughout this book, while noting how Japanese courts deal with similar provisions in the Japanese codes, Dr Teramura warns that certain practices may not be appropriate for Cambodia despite its identical statutory provisions. He explains why in detail, including from time to time pointing out difficulties and obscurities within the approach followed in Japan.

This book is therefore at heart a study in the modern-day reception of the civil law. What Cambodia is experiencing now echoes what many states all over the world have had, at one time or other in their histories, to wrestle with, namely, the question of how much of Roman, French, German, English or some other body of law to adopt in order to establish workable legal and judicial infrastructures for the betterment of their citizenry quickly. The issues with which this book grapples are important, not just for the Cambodian context, but for developing countries in Asia and elsewhere.

The Editors
Kyoto
1 January 2025

PREFACE AND ACKNOWLEDGEMENTS

I acknowledge support from the following institutions and individuals for this book project.

First and foremost, I would like to thank Justice Anselmo Reyes (Singapore International Commercial Court) for inviting me to contribute this volume to the 'Studies in Private International Law – Asia' series. In 2019, Justice Reyes introduced me to Mr BUN Youdy, the founding partner of Bun & Associates in Phnom Penh, Cambodia. This unexpected meeting opened the door for me to explore the vibrant legal scene in Cambodia. In 2020, Mr Bun kindly gave me an opportunity to work at his firm and the National Commercial Arbitration Centre (NCAC) in Phnom Penh which was in the middle of preparing the 2021 NCAC Arbitration Rules. I was inspired by conversation and discussion with senior partners at Bun & Associates, such as Mr BUN, Dr PHIN Sovath and Dr Antoine Fontaine, as well as my colleagues at Bun & Associates and the NCAC – Ms NGORN Rothna, Mr VANN Yuvaktep, Ms LY Mengmely, Ms SENG Puthkarona, Mr SENG Chheanghour and Mr CHHUON Watanak and Ms Ayako Tamiya, to name some. Ms Tamiya introduced me to Japanese legal experts based in Phnom Penh who had worked in the Ministry of Justice of Cambodia and continued helping the Ministry on various capacities – Mr Masao Shimanuki (Tsurugi Solution), Mr Sadao Matsubara (HBS Law) and Mr Issei Sakano (Ministry of Justice of Cambodia). In particular, Mr Sakano helped me interview legal experts at the office of the Japan International Cooperation Agency (JICA) in the Ministry of Justice of Cambodia. Mr Sakano also commented on early drafts of some chapters in this volume, taking advantage of his profound experience in and knowledge of the justice ministry. Those local experts' insights on Cambodian law built the foundation of this book on Cambodian Private International Law, although responsibility for any errors that remain is solely my own.

I am also indebted to Professor Shoichi Hayashi of Doshisha Law School in Kyoto, Japan. Professor Hayashi invited me to Doshisha Law School as a collaborative researcher in June–July 2024, which enabled me to access materials held at Doshisha's library. Institute of Asian Studies (IAS) at Universiti Brunei Darussalam (UBD) then provided me with research leave to visit the library and other research institutes in Japan. The Centre for Asian and Pacific Law within the University of Sydney (CAPLUS) and Professor Luke Nottage (Sydney Law School) enabled me to use their research facilities. Dr Nancy Alas (Sophia University, Japan) helped me obtain copies of various materials kept in university libraries in Japan. I would also like to thank the Hart staff for preparing this volume for press.

Many institutes and people have supported and counselled me during this book project. I hope that I would be forgiven for not naming all of them.

Finally, as always, I would like to thank my parents, Ginichiro and Tomoko Teramura, for their unwavering love and understanding.

Bandar Seri Begawan, Brunei Darussalam — Nobumichi Teramura
December 2024

* Please note that versions of the following chapters of this book are included in other volumes of the 'Studies in Private International Law – Asia' series, with permissions from Hart Publishing.

- Chapter 2: 'Treatment of Foreign Law' as Nobumichi Teramura, 'Treatment of Foreign Law in Cambodia' in Kazuaki Nishioka (ed), *Treatment of Foreign Law in Asia* (Oxford, Hart Publishing 2023) 171–91.
- Chapter 4: 'Direct Jurisdiction' as Nobumichi Teramura, 'Cambodia' in Anselmo Reyes and Wilson Lui (eds), *Direct Jurisdiction: Asian Perspectives* (Oxford, Hart Publishing, 2021) 201–19.
- Chapter 8: 'Family Law' as Nobumichi Teramura, 'Cambodia' in Anselmo Reyes, Wilson Lui and Kazuaki Nishioka (eds), *Choice of Law and Recognition in Asian Family Law* (Oxford, Hart Publishing, 2023) 219–40. (A version of Section III of the latter is included in Chapter 10: 'Recognition and Enforcement' as Section II.C.iv).

** Please also note that this volume relies on the translations of the Act on General Rules for Application of Laws (Act No 78 of 2006; AGRAL) of Japan available at the Japanese Law Translation website run by Japan's Justice Ministry (https://www.japaneselawtranslation.go.jp/en/laws/view/3783/en) and the Private International Law Association of Japan's website (http://www.pilaj.jp/text/tsusokuho_e.html).

*** English translations of the Cambodian Constitution and other statutes tend to treat the word 'Khmer' as synonymous with 'Cambodian'. However, not all Cambodian nationals are of Khmer ethnicity and not all Khmers are Cambodian nationals. Accordingly, in this book, I have used the expression 'Cambodian' to denote a citizen of Cambodia and have avoided using the word 'Khmer' for that purpose.

TABLE OF CONTENTS

PART II
JURISDICTION

PART III
CHOICE OF LAW

LIST OF ABBREVIATIONS

ABLI	Asian Business Law Institute
ADB	Asian Development Bank
ADR	Alternative Dispute Resolution
AGRAL	Act on General Rules for Application of Laws (of Japan)
ALA	ASEAN Law Association
ALAFW	Act on the Law Applicable to the Form of Wills (of Japan)
APOC	Anglo-Persian Oil Company
ASEAN	Association of Southeast Asian Nations
AsianLII	Asian Legal Information Institute
AustLII	Australasian Legal Information Institute
BEA	Bills of Exchange Act (of Japan)
BIT	Bilateral investment treaty
CACJ	Council of ASEAN Chief Justices
CC	(2007) Civil Code (of Cambodia)
CCC	Competition Commission of Cambodia
CCCC	Counter Counterfeit Committee of Cambodia
CCF	Consumer Protection Competition and Fraud Repression (of Cambodia)
CCP	(2006) Code of Civil Procedure (of Cambodia)
CDC	Council for the Development of Cambodia
CGMC	Commercial Gambling Management Commission (of Cambodia)
CHA	Cheques Act (of Japan)
CIS	Commonwealth of Independent States
CISG	United Nations Convention on Contracts for the International Sale of Goods
CLC Convention	International Convention on Civil Liability for Oil Pollution Damage of 1969

CPK	Communist Party of Kampuchea
DK	Democratic Kampuchea
FDI	Foreign direct investment
FTA	Free trade agreement
HCCH	Hague Conference on Private International Law
IAEA	International Atomic Energy Agency
ICA	International commercial arbitration
ICAA	Inter-country Adoption Administration
ICC	International Chamber of Commerce
ICD	International Cooperation Department (of JICA)
ICSID	International Centre for Settlement of Investment Disputes
IFC	International Finance Corporation
ILO	International Labour Organisation
IMO	International Maritime Organisation
IP	Intellectual property
ISDS	Investor-state dispute settlement
JCAA	Japan Commercial Arbitration Association
JICA	Japan International Cooperation Agency
JIDRC	Japan International Dispute Resolution Centre
LCP	Law on Consumer Protection (of Cambodia)
LMQSPGS	Law on Management of Quality and Safety of Products, Goods and Services
LNIPT	Law on Negotiable Instruments and Payment Transactions
LMOG	Law on Management of Commercial Gaming
LOC	Law on the Organisation of the Courts
MIH	Ministry of Industry and Handicraft (of Cambodia)
MLMUPC	Ministry of Land Management, Urban Planning and Construction (of Cambodia)
MOC	Ministry of Commerce (of Cambodia)
MOH	Ministry of Health (of Cambodia)
MOJ	Ministry of Justice (of Cambodia)

MOJJ	Ministry of Justice of Japan
MOSVY	Ministry of Social Affairs, Veterans and Youth Rehabilitation (of Cambodia)
NCAC	National Commercial Arbitration Centre
NCPC	National Consumer Protection Committee
NIOC	National Iranian Oil Company
NUM	National University of Management
OAS	Organisation of American States
ODA	Official development assistance
PIL	Private international law
PRK	People's Republic of Kampuchea
RSJP	Royal School for Judges and Prosecutors
RULE	Royal University of Law and Economics
SIAC	Singapore International Arbitration Centre
SIArb	Singapore Institute of Arbitrators
SOC	State of Cambodia
TIPs	Treaty with investment provisions
UCP	Uniform Customs and Practice for Documentary Credits
UN	United Nations
UNCITRAL	United Nations Commission on International Trade Law
UNIDROIT	International Institute for the Unification of Private International Law
UNTAC	United Nations Transitional Authority in Cambodia
WIPO	World Intellectual Property Organisation

LIST OF CASES

Cambodia

Japan

Other Jurisdictions

ICSID Decisions

LIST OF STATUTES AND LEGISLATIVE INSTRUMENTS

Cambodia

Japan

LIST OF INTERNATIONAL LEGAL INSTRUMENTS

1

Introduction

Private international law, also called conflict of laws, is a set of principles, rules and approaches that indicate how a case or dispute involving a foreign element should be handled. Globalisation has enhanced human beings' cross-border activities through migration, commerce and communication. Legal relationships have thus been increasingly going beyond national and jurisdictional borders, culminating in cross-border or multi-jurisdictional cases and disputes. For instance, a case before a court in Cambodia might involve a person living in Australia, or it might relate to an incident in China or Japan. The legal action in Cambodia might parallel an action in Australia or might be suspended by a judgment issued by a court in China. In dealing with multi-jurisdictional cases like these, the law in common law and civil law jurisdictions typically classify them into one or more of the following three categories.

- **Jurisdiction** – whether the local court (or forum) has the authority to adjudicate the case based on the law, the contract or any other ground at issue.
- **Choice of law** – where the forum court has the jurisdiction to hear the case and determines to exercise the authority, whether the court decides the dispute in accordance with the law of the forum (*lex fori*), or the law of the other state or jurisdiction. Which law then is to be the 'law of the cause (*lex causae*)', 'applicable law' or 'governing law' that disposes of the case, and how does the court in the forum select one or the other? This question will be at stake where the application of the forum law is likely to bring about a different result to that of the foreign law, i.e., where there is a conflict between the forum law and the foreign law – a conflict of laws.
- **Recognition and enforcement of foreign judgments** – where a court in the other state or jurisdiction has already issued a judgment on the case, whether the judgment can be recognised or enforced in the forum.

Cambodian private international law is also concerned with these issues of jurisdiction, choice of law and the recognition and enforcement of foreign judgments. However, the segments of the law that deal with these matters have developed at different paces. For instance, the courts in Cambodia may determine their jurisdiction over international cases by relying on the rules on domestic jurisdiction in the Code of Civil Procedure of Cambodia (CCP) because the Code does not yet contain rules on international jurisdiction, unlike other civil law countries such as Japan. Moreover, Cambodian courts may face challenges in deciding the law governing a cross-border dispute because the law of Cambodia does not have any special statutory body of law dealing specifically with the conflict of laws. There are only some choice of law rules in several independent statutes that deal with specific conflict of laws issues, such as the Civil Code (CC), the Marriage and Family Law, and the

Arbitration Law. The courts will likely be able to decide on the recognition and enforcement of foreign judgments under Article 199 of the CCP. Nevertheless, they have never recognised or enforced judgments issued abroad due to their adherence to the doctrine of strict reciprocity, although such doctrine has already been relinquished in many civil law countries. Thus, Cambodian private international law still has gaps that may prevent the courts from dealing with cross-border disputes efficiently and effectively.

This book aims to fill the gaps, following the methodology proposed by the late Professor Jörg Menzel, a past senior legal and legislative adviser to the Senate of the Kingdom of Cambodia, who played a key role in various international legal technical assistance projects.[1] He acknowledged the lack of a comprehensive framework in Cambodian private international law. Raising the fact that the CC and CCP were influenced by Japanese legal concepts thanks to Japan's legal technical assistance projects,[2] he submitted that 'it might be appropriate to draft legislation largely inspired by Japanese private international law and apply those principles as much as appropriate for the interim period'.[3]

The interim period continues because the country still does not have a comprehensive legal framework that addresses conflict of laws issues, and research on Cambodian private international law is still in its infancy. This book considers how to address the gaps in Cambodian private international law, and takes into account relevant Japanese legal principles, including those imported through foreign donor projects by the Japan International Cooperation Agency (JICA). The discussion is mostly based on English and Japanese literature on Cambodian law and society as a result of the author's limited proficiency in the Khmer language and of the significant volume of Japanese language materials on Cambodian law produced through and related to JICA's legal technical assistance projects.[4] This research approach to Cambodian private international law is experimental and will inevitably attract criticisms from comparative law scholars who might emphasise the significance of the deep knowledge of local language in investigating (any) legal systems.[5] However, perfectionism is unlikely to help ventures into areas of research that have so far not attracted much attention from commentators. The alternative would be to wait until someone who is fluent in English, Khmer and Japanese undertakes research on Cambodian private international law.

This book is divided into five parts.

Part I consists of two chapters and offers an overview of the structure and basic concepts of private international law in the Cambodian legal framework. Chapter 2 considers

[1] https://tu-dresden.de/zis/die-einrichtung/news/news_article-2016-04-22-0137086215?set_language=de (accessed 10 December 2024).

[2] On Japan's legal technical assistant projects in Cambodia, Laos and Vietnam, see generally N Teramura, 'JICA's Legal Technical Assistance Projects in Vietnam, Cambodia and Laos since the 1990s' in LC Kelly and G Sasges (eds), *Vietnam Over the Long Twentieth Century* (Singapore, Springer, 2024) 185ff; N Teramura, 'Japan as a Source of Legal Ideas: A View from the Mekong Subregion of ASEAN' (2021) 13 *New Voices in Japanese Studies* 19.

[3] J Menzel, 'Cambodian Law: Some Comparative and International Perspectives' in H Peng, K Phallack and J Menzel (eds), *Introduction to Cambodian Law* (Phnom Penh, Konrad-Adenauer-Stiftung Cambodia, 2012) 490–91.

[4] See Teramura, '*Japan as a Source of Legal Ideas: A View from the Mekong Subregion of ASEAN*' 28.

[5] For example, see, Ł Biel, '*Linguistic Approaches*' in M Siems and PJ Yap (eds), *The Cambridge Handbook of Comparative Law* (Cambridge, Cambridge University Press, 2024) 91ff; S Skytioti, 'Comparative Law and Language with Reference to Case Law' (2021) 66 *Studies in Logic, Grammar and Rhetoric* 105; B Pozzo, 'Comparative Law and Language' in M Bussani and U Mattei (eds), *The Cambridge Companion to Comparative Law* (Cambridge, Cambridge University Press, 2012) 88ff; O Brand, 'Language as a Barrier to Comparative Law' in F Olsen, A Lorz and D Stein (eds), *Translation Issues in Language and Law* (Cham, Springer, 2009) 18ff.

Cambodian private international law's historical background, sources and foundational principles. The chapter delves into the development of Cambodian private law in the pre-colonisation period, the French colonisation period, the post-colonisation period, the Khmer Rouge period and the Post Pol Pot period, discussing why and how Cambodian private law has been deeply influenced by Japanese civil law since the 1990s. It also reviews the sources of Cambodian law. It examines the (potential) basic conflict of laws methods, doctrines and principles under Cambodian law comprehensively, such as characterisation, incidental questions, *depeçage*, *renvoi* and transmission, among others. Chapter 3 considers the treatment of foreign law. It examines how Cambodian judicial authorities ascertain and interpret foreign law and how they deal with unascertainable foreign law, pondering what remedies are available for the parties to cope with the courts' erroneous application of choice of law rules and foreign law. It also discusses how non-judicial authorities, such as administrative bodies and arbitral tribunals, treat foreign law in Cambodia. Whether and how Cambodian judicial and non-judicial institutions are supportive of providing foreign parties with information on Cambodian law is also considered in this chapter.

Part II of the book concentrates on the international jurisdiction of Cambodian courts in cross-border civil and commercial disputes. As the law of Cambodia does not have explicit rules on the international jurisdiction of Cambodian courts, Chapter 4 proposes that the courts presuppose their international jurisdiction from rules on domestic jurisdiction in the CCP of Cambodia. On the basis of that proposal, the chapter delineates the rules on international jurisdiction in *personam*, international jurisdiction in *rem* (with special focus on shipping claims) and immunities from international jurisdiction in civil and commercial matters.

Part III of the book consists of five chapters and focuses on the principles of choice of law to decide the law governing contractual and non-contractual matters. It considers those choice of law principles by referring to corresponding or relevant provisions in the Act on General Rules for Application of Laws of Japan (AGRAL)[6] due to Cambodian law's lack of clear and comprehensive codification of the conflict of laws rules on cross-border (non-)contractual matters. It does so, of course, bearing in mind the divergences between Cambodian and Japanese legal systems and societies, as well as ambiguities and uncertainties in Japanese private international law.

Chapter 5 discusses how Cambodian courts determine the law governing contractual disputes. Although Article 3 of the CC may serve as a basis for guaranteeing parties with the application of party autonomy, Cambodian law needs more specific choice of law rules on contractual obligations. For instance, the law does not elaborate on how the court in Cambodia should deal with situations in which parties have failed to designate the law governing their contract either explicitly or implicitly. In this type of situation, the court may take advantage of Article 8 of the AGRAL (among other provisions) to identify the law that has the closest connection with that contract. The chapter also considers limits to the choice of proper law and special choice of law rules for specific contracts – e.g., consumer, employment, insurance and sales contracts – based on relevant provisions in Cambodian law and Japanese private international law where applicable.

[6] (Act No 78 of 21 June 2006).

Chapter 6 then offers the readers an insight into how the courts in Cambodia may fill the significant gap in the choice of law for non-contractual obligations, with a focus on torts, because Cambodian law does not have clear rules in this area of law. It draws from Articles 17-22 of the AGRAL, setting out choice of law rules for cross-border torts, including specific torts, such as product liability, defamation, private nuisance, wrongful interference with goods and environmental damage and pollution. It also examines the mechanism of deciphering the law applicable to *negotiorum gestio* and unjust enrichment based on the AGRAL under Cambodian law.

Chapter 7 addresses the need for codification of the rules on choice of law for property issues. It discusses the ways in which Cambodian courts determine the applicable laws of tangible properties and intellectual properties (IPs), grounded upon relevant provisions in the AGRAL and applicable international conventions. It delineates the principles of the Cambodian private international law for issues pertaining to both movable and immovable properties, including expropriation and succession. It also explores the possible use of the international conventions that Cambodia ratified for IP protection, including but not limited to the Paris Convention for the Protection of Industrial Property (the Paris Convention)[7] and the Berne Convention for the Protection of Literary and Artistic Works (Berne, 1886; the Berne Convention),[8] to develop and supplement Cambodian choice of law rules for the protection of copyrights and registered rights (e.g., patents and trademarks).

Choice of law issues arising from family affairs are analysed in Chapter 8. Unlike other areas of Cambodian private international law, one may find the codification of choice of law rules for international marriage and divorce in the Marriage and Family Law of Cambodia. There are indeed some gaps in the codification (for instance, the presumption of death), but they may be covered by (again) invoking relevant Japanese legal principles. However, Cambodian law largely remains silent on choice of law rules for the protection of children's rights, even though Cambodia has the constitutional obligation to protect such rights as per the United Nations Convention on the Rights of the Child (New York, 1989; the 1989 Convention on the Rights of the Child).[9] There are several Hague Conventions for child protection. However, the only Hague Conference on Private International Law (HCCH) instrument that the country has adopted is the Convention of 29 May 1993 on Protection of Children and Co-operation in Respect of Intercountry Adoption (1993 Hague Adoption Convention). Thus, this chapter explores the possible use of relevant provisions in the AGRAL, including the application of the Convention of 2 October 1973 on the Law Applicable to Maintenance Obligations (1973 Hague Maintenance Convention) via those provisions, to harness the gap in Cambodian private international law for family matters.

The final chapter of Part III – Chapter 9 – focuses on the law of corporations, insolvency, antitrust and unfair competition. The chapter analyses the diverging rules governing

[7] World Intellectual Property Organization (WIPO), 'Contracting Parties: Paris Convention (Total Members: 180)' (n.d.), available at www.wipo.int/wipolex/en/treaties/ShowResults?search_what=C&treaty_id=2 (accessed 10 December 2024).

[8] WIPO, 'Cambodia Joins Berne Convention', *News*, 3 April 2023, available at www.wipo.int/about-wipo/en/dg_tang/news/2021/news_0069.html (accessed 10 December 2024).

[9] Constitution of Cambodia, Art 48.

choice of law issues arising from cross-border corporate activities. It first scrutinises whether the 'real seat' theory or the 'incorporation' theory shall determine the law regulating internal corporate affairs. Critically evaluating these theories, the chapter suggests that the former is incompatible with the company law of Cambodia. It therefore suggests that the law of the place of the company's incorporation governs internal corporate affairs, such as the validity of incorporation, the capacity and powers of the company, members' rights and liabilities and the company's internal management. The chapter also investigates the application of Cambodia's Law on Insolvency to cross-border insolvency proceedings, following the *lex concursus* rule. It further attempts to delineate the principles of private international law for the issues of antitrust and unfair competition.

Part IV discusses the recognition and enforcement of foreign judgments in Cambodia. Chapter 10 first considers the recognition and enforcement of foreign judgments under the Agreement on Mutual Judicial Assistance in Civil Matters between the Kingdom of Cambodia and the Socialist Republic of Vietnam (Cambodia–Vietnam Judicial Assistance Treaty) of 2013[10] and the International Convention on Civil Liability for Oil Pollution Damage of 1969 (Brussels, 29 November 1969; the CLC Convention) by the International Maritime Organisation.[11] Confirming the limited scope of application of these international frameworks, the chapter focuses on analysing the principles of judgment recognition and enforcement in the CCP, especially Article 199 of the CCP based on Article 118 of Japan's Code of Civil Procedure (Act No 109 of 26 June 1996). The chapter draws parallels between these two Articles for the sake of utilising relevant Japanese legal principles to deal with Cambodia's lack of experience in the recognition and enforcement of foreign judgments; the courts in Cambodia have reportedly never recognised or enforced foreign judgments due to their strict interpretation of the principle of reciprocity.[12] The chapter therefore also examines whether it is appropriate for the courts to maintain the strict interpretation of reciprocity for the time being.

Part V addresses private international law issues in international arbitration in Cambodia. Chapter 11 considers issues of jurisdiction, choice of law and the recognition and enforcement of arbitral awards in international commercial arbitration and international investment arbitration. The chapter first provides an overview of the legal framework of international commercial arbitration in Cambodia. It reviews various topics on arbitral proceedings, such as the role of courts, the form and scope of arbitration agreements and arbitrability, based on the principles of arbitration derived from the Law on Commercial Arbitration (Arbitration Law) modelling after the 1985 UNCITRAL Model Law on International Commercial Arbitration[13] and the Convention on the

[10] Cambodia ratified the Judicial Assistance Treaty by establishing the Law Approving the Agreement on Mutual Judicial Assistance in Civil Matters between the Kingdom of Cambodia and the Socialist Republic of Vietnam in 2014: Y Bun, 'Country Report: Cambodia' in A Chong (ed), *Recognition and Enforcement of Foreign Judgments in Asia* (Singapore, Asian Business Law Institute, 2017) 41.

[11] https://treaties.un.org/pages/showDetails.aspx?objid=08000002801083db (accessed 10 December 2024).

[12] N Teramura, 'Recognition and Enforcement of Chinese Judgments in Cambodia: Uncertain Foundations of the Rigid Reciprocity Standard in Cambodian Law' in P Sooksripaisarnkit and SR Garimella (eds), *Legal Challenges of China's One Belt One Road Initiative: Private International Law Considerations* (Abingdon, Routledge, 2025) [forthcoming]; E Papp and N Teramura, 'Enforcing Singapore Judgments in Cambodia: Reciprocity under the Loupe' (2025) *Asian Journal of International Law*, First View, 1.

[13] UNCITRAL, 'Status: UNCITRAL Model Law on International Commercial Arbitration (1985), with amendments as adopted in 2006' (n.d.), available at https://uncitral.un.org/en/texts/arbitration/modellaw/

Recognition and Enforcement of Foreign Arbitral Awards (New York Convention).[14] It also investigates arbitration institutions and organisations operating in Cambodia, such as the National Commercial Arbitration Centre (NCAC) and the Arbitration Council. Building upon the discussion on the foundational aspects of arbitration in Cambodia, the chapter examines Cambodia's rules on jurisdiction, choice of law and award recognition and enforcement in international commercial arbitration. It further considers private international law issues in the context of investment arbitration in light of the Convention on the Settlement of Investment Disputes between States and Nationals of Other States (Washington, 18 March 1965; the ICSID Convention) and the United Nations Commission on International Trade Law (UNCITRAL) Arbitration Rules (2021), as these are key investment arbitration frameworks for Cambodia.

Finally, Chapter 12 scrutinises whether Cambodia is actively involved in the works of international organisations, such as the HCCH, UNCITRAL and the International Institute for the Unification of Private Law (UNIDROIT), for the global and regional harmonisation of private international law. The chapter observes that Cambodia apparently has little interest in such works at present and proposes that the country change its attitude for the sound development of Cambodian private international law.

commercial_arbitration/status (accessed 10 December 2024). Note, however, that the Arbitration Law adopted the Model Law without the 2006 amendments: RJW Haw and BJ Slott, 'Cambodia' in MJ Moser and J Choong (eds), *Asia Arbitration Handbook* (Oxford, Oxford University Press, 2011) 536.

[14] UNCITRAL, 'Status: Convention on the Recognition and Enforcement of Foreign Arbitral Awards (New York, 1958)' (n.d.), available at https://uncitral.un.org/en/texts/arbitration/conventions/foreign_arbitral_awards/status2 (accessed 10 December 2024).

PART I

Foundations of Cambodian Private International Law

2

Status of Private International Law in Cambodia and Preliminary Matters

I. Introduction

Private international law (PIL) is still in a state of early development in Cambodia.[1] However, this does not imply a lack of interest in that body of law among Cambodian lawyers and government officials. In fact, they have been attracted to diverse topics of PIL for many years, albeit sporadically. For instance, Cambodian lawyers attempted to elaborate on choice of law rules when they drafted the 2007 Civil Code (CC) with Japanese law scholars working for the Japan International Cooperation Agency (JICA).[2] Their efforts did not result in the establishment of new PIL statutes. However, upward trends in international business transactions in recent years have been generating the interest of Cambodian lawyers in cross-border dispute resolution mechanisms,[3] which typically require knowledge of PIL.[4] Moreover, responding to international criticisms of the Cambodian industry of child adoption,[5] the government of the Kingdom ratified in 2007 the Convention of 29 May 1993 on Protection of Children and Co-operation in Respect of Intercountry Adoption (1993 Hague Adoption Convention),

[1] N Teramura, 'Cambodia' in K Nishioka (ed), *Treatment of Foreign Law in Asia* (Oxford, Hart Publishing, 2023); N Teramura, 'Cambodia' in A Reyes and W Lui (eds), *Direct Jurisdiction: Asian Perspectives* (Oxford, Hart Publishing, 2021).

[2] Industrial Development and Public Policy Department at JICA, *Legal Technical Assistance for Cambodia: The History and Methodology of the Assistance of JICA in Drafting the Civil Code and the Civil Procedure Code [in Japanese]* (2012) 9–11 (noting that the Cambodian lawyers ultimately gave up drafting new choice of law rules due to time constraints).

[3] Post Staff, 'Cambodia Pushes Arbitration as an Alternative Commercial Dispute Resolution Mechanism', *The Phonm Penh Post*, 19 November 2019, available at www.phnompenhpost.com/post-focus/cambodia-pushes-arbitration-alternative-commercial-dispute-resolution-mechanism (accessed 10 December 2024); V Dara, 'NCAC and Singapore's SIAC to Promote International Arbitration', *The Phnom Penh Post*, 24 March 2022, available at www.phnompenhpost.com/national/ncac-and-singapores-siac-promote-international-arbitration (accessed 10 December 2024).

[4] See generally N Blackaby, C Partasides and A Redfern, *Redfern and Hunter on International Arbitration*, 7th edn (Oxford, Oxford University Press, 2022); GB Born, *International Commercial Arbitration*, 3rd edn (Alphen aan den Rijn, Wolters Kluwer, 2020).

[5] The Sydney Morning Herald Staff Writer, 'Babies for Sale: No Warranty', *The Sydney Morning Herald*, 16 December 2003, available at www.smh.com.au/national/babies-for-sale-no-warranty-20031216-gdhzp5.html; S Corbett, 'Where Do Babies Come From?', *The New York Times Magazine*, 16 June 2002, available at www.nytimes.com/2002/06/16/magazine/where-do-babies-come-from.html (accessed 10 December 2024); DM Smolin, 'Child Laundering: How the Intercountry Adoption System Legitimizes and Incentivizes the Practices of Buying, Trafficking, Kidnapping, and Stealing Children' (2006) 52 *The Wayne Law Review* 113.

which was prepared by the Hague Conference on Private International Law (HCCH).[6] The government has also adopted PIL instruments issued by other international institutions, such as the United Nations Commission on International Trade Law (UNCITRAL) and the International Institute for the Unification of Private International Law (UNIDROIT),[7] although the number of such instruments is not outstanding. Overall, PIL has long been discussed for Cambodian law development and reform.

Despite the prolonged debate among Cambodian legal experts, literature on the status and fundamental principles of Cambodian PIL is scanty.[8] This is surprising given the significant number of multinational companies that operate in Cambodia and the solid post-COVID rebound of foreign direct investment (FDI") flowing into the country.[9] This chapter therefore aims to examine the basic concepts of Cambodian PIL, considering the evolution of PIL in the country. It proceeds as follows. Section II surveys the history of Cambodian PIL since the pre-Khmer Rouge period. Section III studies the sources of PIL included in various individual legislation and regulations, as well as in international treaties. Section IV discusses preliminary matters to be considered in dealing with PIL issues: characterisation, incidental questions, *depeçage*, renvoi and transmission. Section V then considers the roles and implications of connecting factors under the Cambodian conflict of laws rules. Section VI discusses the distinction between procedure and substance in Cambodian PIL. Section VII explores debates surrounding other significant PIL notions, such as mandatory rules, public policy and law evasions. Section VIII concludes the chapter.

II. History of Cambodian Private International Law

One may divide the legal history of Cambodia into three phases – (1) the customary law period, (2) the French law period and (3) the mixed law period. This section explores

[6] HCCH, 'Status Table: Convention of 29 May 1993 on Protection of Children and Co-operation in Respect of Intercountry Adoption' (2024), available at www.hcch.net/en/instruments/conventions/status-table/?cid=69 (accessed 10 December 2024); AE Kubo, 'Cambodia to Lift Ban on International Adoptions: The Resumption of Intercountry Adoptions Comes Four Years after Reports of Child Abuse and Trafficking', *The Diplomat*, 10 December 2013, available at https://thediplomat.com/2013/12/cambodia-to-lift-ban-on-international-adoptions/ (accessed 10 December 2024).

[7] Such international legal instruments include the 1958 Convention on the Recognition and Enforcement of Foreign Arbitral Awards (New York Convention) and the 1995 UNIDROIT Convention on Stolen or Illegally Exported Cultural Objects. Cambodia ratified the former in 1960 and the latter in 1995: UNCITRAL, 'Status: Convention on the Recognition and Enforcement of Foreign Arbitral Awards (New York, 1958)' (n.d.), available at https://uncitral.un.org/en/texts/arbitration/conventions/foreign_arbitral_awards/status2 (accessed 10 December 2024); UNIDROIT, 'UNIDROIT Convention on Stolen or Illegally Exported Culutural Objects (Rome, 1995) – Status' (2021), available at www.unidroit.org/instruments/cultural-property/1995-convention/status/# (accessed 10 December 2024).

[8] In fact, there is a paucity of literature addressing Cambodian PIL in general: Teramura, 'Cambodia' in K Nishioka (ed), *Treatment of Foreign Law in Asia*. See also Chapter 3 in this volume.

[9] H Phanet, 'Cambodia-US Trade Rises 32%', *The Phnom Penh Post*, 10 January 2022, available at www.phnompenhpost.com/business/cambodia-us-trade-rises-32 (accessed 10 December 2024); H Phanet, 'Trade with Japan Extends Growth in 2021', *The Phnom Penh Post*, 13 January 2022, available at www.phnompenhpost.com/business/trade-japan-extends-growth-2021 (accessed 10 December 2024); H Pisei, 'South Korea Trade Nearly $870M in Jan-Nov', *The Phnom Penh Post*, 20 December 2021, available at www.phnompenhpost.com/business/south-korea-trade-nearly-870m-jan-nov (accessed 10 December 2024).

these phases of Cambodian legal development, considering the evolution of PIL in each period.

Before the French colonisation of the nineteenth and twentieth centuries, the Cambodian legal system consisted largely of unwritten local customs and social norms.[10] The legal history of this pre-colonisation era may therefore be called the customary law period. The codification of Cambodian laws reportedly started in 1336,[11] adopting a simplified version of the *Dharmaśāstra* – Sanskrit treatises on law and conduct.[12] From the late 16th to 17th centuries, the Khmer Kingdom reportedly established a law code compiling 12 volumes of criminal law, judge's law and other laws.[13] In the 17th to 19th centuries, about 24 codified laws (*Les codes cambodgiens*) were allegedly effective in Cambodia, but they were collections of the past decisions of kings and judges and, therefore, somewhat noncomprehensive and obscure.[14] Accordingly, day-to-day transactions and other affairs were primarily governed by consensus-based customary rules,[15] possibly under the influence of Cambodia's dominant neighbours – the Thai and Vietnamese kingdoms.[16] No discernible materials suggest what PIL principles (if any) were practised during the time.

Next, the French law period commenced when King Norodom signed an agreement with France to turn his Kingdom into a French protectorate in 1863.[17] During this age of French colonisation, Cambodia developed modern statutory laws that closely followed the French civil law system.[18] For instance, the governments of the French protectorate and the Cambodian Kingdom promulgated the 1920 Civil and Civil Procedure Code (*Code civil et de procédure civile*) based on French law. The 1920 Code arguably took into account manners and customs of Cambodia,[19] but the drafting committee for the Code (*la Commission chargé de l'élaboration du Code civil*) consisted of French technocrats (forming a majority) and Cambodian government officers (forming a minority) who were fluent in

[10] K Phallack, 'Overview of the Cambodian Legal and Judicial System and Recent Efforts at Legal and Judicial Reform' in H Peng, K Phallack and J Menzel (eds), *Introduction to Cambodian Law* (Phnom Penh, Konrad-Adenauer-Stiftung Cambodia, 2012) 7; H Peng, 'The Modern Era of Cambodian Constitutionalism: Constitutional Analysis of Historical and Contemporary Development' in H Peng, K Phallack and J Menzel (eds), *Introduction to Cambodian Law* (Phnom Penh, Konrad-Adenauer-Stiftung Cambodia, 2012) 32.

[11] Council of ASEAN Chief Justices, 'Cambodia' (n.d.), available at https://cacj-ajp.org/cambodia/ (accessed 10 December 2024).

[12] Y Kasaya, 'Codification of Law in the French Protectorate of Cambodia (1) [in Japanese]' (2019) 81 *ICD News* 29, 31. See also generally C Geertz, *Local Knowledge: Further Essays in Interpretive Anthropology* (New York, Basic Books, 2000) 195ff.

[13] H Matsuo, *Politics, Economy and Law in Developing Asia: A Reflection on Law and Development* (Tokyo, Keio University Press 2022) 183.

[14] Kasaya (n 12) 31 (introducing the comment by 1900s French colonial officer Albert Tricon that '[*Les codes cambodigiens*] are disorganised compilations lacking clear objectives and just collections of kings' occasional decisions on religious and moral lessons').

[15] See generally C Morris, 'Justice Inverted' in K Brickell and S Springer (eds), *The Handbook of Contemporary Cambodia* (Abingdon, Routledge, 2016) 30–31.

[16] J Holligan and others, 'UPDATE: Overview of the Cambodian History, Governance and Legal Sources' (2019) GlobaLex available at www.nyulawglobal.org/globalex/Cambodia1.html#_CPK/DK_period:_1975 (accessed 10 December 2024).

[17] ibid.

[18] S Umeda, 'Cambodian Law – Global Legal Collection Highlights', *In Custodia Legis: Law Librarians of Congress*, 7 July 2014, available at https://blogs.loc.gov/law/2014/07/cambodian-law-global-legal-collection-highlights/ (accessed 10 December 2024).

[19] SF Low, *Colonial Law Making: Cambodia under the French* (Singapore, NUS Press, 2024) 94.

French, and the committee unsurprisingly discussed and drafted the Code in the French language.[20] Importing the French Civil Code and Civil Procedure Code,[21] the Cambodian legal system likely learnt PIL doctrines from France as these Codes contained rules on international jurisdiction and conflict of laws,[22] although the number of PIL-related rules in French law was not outstanding then.[23]

French colonisation officially ended when Cambodia declared its independence in 1953, following King Norodom Sihanouk's negotiations with France.[24] The Kingdom continued to use French-style legal and judicial systems. Nevertheless, the influence of those old French PIL norms over the current Cambodian PIL is not as pervasive as may be thought, because the Communist Party of Kampuchea (CPK), also known as the Khmer Rouge, almost completely eradicated the French legal system from Cambodia. In 1976, after the civil war, the CPK turned the Cambodian Kingdom into Democratic Kampuchea (DK), which abolished virtually all social systems and institutions existing under previous Cambodian regimes, including the judicial courts.[25] In the same year, the Khmer Rouge regime promulgated a new constitution that provided for the establishment of "People's Courts" and the appointment of judges by "the People's Representative Assembly".[26] However, the available evidence suggests that no judges held office and no laws were enacted from 1976 to 1979. There must be some (if not many) Cambodian lawyers who were equipped with the expertise of PIL derived from France or the French colonisation. But they were highly likely to be killed amid mass atrocities committed by the Khmer Rouge's targeting of intellectuals, which reportedly reduced the number of legal professionals from 600 to six.[27] Hence, the

[20] See generally Y Kasaya, 'Codification of Law in the French Protectorate of Cambodia (3) [in Japanese]' (2021) 86 *ICD News* 20. On French colonial officers' gradual exclusion of traditional Cambodian elites from the drafting processes of modern Cambodian legal codes, see Y Kasaya, 'Codification of Law in the French Protectorate of Cambodia (2) [in Japanese]' (2020) 84 *ICD News* 246. During the French colonisation period, major councils and commissions were controlled by French colonial officers and Cambodian elites who were supportive of the colonisation and knew the French language: H Takahashi, 'The Formation of Central and Local Administrative Systems of the Modern Cambodia and the Political Bodies behind the Reform [in Japanese]' in N Amakawa (ed), *Reconstruction and Development of Cambodia* (Chiba, Institute of Developing Economies, Japan External Trade Organization (IDE-JETRO), 2001) 73ff; Y Kasaya, 'Honorary Titles and Job Titles of Ministers in French Colonial Cambodia: A Study Based on the Royal Ordinances Regulating Membership of the Council of Ministers [in Japanese]' (2016) 1 *Nagoya University Asian Law Bulletin* 58.

[21] K Boren, 'Cambodian Private Law: A Snapshot' in H Peng, K Phallack and J Menzel (eds), *Introduction to Cambodian Law* (Phnom Penh, Konrad-Adenauer-Stiftung Cambodia, 2012) 75 (suggesting the 1920 Civil and Civil Procedure Code was 'almost entirely inspired by the Napoleonic Code of 1804').

[22] J Menzel, 'Cambodian Law: Some Comparative and International Perspectives' in H Peng, K Phallack and J Menzel (eds), *Introduction to Cambodian Law* (Phnom Penh, Konrad-Adenauer-Stiftung Cambodia, 2012) 490. See also generally B Audit, 'Private International Law' in GA Bermann and E Picard (eds), *Introduction to French Law* (Alphen aan den Rijn, Wolters Kluwer, 2008) 453 (suggesting that the 1804 French Civil and Civil Procedure Codes contained rules on conflict of laws and jurisdiction).

[23] According to Cuniberti, 'until the late 20th century, French legislation was essentially silent on [private international law], forepart from three articles of the Civil Code dating back to Napoleonic time: art 3 on choice of law, and arts 14 and 15 on international jurisdiction': G Cuniberti, 'France' in J Basedow and others (eds), *Encyclopedia of Private International Law* (Cheltenham, Edward Elgar Publishing, 2017) 2079.

[24] Holligan and others (n 16).

[25] ibid.

[26] KE Neilson, 'They Killed All the Lawyers: Rebuilding the Judicial System in Cambodia' (1996) Occasional Paper #13, 1, available at www.uvic.ca/research/centres/capi/research/home/researchpublications/papers/Neilson_Killed_Lawyers.pdf (accessed 10 December 2024); Holligan and others (n 16).

[27] Neilson (n 26) 1. See also M Vickery, *Kampuchea: Politics, Economy and Society* (London, Frances Pinter (Publishers) 1986) 120; Phallack (n 10) 8.

CPK forcefully terminated the French law period, destroying by violence the French-style civil law system operating in the Kingdom.

The mixed law period effectively commenced when Vietnamese troops and the Vietnamese-sponsored Cambodian rebel army overthrew the Khmer Rouge regime and established the People's Republic of Kampuchea (PRK) in 1979.[28] The PRK intended to operate under the rule of law. It therefore established a new constitution, recovered the function of a court system, established a legislative organ and ordered several surviving lawyers in the Ministry of Justice to draft new laws.[29] The new judicial and legal systems that emerged during the Vietnamese occupation were heavily influenced by those of Vietnam, reflecting socialist ideologies derived from the Soviet Union.[30] However, the PRK revised the socialist constitution in 1989, denouncing socialism and declaring a transit to a market economy. To facilitate the transition process implementing freedom of contract and party autonomy throughout the country, the State of Cambodia (SOC; officially renamed from the PRK) enacted new laws and regulations, including Decree No. 38 Referring to Contract and Other Liabilities and the Law on Marriage and Family.[31] The latter contained several conflict of laws rules on marriage and family that are still in force under the current Cambodian legal system.[32]

After prolonged conflicts and negotiations between the SOC and the Coalition Government of DK – the government in exile composed of Prince Norodom Sihanouk's royalist party, the Khmer Rouge and the Khmer People' s National Liberation Front (backed by the US) – the Paris Peace Agreements were finally signed in 1991.[33] With the subsequent departure of Vietnamese troops, the United Nations Transitional Authority in Cambodia (UNTAC) assumed responsibility for the ceasefire and administration of Cambodia, to enable free and fair elections for a constituent assembly to be conducted.[34] In 1993, UNTAC held a national election to form the Cambodian Constituent Assembly.[35] This body drafted and approved the Constitution of the Kingdom of Cambodia that turned the country into a constitutional monarchy with a multiparty liberal democracy.

A priority policy of the new coalition government was to reconstruct the social order that had been destroyed by the protracted civil war, to enable the Kingdom to achieve stable

[28] The PRK was later renamed as the State of Cambodia (SOC): Neilson (n 26) 1.

[29] Vickery (n 27) 119.

[30] Phallack (n 10) 8; Vickery (n 27) 118–20; M Mohan, 'Cambodia' in S Chesterman, H Owada and B Saul (eds), *The Oxford Handbook of International Law in Asia and the Pacific* (Oxford, Oxford University Press, 2019) 498; C Forsaith, 'Cambodia' in L Malintoppi and C Tan (eds), *Investment Protection in Southeast Asia: A Country-by-Country Guide on Arbitration Laws and Bilateral Investment Treaties* (Leiden, Brill, 2016) 73 (suggesting the influence of Vietnamese contract law in the current private law of Cambodia).

[31] See generally World Intelligence Partners Japan Co Ltd, *Research Report on Personal Status Law in the Kingdom of Cambodia [in Japanese]* (Tokyo, Ministry of Justice of Japan, 2018) 5.

[32] See Arts 79–81 of the Marriage and Family Law.

[33] The Agreements consist of the Agreement on the Comprehensive Political Settlement of the Cambodia Conflict (with Annexes); the Agreement Concerning the Sovereignty, Independence, Territorial Integrity and Inviolability, Neutrality and National Unity of Cambodia, and the Declaration on the Rehabilitation and Reconstruction of Cambodia; and the Final Act of the Paris Conference on Cambodia.

[34] See generally United Nations, 'Completed Peacekeeping Operations: UNTAC (February 1992 – September 1993)' (2003), available at https://peacekeeping.un.org/sites/default/files/past/untac.htm (accessed 10 December 2024).

[35] Note that the Khmer Rouge was barred from participating in the national election as it did not follow disarmament orders.

economic growth and poverty reduction.[36] Accordingly, in 1994 the government issued the National Programme to Rehabilitate and Develop Cambodia, declaring an intention to re-build the Kingdom's legal and judicial systems,[37] which were outdated or otherwise almost demolished by the Khmer Rouge regime.[38] Unfortunately, however, due to the persistent persecution of lawyers by the Khmer Rouge, the Cambodian legal sector suffered from a serious shortage of human resources that had the specialist capabilities required to draft modern law codes almost from scratch.[39] Accordingly, the government requested international foreign donors for support. The French government agreed to provide support for preparing public laws, such as the Criminal Code and the Criminal Procedure Code. Japan's national ODA agency, JICA, committed to drafting private laws, including but not limited to the 2007 Civil Code (CC) and the 2006 Code of Civil Procedure (CCP),[40] which were perceived by the Cambodian government as being crucial for building the foundation of a sustainable market economy.[41] These Codes closely follow the structures of the Japanese Civil Code (Act No 89 of 27 April 1896) and Civil Procedure Code (Act No 109 of 26 June 1996), and take into account the valid statutory laws and local customs that were effective in Cambodia.[42] The CC and the CCP were important achievements for the development of PIL in Cambodia because the former contains some provisions that govern conflict of laws, and the latter has rules on the direct jurisdiction of the Cambodian courts and on the recognition and enforcement of foreign judgments.[43] Side by side with these projects by the French government and JICA, the Cambodian government requested some international institutions to revise certain laws as per common law principles, in return for obtaining financial aid from their development projects.[44] In sum, the current Cambodian

[36] See generally AV Vathana, 'Keynote Speech: The Establishment of Cambodia's Civil Procedure Code and Japan's Legal Technical Assistance [in Japanese]' (2007) 31 *ICD News* 9.

[37] N Rendak and D Eastman, 'Legal and Judicial Reform: Recent Developments and Prospects' in DT Coe and others (eds), *Cambodia: Rebuilding for a Challenging Future* (Washington DC, IMF, 2006) 102 (noting that the Kingdom's accession to the WTO required the emerging market economy to undertake various law reforms).

[38] I Sakano, 'Various Challenges for Legal Technical Assistance in Cambodia [in Japanese]' (2021) 87 *ICD News* 57.

[39] A Morishima, 'Reflection on the Legal and Judicial Development Project for Drafting the Civil Code of Cambodia [in Japanese]' (2003) 11 *ICD News* 4.

[40] ibid (pointing out the French government's lack of adequate resources (and passion) for helping Cambodia draft new legislation in the area of private law); M Takeshita, 'Reflection on the Technical Assisting for Cambodia to Draft the Civil Procedure Code and Challenges for the Legal Technical Assistance Projects [in Japanese]' (2003) 9 *ICD News* 25.

[41] SH Sen, 'Speech delivered by Samdech Hun Sen, Prime Minister of the Royal Government of Cambodia, at the Opening Ceremony' (2003) 7 *ICD News* 25.

[42] N Teramura, 'Japan as a Source of Legal Ideas: A View from the Mekong Subregion of ASEAN' (2021) 13 *New Voices in Japanese Studies* 19, 26–27. Such bodies of private law relevant to the CC and CCP were the Decree No. 38 Referring to Contract and Other Liabilities (1988), Law on Marriage and Family (1989), Land Law (1992), Law on Enforcement of Judgments (1992), Law on Court Fees (1993) and sub-decrees issued by the Ministry of Justice: Sakano (n 38) 57. French-style laws adopted prior to 1956 arguably remained in effect (Rendak and Eastman (n 37) 100), but a limited amount of literature was available to investigate the old laws because the Khmer Rouge destroyed libraries and burnt law books.

[43] See Section III below.

[44] For instance, the East-West Management Institute – a US not-for-profit organisation for the promotion of rule of law – established the 2001 Land Law, adopting the Torrens title system derived from the common law of South Australia. This law reform was part of the Land Management and Administration Project funded by the Asian Development Bank and World Bank. See Industrial Development and Public Policy Department at JICA, 'Legal Technical Assistance for Cambodia: The History and Methodology of the Assistance of JICA in Drafting the Civil Code and the Civil Procedure Code [in Japanese]' (2012), 39ff, available at https://libopac.jica.go.jp/images/

legal system is an amalgam of French public law and Japanese private law, as well as some common law elements. In terms of PIL, the influence of Japanese law is probably the most salient because major rules on jurisdiction, choice of laws and enforcement of judgments can be found in statutory laws based on Japanese legal principles.

III. Sources of Cambodian Private International Law

One may rank the (primary) sources of Cambodian private law as follows: (1) The Constitution – the supreme law of the Kingdom of Cambodia; (2) Laws (Chbab), such as Codes adopted by the National Assembly and the Senate and then promulgated by the King; (3) Royal Decrees (Preab Reach Kret) – executive regulations proposed by the Council of Ministers (i.e., the Cabinet) and signed by the King; (4) Sub-Decrees (Anu-Kret) – executive regulations normally drafted by relevant ministries, adopted by the Council of Ministers and signed by the Prime Minister; (5) Proclamations (Prakas) – (inter-)ministerial orders signed by the relevant minister(s); (6) Decisions (Sech Kdei Samrach) made by the Prime Minister or relevant ministers (note that decisions issued by the Constitutional Council are final and binding and have supremacy over all laws and regulations within the Cambodian legal system); (7) Circular (Sarachor) – administrative instructions to clarify the works and affairs of government ministries, signed by the Prime Minister and relevant minister(s); and (8) By-laws (deikas) – local regulations issued by Councils at sub-national level.[45] International law is also regarded by the Cambodian legal system as a source of law,[46] so that international treaties and conventions become Cambodian law, upon approval by the National Assembly and the Senate and then signature and ratification by the King.[47] As per Article 31 of the Constitution, certain international instruments on human rights also have the force of law.[48] The Constitution and decisions of the Constitutional Council do not clarify the position of international law in the hierarchy of norms in Cambodia, but it is generally accepted that international instruments (having the force of law in the Cambodian legal system) are below the Constitution but are above or at the very least hold the same authority as Laws (Chbab).[49]

The Kingdom has no legislation accumulating PIL norms either systematically or comprehensively. Sources of Cambodian PIL can be found in various separate statutes,

report/12066494.pdf; The World Bank Group, 'Land Management and Administration Project' (2024), available at https://projects.worldbank.org/en/projects-operations/project-detail/P070875 (accessed 10 December 2024).

[45] Such Councils (from largest to smallest) are the Capital Council, Provincial Councils, Municipal Councils, Districts Councils, Khans Councils, Sangkat Councils and Commune Councils. On the hierarchy of norms in the Cambodian legal system, see Phallack (n 10) 9–10; CHBAB.net, 'About Cambodian Law' (n.d.), available at http://en.chbab.net/about-cambodian-law (accessed 11 April 2022), however, this website is no longer accessible.

[46] Decision of the Cambodian Constitutional Council dated 10 July 2007, available at https://archive.crin.org/en/library/legal-database/decision-cambodian-constitutional-council-dated-10-july-2007.html (accessed 10 December 2024).

[47] Phallack (n 10) 10.

[48] Art 31 of the Constitution provides that 'The Kingdom of Cambodia shall recognize and respect human rights as stipulated in the United Nations Charter, the Universal Declaration of Human rights, the covenants and conventions related to human rights, women's and children's rights'.

[49] Menzel (n 22) 489; P Vanrath, 'The Basics of Substantial Cambodian Criminal Law' in H Peng, K Phallack and J Menzel (eds), *Introduction to Cambodian Law* (Phnom Penh, Konrad-Adenauer-Stiftung Cambodia, 2012) 201.

particularly the CCP and the CC, which were inspired by Japanese legal thinking. For example, the CCP contains in Articles 7-22 the rules on domestic jurisdiction that the courts in Cambodia may adopt to assume their authority to hear cross-border disputes in accordance with Article 4 of the CCP.[50] Article 129 of the CCP governs the taking of evidence abroad. Article 199 of the CCP sets out grounds for determining the effect of a final judgment rendered by a foreign court, while Article 352 provides procedural steps for the courts to issue an execution judgment for a decision issued by a foreign court. Likewise, Article 353 presents the conditions for applying for an execution order for a domestic/foreign arbitral award, listing the grounds for the court to refuse the enforcement of the award. On conflict of laws (or choice of law), Article 3 of the CC on the principle of party autonomy is considered by legal practitioners as the foundation of parties' rights to designate the governing law of a contract.[51] Article 36 of the CC states that the law of the place of residence may not be considered as that of the place of domicile in determining the law governing matters on a Cambodian/foreign individual having no domicile in the Kingdom. The Law on Marriage and Family was mostly repealed upon the enactment of the CC. However, its Articles 79-81 are still valid, offering choice of law rules for international marriages albeit dispersedly. In addition, Cambodia has ratified some international conventions governing certain areas of PIL, such as the 1993 Hague Adoption Convention and the 1958 United Nations Convention on the Recognition and Enforcement of Foreign Arbitral Awards (New York, 10 June 1958; the New York Convention),[52] although the number of such international legal instruments Cambodia has ratified is not large.[53] The general international conventions ratified by Cambodia, like the Convention relating to the Status of Refugees (Geneva, 28 July 1951; the 1951 Refugee Convention), also have conflict of laws rules.[54] Further, some lower-level norms such as Sub-Decrees and Proclamations contain rules that govern certain PIL matters, albeit in conjunction with higher-level sources, such as

[50] Teramura, 'Cambodia' in Reyes and Lui (eds), *Direct Jurisdiction* (2021) (n 1) 203.

[51] Bun & Associates, 'Governing Law and Dispute Resolution [in Japanese]' (2017) *Bun & Associates Newsletter*. On conflict of laws in the context of international arbitration, Art 36 of the Commercial Arbitration Law of Cambodia recognises parties' freedom to choose the law applicable to the merits of the dispute.

[52] UNCITRAL (n 7). Moreover, as Cambodia is a party to the Vienna Convention on Diplomatic Relations (Vienna, 18 April 1961), diplomatic agents in Cambodia shall enjoy immunities from the court's civil jurisdiction: Teramura, 'Cambodia' in Reyes and Lui (eds), *Direct Jurisdiction* (2021) (n 1) 217.

[53] For example, Cambodia has not adopted (or ratified) key PIL treaties, such as the 1961 Hague Convention Abolishing the Requirement of Legalisation for Foreign Public Documents (the Hague Apostille Convention), 1980 United Nations Convention on Contracts for the International Sale of Goods (CISG), 1980 Hague Convention on the Civil Aspects of International Child Abduction (the 1980 Hague Child Adoption Convention), 2005 Hague Convention on Choice of Court Agreements, Singapore Convention on Mediation, among others. See, respectively, HCCH, 'Status Table: Convention of 5 October 1961 Abolishing the Requirement of Legalisation for Foreign Public Documents' (2024), available at www.hcch.net/en/instruments/conventions/status-table/?cid=41 (accessed 10 December 2024); UNCITRAL, 'Status: United Nations Convention on Contracts for the International Sale of Goods (Vienna, 1980) (CISG)' (n.d.), available at https://uncitral.un.org/en/texts/salegoods/conventions/sale_of_goods/cisg/status (accessed 10 December 2024); HCCH, 'Status Table: Convention of 25 October 1980 on the Civil Aspects of International Child Abduction' (2022), available at www.hcch.net/en/instruments/conventions/status-table/?cid=24 (accessed 10 December 2024); HCCH, 'Status Table: Convention of 30 June 2005 on Choice of Court Agreements' (2024), available at www.hcch.net/en/instruments/conventions/status-table/?cid=98 (accessed 10 December 2024); Singapore International Dispute Resolution Academy (SIDRA), 'Singapore Convention on Mediation: Jurisdictions' (2021), available at www.singaporeconvention.org/jurisdictions (accessed 10 December 2024).

[54] 1951 Refugee Convention, Art 12; UNHCR, 'States Parties to the 1951 Convention Relating to the Status of Refugees and the 1967 Protocol' (n.d.) available at www.unhcr.org/media/states-parties-1951-convention-and-its-1967-protocol (accessed 10 December 2024).

Codes.[55] Overall, these statutory rules operate as the sources of PIL under the Cambodian legal system.

As Cambodia is a civil law country, court decisions in general have limited precedent value and are arguably recognised as having effect as a secondary source of law.[56] Case law is expected to play a modest role, such as to fill gaps in the primary sources of law. In practice, however, Cambodian legal practitioners reportedly pay little or no attention (or are unable to pay attention) to past judicial decisions because judgments are not normally published and often lack adequate judicial reasoning,[57] a frequent complaint of local practitioners.[58] To improve the quality of judgments and to increase the transparency of the Cambodian judicial system, JICA launched, as part of its legal technical assistance, the Legal and Judicial Development Project (Phase V) that aimed to undertake the publication of court decisions on civil matters.[59] As a result, the Ministry of Justice (MOJ) of Cambodia started publishing judgments in late 2021.[60] However, the number and scope of judgments available on the MOJ's new database are rather modest – 104 civil verdicts that cover mostly money lending and real estate agreements.[61] Moreover, the MOJ emphasised that delay would be inevitable in judgments publication.[62] Hence, it will still take some time for Cambodian lawyers to accept judicial precedent as a secondary source of law in the context of PIL and beyond.[63]

Accordingly, Cambodia's main secondary sources of law are core legal textbooks and commentaries contributed by foreign donors through their legal technical assistance projects. In the field of private law, JICA has published and disseminated commentaries and materials on the CCP, the CC, the Law on Application of the Civil Code, the Law on Procedures in Actions Relating to Personal Status and the Non-Suit Civil Case Procedural

[55] For example, see the Ministry of Interior Sub-Decree 103 on Civil Status (Civil Registration) 2000 (the Civil Status Sub-Decree) (specifying notification and registration proceedings for (international) couples to have valid marriage in Cambodia as per Art 955 of the CC) and Joint Prakas on Determination of Competence of the Court and Cadastral Commission Regarding Land Disputes: Teramura, 'Cambodia' in Reyes and Lui (eds), *Direct Jurisdiction* (2021) (n 1) 208 and 210.

[56] The University of Melbourne, 'Southeast Asian Region Countries Law: Cambodia – Courts and Cases' (n.d.), available at https://unimelb.libguides.com/c.php?g=930183&p=6721971 (accessed 10 December 2024). Despite having no binding force, the doctrine of precedent has contributed to the development of legal certainty in civil law systems: C Pejovic, 'Civil Law and Common Law: Two Different Paths Leading to the Same Goal' (2001) 32 *Victorian University of Wellington Law Review* 817, 820–21.

[57] Y Shinoda, 'Report on the Investigation of Cambodian Court Judgments (1) [in Japanese]' (2019) 79 *ICD News* 60; A Kamiki, 'Report on the Investigation of Cambodian Court Judgements [in Japanese]' (2011) 48 *ICD News* 25.

[58] L Tayseng, 'Importance of Publicity of Judicial Process and Publication of Judicial Decisions', *The Phnom Penh Post*, 12 April 2022, available at www.phnompenhpost.com/opinion/importance-publicity-judicial-process-and-publication-judicial-decisions (accessed 10 December 2024).

[59] JICA, 'The Legal and Judicial Development Project (Phase V): Outline of the Project' (2017), available at https://www.jica.go.jp/project/english/cambodia/025/outline/index.html (accessed 10 December 2024).

[60] N Chheng, 'Courts' Decisions Now Published as Reference Source', *The Phnom Penh Post*, 4 January 2021, available at www.phnompenhpost.com/national/courts-decisions-now-published-reference-source (accessed 10 December 2024).

[61] MOJ, 'Court Decisions on Actual Civil Cases' (n.d.), available at www.moj.gov.kh/kh/actual-civil-judgments (accessed 10 December 2024); Chheng (n 60).

[62] Chheng (n 60).

[63] Exceptionally, Extraordinary Chambers in the Courts of Cambodia (ECCC) and the Arbitration Council publish precedents on human rights violations during the Khmer Rouge period and collective (mostly domestic) labour disputes (respectively), so their judgments and awards seem to have little relevance to PIL issues. See generally Council of ASEAN Chief Justice, 'Sources of Laws in Cambodia' (n.d.), available at https://cacj-ajp.org/cambodia/legal-system/cambodian-laws/overview/sources-of-laws-in-cambodia/ (accessed 10 December 2024).

Law, and others.[64] Many of these commentaries are available only in Khmer and Japanese because the assistance projects are delivered based on agreements between Cambodia and Japan whose official languages are not English. Guidance in such commentaries is often succinct and merely explains which provisions of a certain statute are based on which corresponding articles of a foreign legal system.[65] Accordingly, when local practitioners interrogate the doctrinal or black letter meaning of a statutory rule in Cambodian law, they often investigate discussions surrounding relevant provisions in foreign legal systems.[66] In the context of private law, they study Japanese law to address ambiguities within Cambodian law codes because the CC and the CCP closely follow the Japanese Civil Code and Civil Procedure Code, and because not a few Cambodian lawyers (especially judges) have experienced legal training designed by Japanese legal experts based on Japanese legal education.[67] Hence, Cambodian legal practitioners incline to perceive legal literature and expert opinions on Japanese law as de-facto (or supplementary) secondary sources of law.[68]

In contrast, it is still being determined to what extent Cambodian lawyers consider legal literature based on local knowledge as reliable because legal research still needs to mature in Cambodia. Several universities have a law department/school/faculty that offers law degree courses at both undergraduate and graduate levels.[69] However, they still need to be ready to undertake high-quality legal research for several reasons. First, most of their law faculty members are part-timers who primarily work as full-time legal professionals.[70] In other words, Cambodian law schools only have a small number of full-time academics who may focus on legal research. This issue may persist for a while as many law schools are now struggling to secure funds to address the underpayment of lecturers' remuneration.[71] For example, a case study shows that a typical salary package for a full-time lecturer at a public university is about a tenth of the package for a professional lawyer working in the private sector.[72] Unless this income gap is addressed, there will be no strong incentives for legal experts to become full-time law faculty staff. Second, Cambodian law schools fail to offer environments that encourage their academic staff to undertake legal research. For instance, there are few research centres in the law schools where Cambodian academics may exchange their insights to develop new research.[73] Some foreign donors

[64] See JICA, 'Portal Site for the Legal Technical Assistance Projects by JICA: Cambodia' (n.d.), available at www.jica.go.jp/activities/issues/governance/portal/index.html (accessed 10 December 2024).

[65] See Teramura (n 42) 27.

[66] The author's interview with lawyers in Cambodia.

[67] Industry Development and Public Policy Department at JICA, *The Final Evaluation Report on the Project for the Improvement of the Training on Civil Matters at the Royal School for Judges and Prosecutors of the Royal Academy for Judicial Professions (Phase 2) [in Japanese]* (2012); A Misawa, 'Supporting the Training of Judges and Prosecutors in Cambodia [in Japanese]' (2004) 18 *ICD News* 1ff.

[68] Teramura (n 42) 34; Teramura, 'Cambodia' in Reyes and Lui (eds), *Direct Jurisdiction* (2021) (n 1) 203.

[69] The universities offering law degrees include: Royal University of Law and Economics (RULE), National University of Management (NUM), Pannasastra University of Cambodia, University of Cambodia, Cambodia University of Specialties, Mekong University and Build Bright University. Only RULE and NUM are public universities. See C Seavmey, 'Challenges of Legal Education in Cambodia [in Japanese]' (2020) 85 *ICD News* 16, 17–18. See also L Zhang, 'Cambodia's Legal Education', *In Custodia Legis: Law Librarians of Congress*, 20 October 2021, available at https://blogs.loc.gov/law/2021/10/cambodias-legal-education (suggesting more than 20 law schools provide four-year LLB programs as of October 2021 (accessed 10 December 2024)).

[70] The author's interview with local lawyers.

[71] Seavmey (n 69) 20.

[72] ibid.

[73] ibid.

maintain research institutions in targeted universities, but their primary focus is the education and training of law students.[74] Moreover, the law schools rarely encourage their faculty staff to publish textbooks or to research articles by providing sufficient research budget or facilities, and the quality of (exceptionally) published materials are unlikely to be top-notch, because no review process has been initiated at institutional levels.[75] Cambodian legal literature might therefore be at too premature a stage to qualify as secondary sources of law.

To summarise, both primary and secondary sources of Cambodian law underpin the pervasive influence of Japanese legal doctrines on the development of Cambodian PIL. The primary sources of PIL can be found in statutory laws developed by Japanese and Cambodian scholars, driven by and attached to Japanese legal ideas. This development process has made Japanese PIL principles an integral part of Cambodian PIL norms, such as in relation to rules on direct jurisdiction and enforcement of foreign judgments in the CCP. On secondary sources, several core textbooks and commentaries have been prepared by Japanese and Cambodian legal experts involved in JICA's legal technical assistance projects. Cambodian legal practitioners frequently consult those materials to address uncertainty within the statutes, studying literature on Japanese law provisions referred to in such materials. These materials on Cambodian and Japanese laws are likely to be influential in the legal interpretation of Cambodian law because the doctrine of precedent is not perceived as either binding or persuasive under the current Cambodian legal practice, and because Cambodian legal experts do not have keen interest in undertaking legal research on Cambodian PIL due to institutional barriers. Hence, for the time being, understanding and developing Cambodian PIL by relying on Japanese legal ideas is likely to be the most plausible approach.[76] The following Sections IV-VII thus consider essential concepts of PIL, and analyse whether their implications under Japanese law are transferrable to Cambodian PIL.

IV. Preliminary Matters

This section deliberates on four basic concepts of PIL that may be discussed at early stages of selecting the applicable law of a dispute. These concepts are "characterisation", "incidental questions", "*depeçage*" and "*renvoi* (transmission)", which may determine which law the court ultimately applies to the dispute.

A. Characterisation

Characterisation (also called classification or qualification) denotes the method through which the court allocates the subject matter of the proceeding (or the cause of action brought

[74] In 2008, Nagoya University (Japan) established the Research and Education Centre for Japanese Law within the Royal University of Law and Economics (RULE), to teach students the Japanese legal system in Japanese: Nagoya University Education and Research Center for Japanese Law, 'Basic Information of the Research and Education Centre for Japanese Law [in Japanese]' (n.d.), available at https://cjl.law.nagoya-u.ac.jp/cb/about/ (accessed 10 December 2024).

[75] Seavmey (n 69) 20.

[76] Menzel (n 22) 490 (suggesting Cambodia apply Japanese PIL principles for the interim period and then draft legislation inspired mainly by Japanese PIL).

by the plaintiff) to one of the established choice of law classifications. Characterisation is not unique in PIL as all legal reasoning and judicial determinations involve some form of categorisation in determining legal norms applicable to the subject matter.[77] However, the method becomes critical in PIL-related disputes because states and territories normally have different choice of law rules for different subject matters, suggesting different definitions of legal concepts and issues.[78] For instance, countries often differ on what constitutes "consumer contracts",[79] and whether a contract is classified into "ordinal contracts" or "consumer contracts" often determines which conflict of laws rule and then which law is to be applied to the contract.[80] Characterisation is thus a gateway issue for the court dealing with conflict of laws.

As Japanese law has no discernible legal provisions regulating how the court shall carry out characterisation, commentators and jurists in Japan advocate the following approaches to characterisation: (1) characterisation based on the (substantive) *lex fori*, (2) characterisation based on the *lex causae*, and (3) characterisation based on the rationale of the Japanese choice of law rules.[81] The first approach suggests characterising the subject matter in accordance with the substantive law of the forum. For example, suppose the parties dispute over the classification of a damage claim as "tortious" or as a "contract violation". In that case, the first approach claims that the classification is to be made by the court as per the definitions of "torts" and "contract violations" under the Japanese Civil Code. The second approach claims to characterise the subject matter by applying the *lex causae* – the law chosen by the forum court from the relevant legal systems to determine the subject matter. Adopting this approach can be tricky because it requires the Japanese court to undertake characterisation based on the governing law of the subject matter (or the cause of action), although the purpose of classifying the subject matter is to designate the governing law. The third approach advocates for characterisation within the framework of Japan's (i.e., the forum's) conflict of laws rules.

Japanese jurists are divided on the implications of the third approach for classification. Some suggest that the approach requires the court to conduct a comparative study of all, or at least all major, legal systems to figure out the common core concept (or definition) of the disputed legal notion that the court may adopt in characterising the subject matter.[82] For example, if the parties have a controversy over whether a property claim is to be categorised as an issue of personal property or real property, the court will be required to identify the least common multiple of the definitions of real properties adopted in different jurisdictions. Some other commentators claim that the court has to perform characterisation in

[77] V Allarousse, 'A Comparative Approach to the Conflict of Characterization in Private International Law' (1991) 23 *Case Western Reserve Journal of International Law* 479, 479.

[78] ibid. For a general discussion about the significance of characterisation for PIL, see also S Jolly and S Khanderia, *Indian Private International Law* (Oxford, Hart Publishing, 2021) 22; R Mortensen, R Garnett and M Keyes, *Private International Law in Australia*, 5th edn, (Chatswood, LexisNexis, 2023) 242ff.

[79] See, e.g., L Nottage and others, 'Chapter 4 – Regulating Consumer Contracts in ASEAN: Variation and Change' in L Nottage and others (eds), *ASEAN Consumer Law Harmonisation and Cooperation: Achievements and Challenges* (Cambridge, Cambridge University Press, 2019).

[80] For example, Japan's statute on choice of law contains special choice of law rules for consumer contracts. See Art 11 of the Act on General Rules for Application of Laws (Act No 78 of 2006).

[81] See generally S Iriinafuku, 'The Characterisation of Legal Relations [in Japanese]' (n.d.), available at (accessed 10 December 2024); Y Sakurada, *Private International Law [in Japanese]*, 7th edn, (Tokyo, Yuhikaku Publishing, 2020) 74–77; T Sawaki and M Dogauchi, *Introduction to Private International Law [in Japanese]* (Tokyo, Yuhikaku Publishing, 2018) 18–21.

[82] Sakurada (n 81) 77–78; Sawaki and Dogauchi (n 81) 20–21.

light of the purpose and objective of Japanese conflict of laws rules, taking into account the cross-border nature of the dispute and the reasonable expectation of the parties.[83] Such method of characterisation arguably requires the court to identify criteria for characterisation by relying on the legislative intention and purpose of the potentially relevant choice of law rules, the competing interests involved and the system of the Act on General Rules for Application of Laws (Act No 78 of 21 June 2006; AGRAL) as a whole.[84] Despite this theoretical divide, the third approach is regarded as the most prevalent among Japanese PIL experts.[85]

However, importing the third approach – characterisation based on the choice of law rules of the forum – to the Cambodian legal system would likely be impractical. Cambodian judges are not always familiar with investigating foreign laws (like their counterparts in foreign jurisdictions) and most of them have rarely been exposed to foreign legal systems and comparative legal studies throughout their professional careers.[86] To force Cambodian judges to conduct a vast comparative legal research for characterisation is to test and challenge the limits of their capacities in each case, which would unlikely lead them to achieve the fundamental objective of Cambodia civil procedure – a fair and efficient dispute settlement.[87] Likewise, ascertaining the rationale of the Cambodian choice of law rules is not the most straightforward task for Cambodian judges because the Kingdom has no statutory law that collects conflict of laws rules either systematically or comprehensively, and because many Cambodian judges only have limited knowledge of PIL.[88] Further, as Cambodia has no statutory law equivalent to Japan's AGRAL, requiring Cambodian judges to discern the implication of the Cambodian system of conflict of laws as a whole is impractical at best, impossible at worst.

Adopting the second approach – characterisation based on the *lex causae* – would pose challenges to the Cambodian legal system. First, this approach entails a circular logic.[89] The ultimate aim of the characterisation process is to decide the law applicable to the cause of action (or subject matter) of the dispute. Characterisation is thus always followed by the court's designation of the *lex causae* but not vice versa. Nevertheless, this approach requires the court to characterise the cause of action based on the governing law of the cause before even choosing it. How would the court be able to apply a law not yet identified by the judge? Regarding it as a logical fallacy, Japanese commentators nowadays do not support the second approach.[90] Cambodian legal practitioners would not find the approach appealing either.[91]

[83] Sakurada (n 81) 78–79; Sawaki and Dogauchi (n 81) 21.

[84] K Nishioka and Y Nishitani, *Japanese Private International Law* (Oxford, Hart Publishing, 2021) 10.

[85] J Yokoyama, *Private International Law in Japan* (Alphen aan den Rijn, Wolters Kluwer 2019) 32; Nishioka and Nishitani (n 84) 9.

[86] Teramura, 'Cambodia' in Reyes and Lui (eds), *Direct Jurisdiction* (2021) (n 1) 203; V Phun, 'Country Factsheet 2: Judicial Training in Cambodia' in A Nababan and others (eds), *Judicial Training in ASEAN: A Comparative Overview of Systems and Programs* (Phnom Penh, Konrad-Adenauer-Stiftung Cambodia, 2014) 34.

[87] CCP, Art 4.

[88] Phun (n 86) 34 (suggesting the judicial training curriculum at the Royal School for Judges and Prosecutors does not cover conflict of laws). See also M Ito, 'Professional Legal Education at the Royal School for Judges and Prosecutors in Cambodia [in Japanese]' (2022) 90 *ICD News* 47.

[89] Iriinafuku (n 81).

[90] Yokoyama (n 85) 33.

[91] The following comment clearly articulates the problem inherent in the second approach, albeit in the context of common law. 'The whole purpose of the choice of law process (including classification) is the identification

In the end, the first approach – characterisation based on the (substantive) *lex fori* – would be the most convenient for Cambodian judges, in light of the current legal environment surrounding conflict of laws in the country. As Cambodian judges are trained to adjudicate civil disputes in accordance with Cambodian law (i.e., the *lex fori*), they may generally tell what may constitute a certain legal concept under the substantive law of Cambodia (comprising of the CC, Law on Application of the Civil Code, Law on Marriage and Family, among others). For such judges familiar with the Cambodian legal concepts, using domestic concepts in characterising subject matter would likely be more probable than conducting a comparative legal analysis and/or inventing conflict-of-laws-specific legal concepts from scratch. Certainly, one may criticise the first approach for prioritising domestic law over foreign law and undermining the internationalisation of PIL. However, this arrangement is somewhat inevitable because PIL is part of municipal law (i.e., Cambodian law) and may, therefore, only achieve its internationalisation within the sphere assumed by the legal system to which it belongs. As Yokoyama rightly points out (albeit in the context of Japanese conflict of laws rules), classification may not be free from the forum's substantive legal principles.[92] Hence, the first approach to characterisation is more viable than the other two approaches that connote the major practical and theoretical challenges.

B. Incidental (or Preliminary) Questions

The incidental (or preliminary) question becomes relevant where the court deals with two legal issues that are related to each other in the sense that one is a prerequisite for the other. For example, the court would not be able to resolve a dispute relating to an inheritance between spouses of a real property overseas before deciding on the validity of their marriage.[93] If this is the case, the court will first have to determine how to choose the law applicable to the preliminary question (i.e., the validity of the marriage), considering whether the choice is to be regulated by the conflict of laws rules governing the main question (i.e., the inheritance).

On the court's general approach towards the incidental question, the Supreme Court of Japan held:

> In a legal relationship with a foreign element, when there is not only a legal question (the main question) before a court but also a preliminary question which needs to be decided in order to solve the main question, and when that preliminary question consists of a different legal relationship from the main question, the law to govern such a preliminary question should be decided by the application of the choice-of-law rules of the forum, that is, the choice-of-law rules of Japan. Neither the substantive law governing the main question nor the law designated by the

of the law of the cause and so, if that is already known at the time of classification, it would be a pointless event to undertake classification in the first place': Mortensen, Garnett and Keyes (n 78) 247. See also P Dirwan and P Diwan, *Private International Law: Indian and English*, 4th edn, (Delhi, Deep & Deep Publications, 1998) 79 cited in Jolly and Khanderia (n 78) 23 (arguing that '[i]f the law which is finally to regulate the matter (ie, the *lex causae*) depends upon classification, how can classification be made according to that law[?]').

[92] Yokoyama (n 85) 33.

[93] Suppose the situation in which a Cambodian widow claims to inherit her deceased husband's real estate in Japan.

> choice-of-law rules of the country to which the law governing the main question belongs should govern the preliminary question.[94]

In other words, the Supreme Court stated that Japanese courts treat the preliminary issue and the main issue as independent of each other unless they derive from the same legal relationship, and that the court should determine each issue in accordance with the independently applicable conflict of laws rule, and should consistently apply the choice of law rules of the forum to the preliminary question. This approach may help the court to ensure consistency of judgments where one of the parties later requests the court to decide the preliminary question as a sole subject matter.[95] If such a request is made, the court shall choose the law governing the preliminary question following the conflict of laws rules of the jurisdiction to which it belongs. Otherwise, if the court subjects the preliminary question to the choice of law rule appliable to the main issue, it may not be possible for the court later to choose the governing law of the preliminary issue as a separate issue based on the forum's conflict rules. This will prompt the court to overlook a case precedent within the forum on the preliminary issue and to undermine legal certainty. The prevailing view among Japanese commentators is in line with the Supreme Court's approach.[96]

Transplanting the Supreme Court's holding on the incidental question to the Cambodian conflict of laws rules is unlikely to cause serious concern among Cambodian jurists. Although the doctrine of precedent is still underdeveloped in Cambodia, Cambodian lawyers value legal certainty and foreseeability brought about by consistency in judicial decisions.[97] They would find the Supreme Court's approach more appealing than subjecting the primary question to the choice of laws rules governing the main question because the former approach would bring greater consistency in the court's selection of law.

C. *Depeçage*

The French word *depeçage* means 'to divide' or 'to split [something] into small pieces'. In the field of conflict of laws, the legal concept (or technique) of *depeçage* 'splits a formerly uniform issue into two or more partial sub-issues [and] subjects these partial sub-issues to different laws'.[98] The courts in Japan have adopted the technique in contractual disputes from time to time. For example, some lower-level courts in Japan have applied English law to the terms of an insurance contract on the basis of the parties' express choice while

[94] *Children v Their Father* [2000] Supreme Court 1995 (O) 1203, 43 Japanese Annual of International Law 197, 199.

[95] S Iriinafuku, 'The Preliminary Question [in Japanese]' (n.d.), available at https://eu-info.jp/IPR/8.html (accessed 10 December 2024); Sakurada (n 81) 150.

[96] Y Tameike, *Lecture on Private International Law [in Japanese]* (Tokyo, Yuhikaku Publishing 2005) 227–32; Yokoyama (n 85) 34; Nishioka and Nishitani (n 84) 13; Sawaki and Dogauchi (n 81) 23–24; M Dogauchi, 'Incidental Questions [in Japanese]' in M Dogauchi and Y Nakanishi (eds), *Leading Cases in Private International Law* (Tokyo, Yuhikaku Publishing, 2021) 7.

[97] See Section III above. In an interview on the judgment publication initiative by the MOJ, a senior Cambodia lawyer said, '[w]e don't want to see similar cases being tried differently. It is not acceptable that one group of judges decides this way and another group of judges decides another way. We want the courts to be able to rule with consistency': Chheng (n 60).

[98] P Mankowski, 'Dépeçage' in J Basedow and others (eds), *Encyclopedia of Private International Law* (Cheltenham, Edward Elgar Publishing, 2017) 526.

relying on Japanese law to determine the validity of the same contract.[99] Indeed, the AGRAL contains no provisions expressly allowing the parties to adopt *depeçage*. However, the drafters of the AGRAL suggest the application of *depeçage* is permissible as long as the parties have agreed to such. As the basis of this argument, they invoke the fact that Article 7 of the AGRAL recognises the principle of party autonomy in conflict of laws without prohibiting the parties from adopting *depeçage*.[100] Thus, *depeçage* is part of the law in Japan.[101]

It is probable that *depeçage* can be imported into Cambodian law. Under Cambodian law, the legal basis of the parties' right to choose the governing law of a contract is Article 3 of the CC, which recognises the principle of party autonomy in private transactions.[102] The Article provides that 'legal relations among private persons, including legal persons, shall be equal and equivalent, respecting the free intentions of such individuals'. Thus, like Article 7 of the AGRAL, Article 3 of the CC does not bar parties from agreeing to apply different laws to separable legal issues. Hence, the broad freedom of contract under the CC may be comprised of the parties' liberty to adopt *depeçage*. This interpretation would possibly enhance international transactions in Cambodia as it conforms with international trends in choice of governing law methodology in cross-border transactions.[103]

D. *Renvoi* and Transmission

The original meaning of *renvoi* in French is to "send back" or "return unopened". Sonnentag explains the notion of *renvoi* in the context of conflict of laws as follows:

> The problem of *renvoi* concerns the question of whether a reference to a foreign legal system encompasses that system's substantive law or its conflict-of-laws rules. In the first case, the substantive law of the designated state is applicable. However, if the reference directs to the conflict-of-laws rules, there are three possibilities. First, this law may refer to itself .... In such a case, the substantive rules of the law, designated by the law of the forum, are applicable. The so-designated law accepts the reference by the law of the forum. ... Second, it is possible that the designated law itself refers back to the law of the forum, or as a third possibility refers further to a yet third law. In the latter case, the additional question arises of whether only remissions to the law of the forum ... or also transmissions to the law of a third country have to be observed.[104]

Sonnentag then states that these issues – the question of whether a reference to a foreign legal system encompasses the system's substantive law or its choice of law rules and the problem concerning remissions and transmissions – are collectively called *renvoi*.

[99] Y Nishitani, 'Party Autonomy in Contemporary Private International Law: The Hague Principles on Choice of Law and East Asia' (2016) 59 *Japanese Yearbook of International Law* 300, 331; Sawaki and Dogauchi (n 81) 189; F Masuda, 'Depeçage' in M Dogauchi and Y Nakanishi (eds), *Leading Cases in Private International Law* (Tokyo, Yuhikaku Publishing, 2021) 56–57.

[100] K Koide, *Commentary on the Act on General Rules for Application of Laws [in Japanese]* (Tokyo, Shojihomu Publishing 2014) 82, 90–91; Yokoyama (n 85) 23.

[101] According to some Japanese commentators, failing to designate the law applicable to a contract does not deter the parties from applying *depeçage* to the contract. See Yokoyama (n 85) 24; Nishioka and Nishitani (n 84) 14.

[102] Bun & Associates (n 51) 1.

[103] For example, Art 2 of the Hague Principles on Choice of Law in International Commercial Contracts reads: '[t]he parties may choose ... the law applicable to the whole contract or to only part of it; and different laws for different parts of the contract'. Thus, the Article recognises the parties' freedom to opt for *depeçage* explicitly.

[104] M Sonnentag, 'Renvoi' in Jürgen Basedow and others (eds), *Encyclopedia of Private International Law* (Cheltenham, Edward Elgar Publishing, 2017) 1537.

Renvoi is basically the law in Japan. The AGRAL recognises remissions in cases where the court applies the relevant Japanese choice of law rule to decide the governing law of the status of a person.[105] The matters that the court is allowed to adopt remissions in such cases are limited to:[106] a person's capacity to act,[107] requirements for the formation of marriage,[108] parentage of a child born out of wedlock,[109] legitimation of a child,[110] adoption of a child,[111] other family affairs such as relationships between relatives,[112] formalities of a legal act involving family relationships,[113] guardianship,[114] succession and formation and effects of a will.[115] Effects of marriage, matrimonial property regimes, divorce and parent-child relationships are excluded from the list.[116] Moreover, the AGRAL does not recognise transmission.[117] Thus, the scope of *renvoi* under Japanese law is rather modest.

Careful considerations are required before introducing Japanese legal thinking on the doctrine of *renvoi* to the Cambodian conflict of laws rules. For instance, an acute challenge for those intending to import the Japanese model of *renvoi* is that there needs to be a discernible statutory provision or case law applying the doctrine under Cambodian law. Accordingly, the basis of the application of *renvoi* would highly likely be the interpretation of certain rules in the Cambodian legal system, which might be highly artificial, theoretical or technical. The discussion surrounding *renvoi* is theoretical and technical, too. For example, Japanese commentators are divided on whether the court should admit an indirect remission as the result of a transmission and whether the indirect remission is admissible in certain situations.[118] Assigning these technical exercises to Cambodian judges (most of whom are not familiar with the conflict of laws)[119] would likely not help them achieve their primary duty in civil litigation – fair and expeditious dispute resolution.[120]

Moreover, the legislative history of Article 41 AGRAL is unable to provide strong justification for transferring the Japanese concept of *renvoi* to Cambodian PIL. Though the origin of Article 41 dates to the time of the old AGRAL, not a few members of the drafting committee of the current AGRAL opposed maintaining the *renvoi* provision.[121] The committee

[105] AGRAL, Art 41 (providing that '[w]here a person's national law applies and the rules of that law require that Japanese law should apply, then Japanese law shall apply').

[106] Koide (n 100) 372; AGRAL, Art 41.

[107] AGRAL, Art 4(1).

[108] ibid, Art 24.

[109] ibid, Art 29. However, some Japanese commentators suggest excluding the application of *renvoi* for Arts 29(1) and 31(1) of the AGRAL if doing so would be in the best interests of the child: Yokoyama (n 85) 37.

[110] AGRAL, Art 30.

[111] ibid, Art 31.

[112] ibid, Art 33.

[113] ibid, Art 34(1).

[114] ibid, Art 35(1).

[115] ibid, Arts 36–37.

[116] ibid, Art 41; Yokoyama (n 85) 38.

[117] Nishioka and Nishitani (n 84) 15.

[118] An indirect remission takes place, for example, 'where the Japanese choice of law rule refers to the law of state A, the conflicts rule of state A then refers to the law of state B, and the choice of law rule of state B refers back to Japanese law': ibid, 14; Tameike (n 96) 164–65; R Yamada, *Lectures on Private International Law [in Japanese]*, 3rd edn, (Tokyo, Yuhikaku Publishing 2004) 71; A Kitazawa, 'Article 41' in M Dogauchi and Y Sakurada (eds), *Private International Law Annotated [in Japanese]*, vol 2 (Tokyo, Yuhikaku Publishing, 2011) 327; Sakurada (n 81) 122.

[119] Ito (n 88).

[120] CCP, Art 4.

[121] On the drafting history of Art 41 of the AGRAL, see generally Yokoyama (n 85) 37ff; Koide (n 100) 372.

finally approved the inclusion of the provision to the new AGRAL because several career judges in the committee emphasised the utility of *renvoi* for the succession of lands owned by North Korean nationals.[122] The AGRAL provides in Article 36 that '[s]uccession shall be governed by the national law of the decedent'. Thus, North Korean law would be applied to the succession if the deceased was a North Korean national and the subject of the succession was a piece of land in Japan. However, the North Korean legal system lacked substantive norms regulating land succession due to the country being socialist. Thus, Japanese judges had to circumvent the legal vacuum by adopting remission to refer the matter back from North Korean to Japanese law.[123] In other words, Article 41 and the doctrine of *renvoi* were crucial for Japanese judges to handle a succession dispute involving a deceased person from a jurisdiction that had no substantive law on land succession. However, this would unlikely be the case in Cambodia, where land ownership by foreign nationals is prohibited by law.[124] The succession to Cambodian real property owned by a foreign national is not legally plausible as there are virtually no pieces of land under the possession of foreigners who do not have citizenship of the Kingdom. Hence, the doctrine of *renvoi* would not promise practical benefits to Cambodian jurists, unlike in the case of the AGRAL in Japan.[125]

V. Connecting Factors

The purpose of conflict of laws rules is to decide which law is applicable for solving legal problems arising from specific fact patterns. The word 'connecting factor' refers to 'the element of a conflict rule that connects a factual situation with the laws of a specific jurisdiction'.[126] Connecting factors exist in Cambodian PIL. Article 79 of the Law on Marriage and Family provides that a marriage performed overseas (whether between Cambodian citizens or a Cambodian and a foreign national) shall be recognised in Cambodia if the marriage satisfies the formalities set out in the law of the place of the ceremony. In this case, the connecting factor is the place of the ceremony, and it connects the marriage held abroad with the law of the country where the marriage was performed.

As opposed to Japanese law, which has embedded various connecting factors in the AGRAL,[127] the Cambodian legal system has only a handful of statutory conflict rules,[128]

[122] Yokoyama (n 85) 37.

[123] The PIL of North Korea designates the *lex situs* (i.e., the law of the place in which property is situated) as the law governing the succession of real property: ibid 37; C Kim, 'The 1995 Private International Law of North Korea' (1998) 29 *California Western International Law Journal* 205, 210.

[124] Art 8 of the 2001 Land Law reads, '[o]nly natural persons or legal entities of [Cambodian] nationality have the right to ownership of land in the Kingdom of Cambodia'. "Indirect ownership" is also prohibited by Art 9, which provides that '[a]n enterprise registered in Cambodia, in respect of which 51% or more of the shares are held by natural persons of Cambodian nationality or by Cambodian legal entities recognized pursuant to the laws of Cambodia, may be the owner of land … Any private agreement signed by a shareholder that is contrary to this article is null and void.'

[125] The default exclusion of *renvoi* conforms with Art 36 of the Commercial Arbitration Law providing that 'Any designation of the law or legal system of a given state shall be construed, unless otherwise expressed, as directly referring to the substantive law of that state and not to its conflict of laws rules'.

[126] H-P Mansel, 'Connecting Factor' in J Basedow and others (eds), *Encyclopedia of Private International Law* (Cheltenham, Edward Elgar Publishing, 2017) 441.

[127] Nishioka and Nishitani (n 84) 13–17; Yokoyama (n 85) 25–30.

[128] See Section III above.

incorporating relatively few connecting factors: the intention of the parties as an expression of the principle of party autonomy (as the connecting factor for the law governing a contract),[129] the place of the celebration of marriage (as the connecting factor for deciding the law applicable to the formalities of the marriage),[130] the place where a couple resides (as the connecting factor for deciding the governing law of the validity of their divorce),[131] and domicile and residence (as connecting factors for deciding the personal status of a refugee).[132] The following sections consider how the courts in Cambodia would likely treat the connecting factors that have been traditionally discussed by Japanese jurists.[133]

A. Nationality

Japanese law has regarded nationality as the primary connecting factor for personal matters since the establishment of Japanese conflict of laws rules.[134] Japan's PIL presupposes that the 'personal law' – the proper law of each natural person – is to govern the questions of personal status and family relations,[135] and that the personal law of each person is to be determined by their nationality.[136] This is because the personal law based on the individual's nationality arguably reflects the culture and custom that they are familiar with, and because nationality is relatively stable as a connecting factor, compared with domicile and residence that may change upon the individual's movement.[137] Moreover, it is suggested that law enforcement officers may identify one's nationality easily, by checking identity documents or records in resident registers.[138]

Cambodian PIL has several conflict rules that adopt nationality as a connecting factor. Article 79 of the Law on Marriage and Family reads that 'a [m]arriage between … Cambodian citizen[s] … living in a foreign country must be held before the registrar of the embassy or consulate of the [Kingdom] of Cambodia which is located in the country where both part[ies] reside'. The couple is required to file a request for marriage to the registrar/consulate,[139] and then the registrar/consulate shall examine the application to check whether the marriage is in compliance with the conditions of marriage provided in the family law of Cambodia (i.e., the Civil Code and the Law on Marriage and Family).[140] It follows that Article 79 designates the personal law of the couple (i.e., Cambodian family law) as the law applicable to the validity of the marriage, albeit somewhat indirectly via the Civil Status Sub-Decree. Article 34 of the Sub-Decree provides that '[a]n immigrant and a foreigner living lawfully in the territory of the Kingdom of Cambodia may [marry] another

[129] CC, Art 3; Bun & Associates (n 51); Art 36 of the Commercial Arbitration Law of Cambodia.

[130] Law on Marriage and Family, Arts 79–80.

[131] ibid, Art 81.

[132] 1951 Refugee Convention, Art 12.

[133] Nishioka and Nishitani (n 84) 13ff; S Iriinafuku, 'Connecting Factors [in Japanese]' (n.d.), available at https://eu-info.jp/IPR/4.html (accessed 10 December 2024).

[134] Nishioka and Nishitani (n 84) 14.

[135] See, AGRAL, Arts 4, 24–25, 28–33, 35–38, among others.

[136] Iriinafuku (n 133); Nishioka and Nishitani (n 84) 14.

[137] Iriinafuku (n 133); Nishioka and Nishitani (n 84) 14.

[138] Nishioka and Nishitani (n 84) 14.

[139] Civil Status Sub-Decree, Art 32.

[140] ibid, Art 28; Law on Implementation of the Civil Code, Art 78.

foreigner or immigrant by abiding by the law on marriage of their own country'. Therefore, the Article designates the non-Cambodian couple's personal law as the law governing their marriage formation, using their nationality as the connecting factor. Nationality is a key connecting factor under Cambodian PIL rules on family matters.

Complications may arise when a person has no citizenship or dual nationality. For the former, Article 38(2) of the AGRAL provides that the law of the person's habitual residence shall become his/her national law, except where the subject matter is the effect of marriage, a matrimonial property regime, divorce or a parental relationship. An obstacle to importing this rule to Cambodian PIL is Cambodian lawyers' unfamiliarity with the idea of habitual residence because no discernible Cambodian statutory norms adopt this connecting factor. The challenge is unlikely to be alleviated by Cambodia's membership of the 1993 Hague Adoption Convention. The Convention indeed uses the words "habitual residence", but it does not contain either a definition of habitual residence or specific factors that must be considered by the court to determine the person's habitual residence. Further, the HCCH suggests, 'habitual residence is an autonomous concept that is determined based upon the facts of each particular case, and in light of the objectives of the particular Hague Convention rather than each State's domestic law constraints'.[141] Thus, expanding the doctrine of habitual residence to PIL issues other than inter-country adoptions is unlikely to be plausible under the current Cambodian legal system. A more practical arrangement for Cambodian judges to deal with the absence of nationality is to rely on domicile and residence, both of which are defined in the CC.[142] The arrangement would be in conformity with the 1951 Refugee Convention designating those as connecting factors for determining the law governing the status of refugees and stateless people.[143]

On dual/multiple citizenships, the AGRAL distinguishes those involving Japanese nationality from other situations.[144] For instance, the personal law of a person having multiple citizenships, including Japanese, is to be Japanese law, while that of an individual with multiple nationalities other than Japanese is to be the law of their habitual residence in one of their countries of nationalities. If the individual has no such habitual residence, the law of the state that they have the closest connection to is deemed their national law.

Cambodian PIL does not contain rules regulating multiple nationalities. However, some adjustments are required to import the Japanese conflict rules because the concept of habitual residence is not widely adopted in the context of Cambodian private law, as discussed above. If a person has Cambodian citizenship as one of their multiple citizenships, the court in the Kingdom may regard Cambodian law as their personal law. Giving priority to Cambodian citizenship would alleviate the burden on Cambodia's administrative authorities as they have no difficulties in ascertaining the person's Cambodian nationality.[145] If the person with multiple citizenships does not have Cambodian nationality, without resorting to the under-used concept of habitual residence, Cambodian jurists would need to identify the person's national law through examining which state is the most closely connected with

[141] HCCH, *Note on Habitual Residence and Scope of the 1993 Hague Convention on Protection of Children and Co-operation in Respect of Intercountry Adoption* (HCCH – Permanent Bureau 2018) 8.

[142] CC, Arts 34–35.

[143] 1951 Refugees Convention, Art 12.

[144] AGRAL, Art 38(2).

[145] Yokoyama (n 85) 27 (suggesting as such on Japanese authorities under Art 38(2) of the AGRAL).

the person among their multiple countries of nationalities. Then, they would be required to determine the closest connection in each individual case, taking into account the factual circumstances of the case.[146] For Cambodian judges, domicile and residence are likely the most convenient indicators of the most closed connection because they are used to adopt the concepts in handling private disputes.

The courts in Cambodia may apply different connecting factors in seeking the proper law of non-natural persons such as corporations, ships and aircraft. Regarding corporations, Article 48 of the CC defines foreign corporations as juristic persons incorporated under foreign law, highlighting juristic persons' strong connection with their *lex societatis* (the law of the place of incorporation) under Cambodian law. Like Japanese jurists and commentators,[147] Cambodian judges would likely thus uphold the incorporation theory. Regarding ships, the concept of "flag state" is generally accepted in the Kingdom, so that Cambodian jurists would regard a vessel's flag as the evidence of its nationality conferred by the state on which the vessel was registered as per the state's national legislation.[148] Accordingly, the judges would presuppose that the law and regulations of the flag state apply to matters pertaining to the vessel.[149] The flag state principle applies to aircraft too, as is evident from the Law on Civil Aviation, which states in Article 6 that '[a]ny aircraft registered in the Kingdom of Cambodia shall have Cambodian nationality'.

B. Domicile and Residence

The CC offers different concepts of domicile for natural persons and corporations. According to Article 34 of the CC, the domicile of a natural person is their principal place of daily activities. The principality is to be determined on a case-by-case basis without entirely depending on the Civil Registration Records.[150] If the principal place of daily activities

[146] ibid 26 (suggesting the courts in Japan are required to determine the closest connection as such under the AGRAL).

[147] Nishioka and Nishitani (n 84) 15.

[148] See generally M Busssat, 'Ship Registration in Cambodia' (2021) *HBS Law: Legal Brief*, available at www.hbslaw.asia/images/Related-Publications/2021/Ship-Registration-in-Cambodia.pdf (accessed 10 December 2024). Note, however, the Kingdom signed but has not ratified the United Nations Convention on the Law of the Sea, which offers rules on flag state: United Nations, 'United Nations Convention on the Law of the Sea (Montego Bay, 10 December 1982): Status' (2024), available at https://treaties.un.org/Pages/ViewDetailsIII.aspx?src=TREATY&mtdsg_no=XXI-6&chapter=21&Temp=mtdsg3&clang=_en (accessed 10 December 2024).

[149] Busssat (n 148) 1–2. On ship registration in Cambodia, see generally BNG Legal, 'Ship Registration in Cambodia' (2021) *BNG Newsletter*, available at https://bnglegal.com/wp-content/uploads/2021/02/Newsletters_of_Ship-Registration-in-Cambodia.pdf (accessed 10 December 2024). The royal government previously granted the International Ship Registry of Cambodia (ISROC), a South Korean company, the sole and exclusive authority to register foreign-owned vessels as Cambodian-flagged ones. However, the government terminated the license in 2015 as it realized that the ISROC turned the Cambodian flag into a "flag of convenience", enabling ship owners who registered under the flag to avoid complying with more stringent regulations applicable elsewhere. In 2016, the Cambodian government notified the International Maritime Organisation, 'any ship claimed to be under Cambodian flag [by registry certificate issued by the ISROC] after [the end of August 2016] is considered illegal and subject to applicable international law and regulations': Ministry of Foreign Affairs and International Cooperation, 'Clarification' (2017), available at https://pressocm.gov.kh/wp-content/uploads/2017/10/ENG-Ministry-of-Foreign-Affairs-and-International-Cooperation-201710-1-5.pdf (accessed 10 December 2024).

[150] JICA, *Commentary on the Civil Code of the Kingdom of Cambodia [in Japanese]* (JICA, 2011) 12.

is unknown, the person's place of residence is deemed to be their domicile.[151] Regarding corporations, the CC provides that the domicile of a company shall be the location of the head office, which the company is required to designate upon its registration with the Ministry of Commerce.[152] These concepts of domicile and residence, albeit provided by the CC, shall apply to PIL issues, because the courts in Cambodia are expected to characterise subject matters based on the substantive law of the forum.[153]

VI. Substance and Procedure

Like other modern legal systems, Cambodian law distinguishes procedure from substance – i.e., rights and obligations.[154] The distinction is maintained in the context of conflict of laws because PIL is part of the domestic law of Cambodia. Thus, procedural matters are governed by the (procedural) law of the forum (i.e., the *lex fori*), and substantive matters are subject to the law of the cause of action or obligation (i.e., the *lex causae*) that is selected through the application of the appropriate conflict rules of the forum (i.e., the Cambodian choice of law rules applicable to the subject matter in dispute).[155] Drawing a clear line between substance and procedure is not easy because some procedural rules of a legal system are closely linked to substantive rules of the same system,[156] and because certain subject matters (appear to) have both procedural and substantive natures.[157] In discussing PIL in general, Garnett suggests that:

> The distinction between substance and procedure must … be analysed against the wider context of private international law, whose objectives are the pursuit of uniformity of outcome in decisions of national courts and the discouragement of forum shopping. Such aims are compromised when national systems of choice of law allow too wide a scope for the operation of forum law at the expense of foreign rules. *Accordingly, a narrow and limited definition of procedure focusing on the idea of the conduct or regulation of court proceedings is increasingly being adopted by most national and transnational legal systems in recognition of these concerns.*[158]

Cambodian jurists may also be encouraged to adopt this narrow interpretation of procedure when they consider the distinction between procedure and substance, because of the CCP's general observance of the doctrine of forum non convenience to prevent forum shopping.[159]

[151] CC, Art 35.

[152] ibid, Arts 49–51. See also generally Ministry of Commerce, 'Business Registration' (n.d.), available at www.businessregistration.moc.gov.kh/starting-a-business-2/register/ (accessed 10 December 2024).

[153] See Section IV.A above.

[154] See generally K Phallack, 'Overview of Contemporary Civil Procedures of Cambodia' in H Peng, K Phallack and J Menzel (eds), *Introduction to Cambodian Law* (Phnom Penh, Konrad-Adenauer-Stiftung Cambodia, 2012).

[155] Almost all major systems of PIL (including Japanese PIL) adopt the distinction between substance and procedure: R Garnett, 'Substance and Procedure' in J Basedow and others (eds), *Encyclopedia of Private International Law* (Cheltenham, Edward Elgar Publishing, 2017) 1668; Yokoyama (n 85) 35; Nishioka and Nishitani (n 84) 17–18.

[156] Nishioka and Nishitani (n 84) 18.

[157] Yokoyama (n 85) 35.

[158] Garnett (n 155) 1667 (emphasis added).

[159] See generally Teramura, 'Cambodia' 205; CCP, Art 19(1).

VII. Exclusion of Foreign Law

The principle of party autonomy is indispensable for conflict of laws and PIL. However, the choice of foreign law is not without safeguards. Most legal systems have certain rules that allow the forum court to exclude the application of foreign law in specific circumstances. This section considers such circumstances in the context of Cambodian law, focusing on mandatory rules and public policy.

A. Mandatory Rules

It is generally accepted by PIL commentators, including experts of Japan's AGRAL, that mandatory rules – rules not subject to contrary agreements – may be classified into two categories: non-derogable rules and overriding mandatory rules.[160] The first category is composed of rules that the parties may not depart from in a purely domestic context. For instance, if the *lex causae* is Japanese law, the parties would find that the principle of party autonomy is restricted to some extent by provisions for protecting weaker parties in relation to employment and consumer transactions, among others. These mandatory provisions, however, would not affect the status of Japanese law as governing law, in that they are non-derogable within the framework of the Japanese legal system. In other words, such mandatory rules only apply where they form part of the *lex causae*. Parties have the liberty not to choose a law containing those mandatory rules. In contrast, the second category, overriding mandatory rules (also referred to as internationally mandatory provisions or *lois de police*), are provisions that uphold the forum's fundamental legal principles embodying its social, economic, or political interests. These provisions apply to a given circumstance regardless of the law designated by the forum's conflict of law rules, and thus they override the foreign *lex causae*.

No discernible laws or regulations present the concept of overriding mandatory rules applicable under Cambodian law. Japanese law is not helpful either for filling the legal vacuum because the drafters of the AGRAL abstained from introducing provisions on overriding mandatory rules due to the difficulty in defining such rules, and the conditions of application for the rules,[161] and because either Japanese case law or academic debate on the subject had not yet fully developed.[162] Probably, a reasonable option for Cambodian jurists is to approach the identification of overriding mandatory rules based on the Kingdom's core values highlighted in the Constitution, such as national unity, democracy, guarantee of human rights, and rule of law.[163]

[160] M Wilderspin, 'Overriding Mandatory Provisions' in J Basedow and others (eds), *Encyclopedia of Private International Law* (Cheltenham, Edward Elgar Publishing, 2017) 1331; Yokoyama (n 85) 42–43; Nishioka and Nishitani (n 84) 20–22.

[161] Koide (n 100) 88–89; Yokoyama (n 85) 42.

[162] Koide (n 100) 86–87; Nishioka and Nishitani (n 84) 21.

[163] Preamble of the Constitution of the Kingdom of Cambodia.

B. *Ordre Public* or Public Policy

When it comes to PIL, public policy (or *ordre public*) is a general and abstract notion that is specified by judges for setting limits on the application of foreign law in a forum, based on local morality and social order.[164] The judges may adopt these limits when they consider choice of law and the recognition and enforcement of a foreign judgment and arbitral award. A foreign rule, judgment/decree, and award deemed contrary to the forum's public policy has no effect under the domestic legal system, notwithstanding the principle of international comity.

Nonetheless, implications of public policy under Cambodian conflict of laws rules are not quite conceivable as no discernible legal provisions, cases or academic commentaries address the concept in the context of choice of law. Should Cambodian jurists intend to develop a Cambodian concept of public policy that relies on Japanese PIL, they would need to overcome the following theoretical complications.

The first issue is whether they should develop a concept of public policy unique to Cambodian conflict rules and somewhat distinguishable from substantive legal norms of the forum. On public policy under Japanese law, commentators suggest that the concept of public policy at the choice of law level differs from the concept at the substantive law level, say, under the Civil Code.[165] The objectives of these concepts are different at two levels, in that public policy at the choice of law level focuses on the result of applying a foreign legal norm, whereas *ordre public* at the substantive law level deals with a certain legal act (issue) raised by a domestic law provision. This distinction is crucial for the proper function of conflict of laws, because, otherwise, any foreign law against non-overriding mandatory rules of the forum will be excluded from application.[166]

Regarding the issue as to when judges may trigger the public policy exception at the choice of law level, Japanese jurists posit the satisfaction of the following requirements.[167] First, the application of foreign law to an individual case must be unacceptable from the standpoint of Japanese law, in light of fundamental differences between the foreign and Japanese legal systems. Second, the facts of the case demonstrate sufficient proximity to Japan (i.e., the forum). The two requirements are in an inverse relationship, meaning that the closer the connection between the case and the forum is, the lower the threshold for the public policy intervention becomes. Cambodian jurists might find this approach to public policy useful when they establish their PIL concept of *ordre public* in due course.

The second issue is how to fill the lacuna caused by applying the public policy exception and the exclusion of the resulting application of foreign law. Japanese legal experts are divided on whether the legal vacuum is to be supplemented by (1) the (substantive) law of the forum, (2) the method for dealing with unknown foreign law, (3) *naturalis ratio* (*jôri*) based on the general ideas of fairness, and (4) the law having the closest connection

[164] I Thoma, 'Public Policy (*Ordre Public*)' in J Basedow and others (eds), *Encyclopedia of Private International Law* (Cheltenham, Edward Elgar Publishing, 2017) 1453–60.

[165] Nishioka and Nishitani (n 84) 22; T Kono, 'Public Policy [in Japanese]' in Y Sakurada and M Dogauchi (eds), *Private International Law Annoted, Vol 2* (Tokyo, Yuhikaku Publishing, 2011) 334; Sakurada (n 81) 136.

[166] Nishioka and Nishitani (n 84) 22.

[167] Yokoyama (n 85) 40; Nishioka and Nishitani (n 84) 22–23; Kono (n 165) 335–42; Sawaki and Dogauchi (n 81) 57–8; Sakurada (n 81) 137–39.

to the forum next to the excluded foreign law.[168] Further, a recent majority view among Japanese commentators denies the existence of such a legal lacuna, suggesting that the judge has already rendered a substantive decision and demonstrated certain value standards by excluding the application of foreign law based on the forum law.[169] The discussion has not been settled yet, but many cases have filled in the legal vacuum by adopting the substantive law of the forum – Japanese law.[170] Cambodian judges will possibly find this solution most convenient as they are most familiar with the Cambodian legal system, as discussed elsewhere in this chapter.

C. Evasion of Law

Evasion of law (*fraus legis*) in PIL is the circumvention of mandatory rules of law by either using law for purposes for which it is not designed or by avoiding the application of the law by intentionally not fulfilling the requirements for application.[171] A typical example of evasion of law is the incorporation of a shell company in a jurisdiction favourable to corporate activities to achieve specific financial objectives, such as the reduction of corporate tax payments and the avoidance of environmental regulations in producing goods or providing services. Statutory provisions and accessible resources do not clarify whether the law prohibits evasion of law in Cambodia. Japanese PIL has abolished rules regulating law evasion because choice of law under Japanese law is, as far as possible, to be determined solely on the basis of objective criteria. This is due to the difficulty of proving someone's intention to avoid the application of mandatory rules, regardless of whether the person acts in good or bad faith.[172] There would be no strong reason for complicating Cambodian PIL by adopting the vague requirements of law evasion that Japanese law itself has relinquished.

VIII. Conclusions

This chapter has examined the status and basic concepts of PIL in Cambodia. Though the country has a modern legal system, the history of Cambodian PIL is rather short. No accessible materials suggest a French-style system of PIL had been sufficiently developed during the French colonisation period. Rather, Cambodia started putting salient efforts into developing PIL rules after the collapse of the Khmer Rouge regime. The move accelerated when the modern Kingdom of Cambodia was established, and when the country signed a partnership agreement with JICA on legal technical assistance. However, the country still needs to establish a structured PIL system. For instance, sources of PIL are dispersed unsystematically in various statutes and international instruments, such as the CC, the CCP,

[168] Koide (n 100) 374–75; Sawaki and Dogauchi, (n 81) 59–60; Sakurada (n 81) 139–40.

[169] Koide (n 100) 375; Nishioka and Nishitani (n 84) 23; Sakurada (n 81) 139–40.

[170] Kono (n 165) 342; S Hayakawa, 'Public Policy (4): South Korean Law Not Recognising the Division of Property in Divorce' in M Dogauchi and Y Nakanishi (eds), *Leading Cases in Private International Law* (Tokyo, Yuhikaku Publishing, 2021) 29.

[171] K Siehr, 'Evasion of laws (fraus legis)' in J Basedow and others (eds), *Encyclopedia of Private International Law* (Cheltenham, Edward Elgar Publishing, 2017) 698ff.

[172] Yokoyama (n 85) 43; Nishioka and Nishitani (n 84) 24–25.

the Marriage and Family Law, the Commercial Arbitration Law and the Hague Adoption Convention. PIL legal provisions in these legal instruments often fail to address the preliminary matters and basic concepts of conflict of laws. Nonetheless, secondary sources of law are unlikely to fill the gaps because the doctrine of precedent has no outstanding effect on the Cambodian legal system, and because Cambodian jurists do not take legal research seriously yet. Such fundamental legal vacuums may be covered by borrowing relevant legal ideas from Japanese PIL since Cambodian private law is interwoven with Japanese legal thinking, thanks to JICA's long-term legal technical assistance.

3

Treatment of Foreign Law*

I. Introduction: Status of Choice of Law Rules

Choice of law rules are only at an early stage of development in the Kingdom of Cambodia. As discussed in Chapters 1 and 2, Cambodian private law is largely based on Japanese law thanks to the Legal Technical Assistance Project (the Project) by the Japan International Cooperation Agency (JICA), in which experienced Japanese legal experts guided Cambodian legal elites in drafting the main codes and laws regulating civil matters.[1] Nevertheless, the Project did not establish a set of conflict of laws rules like Japan's 2006 Act on General Rules for Application of Laws (AGRAL). The Cambodian legal experts were at first passionate about a plan for codifying choice of laws rules in the 2007 Civil Code of Cambodia (CC), and the Japanese advisors agreed to materialise that plan.[2] The Cambodian lawyers' idea was to establish a comprehensive framework of choice of laws based on private international law (PIL) norms that arguably existed in the country before the Khmer Rouge period.[3] However, the Cambodian lawyers ultimately dismissed the plan as a result of alleged time constraints.[4]

It is notable that Cambodian legal elites insisted on adopting such old choices of law norms. First, the Communist Party of Kampuchea's persistent persecution and execution of legal professionals during the Khmer Rouge period turned the country into a legal vacuum with only a few lawyers and the near-total destruction of legal documents.[5] Consequently, when the new Cambodian Government was established in 1993, only a limited amount of literature was available for the surviving Cambodian lawyers to investigate the pre-Khmer

* A version of this chapter is available as N Teramura, 'Cambodia' in K Nishioka (ed), *Treatment of Foreign Law in Asia* (Oxford, Hart Publishing, 2023) 171–90.

[1] N Teramura, 'Cambodia' in A Reyes and W Lui (eds), *Direct Jurisdiction* (Oxford, Hart Publishing, 2021); N Teramura, 'Japan as a Source of Legal Ideas: A View from the Mekong Subregion of ASEAN' (2021) 13 *New Voices in Japanese Studies* 19; Y Kaneko, 'Japan's Civil Code Drafting Support for Socialist Reform Countries: Diversity of Normative Choice' in Y Kaneko (ed), *Civil Law Reforms in Post-Colonial Asia: Beyond Western Capitalism* (Cham, Springer, 2019).

[2] Industrial Development and Public Policy Department at JICA, *Legal Technical Assistance for Cambodia: The History and Methodology of the Assistance of JICA in Drafting the Civil Code and the Civil Procedure Code [in Japanese]* (2012) 9.

[3] ibid 10–11.

[4] ibid.

[5] M Vickery, *Kampuchea: Politics, Economy and Society* (London, Frances Pinter, 1986) 120; K Phallack, 'Overview of the Cambodian Legal and Judicial System and Recent Efforts at Legal and Judicial Reform' in H Peng, K Phallack and J Menzel (eds), *Introduction to Cambodian Law* (Phnom Penh, Konrad-Adenauer-Stiftung Cambodia, 2012) 8; DA Donovan, 'Cambodia: Building a Legal System from Scratch' (1993) 27 *The International Lawyer* 445.

Rouge statutory norms such as the old Civil Code and the old Code of Civil Procedure.[6] Thus, the government requested that the JICA help to rebuild its legal infrastructure.[7] Second, a few commentators suggested in the early 1970s that certain French legal principles applied to choice of law issues in Cambodia as the Kingdom did not have relevant legislation.[8] However, they did not clarify the source of such principles, probably because French law only had a few provisions on choice of law.[9] Third, it would be more appropriate to draft choice of law legislation based on inspirations from Japanese PIL because the CC and the 2006 Code of Civil Procedure of Cambodia (CCP),[10] as well as other main bodies of private law, are built upon Japanese legal concepts and principles, and because, '[i]n contrast to France, which has no codified private international law, Japan [has] modern legislation in the field'.[11] In the end, virtually no traditional PIL principles deriving from the French colonisation are available to supplement the lack of codification of Cambodian choice of law rules. In contrast, Japanese PIL doctrines may play a gap-filler role for Cambodian PIL because of Japanese private law's role as the foundation of modern Cambodian civil law.

One may find Cambodia's sources of choice of law rules in various codes and laws. For instance, Article 3 of the CC (recognising the principle of party autonomy in private legal relationships) is regarded by practitioners as the basis of parties' rights to designate the governing law of a contract.[12] Likewise, Article 36 of the Commercial Arbitration Law of Cambodia (Arbitration Law) confers the parties freedom to agree on the rules of law to be applied to the merits of the dispute, allowing the arbitral tribunal to choose the appropriate applicable law voluntarily in case the parties are unable to reach such an agreement. Article 46 of the Arbitration Law confers the Appeal Courts of Cambodia with the power to refuse the recognition and enforcement of a foreign arbitral award that has not yet become binding on the parties under the law of which the award was made.[13] Moreover, the Law on the Marriage and Family sets out in Articles 79–81 a couple of conflict of laws rules pertaining to marriage between Cambodian citizens in a foreign country and that between a Cambodian citizen and a foreign national in Cambodia. Hence, the legal system of Cambodia indeed contains norms on conflict of laws, but these are not as comprehensive and organised as the AGRAL.

Nevertheless, the fact that those choice of law rules constitute some parts of the Cambodian legal system implies the significance of the treatment of foreign law for the Cambodian justice system. Because judges have the duty to observe the legal procedures

[6] Teramura (n 1) 201–03; I Sakano, 'Reflection on the Legal and Judicial Development Project for Drafting the Civil and Civil Procedure Codes of Cambodia [in Japanese]' (2003) 7 *ICD News* 91, 97.

[7] Teramura (n 1) 26–27.

[8] J Menzel, 'Cambodian Law: Some Comparative and International Perspectives' in H Peng, K Phallack and J Menzel (eds), *Introduction to Cambodian Law* (Phnom Penh, Konrad-Adenauer-Stiftung Cambodia, 2012) 490.

[9] ibid; G Cuniberti, 'France' in Jürgen Basedow and others (eds), *Encyclopedia of Private International Law* (Edward Elgar Publishing 2017) 2079.

[10] Unless otherwise stated, this chapter relies on the unofficial English translation of the CC and CCP prepared by the JICA through the Legal Technical Assistance Project, which are available at (respectively): www.jica.go.jp/project/cambodia/0701047/04/ku57pq00001spnva-att/01_02e.pdf; www.jica.go.jp/project/english/cambodia/0701047/materials/c8h0vm000000zsb2-att/01_01e.pdf (accessed 10 December 2024).

[11] ibid 490–91.

[12] Bun & Associates, 'Governing Law and Dispute Resolution [in Japanese]' (2017) *Bun & Associates Newsletter*.

[13] Commercial Arbitration Law, Art 46(1)(e). Note that the Appeal Courts may refuse the enforcement/recognition of an award only where the party against whom the enforcement/recognition is invoked requests the refusal, furnishing proof that the ground of refusal has been met.

and laws in force in the country,[14] and those PIL rules form parts of the domestic law of the Kingdom, the application of the rules in the courts is not facultative but mandatory. Cambodian judges would thus need to consider how to treat foreign law (if the choice of law rules apply to their proceedings) as the PIL rules in the national law may lead to the application of foreign legal norms.

Nonetheless, examining features of Cambodian treatment of foreign law is more complicated than it seems. For example, in contrast to the situation in other Southeast Asian jurisdictions, such as Singapore and Brunei Darussalam, where past judgments are publicly available,[15] it is difficult (and probably pointless) for commentators to try to discern judicial reasoning behind the application of foreign law in Cambodia. The reason for this is that Cambodian lawyers, including judges, do not regard the doctrine of precedent as being significant or convincing, as seen from their reluctance to perceive judgments as sources of law and their lack of passion for publishing judgments.[16] However, one may still obtain useful information from relevant statutes and other vital legal documents, such as official commentaries and textbooks, as well as notes and reports prepared by those legal experts involved in the drafting process of codes and laws. A great deal of these secondary authorities on Cambodian private law are written only in Khmer and/or Japanese,[17] as discussed in Chapters 1 and 2. Thus, this chapter explores the treatment of foreign law in Cambodia, taking into consideration relevant documents written not only in English but also in Japanese. In case such materials fall short of the information needed, the chapter will have recourse to the PIL concepts and principles of Japanese law because modern Cambodian private law has its roots in Japanese civil law.

II. Foreign Law before Judicial Authorities

A. Nature of Foreign Law

Whether a court characterises foreign law as 'law' or 'fact' may determine how the court treats foreign law.[18] Characterising foreign law as 'law' means that the court regards foreign law as part of or equivalent to domestic law, and that arguably leads to the mandatory application of foreign law by judges.[19] Characterising foreign law as 'fact' means that the court treats foreign law like other facts, so it will apply foreign law facultatively, relying primarily on evidence provided by parties.[20] Accordingly, the classification that the court takes will influence how foreign law is introduced, examined and applied in legal proceedings.[21]

[14] Constitution of Cambodia, Art 129.

[15] State Judiciary Department: Brunei Darussalam, 'Judgments Search' (n.d.), www.judiciary.gov.bn/SJD%20Site%20Pages/Judgment%20Search.aspx (accessed 10 December 2024); Singapore Courts: The Judiciary, 'Judgments' (2024), available at www.judiciary.gov.sg/judgments (accessed 10 December 2024).

[16] Teramura (n 1) 201–03; and the author's interview with local practitioners.

[17] Teramura (n 1) 202; Teramura (n 1) 28; S Leng, 'Problems in Translating Cambodian Civil Code and Civil Procedure Code and Future Prospects [in Japanese]' (2016) 68 *ICD News*.

[18] Y Nishitani, 'Treatment of Foreign Law: Dynamics Towards Convergence? – General Report' in Y Nishitani (ed), *Treatment of Foreign Law – Dynamics towards Convergence?* (Cham, Springer, 2017) 17.

[19] ibid.

[20] ibid.

[21] ibid.

The classification of foreign law under Cambodian law is not clear-cut. In explaining the rules of evidence under the CCP, the official commentary states:

> In civil lawsuits, the major subjects of proof are facts. However, *depending on the circumstances*, empirical principles and *legal norms may also be the subjects of proof*. ... Since judges are experts of law, they have the authority to apply laws and regulations based on their expertise, and they shall exercise such power in most cases. Nevertheless, *foreign law, local government ordinances and customs are not always clear and unambiguous to judges, so that the contents of these norms may have to be identified [by parties] based on evidence*.[22] [emphasis added]

This comment suggests as a basic rule categorising foreign law as 'law' provided that the law is clear to judges. However, it does not eliminate the possibility to treat foreign legal norms as 'facts' because the contents of these norms may be based on evidence. Therefore, foreign law is likely to be categorised as 'tertium genus' or of 'hybrid nature' in Cambodia.

B. Ascertainment of Foreign Law

i. Who Owes the Duty to Ascertain Foreign Law?

One might argue that a hybrid categorisation of foreign law is unusual for Cambodia since it follows a civil law system. Based on comparative research mainly targeting Europe, the Americas, and Northeast Asia, Nishitani claims that almost all civil law jurisdictions, including Japan, consider foreign law as 'law'.[23] Indeed, not a few Japanese PIL academics, as well as some judges, justify the characterisation of foreign law as 'law', relying on a thesis that foreign law is treated equally as domestic law (i.e., it can be applied without incorporation to Japanese law) so as to ensure international harmony of judicial decisions – arguably the main objective of Japanese PIL.[24] Thus, they claim that judges owe a professional obligation to investigate and apply foreign law. However, the central authority on Japanese civil procedure, Mikazuki, disagrees. He correctly points out that most Japanese judges are not trained in foreign law and are unlikely to have sufficient expertise in foreign legal systems to deal with random cross-border issues in litigation.[25] For better procedural efficiency and economy, Mikazuki refuses to impose on judges a duty to investigate the content of foreign law, suggesting that courts are only entitled to ascertain foreign law based on, but not limited to,

[22] JICA, 'Commentary on Cambodian Code of Civil Procedure: Judgment Procedure [in Japanese]' (n.d.), 58ff, available at www.moj.go.jp/content/000122394.pdf (accessed 10 December 2024) [This author's translation].

[23] Nishitani (n 18) 17. Among the jurisdictions investigated by the comparative research, other civil law jurisdictions adopting a hybrid categorisation of foreign law are Macau and Spain only, although the Spanish approach is different from Cambodia's as parties have the primary duty of proving foreign law (ibid 19); CA Monzonís, 'Spain: The Application of Foreign Laws in Spain – Critical Analysis of the Legal Novelties of 2015' in Y Nishitani (ed), *Treatment of Foreign Law – Dynamics towards Convergence?* (Cham, Springer, 2017) 331; G Tu, 'Macau: Proof and Information About Foreign Law in Macau' in Y Nishitani (ed), *Treatment of Foreign Law – Dynamics towards Convergence?* (Cham, Springer, 2017) 543.

[24] Y Nishitani, 'Treatment of and Access to Foreign Law in Japan' (2018) 23 *Journal of Japanese Law* 69, 75; Y Sakurada, *Private International Law [in Japanese]* (7th edn, Tokyo, Yuhikaku Publishing, 2020) 126.

[25] A Mikazuki, 'The Application of Foreign Law and the Court [in Japanese]' in T Sawaki and Y Aoyama (eds), *Theories of International Civil Procedure Law* (Tokyo, Yuhikaku Publishing, 1987) 250–53. Some French commentators also state that the strict application of the *iura novit curia* principle to foreign law is deemed to be unrealistic: S Corneloup, 'France – The Evolving Balance Between the Judge and the Parties in France' in Y Nishitani (ed), *Treatment of Foreign Law – Dynamics towards Convergence?* (Cham, Springer, 2017) 170.

the evidence submitted by parties.[26] According to Nishitani and Nakano, Mikazuki's practical approach that allegedly draws on common law is likely to be a minority view in Japan.[27] Nevertheless, his thesis is compatible with the Cambodian categorisation of foreign law advocated by the official commentary of the CCP.[28]

Moreover, the Cambodian judicial system should not underestimate the procedural efficiency and economy Mikazuki emphasises. This is because the strict extension of the principle of *iura novit curia* to the ascertainment of foreign law may create an additional burden on the Cambodian judicial officers who are already overwhelmed by their daily case management tasks. For example, as part of the Project, the JICA closely reviewed 14 first-instance judgments on divorce and loan refund cases issued between 2016 and 2017.[29] The salient challenge that the Japanese legal experts found in the judgments was that some judges did not manage to apply major codes and laws of Cambodia properly, despite these having been established about a decade ago.[30] According to Shinoda, a long-term JICA Legal Expert stationed in the Ministry of Justice of Cambodia (MOJ), some courts in loan refund cases failed to reflect in their judgments a precise understanding of interest and late payment damage/interest.[31] Under Cambodian law, interest is the monetary charge for borrowing money.[32] On the other hand, a party is entitled to claim damage/interest for late payment if the other party has paid back borrowed money after considerable delay.[33] The distinction between interest and late payment damage/interest has practical consequences for parties as the annual interest rate cap for interest on borrowed money is 18 per cent, while the same for late payment damage/interest is 27 per cent.[34] Nevertheless, the courts sometimes ordered a party to pay 'interest' on borrowed capital that was overdue and other times described late payment damage/interest as 'fine' (i.e., criminal penalty).[35] In other cases, the courts voluntarily decided on non-ex-officio matters not claimed by the parties despite Article 182(2) of the CCP prohibiting the court from adjudicating issues that the parties did not raise.[36] Such struggle of Cambodian judges with applying domestic law and Cambodia's international reputation of being a state with limited legal certainty and a weak rule of law,[37] will not warrant the strict inclusion of foreign law into the *iura novit curia*

[26] Mikazuki (n 25) 259–65 (pointing out that applying the *iura novit curia* principle to foreign law may overburden national courts that are unlikely to have sufficient capacities and resources, as well as time, to thoroughly investigate foreign legal systems).

[27] Nishitani, (n 24); S Nakano, 'Japan: Proof of and Information about Foreign Law in Japan' in Y Nishitani (ed), *Treatment of Foreign Law – Dynamics towards Convergence?* (Cham, Springer, 2017). See also K Yamamoto, 'Application of Foreign Law [in Japanese]' in Y Sakurada and M Dogauchi (eds), *Private International Law Annotated, Vol 2* (Tokyo, Yuhikaku Publishing, 2011) 353.

[28] JICA (n 22) 58ff.

[29] Y Shinoda, 'Report on the Investigation of Cambodian Court Judgments (1) [in Japanese]' (2019) 79 *ICD News* 60.

[30] ibid.

[31] ibid.

[32] CC, Arts 578 and 583.

[33] ibid, Arts 389 and 390.

[34] Arts 1 and 2 of the Prakas (Ministerial Ordinance) No 128 MoJ.PK/11 of the Ministry of Justice on the Maximum Interest Rate.

[35] Shinoda (n 29) 68.

[36] ibid 65ff.

[37] The Rule of Law Index 2024 ranked Cambodia 141th across 142 countries, and the Corruption Perception Index 2023 ranked Cambodia 158th across 180 states: World Justice Project, 'WJP Rule of Law Index®' (2024), available at https://worldjusticeproject.org/rule-of-law-index/global (accessed 10 December 2024);

doctrine in the Cambodian courts. Because of the hybrid status of foreign law, Cambodian judges may investigate and apply (but not be bound by) foreign legal norms based on evidence submitted by the parties.[38]

ii. Means for the Ascertainment of Foreign Law

As discussed above, Cambodian judges treat foreign law as law and evidence (fact). The legal aspect allows the judges to investigate foreign legal systems *sua sponte*, while no legal texts on Cambodian law define the authority of the judges in such a context. The factual aspect is likely to lead to the application of the rules of evidence to the ascertainment of foreign law. Then, the courts will find the following evidence of foreign law admissible: documentary evidence, including documents comprised of transcriptions of tape recordings or other recording media;[39] objects equivalent to documents 'such as drawings, photographs, audio and video tapes, or other items that are not documents but were created to express information';[40] expert witnesses designated by the court upon request by a party;[41] and evidence located abroad (that would be examined by an institution commissioned by the court to conduct the investigation, such as a competent government agency of the foreign country or an embassy, that is, an ambassador, minister or counsel, of Cambodia stationed in the foreign country).[42] Also, the courts may request competent foreign administrative institutions and Cambodia's diplomatic missions to conduct evidence investigation abroad,[43] even though Cambodia is not a party to the Convention of 18 March 1970 on the Taking of Evidence Abroad in Civil or Commercial Matters (the 1970 Hague Evidence Convention).[44] In addition, it is uncertain whether Cambodian judges can communicate directly with foreign judges on official channels because none of the Cambodian judicial

Transparency International, 'Corruption Perceptions Index 2023' (2024), available at www.transparency.org/en/cpi/2023?gad_source=1&gclid=Cj0KCQjwncWvBhD_ARIsAEb2HW8duSXLuItQiYOCFteUBFHBTSnXfSqT699mD3B6EiXzvD0EjVX_hT4aAt-KEALw_wcB (accessed 10 December 2024).

[38] This view is compatible with Arts 46(1)(a) and (e) of the Commercial Arbitration Law. The Articles provide the Appeal Courts with the power to decide the enforceability and recognisability of a foreign arbitral award where: (1) a party proves that the original arbitration agreement is not valid under the law applicable to the agreement; and (2) the award has not become binding on the parties under the law of which the award was made. In other words, the Articles allow the Appeal Courts to determine the enforceability/recognisability based on but not limited to the party's proof of the foreign law applicable to the arbitration agreement/award.

[39] CCP, Arts 148 and 159.

[40] ibid, Art 158.

[41] ibid, Arts 143 and 144. The expert witness is to testify matters specified by the parties and court.

[42] ibid, Art 129(1). The Article suggests in its official note (in Japanese) that the court intending to undertake the examination of evidence abroad needs to obtain permission from the host country based on international conventions and/or bilateral agreements (if any). Nevertheless, Art 129(2) of the CCP provides that '[a]n examination of … evidence conducted in a foreign [country], even [if] it contravenes [the] laws of [that country], [is still valid] if it does not contravene [the CCP]. It is unclear whether the host country will permit an institution commissioned by the court to undertake such illegal evidence taking.

[43] CCP, Art 130. However, the Article provides in its official note (in Japanese) that the court may commission a (foreign) government agency to conduct the necessary evidence examination only where the purpose of the examination is to ascertain an objective fact that may not lead to any fairness concern. For example, the note raises commissioning to a foreign meteorological bureau to investigate past weather in the country. Thus, the court is unlikely to rely on this Article to investigate controversial or complicated foreign legal issues, while it may request a foreign government agency to send non-contentious legal information such as statutes and judgments.

[44] HCCH, 'Status Table: Convention of 18 March 1970 on the Taking of Evidence Abroad in Civil or Commercial Matters' (2023) www.hcch.net/en/instruments/conventions/status-table/?cid=82 (accessed 10 December 2024).

officers have participated in the International Hague Network of Judges.[45] Moreover, in the age of information technology, it is hard to assume that Cambodian judges and attorneys hesitate to rely on accessible internet sources and electronic documents – foreign statutes, commentaries, textbooks and other publications – in searching for relevant information.[46] In fact, many courts in civil law countries utilise internet sources.[47] However, as webpages and e-documents can be easily modified and even forged,[48] it might not always be appropriate for Cambodian lawyers to depend on internet sources in ascertaining foreign law. Nonetheless, no statutory provisions in Cambodian law explicitly require judges to rely on authentication in determining the admissibility of internet sources.

Further, that foreign law is subject to proof in legal proceedings means that parties need to provide voluntary assistance to the court in examining the content of relevant foreign law, as per the evidence procedures under the CCP. Thus, following the principle of evidence-based decision-making, the court owes a duty to examine evidence offered by parties.[49] To support their argument and persuade the court, a party who intends to make a claim based on applicable foreign law needs to submit to the court evidence demonstrating the content of the foreign law. The court may then examine the evidence by its authority,[50] but the examination is to be conducted on evidence submitted by the parties only. The court is not allowed to undertake evidence collection on its motion.[51] Moreover, if a party submits as evidence a document written in a foreign language, the party shall attach the translation of the part of the document for which examination is sought.[52] The counterparty having any opinion on the accuracy of the translation shall express the opinion to the court in writing.[53] In addition, a party may file a request for the court to order the person (or party) possessing an evidentiary document to submit it to the court.[54] If the party does not comply with the document submission order, the court may find the other party's allegations on the document to be true.[55] Hence, those who rely on foreign law in Cambodian legal proceedings are advised to submit and/or specify evidence showing the content of the law.

Despite the evidence procedure under the CCP, the hybrid nature of foreign law may enable Cambodian judges to determine the law's substance without being bound by evidence submitted by parties. For example, the judges may adopt any other means to investigate foreign law independently, such as inquiries to (foreign) judicial/administrative

[45] HCCH, 'International Hague Network of Judges (IHNJ)' (2022), available at https://assets.hcch.net/docs/665b2d56-6236-4125-9352-c22bb65bc375.pdf (accessed 10 December 2024).

[46] See, e.g., Nishitani (n 18) 23.

[47] For example, German and Japanese courts: O Remien, 'Germany: Proof of and Information about Foreign Law – Duty to Investigate, Expert Opinions and a Proposal for Europe' in Y Nishitani (ed), *Treatment of Foreign Law – Dynamics towards Convergence?* (Cham, Springer, 2017) 193; Nakano 532.

[48] H Brander, 'Fake or Fact? (1) Digital Docs Manipulation and How to Spot It', *Counsel*, 15 January 2021, available at www.counselmagazine.co.uk/articles/fake-or-fact-digital-docs-manipulation-how-to-spot-it-(1) (accessed 10 December 2024).

[49] CCP, Arts 123–25.

[50] ibid, Art 124(2).

[51] ibid, Art 124(1).

[52] ibid, Art 149(1). See also Art 5 of the Constitution of Cambodia stating that '[t]he official language and script [of Cambodia] are Khmer'.

[53] CCP, Art 149(2).

[54] ibid, Art 148(1).

[55] ibid, Art 153(1).

institutions,[56] without being restricted to the result they obtained.[57] Indeed, ambiguity exists between the court's right to call for the assistance of the parties in the ascertainment of foreign law and the parties' obligation (or willingness) to satisfy such a request.[58] However, the court is unlikely to be deterred from exercising such a right, and the parties should endeavour to fulfil the assistance request expeditiously. This is because Article 4 of the CCP provides the court's general duty to proceed with civil actions fairly and speedily, mandating the parties to participate in such actions honestly and in good faith. Timely ascertainment of foreign law may help both judges and parties satisfy their obligations imposed by that Article. However, the assistance request does not force the judges to be bound by evidence offered by the parties since the court may determine the reliability of the legal information by itself.[59] In the end, it is at the judges' discretion whether to adopt in their judicial reasoning the evidence of foreign law submitted by the parties. Nevertheless, no statutory provisions in Cambodian law set out rules for the courts' examination of the legal information submitted by the parties.

iii. Qualifications to Provide Foreign Legal Information

In accordance with Article 144 of the CCP, the court shall appoint as an expert witness a person with the knowledge and experience needed to provide expert testimony on foreign law matters. However, the Article prohibits the following persons from serving as expert witnesses:

- a person whose expert testimony may lead to the criminal prosecution, conviction, reputational cost or family breakdown of the person, their spouse or another relative;[60]
- a (former) public officer, if they are required by the court to testify about matters related to their professional secret unless their supervisory government agency has approved them to provide the witness testimony;[61]
- an attorney at law, doctor, dentist, birth assistant, nurse, pharmacist, clergyman or any other person, if the witness testimony they are required by the court to provide is related to their professional secret or any fact that they learned in the course of their professional duties;[62] and
- any other person, if they are asked by the court to testify matters on their technological or professional secret.[63]

[56] ibid, Art 130. See also Mikazuki (n 25) 264–65.

[57] Mikazuki (n 25) 259–63; Nishitani (n 24) 75 (discussing Mikazuki's thesis).

[58] Mikazuki (n 25) 264.

[59] Art 124(2) of the CCP provides that '[t]he court may conduct an examination of the evidence on its own authority in cases where it finds that it cannot reach a conclusion on whether or not the factual allegations made by a party are true on the basis of the evidence offered by the parties, or in any other case where the court finds such examination necessary'.

[60] CCP, Art 144(3)(a).

[61] ibid, Art 144(3)(b) (noting that '[t]he supervisory government agency may not refuse to [grant] approval, except where such approval is likely to harm the public interest or significantly hinder the performance of public duties').

[62] ibid, Art 144(3)(c).

[63] ibid, Art 144(3)(d).

Moreover, a party may challenge the expert witness if there are circumstances that could prevent the witness from giving expert testimony in good faith.[64] Unless one of these grounds exists, the court may appoint as an expert witness any specialist who is knowledgeable about the disputed topic.

iv. Who Bears the Costs of Ascertaining Foreign Law?

Under Cambodian law, parties are primarily responsible for bearing the costs of ascertaining foreign law. For example, Article 62 of the CCP requires the parties or other persons related to the case to compensate for:

(a) an amount [of cost for] the court to investigate … evidence, serve documents, and conduct any other procedural act during the civil action; and
(b) an amount [of cost] equivalent to … travel and lodging costs for a judge and a court clerk should [they need to carry out] the investigation of evidence, investigation of facts, or other act … carried out outside of the courtroom.

As these provisions demonstrate, judges may order parties to pay the court's costs of ascertaining foreign law, and the unsuccessful party usually bears such costs.[65] Moreover, each party to a lawsuit shall pay its own attorney's fees.[66] In practice, it is common among Cambodian lawyers to claim the time they spent investigating foreign legal systems as part of their billable hours.[67]

C. Interpretation and Application of Foreign Law

A corollary of judges' obligation to apply choice of law rules under Cambodian law is that Cambodian judges are required to apply foreign law *ex officio* if the applicable choice of law rules lead to the application of such law.[68] The judges also have the power to ascertain the content of foreign law *ex officio* because of the hybrid nature of foreign law in the Cambodian legal system.[69] Requesting the application of foreign law, the parties may indeed plead and prove the content of foreign law as per the evidence rules in the CCP, and the judges take into account suggestions by the parties.[70] However, without being fully bound by the parties' pleadings and proof, the judges may exercise their professional right and authority to examine, determine and apply relevant foreign legal norms.[71]

There are no evident laws or regulations that define how judicial officers shall interpret and apply foreign law in the Cambodian civil courts. In Japan, the prevailing PIL theory suggests that judges shall interpret and apply foreign law in the ways courts of the country

[64] ibid, Art 145.
[65] ibid, Art 64.
[66] The official note on Art 63 of the CCP [in Japanese].
[67] The author's interview with Cambodian practitioners.
[68] See section I above.
[69] See sections II.A and II.B.i above.
[70] See section II.B.ii above.
[71] ibid.

of origin take.[72] It also claims that the doctrine is extended to the situations in which there is a gap in foreign law, that is, where the applicable foreign law fails to cover issues submitted to the courts.[73] There is no noticeable evidence that the Japanese legal theory has been incorporated into the Cambodian legal system. However, comparative research justifies the Cambodian courts to follow the doctrine. Investigating the treatment of foreign law in 29 major common and civil law jurisdictions, Nishitani concludes that 'it is generally accepted that foreign law ought to be interpreted and applied in accordance with the rules of interpretation established in the country of origin'.[74] Nishitani upholds this principle, invoking the purpose of the conflict of laws as follows:

> Where conflicts rules designate foreign law as the applicable law, it ought to be interpreted and applied correctly – in the same manner that a judge in that country would – to achieve international harmony and respect the parties' interests.[75]

Nishitani further claims that the general principle is naturally extended to gaps in foreign law, suggesting these are 'filled pursuant to the criteria in the country of origin to ensure the coherence of the foreign legal system'.[76] Because the majority of civil law countries, including Japan, opt for the approach elucidated by Nishitani,[77] and because Cambodia adopts a civil law system based on Japanese law,[78] it will not be unreasonable for Cambodian judicial officers to put on the shoes of the judges of the country of origin when they interpret foreign legal norms and fill their gaps.

However, mandating Cambodian judges to follow Nishitani's thesis is likely to be impractical, given the current situation of the Cambodian judiciary. The reason for this is that Cambodian judicial officers are (understandably) trained in adjudicating disputes under Cambodian domestic law. In the Kingdom, most new judges are appointed from judge students who have passed 'the examination for the selection of judges students' and have completed the professional training organised by the MOJ.[79] The institution responsible for conducting the professional training is the Royal School for Judges and Prosecutors (RSJP),[80] which was established by the Government of Cambodia in 2002.[81] The objective

[72] Nakano (n 27) 533; Y Tameike, *Lecture on Private International Law* [in Japanese] (Tokyo, Yuhikaku Publishing, 2005) 244; R Yamada, *Lectures on Private International Law* [in Japanese], 3rd edn (Tokyo, Yuhikaku Publishing, 2004) 133; Yamamoto (n 27) 357–58; Sakurada (n 24) 128.

[73] Tameike (n 72) 250; S Ikehara, H Egawa and R Yamada, *The General Theory of Private International Law and Nationality Law [in Japanese]* (Tokyo, Yuhikaku Publishing, 1973) 240; Yamada (n 72) 134.

[74] Nishitani (n 18) 31, noting that 23 of the 29 jurisdictions investigated and the Inter-American Convention on General Rules of Private International Law support that principle. Note, however, that the 23 jurisdictions are civil law jurisdictions, and the signatories of and parties to the Inter-American Convention are South and Central American countries that follow the civil law tradition: www.oas.org/juridico/english/sigs/b-45.html (accsessed 10 December 2024). Thus, the principle is generally accepted among civil law countries.

[75] ibid.

[76] ibid.

[77] ibid.

[78] See section I above.

[79] Law on the Status of Judges and Prosecutors, Arts 19ff.

[80] Also sometimes referred to as the Royal School for Magistracy (RSM): V Phun, 'Country Factsheet 2: Judicial Training in Cambodia' in A Nababan and others (eds), *Judicial Training in ASEAN: A Comparative Overview of Systems and Programs* (Phnom Penh, Konrad-Adenauer-Stiftung Cambodia, 2014) 31.

[81] M Ito, 'The History of JICA's Legal Technical Assistance in Cambodia [in Japanese]' (2021) 87 *ICD News* 47, 50; C Huot and S Rith, 'Hope of Justice Lies in School for Judges', *The Phnom Penh Post*, 21 November 2003, available at www.phnompenhpost.com/national/hope-justice-lies-school-judges (accsessed 10 December 2024).

of the RSJP is to provide judge students with opportunities to learn about Cambodian judicial proceedings to adjudicate domestic disputes.[82] Thus, the RSJP's training curriculum for judges focuses on the Cambodian legal system.[83] In fact, major private law subjects taught in the RSJP are (Cambodian) civil proceedings, judgment writing, family law and land law, among others.[84]

The judicial training curriculum does not systematically cover foreign law related topics like the Association of Southeast Asian Nations (ASEAN) legal framework, international law, comparative law or conflict of laws.[85] During the RSJP's one-year practical judicial traineeship,[86] some selected trainees are reportedly placed at courts abroad based on the frameworks of international cooperation that Cambodia concluded with foreign donors.[87] In addition, some donor countries offer special training programmes for senior judges and instructors teaching at the RSJP. For example, the JICA has trained Cambodian judicial elites for many years as part of the Legal and Judicial Development Project. It has sent elite legal officers (including those working for the RSJP) to Japan to enrol them in special capacity-building programmes on Japanese judicial proceedings, which have been taught by senior Japanese judges, experienced lawyers and famous professors.[88] This initiative aims to help those elite officers make use of the practical knowledge of Japanese law to enrich their understanding of the Cambodian justice system. The duration of the programmes is normally several weeks. Whether junior or senior, ordinal Cambodian judges are thus unlikely to have opportunities to study foreign legal systems comprehensively and systematically.

Certainly, some judges might be able to have intensive training on foreign judicial proceedings in Cambodia and abroad. However, such special programmes organised by Cambodia's official development assistance (ODA) partners are optimised for guest students who learn about specific topics on foreign law on a short-term basis. The programmes are not designed to let Cambodian trainees undergo 'real' professional training for judges who are expected to handle disputes under the foreign legal system. This is legitimate for these kinds of cooperation projects, most of which have small budgets and are delivered based on agreements between Cambodia and donor countries whose official languages are different.[89]

[82] A Misawa, 'Supporting the Training of Judges and Prosecutors in Cambodia [in Japanese]' (2004) 18 *ICD News* 1, 7.

[83] Phun (n 80) 34.

[84] Misawa (n 82) 7.

[85] Phun (n 80) 34.

[86] The judicial training programme of the RSJP consists of: (1) in-class training on legal theory for eight months; (2) practical judicial traineeship for one year; and (3) specialised training for four months: ibid 33.

[87] ibid 33.

[88] See, e.g., Social Development Department at JICA, *The Final Evaluation Report on the Project for the Improvement of Training on Civil Matters at the Royal School for Judges and Prosecutors of the Royal Academy for Judicial Professions [in Japanese]* (2008); Public Policy Department at JICA, *The Ex-ante Evaluation Report on the Project for the Improvement of the Training on Civil Matters at the Royal School for Judges and Prosecutors of the Royal Academy for Judicial Professions (Phase 2) [in Japanese]* (2009); Public Policy Department at JICA, *The Mid-term Review Report on the Project for the Improvement of the Training on Civil Matters at the Royal School for Judges and Prosecutors of the Royal Academy for Judicial Professions (Phase 2) [in Japanese]* (2010); Industry Development and Public Policy Department at JICA, *The Final Evaluation Report on the Project for the Improvement of the Training on Civil Matters at the Royal School for Judges and Prosecutors of the Royal Academy for Judicial Professions (Phase 2) [in Japanese]* (2012).

[89] P Nicholson and T Kuong, 'Japanese Legal Assistance: An East Asian Model of Legal Assistance and Rule of Law?' (2014) 6 *Hague Journal on the Rule of Law* 141.

Demanding Cambodian trainees to pass a professional training course whose participants are expected to be equipped with specialist (non-Khmer) language skills and expertise is unreasonable at best and unrealistic at worst.

In the end, the situation of the judicial training in Cambodia confirms Mikazuki's thesis – judges of a certain legal system are not trained in adjudicating disputes based on foreign legal norms.[90] In theory, Cambodian judges may thus be required to interpret and apply foreign law in the manner adopted by courts of the country of origin, following their reasonable knowledge and investigation of that country's legal practice. However, it is likely to be impractical for the judges to replicate foreign judicial reasonings in Cambodian judgments.

D. Unascertainable Foreign Law

No available materials suggest how Cambodian courts cope with a case in which the parties and the judges are unable to establish the content of the foreign law applicable to the case. In Japan, the courts and academics are divided on how to fill such a legal vacuum reasonably and effectively.[91] For example, many courts hand down decisions, referring to the *lex fori*[92] (i.e., Japanese law) in filling a gap in applicable foreign law.[93] On the other hand, a significant number of judgments rely on the so-called 'reasonable test' approach that seeks to deduce and apply relevant norms presumably in force in the country of origin, considering the fundamental principles of the foreign legal system and appropriate solutions for the case at hand.[94] However, judicial and academic opinions have yet been settled as to whether the reasonable deduction of the content of applicable foreign law is based on the *lex fori*,[95] the presumed foreign law,[96] or the general reasonableness test.[97] Further, several judges and scholars recommend relying on the legal system most similar to the applicable foreign law in presuming the non-ascertainable content of the law.[98]

[90] Mikazuki (n 25) 251ff.

[91] Nishitani (n 24) 80; Nakano (n 27) 533–34; Yamamoto (n 27) 358–62; Sakurada (n 24) 129-132; T Sawaki and M Dogauchi, *Introduction to Private International Law [in Japanese]* (Tokyo, Yuhikaku Publishing 2018) 53–55; T Morishita, 'Dealing with Unascertainlable Foreign Law [in Japanese]' in M Dogauchi and Y Nakanishi (eds), *Leading Cases in Private International Law* (Tokyo, Yuhikaku Publishing, 3rd edn, 2021) 210–11.

[92] *Lex fori* means the law of the jurisdiction or authority seized with a case.

[93] See, e.g., *Takechi v Hayashi* [1987] Yamaguchi Family Court (Shimonoseki Branch) Showa 62 (Ka) No 163, 40/3, Kateisaiban Geppo [in Japanese] 90; *XX v YY* [1987] Kyoto District Court Showa 61 (Wa) No 2444, 1275 Hanrei Jiho [in Japanese] 107; *Kin v Gen* [1984] Tokyo High Court Showa 59 (Ne) No 58, 37/9 Kaiteisaiban Geppo [in Japanese] 87. See also Nishitani (n 24) 81.

[94] Nishitani (n 24) 81.

[95] *Tokio Marine Fire Insurance Co Ltd v The Shipping Corporation of India Ltd* [1983] Kobe District Court Showa 51 (Wa) No 908, 1092 Hanrei Jiho [in Japanese] 114; *Tei v Pak* [1982] Nagano Family Court Showa 51 (Ka) No 131, 35/1 Kateisaiban Geppo [in Japanese] 105.

[96] *XX v YY* [1987] Tokyo District Court Showa 58 (Wa) No 7218 / Showa 60 (Wa) No 162 / Showa 61 (Wa) No 1748, 1278 Hanrei Jiho [in Japanese] 97; *Son Phong v Champassak* [1986] Hiroshima District Court Showa 60 (Ta) No 18, 38/6 Kateisaiban Geppo [in Japanese] 43. See also Nishitani (n 24) 81.

[97] *XX v YY & others* [1985] Osaka District Court Showa 60 (Ta) No 4, 1179 Hanrei Jiho [in Japanese] 94; *Doihara v The Superintending Prosecutor of the Tokyo High Public Prosecutors Office* [1981] Tokyo High Court Showa 55 (Ne) No 1051, 34/9 Kateisaiban Geppo [in Japanese] 72.

[98] *Takahara v Ryu* [1983] Nagoya Family Court Showa 58 (Ka) No 1493, 36/11 Kateisaiban Geppo [in Japanese] 138; *XX v YY* [1975] Naha Family Court Showa 49 (Ka I) No 21 / Showa 49 (Ka I) No 22, 28/2 Kateisaiban Geppo [in Japanese] 115; Ikehara, Egawa and Yamada (n 73) 243; Yamada (n 72) 136; Nakano (n 27) 533–34; Nishitani (n 24) 81.

For instance, the Tokyo District Court determined in 2015 the rules of tort and unjust enrichment in Myanmar, relying on the corresponding rules in English law.[99]

This diversity of opinions among Japanese judges and scholars will likely spark controversy among the Cambodian legal profession when the issue of unascertainable foreign law has caught more attention from lawyers in Cambodia. In the age of the internet, Cambodian judges will probably seldom declare foreign law as inaccessible because many countries have improved means of accessing their laws by publishing their legislation and cases online. Nevertheless, the judges may not eliminate the possibility as Cambodia is surrounded by countries whose legal systems do not strictly follow the doctrine of precedent and publish only a small number of judgments.[100]

E. Judicial Review/Appeal

i. Erroneous Application of Choice of Law Rules

In Cambodia, choice of law rules form part of domestic law.[101] A court's erroneous application of such rules may thus constitute an error on a question of law that may become a cause for reversal by a higher court, provided that the judgment has not yet become final and binding.[102] Those who intend to challenge a court's holding on choice of law need to prepare an *Uttor* appeal and/or *Satuk* appeal.[103] Parties may file an *Uttor* appeal against a judgment rendered by a court of first instance[104] within one month from the day when service of the written judgment was made to the parties.[105] Such an appeal is permissible where the parties have not agreed in writing to exclude their right to appeal to an *Uttor* appellate court,[106] and where the judgment was handed down on a civil or commercial matter whose value exceeded 5,000,000 Riel (around US$1,230).[107] Then, the parties may request a second instance court to re-examine both legal and factual determinations in a judgment rendered at the first instance.[108] Incidentally, the parties may apply to the Supreme Court in Phnom Penh for a *Satuk* appeal on a judgment issued by an *Uttor* appellate court.[109] The parties may file the appeal only 'on the grounds of a violation of the Constitution, laws, or regulations that influence the judgment'.[110] Thus, they are not allowed to request the

[99] *XX v YY* [2015] Tokyo District Court Heisei 25 (Wa) No 32882, LEX/DB 25532655 [in Japanese] 1.

[100] N Sakai and S Kamata, 'The Doctrine of Precedent in Vietnam [in Japanese]' (2017) 73 *ICD News* 29; A Ito, 'Legal Education and Professional Legal Training in Laos: Towards the Birth of Lao Jurisprudence [in Japanese]' (2020) 82 *ICD News* 40, 47.

[101] See section I above.

[102] CCP, Art 259ff.

[103] ibid, Art 259(1).

[104] ibid, Art 259(1)(a).

[105] ibid, Art 264.

[106] ibid, Arts 260(1)(a), 260(2), 263.

[107] ibid, Arts 260(1)(b).

[108] JICA (n 22) 127.

[109] CCP, Art 283 and Arts 259(1)(a)–(b). Note that the parties may file a *Satuk* appeal against a judgment rendered by a first instance court if they have agreed not to have an *Uttor* appeal but have agreed to, reserve the right to file a *Satuk*/final appeal: ibid, Arts 259(1)(a) and 260(1).

[110] ibid, Art 284; JICA (n 22) 129. The Supreme Court shall transfer a claim of unconstitutionality to the Constitutional Council, except where it deems the claim is inadmissible: Law on the Organisation and the Functioning of the Constitutional Council 2018, Art 19.

Supreme Court to review a lower court's factual determinations.[111] The Supreme Court only re-examines an *Uttor* judgment's specific legal issues – including matters on choice of law – raised by the parties because the court is bound by the facts lawfully determined in the original judgment.[112] Therefore, when a Cambodian court misapplies choice of law rules, the parties would be allowed to file an appeal to a higher court.

ii. Erroneous Application of Foreign Law

A party would possibly consider an option to challenge a judgment when the court that issued the decision correctly applied conflict of law rules and nevertheless misinterpreted the foreign law applicable to the dispute. As discussed in section II.A, Cambodian law perceives foreign law as a question of fact and law. The hybrid nature of foreign law does not prevent the party from appealing against a judgment rendered by a first instance court because they may file an *Uttor* appeal to request for review of both factual and legal issues in that judgment.[113] One might argue that the hybrid nature will pose a difficulty to the party when they plan to undertake a *Satuk* appeal. However, the Supreme Court is unlikely to reject such an appeal by emphasising the factual aspect of foreign law. Article 297 of the CCP provides that judges in a *Satuk* appeal case are not obliged to follow facts determined in the original judgment when they intend to examine *ex officio* matters.[114] Accordingly, the Supreme Court is not constrained by the determination of foreign law in the previous instance (even where the decision emphasises the factual aspect of the foreign law) because Cambodian judges have the authority to investigate the content of foreign law on their own motion.[115] Hence, the Cambodian legal system is likely to allow the appellate courts and the Supreme Court to review the erroneous application of foreign law.

III. Foreign Law in Other Instances

A. Administrative and Non-judicial Authorities

Local government officials and diplomats at Cambodian embassies/consulates are sometimes required to ascertain foreign law as part of their daily duty. For instance, Sub-Decree No 103 S-D/BK on Civil Status (the Civil Registration Sub-Decree) mandates in Article 3 all Cambodian citizens to register their civil status in Civil Status Books.[116] Each

[111] Note that parties must file a *Satuk* appeal within one month of receiving the written judgment by an appeal court: CCP, Art 286.

[112] ibid, Arts 295–96; K Phallack, 'Overview of Contemporary Civil Procedures of Cambodia' in H Peng, K Phallack and J Menzel (eds), *Introduction to Cambodian Law* (Phnom Penh, Konrad-Adenauer-Stiftung Cambodia, 2012) 166.

[113] See section II.E.i above.

[114] CCP, Art 296.

[115] See section II.B.i above.

[116] An unofficial English translation of the Sub-Decree is available at: www.skpcambodia.com/storage/uploads/files/Nationality_Immegration_Civil%20Registration/Sub-dree%20No103%20on%20Civil%20Registration-Eng.pdf (accessed 10 December 2024).

commune/sangkat shall keep the Books to record the birth, marriage and death of Cambodian citizens and foreigners living in the jurisdiction.[117] The Chief of the commune/sangkat,[118] as the Registrar of the administrative division,[119] has the professional obligation to maintain the Books for the commune/sangkat.[120] The Registrar has to examine and record essential facts related to the birth, marriage and death of those registered in the Books.[121] To keep records on Cambodian citizens residing in foreign countries, the embassies and consulates of Cambodia also keep the Books,[122] and each embassy/consulate must have one officer who takes the role of Registrar to update the Books upon nomination by the Ministry of Foreign Affairs and International Cooperation.[123] Hence, Cambodian Registrars, particularly those working at diplomatic missions overseas, will have to discern foreign law when they undertake civil registrations involving foreign elements.

In fact, the Registrars, whether working at local governments or diplomatic offices, are required to investigate foreign law in handling marriages performed overseas. On Registrars at embassies/consulates, Article 79 of the Law on the Marriage and Family provides:

> [A] [m]arriage between [Cambodian citizens] or between a Cambodian citizen and [a] foreigner living in a foreign country must be held before the [R]egistrar of the embassy or consulate of the State of Cambodia which is located in the [foreign] country where both part[ies] reside. … [A] [m]arriage between [Cambodian citizens] or [between a] Cambodian citizen and [a] foreigner, which is formally held [in accordance with] marriage procedure[s] described by the law of the marriage [in the foreign country where both parties reside], shall be recognized as being valid in the [Kingdom] of Cambodia as long as such a marriage is not against … the laws of the [Kingdom] of Cambodia. A marriage certificate or a copy of the marriage certificate must be registered in a [Civil Status Book kept at] the embassy or consulate of the [Kingdom] of Cambodia [in the foreign country].[124]

Accordingly, the Registrars must examine whether the marriage has complied with the law of the foreign country where the couple resides. On Registrars in communes/sangkats, Article 79 states that:

> The [Kingdom] of Cambodia shall enter the marriage certificate [issued by the authority of the country where the couple held the marriage] or [a] copy of the marriage certificate in the [Civil Status Book] of the [c]ommune or [sangkat] where both [parties] reside.[125]

[117] Civil Registration Sub-Decree, Art 12.

[118] The sub-national administration of Cambodia consists of: (1) capital city/province; (2) district/municipality/khan; and (3) sangkat/commune. As at 10 December 2024, Cambodia has 1,378 communes and 274 sangkats: National Committee for Sub-National Democratic Development, 'Gazetteer Database Online' (n.d.) http://db.ncdd.gov.kh/gazetteer/view/index.castle (accessed 10 December 2024). Each commune/sangkat has a commune council consisting of a president (also called commune/sangkat chief), a few deputies and other members. All members of the council are elected directly by Cambodian citizens living in the commune/sangkat: Open Development Cambodia, 'Administration' (2015) https://opendevelopmentcambodia.net/topics/administration/#ref-79177-3 (accessed 10 December 2024).

[119] Civil Registration Sub-Decree, Art 8.

[120] ibid, Arts 9 and 15.

[121] ibid, Arts 9 and 15.

[122] ibid, Art 14.

[123] ibid, Art 11 (noting that the Ministry of Interior shall be informed of the nomination of Registrar).

[124] An unofficial English translation of the Law on the Marriage and Family is available at https://faolex.fao.org/docs/pdf/cam208228.pdf (accessed 10 December 2024). See also Civil Registration Sub-Decree, Art 32.

[125] https://faolex.fao.org/docs/pdf/cam208228.pdf (accessed 10 December 2024).

Then, the local Registrars may have to discern whether the marriage and its certificates comply with the matrimonial law of the state where the marriage took place and the document was issued.[126]

B. Alternative Dispute Resolution

The two types of arbitration popular in Cambodia are international commercial arbitration (ICA) and labour arbitration.[127] Because ICA is a means of solving cross-border business disputes, international arbitrators are used to dealing with issues on conflict of laws and application of foreign law. The Arbitration Law recognises party autonomy to choose the rules of law governing the merits of the dispute, mandating the arbitral tribunal to designate and apply the rules it considers appropriate where the parties are unable to agree on the governing law.[128] Cambodia's top ICA institution, the National Commercial Arbitration Centre (NCAC), also articulates such norms in its Arbitration Rules.[129] In contrast, the main aim of labour arbitration in Cambodia is to settle differences between employers and employees following domestic labour law. In fact, the mission of the Arbitration Council – Cambodia's flagship labour arbitration body established in 2003 with the support of the Ministry of Labour[130] – is to facilitate parties to settle collective employment disputes in Cambodia, in accordance with the Labour Law of the Kingdom.[131] Thus, both conflict of laws and ascertainment of foreign law may rarely arise in labour arbitration held in Cambodia, while arbitrators are expected to come across such issues in ICA proceedings.

The complexity is that no discernible legal instruments and materials define how international arbitrators ascertain foreign legal norms under Cambodian law. The ambiguity is exacerbated by a widely accepted theoretical justification of international arbitration. The thesis suggests that international arbitration is not anchored in any municipal legal system, claiming that international arbitration is underpinned by the autonomous arbitral order that exists outside states.[132] Adopting the thesis, arbitrators will regard any applicable

[126] Moreover, Art 34 of the Civil Registration Sub-Decree allows a couple between immigrants/foreigners living lawfully in the territory of Cambodia to have a marriage in accordance with the law on marriage of the couple's country, provided that the Registrar of the couple's commune/sangkat has approved the marriage. Following the marriage, the couple may request either the embassy/consulate of their home country to Cambodia or the Registrar of their commune/sangkat to record the marriage in the Civil Status Book. Then, the Registrar may need to study the foreign law applied to the marriage. Other instances where the Registrar may be expected to investigate foreign law include the registration of the birth of a child between Cambodian parents or between a Cambodian citizen and a foreign national living abroad, as well as the registration of the death of a Cambodian citizen who was residing in a foreign country. See Civil Registration Sub-Decree, Arts 26 and 41.

[127] The author's interview with Cambodian practitioners while working at a top Cambodian law firm in 2020.

[128] Commercial Arbitration Law, Art 36.

[129] 2021 NCAC Arbitration Rules, Art 32.

[130] Arbitration Council, 'The Arbitration Council: Background' (n.d.), available at www.arbitrationcouncil.org/about-ac/the-arbitration-council/ (accessed 10 December 2024); S Tamagaki, 'The Arbitration Council in Cambodia: Impacts of the 2016 Law on Trade Unions and Prakas No. 303 by the Ministry of Labour and Vocational Training [in Japanese]' (2019) 80 *ICD News* 56.

[131] Arbitration Council, 'Law' (n.d.), available at www.arbitrationcouncil.org/resources/laws-regulations/law/ (accessed 10 December 2024) (noting that '[t]he Labour Law is pivotal to all decision making by the Arbitration Council').

[132] E Gaillard, *Legal Theory of International Arbitration* (Leiden, Martinus Nijhoff Publishers, 2010); N Teramura, *Ex Aequo et Bono as a Response to the 'Over-Judicialisation'of International Commercial Arbitration* (Alphen aan

national law as foreign law. They will unlikely distinguish Cambodian law from other legal systems in that respect, even where the seat of their arbitration is in Cambodia. This is because the arbitration will be presumed to be independent of the Cambodian legal order, and both Cambodian and other foreign legal norms will be equally foreign to the arbitrators. Thus, pondering international arbitrators' treatment of 'foreign law' under 'Cambodian law as domestic law' is theoretically complex and difficult.

In the context of the general practice of international arbitration, commentators are inclined to discuss arbitrators' duty to ascertain the content of the applicable law without drawing a sharp line between domestic and foreign laws.[133] The Arbitration Committee of the International Law Association (ILA) supports the lack of distinction, suggesting that '[u]nlike before national courts where there is a distinction between national and foreign law, in arbitration one can only speak of applicable law'.[134] Applying this to the context of Cambodia, international arbitrators in the Kingdom have to tailor their approach to assessing the 'applicable law' instead of the applicable foreign law. However, no harmonised rules have yet been established to regulate such a field of arbitration practice.[135]

The Arbitration Committee of the ILA has recognised the need for guidance and development of best practices for arbitrators to investigate the contents of the applicable law.[136] In 2010, the Committee published *the Report on Ascertaining the Contents of the Applicable Law in International Arbitration* to set out basic principles that international arbitrators are encouraged to follow in discerning the substance of the applicable law.[137] Taking into account various arbitration acts, institutional rules and arbitral awards, the Report comments that arbitrators deciding a matter based on a legal norm not invoked by the parties may be subject to the accusation from the parties of exceeding their mandate, even where such an approach would have been acceptable in a court adopting the *jura novit curia* doctrine.[138] The reason for this comment is that arbitrators are not allowed to stray beyond their mandate agreed by the parties.[139] In addition, the Report articulates what it calls 'the most acceptable general approach' for arbitrators to determine the content of the applicable law as follows:

> Arbitrators should primarily rely on the parties to articulate legal issues and to present the law, and disputed legal issues. They should give parties appropriate directions in relation thereto and should give appropriate weight to information so obtained. Arbitrators must through the

den Rijn, Wolters Kluwer, 2020) 153ff; N Teramura, 'Ex Aequo et Bono and Arbitration Theories: an Arbitrator's Subjective Perspective of Fairness as the Final 'Gap-Filler'' (2020) 38 *ASA Bulletin* 350.

[133] GB Born, *International Commercial Arbitration*, 3rd edn (Alphen aan den Rijn, Wolters Kluwer, 2020) 2141; N Blackaby and others, *Redfern and Hunter on International Arbitration*, 7th edn, (Oxford, Oxford University Press, 2022) para 5.15; G Kaufmann-Kohler, 'The Arbitrator and the Law: Does He/She Know It? Apply It? How? And a Few More Questions' (2005) 21 *Arbitration International* 631.

[134] FD Ly, MW Friedman and LGR di Brozolo, 'International Law Association International Commercial Arbitration Committee's Report and Recommendations on Ascertaining the Contents of the Applicable Law in International Commercial Arbitration' (2010) 26 *Arbitration International* 193, 206.

[135] P Baysal and M Atar, 'A Comparative Analysis of Content-of-Laws Inquiry and Its Importance for International Commercial Arbitration', *Kluwer Arbitration Blog*, 25 January 2020, available at http://arbitrationblog.kluwerarbitration.com/2020/01/25/a-comparative-analysis-of-content-of-laws-inquiry-and-its-importance-for-international-commercial-arbitration/ (accessed 10 December 2024).

[136] Blackaby and others (n 133) 219.

[137] Ly, Friedman and Brozolo (n 134) 193.

[138] ibid 214.

[139] ibid.

> proceeding develop a sufficient understanding of the applicable law that they can fulfill their mandate to decide the dispute according to law. Arbitrators who attempt to develop legal issues in a strict application of *iura novit curia* approach risk taking the arbitration from the parties and appearing partial. Yet arbitrators who completely fail to seek clarification of legal issues in a strict *laissez faire* approach risk not having sufficient guidance when they go to render an award, or risk making an award that is incorrect on the legal issue in question. Accordingly, arbitrators should inquire about the applicable law within the general parameters of the arbitration defined by the parties and, considering costs, time and relevance of issues, may conduct their own research, provided the parties are given an opportunity to be heard on material that goes meaningfully beyond the parties' submissions.[140]

International arbitrators in Cambodia are possibly willing to adopt this balanced approach when researching applicable law. They are keen to follow the international best practice of arbitration,[141] and global legal experts perceive the approach advocated by the ILA's Report as part of the best practice.[142] Hence, compared with Cambodian judges, international arbitrators in Cambodia have limited authority to invoke their independent investigation in the application of municipal law.

IV. Access to Cambodian Law

Some government ministries and departments whose duties are related to the activities of foreign companies have websites that provide, in English, information on the laws and regulations of Cambodia. For example, the Council for the Development of Cambodia (CDC) has a webpage that aims at helping foreign investors access business-related legislation and government orders.[143] Noting that the translation is unofficial,[144] the page offers in English a comprehensive set of such legislation and orders in the fields of: agriculture, fisheries, general business, construction, customs, development, education, environment, finance, forestry, government, industry, infrastructure, intellectual property rights, investment, labour and employment, land, mining, society special economic zones, tax and accounting, telecommunications, tourism, trade, transportation and logistics, among others. Moreover, the Consumer Protection Competition and Fraud Repression (CCF) Directorate-General of the Ministry of Commerce has a webpage that lists the English language versions of laws, regulations and other legal documents related to its roles and functions. Such laws include the Law on Consumer Protection, Law on the Management of Quality and Safety of Products and Services, Law on E-Commerce, Law on Trademark and Acts of Dishonest Competition and

[140] ibid 217–18.

[141] S Sarath, 'Arbitration Rules Under Review', *Khmer Times*, 28 July 2020, available at www.khmertimeskh.com/50749327/arbitration-rules-under-review/ (accessed 10 December 2024).

[142] S Loizou, 'Revisiting the "Content-of-Laws" Enquiry in International Arbitration' (2018) 78 *Louisiana Law Review* 811; CP Alberti and DM Bigge, 'Ascertaining the Content of the Applicable Law and Iura Novit Tribunus: Approaches in Commercial and Investment Arbitration' (2015) 70 *Dispute Resolution Journal* 1; J Waincymer, 'International Arbitration and the Duty to Know the Law' (2011) 28 *Journal of International Arbitration* 201.

[143] CDC, 'Laws and Regulations' (n.d.), available at http://cdc.gov.kh/laws-and-regulations/ (accessed 10 December 2024).

[144] Art 5 of the Constitution provides that '[t]he official language and script [of the Kingdom of Cambodia] are Khmer'.

the Law on Competition.[145] The CDC and the CCF Director-General regularly update their websites to assist foreign businesses in obtaining the latest Cambodian legal instruments.

The ODA partners of Cambodia also maintain websites collecting the non-Khmer language versions of principal legislative documents. For example, the Ministry of Justice of Japan ("MOJJ") has a page dedicated to the Legal and Technical Assistance Project implemented by its International Cooperation Department (ICD) and JICA.[146] The unofficial Japanese translation of many laws and regulations of various fields is available on the Japanese language website. In addition, the JICA has a webpage exhibiting materials that Japanese and Cambodian legal experts prepared through the Legal Technical Assistance Project.[147] Such materials include the unofficial Japanese and English versions of the CCP, CC and other relevant bodies of law.[148] Thus, the websites of the ICD and JICA are valuable tools for Japanese investors to learn about Cambodia's statutory documents.

While many online platforms introduce the laws and regulations of the Kingdom in non-Khmer languages, few platforms touch upon the decisions of the Cambodian courts. A database of the Asian Legal Information Institute (AsianLII), which was developed by the Australasian Legal Information Institute (AustLII), provides the English translation of judgments rendered by the Constitutional Council of Cambodia between 2003 and 2009.[149] Moreover, some project reports authored by JICA legal experts present selected civil court judgments in Japanese.[150] However, the vast majority of court decisions are not available in foreign languages because the courts in Cambodia are not expected to publish their rulings.[151] It was only around the end of 2020 that the MOJ started publishing some judicial decisions as points of reference, thanks to the JICA's long-term support.[152] However, the MOJ's new database contains only a handful of verdicts from civil litigation cases, and these decisions are not regarded as sources of law.[153] In the end, the most plausible method for foreign entities to access Cambodian court decisions is likely to seek assistance from local law firms that maintain close connections with Cambodian judicial officers and have the capacity to provide legal services in English.[154]

[145] CCF Director-General, 'Laws & Regulations: Laws, Regulations and Other Legal Documents Related to the Roles and Functions of the CCF Directorate-General' (2021), available at www.ccfdg.gov.kh/en/laws-regulations/ (accessed 10 December 2024).

[146] MOJJ, 'Cambodia [in Japanese]' (n.d.), available at www.moj.go.jp/housouken/houso_houkoku_cambo.html (accessed 10 December 2024).

[147] JICA, 'The Legal and Judicial Development Project (Phase 3): Materials' (n.d.), available at www.jica.go.jp/project/english/cambodia/0701047/materials/index.html (accessed 10 December 2024).

[148] ibid.

[149] Asian Legal Information Institute, 'Constitutional Council of Cambodia' (n.d.), available at www.asianlii.org/kh/cases/KHCCl/ (accessed 10 December 2024).

[150] A Kamiki, 'Report on the Investigation of Cambodian Court Judgements [in Japanese]' (2011) 48 *ICD News* 25; Shinoda (n 29).

[151] See section I above.

[152] N Chheng, 'Courts' Decisions Now Published as Reference Source', *The Phnom Penh Post*, 4 January 2021, available at www.phnompenhpost.com/national/courts-decisions-now-published-reference-source (accessed 10 December 2024).

[153] ibid.

[154] Teramura (n 1) 218. In contrast, the Arbitration Council has published many past arbitral awards: Arbitration Council, 'Arbitral Awards' (n.d.), available at www.arbitrationcouncil.org/arbitral-decision/arbitral-award/ (accessed 10 December 2024).

V. Conclusions

Cambodian legal norms on the ascertainment and treatment of foreign law have not yet been fully developed. This is somewhat inevitable since the Kingdom has no comprehensive set of choice of law rules, and many Cambodian lawyers are unfamiliar with PIL. There has thus been little discussion on how the courts in Cambodia investigate and apply foreign law in cross-border disputes. Fortunately, however, the treatment of foreign law is not a complete legal vacuum under Cambodian law. As this chapter has demonstrated, the CCP and other statutes regulate how judges are expected to manage major legal issues related to the ascertainment of foreign law. The judges can deal with the complicated and theoretical problems by referring to the official commentaries of the principal statutes and relevant Japanese legal principles on which the statutes are based.

The lack of international insights (apart from those imported via Japanese law) in the treatment of foreign law is possibly due to Cambodia's reluctance to adopt international frameworks governing that area of law. In fact, the country has not signed any international instruments on administrative cooperation for the facilitation of access to foreign law, including but not limited to the European Convention on Information on Foreign Law (London, 7 June 1968; the London Convention);[155] the Inter-American Convention on Proof of and Information on Foreign Law (Montevideo, 5 August 1979; the Montevideo Convention);[156] and the Convention on Legal Aid and Legal Relations in Civil, Family and Criminal Cases (Minsk, 22 January 1993; the Minsk Convention).[157] Cambodia's lack of interest in these multilateral agreements is not absurd because the country has no territorial links with them. While being open to any country for participation, these Conventions are byproducts of regional institutions such as the Council of Europe, the Organisation of American States (OAS) and the Commonwealth of Independent States (CIS), all of which are far from the Mekong subregion. It is unreasonable to criticise Cambodia for having little interest in those regional arrangements that are not well-known even among legal practitioners based within the geographical reach of those regional organisations.[158] After all, the dearth of globally harmonised rules is linked to Cambodian lawyers' lack of passion for pursuing internationally accepted principles on the treatment of foreign law. New formal instruments by the Hague Conference (if any) might change the mindset of Cambodian legal experts, despite Southeast Asian nations having been excluded from the latter's Access to Foreign Law in Civil and Commercial Matters Conference in 2012.[159] Otherwise, Cambodian lawyers will find ASEAN-focused instruments on the information

[155] Council of Europe, 'Treaty Office: Chart of Signatures and Ratifications of Treaty 062' (2024), available at www.coe.int/en/web/conventions/full-list?module=signatures-by-treaty&treatynum=062 (accessed 10 December 2024).

[156] OAS: Department of International Law, 'Multilateral Treaties: Inter-American Convention on Proof of and Information on Foreign Law' (n.d.), available at www.oas.org/juridico/English/sigs/b-43.html (accessed 10 December 2024).

[157] UNHCR, 'Convention on Legal Aid and Legal Relations in Civil, Family and Criminal Cases, Adopted in Minsk on 22 January 1993 (The Minsk Convention)' (n.d.), available at www.unhcr.org/protection/migration/4de4edc69/convention-legal-aid-legal-relations-civil-family-criminal-cases-adopted.html (accessed 10 December 2024).

[158] Nishitani (n 18) 49–50.

[159] European Commission and Hague Conference on Private International Law, 'Access to Foreign Law in Civil and Commercial Matters: Conclusions and Recommendations' (2012), available at https://assets.hcch.net/docs/b093f152-a4b3-4530-949e-65c1bfc9cda1.pdf (accessed 10 December 2024).

on foreign law more useful to absorb external perspectives on the topic, although no such legal documents are available yet.

Probably, the first step for ASEAN to establish new uniformed frameworks for access to the treatment of foreign law is to improve the regional networks currently available. For instance, the Council of ASEAN Chief Justices (CACJ), accredited by the ASEAN Charter, 'provides a regular forum for the *Chief Justices* to discuss and exchange views on common issues facing the ASEAN Judiciaries' and 'facilitates judicial cooperation and collaboration to enhance economic growth [in the region]'.[160] However, the CACJ does not aim to promote direct and general communications between judges in different Member States, unlike the International Hague Network of Judges. Moreover, the ASEAN Law Association (ALA) aspires to be the framework for regional cooperation in exchanging and disseminating information on the laws of the ASEAN states.[161] Nonetheless, its Standing Committee on Legal Information has yet to issue noticeable recommendations on access to foreign law.[162] New initiatives that addresss those gaps in the existing regional frameworks will hopefully build the foundation of legal instruments that improve and harmonise the treatment of foreign law in ASEAN. Active participation in such initiatives will help Cambodia shake off its stereotypical reputation for having limited legal certainty and a weak rule of law.[163]

[160] Council of ASEAN Chief Justice, 'About CACJ: Mission Statement' (n.d.), available at https://cacj-ajp.org/about-cacj/mission-statement/ (accessed 10 December 2024) (emphasis added).

[161] ASEAN Law Association, 'About ALA: Objectives' (n.d.), available at www.aseanlawassociation.org/about-ala/#1571425345512-313f5198-86e5 (accessed 10 December 2024).

[162] ASEAN Law Association, 'About ALA: Standing Committees' (n.d.), available at www.aseanlawassociation.org/about-ala/#1572932443790-bff759c2-d61d (accessed 10 December 2024).

[163] World Justice Project (n 37).

PART II

Jurisdiction

4

Direct Jurisdiction*

I. Introduction

Because of long-term legal technical assistance by Japan in Cambodia, one may need to have knowledge of Japanese law when learning about Cambodian private laws,[1] such as the Code of Civil Procedure of Cambodia (CCP) in 2006[2] and the Civil Code of Cambodia (CC) in 2007.[3] Accordingly, this chapter provides concise guidance of direct jurisdiction in Cambodia, taking into account relevant documents written not only in English, but also in Japanese. It assumes that rules on domestic jurisdiction in the CCP may apply to decide the international jurisdiction of Cambodian courts. This idea derives from previous legal practice in Japan on international jurisdiction surrounding the old version of the Japanese Code of Civil Procedure – the foundation of the current CCP. The theory behind the practice is summarised by Nishitani as follows:

> Prior to [2011], there were no written rules on international jurisdiction except for limited special rules in international instruments. Hence, jurisdiction rules have been principally established by case law …, referring to *naturalis ratio (jôri) based on the ideas of fairness between the parties and an equitable and expeditious administration of justice.* … In the concrete application of *jôri*, courts granted international jurisdiction insofar as a specific court in Japan … had local jurisdiction pursuant to the domestic jurisdiction rules provided in the [Japanese] CCP. The local jurisdiction of a particular court in Japan was considered to presuppose the existence of international jurisdiction.[4]

The doctrine of *jôri* is unlikely to exist in Cambodia as it is a Japanese legal concept proclaimed by the *Daijokan* (Grand Council of State) during the *Meiji* period. No evidence suggests that the doctrine has been imported into the Cambodian legal system. However, Article 4 of the CCP requires Cambodian courts to make efforts to proceed with civil actions fairly and speedily, while obliging parties to pursue civil actions honestly and in good faith.[5]

* A version of this chapter is available as N Teramura, 'Cambodia' in A Reyes and W Lui (eds), *Direct Jurisdiction: Asian Perspectives* (Oxford, Hart Publishing, 2021) 201–19. The author is grateful to Mr Issei Sakano, Advisor of the Ministry of Justice of Kingdom of Cambodia, and other legal practitioners working in Phnom Penh for their insightful comments that helped completing the manuscript. Note that responsibility for any errors that remain is solely my own.

[1] See generally Chapter 2 in this volume.

[2] An unofficial English translation prepared by the JICA as part of the project is available at www.jica.go.jp/Resource/project/english/cambodia/0701047/materials/c8h0vm000000zsb2-att/01_01e.pdf (accessed 10 May 2025).

[3] An unofficial English translation prepared by the JICA as part of the project is available at www.jica.go.jp/Resource/project/english/cambodia/0701047/materials/c8h0vm000000zsb2-att/01_02e_1.pdf (accessed 10 May 2025).

[4] Y Nishitani, 'International Jurisdiction of Japanese Courts in a Comparative Perspective' (2013) 60 *Netherlands International Law Review* 251, 252–53 (emphasis added).

[5] CCP, Art 4.

In other words, the Article may play a similar role to *jôri*, and, therefore, there seems to be no real problem in presupposing the existence of international jurisdiction from the local jurisdiction of a particular court in Cambodia.

II. Jurisdiction *in Personam*

A. General Principles

Article 8 of the CCP sets out general rules of jurisdiction *in personam*, under which the Court of First Instance having territorial jurisdiction over 'the address of the defendant' shall hear a case. The address of the defendant is defined according to the type of the defendant as follows:

(a) **Natural person**: (1) his/her domicile; (2) the location of residence, where such a natural person does not have a domicile within Cambodia, or where his/her domicile is unknown; or (3) his/her last known domicile, where such a natural person does not have a location of residence within Cambodia, or where the location of his/her residence is unknown.
(b) **Cambodian juridical person (corporation)**: (1) the location of its administrative headquarters or business office; or (2) the location of the domicile of the entity's representative or another principal person in charge of the operations of the entity, where there is no administrative headquarters or business office.
(c) **Foreign juridical person (corporation)**: (1) the location of the entity's administrative headquarters or business office in Cambodia; or (2) the location of the domicile of the entity's representative or another principal person in charge of the operations of the entity in Cambodia, where there is no administrative headquarters or business office within Cambodia.

Under Cambodian law, juridical persons (corporations) mean either (profit and non-profit) associations (companies) or foundations (including public and charitable foundations).[6]

i. *Jurisdiction of Courts within the Territory*

Cambodia has a unified judicial system. According to the Law on the Organisation of the Courts (LOC),[7] Cambodian courts are classified as the Court of First Instance (first level courts), the Court of Appeal (second level courts) and the Supreme Court.[8] Cambodia consists of 25 provinces (including the autonomous municipality of the capital Phnom Penh), and the capital of each province, other than Kep Province, has a Court of First

[6] CC, Art 46.

[7] An unofficial translation, prepared by Cambodian Centre for Human Rights is available at https://sithi.org/medias/files/projects/sithi/law/02_CCHR_Draft_of_Law_of_the_Organization_the_Courts_English.pdf (accessed 9 February 2025). Although it is a translation of the draft version, the document seems to be the only available English translation of the Law on the Organisation of the Courts revised in 2014.

[8] LOC, Art 3 (referring the Military Court that is in the same hierarchical level as the Court of First Instance and has special jurisdiction over military matters).

Instance.[9] A Court of First Instance may exercise jurisdiction over the case if the defendant has an address in the province.[10] Moreover, the Court of Appeal in Phnom Penh had been the only second-level court in the country and handled all appeal cases until March 2020. Since the establishment of new regional appeal courts on 1 April 2020, the four second-level courts have been dealing with appeal cases from their respective regions.[11] Finally, the Supreme Court is in Phnom Penh.

Those courts have general judicial jurisdiction over all cases, including administrative ones,[12] though courts of each level are divided into special courts and chambers. The Court of First Instance consists of the Civil Court, Criminal Court, Commercial Court, and Labour Court.[13] How these special courts share jurisdiction is unclear as the LOC merely provides that the Civil, Criminal, Commercial, and Labour Courts are competent to hear civil, criminal, commercial, and labour cases respectively.[14] To deal with the potential conflict of jurisdiction among specialised courts, Article 19 of the LOC requires the President of the Court of First Instance to hold a meeting with the Presidents of the concerned specialised courts and to decide issues of competing jurisdiction, at the President's discretion or upon request by the President(s) of any relevant specialised court(s). It seems that the lack of standards has not caused any jurisdictional issues – at least in practice – as neither the Commercial Courts nor the Labour Courts have been established yet.[15] The LOC also requires the Court of Appeal to have Civil, Criminal, Investigating, Commercial, and Labour Chambers,[16] but only the Criminal and Civil Chambers appear to have been accepting new cases.[17]

[9] A Uchiyama, 'Cambodian Judiciary: The Court of First Instance [in Japanese]' (2017) 73 *ICD News* 48, 48. Cases arising in Kep Province fall under the jurisdiction of Kampot Provincial Court: https://cacj-ajp.org/cambodia/judiciary/description-of-cambodian-courts/ (accessed 9 February 2025).

[10] CCP, Art 8.

[11] T Vida, 'Regional Appeal Courts Open on April 1', *Khmer Times*, 25 March 2020, available at www.khmertimeskh.com/50705314/regional-appeal-courts-open-on-april-1/ (accessed 10 May 2025). Respectively: (1) the Tboung Khmum Appeal Court (covering Kampong Cham, Kampong Thom, Preah Vihear, Kratie, Stung Treng, Ratanakiri, Mondulkiri, and Tboung Khmum); (2) the Battambang Appeal Court (covering Pursat, Battambang, Pailin, Banteay Meanchey, Oddar Meanchey, and Siem Reap); and (3) Preah Sihanouk Appeal Court (covering Kampot, Kep, Koh Kong, and Preah Sihanouk). The Phnom Penh Appeal Court is now responsible for appeals from cases in the provincial courts of Phnom Penh, Kandal, Kampong Chhnang, Kampong Speu, Takeo, Prey Veng, and Svay Rieng.

[12] LOC, Art 4.

[13] Note that local practitioners call them 'Chambers' since no organised independent Special Courts have been established yet. Typically, in practice, each Court of First Instance consists of a Civil Law Division (Chamber) and a Criminal Law Division (Chamber) only.

[14] LOC, Arts 20–22, 25.

[15] See, e.g., Uchiyama (n 9) 50, fn 4; JETRO, 'Enforcement of Intellectual Property Rights in Cambodia [in Japanese]' (2018), 15, available at www.jetro.go.jp/ext_images/world/asia/kh/ip/pdf/survey_201810_kh.pdf. See also the author's interview with local practitioners. In January 2021, the MOJ of Cambodia set up a commission to investigate the formation of Commercial Courts, to attract more foreign investments in Cambodia: BR Kongkea, 'Commercial Courts in the Pipeline to Attract More Investors', *Khmer Times*, 25 January 2021, available at www.khmertimeskh.com/50806501/commercial-courts-in-the-pipeline-to-attract-more-investors/ (accessed 10 May 2025). In February 2023, a justice ministry adviser Ly Tayseng commented that the Commercial Court could be established and start operation as early as 2024: O Bunthoeurn, 'Commercial Court Could Function 'As Early As 2024': Justice Ministry Officials', *The Phnom Penh Post*, 3 February 2023, available at www.phnompenhpost.com/business/commercial-court-could-function-early-2024-justice-ministry-officials (accessed 10 December 2024).

[16] LOC, Art 42.

[17] The author's interview with local practitioners.

ii. Forum Non Conveniens, Lis Alibi Pendens, *Anti-suit Injunctions, Interim Measures and Choice of Court Agreements*

There are several legal principles with similar effects to certain common law doctrines of direct jurisdiction. For example, a variation of *forum non conveniens* is stipulated in Article 19.1 of the CCP, allowing a Court of First Instance, upon a party's motion or on its own authority, to transfer all or part of an action under its jurisdiction to another court, if such a transfer is necessary to avoid significant delay or to ensure procedural fairness. The Article is unlikely to be applied to transnational transfers as it is based on Article 17 of the Japanese Civil Code that does not apply to cross-border cases.[18] In addition, *lis alibi pendens* is expressly prohibited by Article 83 of the CCP ('A party may not file suit regarding a case that is already before the court') for purely domestic cases. But the Article may not apply to a domestic case that is already before a foreign court and a foreign case that is already before the Cambodian court. The reason is that the Article does not take cross-border cases into consideration,[19] and foreign courts do not always pay attention to whether their cases have been referred to Cambodian courts.

As for procedural orders, courts do not issue anti-suit injunctions, contrary to what is prevalent in common law countries. However, courts have authority to issue interim measures (preservative reliefs) such as provisional attachment, provisional disposition of the subject matter of the dispute and, provisional disposition establishing a provisional legal status.[20] These preservative measures belong to the exclusive jurisdiction of the court having jurisdiction over merits of the case, or the Court of First Instance having jurisdiction over the objects to be attached or the subject matter of the dispute.[21]

Finally, parties may have a valid choice of court agreement upon satisfying certain conditions. According to Article 13.1 of the CCP, such a jurisdictional agreement is valid only where: (1) 'it is made between merchant(s) and/or juristic person(s) with regard to the court of first instance'; (2) it pertains to an action on a specific legal relationship; and (3) it is made in writing.

iii. Service of Process

Cambodia has not ratified key service conventions such as the Convention of 15 November 1965 on the Service Abroad of Judicial and Extrajudicial Documents in Civil or Commercial Matters (the 1965 Hague Service Abroad Convention)[22] and the Convention of 1 March 1954 on Civil Procedure (the 1954 Hague Civil Procedure Convention).[23] Therefore, the service of process is conducted following domestic norms.

[18] See the note on Art 19 in the Japanese language edition of the CCP of Cambodia, available at www.jica.go.jp/project/cambodia/0701047/04/pdf/clause/clause01_j.pdf (accessed 10 December 2024). An English translation of Code of Civil Procedure of Japan is available at www.japaneselawtranslation.go.jp/en/laws/view/2834/en (accessed 10 December 2024).

[19] See the note on Art 83 in the Japanese language edition of the CCP of Cambodia.

[20] CCP, Art 531.

[21] CCP, Arts 540(1), 533.

[22] The status table is available online: www.hcch.net/en/instruments/conventions/status-table/?cid=17 (accessed 10 December 2024).

[23] The status table is available online: www.hcch.net/en/instruments/conventions/status-table/?cid=33 (accessed 10 December 2024).

For instance, the basic rules of service of process outside the territory of Cambodia are provided in Article 253 of the CCP, according to which such service shall be made by the court through entrusting a service document to a competent governmental authority of the country, or the Cambodian ambassador, envoy, or consul to that foreign country. Where the service cannot be made in this way, or where the competent authority has not delivered the proof of service within six months, the court clerk may opt for service by a publication upon a party's motion and with permission from the court.[24] The publication can be made by posting on the court's notice board an announcement stating that the service document is kept by the clerk and is ready for delivery at any time.[25] To maximise the impact, the clerk may send a notice about the publication to the defendant abroad.[26] In any event, service by publication in respect of a defendant abroad shall take effect after six weeks have passed since the posting of the announcement on the court's notice board.[27]

B. Special Rules for Establishing Jurisdiction

i. Law of Obligations

a. Contracts

Article 9 of the CCP provides additional grounds of jurisdiction to determine obligations.[28] Parties may bring actions demanding: (1) performance of obligations, to the court having the territorial jurisdiction over the location where the obligations are to be performed;[29] (2) payment of money on bills or checks, to the court having the territorial jurisdiction over the location where payment on the bill or check is to be made;[30] (3) performance of obligations against a person whose domicile is not in Cambodia or is unknown, to the court having the territorial jurisdiction over the location of the defendant's property which is the subject of the claim or security interest, or which may be seized;[31] and (4) performance of obligations against juridical persons whose administrative headquarters or business office are not in Cambodia or are unknown, to the court having the territorial jurisdiction over the location of the defendant's property which is the subject of the claim or security interest, or which may be seized.[32] Those grounds are additional to the jurisdictional bases in Article 8 of the CCP, so that parties involved in contract disputes may rely on either Article 8 or 9 to bring their claims of obligations before the court.

As the CCP does not provide jurisdictional standards for any specific types of contracts, the default rule is that disputes concerning consumer or labour contracts may be referred to the court designated by grounds of jurisdiction over contractual disputes under Article 9

[24] CCP, Arts 255(1)(c)–(d).
[25] ibid, Art 256(1).
[26] ibid, Art 256(3).
[27] ibid, Art 257.
[28] According to CC Art 309, causes of obligation are: contracts, unilateral legal acts, management of affairs without the mandate, unjust enrichment, tortious act, and legal provisions.
[29] CCP, Art 9(a).
[30] ibid, Art 9(b).
[31] ibid, Art 9(c).
[32] ibid, Art 9(d).

of the CCP. However, there are other options for consumers and employees to decide where to seek remedies.

For instance, according to the Law on Consumer Protection,[33] consumers and consumer associations are expected to bring to the National Consumer Protection Committee (NCPC) their complaints about an alleged infringement of consumer rights.[34] The ombudsperson in the institution first investigates the alleged infringement, and then the NCPC issues decisions that are, if necessary, accompanied by administrative sanctions against the infringement.[35] State courts are unlikely to be involved in the complaints procedures.

Moreover, alternative dispute resolution (ADR) is recommended as a means to resolve labour disputes in Cambodia. For example, the Labour Code[36] recommends parties to refer an individual labour dispute to a preliminary conciliation by the Labour Inspector of their province, capital, or municipality.[37] If the preliminary conciliation fails, the parties can file a complaint in a court of competent jurisdiction.[38] Accordingly, should parties not opt for conciliation to resolve an individual labour dispute, they can refer the case to a competent court, although such a choice has been perceived as impractical in Cambodia.[39] The Code also requires parties to have a compulsory conciliation by the Labour Inspector in order to solve a collective labour dispute.[40] If the conciliation fails, the parties are required to settle the dispute through arbitration by the Arbitration Council or any other dispute resolution proceedings as they have agreed.[41] Litigation then may be a choice but it is not one that is appealing to many employees and employers.

b. Torts

Article 9 of the CCP also stipulates the jurisdictional rules of tort claims, stating that parties may bring a tort action to the court having jurisdiction over the place where the alleged tort occurred.[42] The plaintiff is not required to prove the tort but the provision of *prima facie* evidence of the occurrence of the tort may be encouraged.[43] In addition, the CCP is silent as to the definition of the place of a tort, probably following the Japanese Code of Civil Procedure before the 2011 law reforms in Japan.[44] It is therefore unclear whether the

[33] An unofficial English translation is available online: https://ibccambodia.com/wp-content/uploads/2020/01/Law-on-Consumer-Protection_EN.pdf (accessed 10 May 2025).

[34] Law on Consumer Protection, Art 28.

[35] ibid, Arts 29–32.

[36] An unofficial English translation is available online: https://natlex.ilo.org/dyn/natlex2/natlex2/files/download/46560/KHM46560.pdf (accessed 10 May 2025).

[37] Labour Code, Art 300. See also K Phallack, 'Cambodian Labour and Employment Law' in H Peng, K Phallack and J Menzel (eds), *Introduction to Cambodian Law* (Phnom Penh, Konrad-Adenauer-Stiftung Cambodia, 2012) 290–91.

[38] Labour Code, Art 301.

[39] S Tamagaki, 'The Arbitration Council in Cambodia: Impacts of the 2016 Law on Trade Unions and Prakas No. 303 by the Ministry of Labour and Vocational Training [in Japanese]' (2019) 80 *ICD News* 56, 60.

[40] Labour Code, Art 302. The complaint must be submitted within two months.

[41] Labour Code, Art 309. For the details of the Arbitration Council, see generally K Phallack, 'Labour Arbitration in Cambodia: Law and Practice' (2010) 1 *Cambodian Yearbook of Comparative Legal Studies* 163; the Arbitration Council's website, available online at www.arbitrationcouncil.org/ (accessed 10 December 2024).

[42] CCP, Art 9(e).

[43] See the note on Art 9 in the Japanese language edition of the CCP of Cambodia.

[44] K Takahashi, 'Japan's Newly Enacted Rules on International Jurisdiction: with a Reflection on Some Issues of Interpretation' (2011) 13 *Japanese Yearbook of Private International Law* 146; K Takahashi, 'The Jurisdiction of Japanese Courts in a Comparative Context' (2015) 11 *Journal of Private International Law* 103.

place of tort under Cambodian law means the place where the alleged tort was committed, the place where the alleged damage occurred, or both. Moreover, the place of the alleged damage has to be defined, as it is sometimes difficult for the defendant to know the place where the alleged damage occurred, especially in the context of product liability cases, but that is left to the discretion of the court in each individual case.[45]

c. Trusts

There are no special rules of jurisdiction for trust disputes. Accordingly, the court having jurisdiction over a trust case is the Court of First Instance of the place where the trust contract concluded between a merchant/corporation and a merchant/corporation has been executed,[46] or otherwise where: (1) the defendant maintains an address; (2) the (real) property subject to the trust agreement is located; or (3) the tort related to the trust was allegedly committed.[47] However, this may change over time. The Trust Law was newly promulgated in early 2019, and trusts are now subject to registration and supervision with the Ministry of Economy and Finance.[48] The scope of supervision is not defined, and therefore, it is still unclear how the government body is willing to intervene in trust disputes.

ii. Law of Property

a. Immovable Property

In Cambodia, real or immovable properties are classified into two categories, namely, registered lands that are with any types of titles issued by cadastral administration and non-registered lands that are without such titles.[49] As for the former, Article 9(g) of the CCP allows parties to bring claims to the court that has territorial jurisdiction over the disputed real property.[50] As for the latter, the Joint Prakas on Determination of Competence of the Court and Cadastral Commission Regarding Land Disputes (Joint Prakas)[51] provides that disputes over unregistered land shall be subject to the competence of the Cadastral

[45] The current Japanese Civil Procedure Code states that the Japanese courts have jurisdiction over an action for a tort 'if the place where the tort occurred is within Japan (excluding if the consequences of a wrongful act committed in a foreign country have arisen within Japan but it would not ordinarily have been possible to foresee those consequences arising within Japan)' (Art 3-3(viii)). It is unclear whether the Cambodian courts will follow suit.

[46] CCP, Art 13.

[47] CCP, Arts 8, 9, 13.

[48] PJ Smith and T Tavsothaly, 'Cambodian Trust Law', *BNG Legal*, December 2019, available at http://bnglegal.com/wp-content/uploads/2019/12/191219-BNG-Newsletter-December-Trust-law.pdf (accessed 9 February 2025).

[49] Joint Prakas, Praka 1.

[50] According to CC Art 120, immovable properties are land and any other objects that are immovably fixed to the land such as buildings, constructions, crops, timber, and other similar objects, which means that buildings are generally treated as part of the land to which they are attached. Note that CC Art 122 provides that '[s]hould the right holder bear a right in relation to another person's land enforces his/her right upon any constructed buildings or structures, grown timber, crops or other such objects on the land, those objects shall not be deemed to be components of said land'.

[51] An unofficial English translation is available online: www.huskyandpartners.com/images///Law%20Library/Real%20Property%20and%20Construction/20190604-Joint%20Prakas%20on%20Determination%20of%20Competence%20of%20the%20Court%20and%20Cadastral%20Commission%20Regarding%20Land%20Disputes_2003_En.pdf.pdf (accessed 9 February 2025).

Commission (or Committee) in the Ministry of Land Management,[52] while conferring on the court the authority to hear contractual disputes over unregistered land.[53] During the Khmer Rouge period, all property rights were abolished and most of the land registries were destroyed.[54] As a consequence, around 22 per cent of lands in the country (assuming there were seven million properties) was still unregistered in November 2019,[55] which means that there is still potential for foreign companies to be involved in disputes over non-registered immovable properties, even though foreign individuals and companies are prohibited from owning land in Cambodia.[56]

b. Intangible Property: Intellectual Property

In Cambodia, the following intellectual property (IP) rights are legally protected: copyrights and neighbouring rights, patents, trademarks, utility models, industrial designs and new plant varieties.[57] IP rights other than copyrights and neighbouring rights shall be registered at the respective government bodies. Patents, utility models, industrial designs and new plant varieties must be registered at the Department of Industrial Property of the Ministry of Industry, Science, Technology and Innovation (MISTI).[58] Trademarks must be registered at the IP Department of the Ministry of Commerce (MOC).[59] Parties may seek remedy from a competent court for the disputes and infringements of their IP rights, but no special rules of jurisdiction are provided.[60] The competent court is thus designated in accordance with rules for establishing the courts' jurisdiction in Articles 8 and 9 of the CCP.

c. Succession to Property

In terms of actions over succession to property, it is important to examine where the deceased was living at the point of death. Article 9(i) of the CCP provides that such actions may be brought in the court having jurisdiction over 'the location of the domicile of the

[52] Joint Prakas, Praka 1. For the function of the Cadastral Commission, see generally GTZ-Cambodia Land Management Project and the World Bank Justice for the Poor Program, 'Towards Institutional Justice? A Review of the Work of Cambodia's Cadastral Commission in Relation to Land Dispute Resolution' (2006) *The World Bank Justice for the Poor Program*, available at http://documents.worldbank.org/curated/en/309161468222269820/pdf/408230Towards01nal0Justice01PUBLIC1.pdf (accessed 9 February 2025).

[53] Joint Prakas, Praka 4. The contracts include succession, sale/purchase contract, lease agreement, and mortgage.

[54] M Isoi, 'Real Property Registration in Cambodia [in Japanese]' (2014) 60 *ICD News* 33.

[55] Ministry of Land Management Urban Planning and Construction and United Nations Cambodia, *Cambodia Urban Forum: Smart, Sustainable and Inclusive Urban Development* (Ministry of Land Management, Urban Planning and Construction and United Nations Cambodia 2019) 4.

[56] Law on Investment, Art 16. An unofficial English translation is available at www.wto.org/english/thewto_e/acc_e/khm_e/WTACCKHM3A3_LEG_45.pdf (accessed 9 February 2025).

[57] P Sovath, 'Economic Law: Intellectual Property Rights' in H Peng, K Phallack and J Menzel (eds), *Introduction to Cambodian Law* (Phnom Penh, Konrad-Adenauer-Stiftung Cambodia, 2012) 271ff.

[58] Previously called Ministry of Industry, Mines and Energy (MIME) and then Ministry of Industry and Handicraft (MIH). For the structure of the Department of Industrial Property, see www.cambodiaip.gov.kh/en/department-of-industrial-property/ (accessed 9 February 2025). Precisely, if one claims for protection of utility models, s/he shall obtain a 'protectable utility certificate' from the Industrial Design Office in the Department of Industrial Property: Law on the Patents, Utility Model Certificates and Industrial Designs (Patent Law), Arts 69 and 117. For the registration of industrial designs, see Patent Law, Art 95. As for the grant of plant variety protection, see the Law on Seed Management and Plant Breeder's Rights, Arts 6–38.

[59] www.cambodiaip.gov.kh/en/ (accessed 9 February 2025).

[60] See the note on Art 9 in the Japanese language edition of the CCP of Cambodia.

deceased at the time the inheritance commences, or if such person does not have a domicile in Cambodia or his/her domicile is unknown, the location of his/her residence, or if such person does not have a location of residence in Cambodia or his/her location of residence is unknown, the location of his/her last known domicile'.[61] Though not expressly stated in the CCP, it is reasonable to assume that the 'the last known domicile' shall be in Cambodia as the CCP is not supposed to deal with cross-border cases.

Also, the Annex of the Non-Suit Civil Case Procedural Law (the Annex) contains special rules for courts to establish jurisdiction for non-contentious succession cases.[62] The Annex determines the jurisdiction of courts, which depends on the matters of succession that are listed in Chapter 8 of the CC. Most of those matters are to be determined by the court of the place where the succession commenced, while other courts have jurisdiction only in exceptional cases. For example, the court having territorial jurisdiction over the deceased's address or the place where the succession commenced shall decide who will succeed the ownership of ceremonial implements, graves and movable ancestral heirlooms, if the deceased did not designate such a successor, and if there is no custom for making the decision.[63] Such a court also has the competence to hear matters related to the disqualification of presumptive successors under Articles 1151, 1152, and 1154 of the CC.[64] Moreover, the court having jurisdiction over the successor's address shall determine whether the person may renounce his or her legally reserved portion of inherited wealth.[65]

iii. Family Law

Certain proceedings are required for couples to have a valid marriage in Cambodia, as stipulated generally in Article 955 of the CC and more specifically in the Ministry of Interior Sub-Decree 103 on Civil Status (Civil Registration) (2002) (Sub-Decree 103).[66] For example, a marriage between Cambodian citizens comes into effect when the following conditions are satisfied: (1) the couple has applied for permission to marry to the Commune/Sangkat registrar at the prospective wife's residence;[67] (2) the registrar has made an announcement to the public of the scheduled marriage ceremony;[68] (3) the couple has entered into a marriage contract before the registrar at the prospective wife's residence;[69] and (4) the registrar has

[61] Note that neither 'domicile' nor 'residence' is defined by the CCP.

[62] The Annex of the Non-Suit Civil Case Procedural Law (in Japanese) is available online: www.jica.go.jp/activities/issues/governance/portal/cambodia/ku57pq00002khh0b-att/non_suit_civil_case_procedural_law_ja.pdf (accessed 9 February 2025). See also Non-Suit Civil Case Procedural Law, Art 1. An unofficial English translation is available online: www.jica.go.jp/project///cambodia/0701047/04/ku57pq00001spnva-att/non-suit_civil_case_procedural_law_03_en.pdf (accessed 9 February 2025).

[63] Annex of the Non-Suit Civil Case Procedural Law, s 5.1; CC, Art 1147(2).

[64] Annex of the Non-Suit Civil Case Procedural Law, s 5.2; CC, Art 1151, 1152, 1154.

[65] Annex of the Non-Suit Civil Case Procedural Law, s 5.10; CC, Art 1246.

[66] An unofficial English translation of Sub-Decree 103 is available at www.skpcambodia.com/storage/uploads/files/Nationality_Immegration_Civil%20Registration/Sub-dree%20No103%20on%20Civil%20Registration-Eng.pdf (accessed 9 February 2025). See also CC, Arts 948–68; D van der Keur, 'Legal and Gender Issues of Marriage and Divorce in Cambodia' (2014) 3 *Cambodia Law and Policy Journal* 1, 4 (explaining basic rules of marriage registration in Cambodia); generally S Serena, 'Cambodian Family Law: Development and Challenges Ahead' in H Peng, K Phallack and J Menzel (eds), *Introduction to Cambodian Law* (Phnom Penh, Konrad-Adenauer-Stiftung Cambodia, 2012) 135ff.

[67] Sub-Decree 103, Art 28.

[68] ibid, Art 29.

[69] ibid, Art 30.

registered the marriage in the Marriage Book.[70] Satisfying these conditions, a couple being a Cambodian citizen and a foreigner, or an immigrant living lawfully in the country, may also have a legally binding marriage.[71] In addition, a marriage that took place abroad between Cambodian citizens, or a Cambodian citizen and a foreigner, is also to be deemed valid in Cambodia, provided that the marriage observed the law of the place of marriage and had been registered in the Marriage Books maintained in a Cambodian diplomatic office attached to the respective jurisdiction.[72]

According to the Law on Procedures in Actions Relating to Personal Status (Personal Status Procedures Law),[73] actions relating to other aspects of marriage – divorce, nullity and separation – are to be heard by the Court of First Instance of the place where the parties reside.[74] A potential theoretical problem is how to determine jurisdiction if the respective spouses have already started living separately in different addresses. As it is difficult for such parties to invoke their residence as a basis of jurisdiction,[75] the Court of First Instance of Phnom Penh is presumed to have exclusive jurisdiction to hear the matter.[76] In any event, if the couple has agreed to divorce, they may file a petition to the court that has territorial jurisdiction over the address of the husband or wife.[77] The couple may do the same in the situation where they are unable to reach a consensus on the distribution of property.[78]

The Personal Status Procedures Law also covers matters relating to the well-being of the child, including the confirmation of paternity, confirmation of maternity, confirmation of the absence of parenthood, and dissolution of adoption.[79] These matters may be referred to the Court of First Instance having territorial jurisdiction over the place where the parties reside; if the parties are living separately, the Court of First Instance of Phnom Penh will have exclusive jurisdiction.[80] The jurisdiction is not exclusive in *sensu stricto* since the court is allowed to transfer the case to another court upon a party's motion or on its own authority, in order to avoid significant delays and to ensure fairness, taking into account the circumstance of the case.[81] The court is probably encouraged to determine the transfer in light of the best interests of the child as Cambodia is a party to the United Nations Convention on the Rights of the Child (New York, 1989),[82] despite its limited interest in ratifying private international law treaties for child protection.[83] Such interpretation also

[70] ibid, Arts 30, 31.
[71] ibid, Art 33.
[72] ibid, Art 32.
[73] An unofficial English translation is available online: www.jica.go.jp/project/cambodia/0701047/04/ku57pq00001spnva-att/action_relating_to_personal_status_02_en.pdf (accessed 9 February 2025).
[74] Personal Status Procedures Law, Art 5; CCP, Art 10(1). Note that the jurisdiction is not absolutely exclusive as the court may invoke the doctrine of *forum non conveniens* under Art 6 of the Personal Status Procedures Law, depending on the circumstances of the case.
[75] Personal Status Procedures Law, Art 5.2.
[76] ibid, Art 5.4.
[77] Annex, s 4.5.
[78] Annex, s 4.6.
[79] Personal Status Procedures Law, Art 3.
[80] ibid, Art 5.
[81] ibid, Art 6.
[82] The status of ratification is available online: https://indicators.ohchr.org/ (accessed 10 May 2025).
[83] Cambodia has not yet ratified the Convention of 19 October 1996 on Jurisdiction, Applicable Law, Recognition, Enforcement and Co-operation in Respect of Parental Responsibility and Measures for the

conforms with specifications in the Non-Suit Civil Case Procedural Law that designates the court having territorial jurisdiction over the address of the child as the appropriate court to hear child-related cases.[84]

iv. Law of Corporations, Insolvency and Bankruptcy

In contrast to the revised Japanese Code of Civil Procedure,[85] the CCP does not provide any special rules for establishing jurisdiction to hear corporate matters. Cambodian courts may therefore decide their jurisdiction over corporate cases in light of the rules of personal jurisdiction in Article 8 of the CCP or the jurisdictional rules of contracts and torts in Article 9 of the CCP.[86] Note, however, that the Non-Suit Civil Case Procedural Law confers on the court having territorial jurisdiction over the address of the company, exclusive jurisdiction in respect of: (1) the appointment of a special director;[87] (2) the appointment of a special representative;[88] (3) the appointment of an inspector for the inspection of capital contribution;[89] (4) the amendment of the Articles of Incorporation;[90] and (5) permission for the stakeholders to convene an extraordinary general stakeholders meeting.[91] It should also be noted that the Law on Commercial Enterprises has provisions allowing parties to refer to the arbitral tribunal matters including, but not limited to, appraisal disputes and controversies over the duty of care.[92]

Moreover, neither the CCP nor the Insolvency Law contain specific rules of jurisdiction for insolvency cases.[93] However, the Non-Suit Civil Case Procedural Law mandates

Protection of Children (the 1996 Hague Convention on Parental Responsibility and Protection of Children) and the Convention of 25 October 1980 on the Civil Aspects of International Child Abduction (the 1980 Hague Abduction Convention). The status tables of the Conventions are available online, respectively: www.hcch.net/en/instruments/conventions/status-table/?cid=69; www.hcch.net/en/instruments/conventions/status-table/?cid=24 (accessed 10 December 2024). Note that Cambodia has ratified the 1993 Hague Convention on Protection of Children and Co-operation in Respect of Intercountry Adoption. The status table is available at www.hcch.net/en/instruments/conventions/status-table/?cid=69 (accessed 10 December 2024).

[84] According to Section 4 of the Annex of the Non-Suit Civil Case Procedural Law, the following matters shall be applied to the court having jurisdiction over the address of the child: petitions for simple adoption, dissolution of simple adoption by agreement, designation of the person parental authority, change of the person with parental authority, petitions for rights and obligations of the parent who does not live with the minor child, determination of the manager of a child's property provided by a third person, and appointment of a special representative for the minor whose interests conflict with the parental authority holder.

[85] Code of Civil Procedure (Japan), Arts 3–3 and 5(viii).

[86] Foreign businesses operating in Cambodia in any form are subject to the laws and jurisdictions of Cambodia. See Law on Commercial Enterprises, Arts 270–273.

[87] Annex of the Non-Suit Civil Case Procedural Law, Art 1.11; CC, Art 60.

[88] Annex of the Non-Suit Civil Case Procedural Law, Art 1.12; CC, Art 61.

[89] Annex of the Non-Suit Civil Case Procedural Law, Art 1.19; CC, Art 85(2).

[90] Annex of the Non-Suit Civil Case Procedural Law, Art 1.20; CC, Art 85(4).

[91] Annex of the Non-Suit Civil Case Procedural Law, Art 1.21; CC, Art 93(3). CC Art 93(2) provides that the stakeholders who hold no less than 10 per cent of total voting rights (or other percentage as provided in the Articles of Incorporations) may request the directors to convene an extraordinary general stakeholders meeting, and the directors must follow the request without delay. CC Art 93(2) is for the stakeholders to seek permission for the court to hold the stakeholders meeting, in case the directors cannot make it on time.

[92] Law on Commercial Enterprises, Arts 250 and 289. An unofficial English translation is available at www.wipo.int/edocs/lexdocs/laws/en/kh/kh011en.pdf (accessed 9 February 2025).

[93] An English translation of the Insolvency Law is available at https://cdc.gov.kh/wp-content/uploads/2022/04/Law-on-Insolvency_full-text_071016.pdf (accessed 10 December 2024). Note that Cambodia has not adopted

the court of the address of the company to handle matters concerning the dissolution and liquidation of companies, including: (1) a petition for the dissolution of a legal person that is undermining the public interest;[94] (2) the appointment of a liquidator upon a petition by an interested person or the Ministry of Justice;[95] (3) the removal of a liquidator for grave reasons upon a petition by an interested person;[96] (4) permission for a liquidator to settle claims by creditors within the presentation period;[97] (5) the appointment of a valuer to determine the sum of uncertain claims;[98] and (6) the appointment of a custodian of the legal person's documents.[99]

v. *Competition Law*

The Law on Competition of Cambodia (Competition Law), which the MOC drafted, was promulgated by King Norodom Sihamoni in October 2021.[100] An innovative aspect of the Competition Law is that it intends to establish the first Competition Commission of Cambodia (CCC) – an inter-ministerial body led by the MOC to ensure fair competition.[101] According to Article 5 of the Competition Law, '[t]he CCC shall be led by the Minister of Commerce as Chairman with Vice-Chairmen and other representative members from relevant ministries/institutions, as necessary'.[102] The CCC shall also have independent members with a five-year term consisting of one former judge, two legal experts and two economic experts.[103] Establishing the CCC may be a significant step for the Cambodian economy and for consumers, although many other southeast Asian nations have such a commission already.[104] The CCC is expected to perform various functions to restore and promote competition in the Cambodian market,[105] including issuing various sanctions against violations of the Competition Law[106] and filing lawsuits against people who do not pay pecuniary penalties, before a competent court – typically the Phnom Penh Municipal Court.[107]

the 1997 UNCITRAL Model Law on Cross-Border Insolvency: see https://uncitral.un.org/en/texts/insolvency/modellaw/cross-border_insolvency/status (accessed 10 December 2024).

[94] Annex of the Non-Suit Civil Case Procedural Law, Art 1.13; CC, Art 65(3).

[95] Annex of the Non-Suit Civil Case Procedural Law, Art 1.14; CC, Arts 68(2)–(3).

[96] Annex of the Non-Suit Civil Case Procedural Law, Art 1.15; CC, Art 69(1).

[97] Annex of the Non-Suit Civil Case Procedural Law, Art 1.16; CC, Art 74(2).

[98] Annex of the Non-Suit Civil Case Procedural Law, Art 1.17; CC, Art 76(2).

[99] Annex of the Non-Suit Civil Case Procedural Law, Art 1.18; CC, Art 81.

[100] An unofficial English translation prepared by the Consumer Protection Competition and Fraud Repression Directorate-General (CCF) of Cambodia is available at www.aseanconsumer.org/file/post_image/Final-08112021ENG_CAM_Law-on-Competition.pdf (accessed 10 December 2024).

[101] Competition Law, Arts 5, 6.

[102] However, the Law needs to be clarified about which ministries and institutions may send their representatives to the CCC.

[103] Competition Law, Article 5.

[104] See ASEAN Secretariat, *Handbook on ASEAN Consumer Protection Laws and Regulation* (Jakarta, ASEAN Secretariat 2018) 17ff.

[105] Competition Law, Arts 6.

[106] Such sanctions are 'written warning, suspension, revocation or withdrawal of business registration certificates, business licenses, or business permits, pecuniary fine, financial penalty and imprisonment': Competition Law, Art 34.

[107] ibid, Art 34.

III. Jurisdiction *in Rem* with Special Focus on Shipping Claims

A. Jurisdiction *in Rem* of the Courts within the Territory

Jurisdiction *in rem* was once understood as the competence of a court over a thing or property based on its presence in the country's territory and was therefore distinguished from the jurisdiction *in personam*.[108] However, Michaels suggests that *in rem* jurisdiction should ultimately be construed as part of *in personam* jurisdiction, and the presence of a thing or property merely constitutes the basis of jurisdiction over a person.[109] This chapter respectfully follows his argument.

The CCP contains several provisions setting out explicit rules of jurisdiction *in rem*. Article 9(c) concerns actions for specific performance against persons who have no known domicile in Cambodia. It specifies the location of the person's property that is subject to the claim, security or seizure as a basis of jurisdiction. Similarly, Article 9(d) covers actions for specific performance against corporations that have no known administrative headquarter or business office in Cambodia. It designates the location of the legal person's property that is subject to the claim, security, or seizure as the basis of jurisdiction. Moreover, Article 9(g) deals with actions involving immovables, stating that the location of the real property determines which court has the competence to handle the case.

Note, however, that Article 9(i) concerning actions over a deceased's estate may not be regarded as a rule for *in rem* jurisdiction, as it does not decide jurisdiction based on the location of the deceased's estate, but on the address of the deceased. Moreover, the CCP does not have special jurisdictional rules for claims relating to ships, in contrast to the Japanese Civil Procedure Code containing rules of jurisdiction *in rem* for an action based on a ship claim or any other claim secured by a ship.[110] The reason for omission is unclear, even though the Cambodian CCP was inspired by that of Japan, as mentioned elsewhere in this chapter.

B. Process of Ship Arrest in the Territory

In Cambodia, ship arrest as a measure to secure a maritime claim is governed by the International Convention for the Unification of Certain Rules relating to Arrest of Sea-going Ships (Brussels, 10 May 1952; the 1952 Arrest Convention) and the CCP.[111] Ship arrest may

[108] R Michaels, 'Jurisdiction, Foundations' in Jürgen Basedow and others (eds), *Encyclopedia of Private International Law* (Cheltenham, Edward Elgar Publishing, 2017) 1043.

[109] ibid.

[110] Code of Civil Procedure (Japan), Art 5(vii).

[111] H Darwin and C Rithy, 'Ship Arrest in Cambodia', *BNG Legal*, June 2016, available at http://bnglegal.com/cn/wp-content/uploads/2016/08/160729-Ship-Arrest-In-Cambodia-June-2016.pdf (accessed 10 December 2024). The Arrest Convention came into force in Cambodia on 12 May 1957: see https://treaties.un.org/pages/showDetails.aspx?objid=08000002801338ba (accessed 10 December 2024). However, Cambodia is not a member of the United Nations International Convention on Arrest of Ships (Geneva, 12 March 1999): see https://treaties.un.org/Pages/ViewDetails.aspx?src=TREATY&mtdsg_no=XII-8&chapter=12&clang=_en (accessed 10 December 2024).

take place as part of the enforcement of an adjudicatory decision (that is, a court judgment or an arbitral award) or a provisional remedy.

i. Ship Arrest for Judgment Enforcement

The process of ship arrest for judgment and award enforcement is specified in Book Six (Compulsory Execution) of the CCP. The Arrest Convention is then not applicable as it does not cover the seizure of a ship in execution or satisfaction of a judgment.[112] Under the CCP, such ship arrest may take place over any ships (or vessels, including hovercrafts and hydrofoils) of any nationality that are heavier than 20 gross tonnages and within Cambodian territorial waters.[113]

Ship arrest for judgment enforcement proceeds as follows. First, the judgment creditor must file a request (motion) of compulsory execution against a vessel to the court having territorial jurisdiction over the ship.[114] The request, which must be in writing, shall contain: (1) the name and address of the creditor and his/her representative; (2) description of the title of obligation; (3) type of judgment execution to be requested (that is, direct compulsory execution, indirect compulsory execution, or execution by a substitute); (4) detail of the property subject to direct compulsory execution; (5) detail of the requested decision on indirect compulsory execution or execution by a substitute; (6) location of the vessel; (7) and name and current location of the captain.[115] The request shall also be accompanied by an authenticated copy of the title of obligation and an authenticated copy of the certificate of ship registration issued by the Cambodian authority, or documents showing that the ship is more than 20 gross tonnage and is in the judgment debtor's possession.[116]

After receiving the request, the competent court issues an order for commencement of compulsory auction of the ship, ordering a bailiff (enforcement agent) to confiscate the certificate of ship registration and submit it to the competent court.[117] In the order, the court shall declare its intention to attach the ship on behalf of the judgment creditor and its willingness to prohibit the judgment debtor from letting the ship leave the current location (port).[118] The order shall be served to the judgment debtor and come into effect as soon as the service process has been completed.[119] However, if the registration of the attachment has been made prior to the issuance of the order for commencement of ship auction, the ship arrest becomes effective at the time of such registration.[120] Somewhat similarly, if the bailiff confiscates the certificate of ship registration and other relevant documents prior to the service of the order for commencement of ship auction, or prior to the registration of the attachment by the registrar, the ship arrest becomes effective at the time of such confiscation.[121] Moreover, if the ship was registered in Cambodia, the court clerk

[112] Arrest Convention, Art 1(2).

[113] CCP, Art 454; JICA, 'Commentary on Cambodian Code of Civil Procedure: Compulsory Execution and Provisional Remedies [in Japanese]' (n.d.), 80, available at www.moj.go.jp/content/000122393.pdf (accessed 10 May 2025).

[114] CCP, Arts 455, 466.

[115] ibid, Art 455(2). See also ibid, Art 349(2).

[116] ibid, Art 455(3).

[117] ibid, Art 457(1).

[118] ibid, Art 457(2).

[119] ibid, Arts 457(3), 457(5).

[120] ibid, Art 457(5).

[121] ibid, Art 457(6).

would immediately have to direct the registrar to record the attachment.[122] Further, should the ship move outside the jurisdiction of the competent court, the court may transfer the case to the Court of First Instance that has territorial jurisdiction over the new location of the ship.[123]

ii. Ship Arrest as a Provisional Measure

Ship arrest as a provisional measure is governed by the Arrest Convention and Book Seven (Preservative Disposition) of the CCP. The Convention, however, plays a limited role in defining the process of provisional ship arrest as it provides in Article 6 that:

> The rules of procedure relating to the arrest of a ship, to the application for obtaining the authority of [a Court or of the appropriate judicial authority of the contracting State in which the arrest is made], and to all matters of procedure which the arrest may entail, shall be governed by the law of the Contracting State in which the arrest was made or applied for.

Accordingly, the process shall observe the procedural steps defined in the CCP and proceed as follows.

First, the claimant shall file a request of provisional (preservative) relief to the court having jurisdiction over the merits of the case, or the Court of First Instance having jurisdiction over the object to be attached or the subject matter of the dispute.[124] The request of provisional relief must contain: (1) names and addresses of the parties and their representatives; (2) details of the preservative relief to be sought; (3) details of the rights or legal relationship that are requested to be protected; and (4) the necessity of such preservative relief.[125]

Second, the court decides whether to issue a ruling for such provisional relief that can be either provisional disposition or provisional attachment.[126] To proceed with ship arrest, the claimant needs to obtain a ruling for provisional attachment, convincing the court that the subject matter of the claim is money, and compulsory execution at a later stage is likely to become impossible or extremely difficult without such provisional attachment.[127] In issuing the ruling, the court shall specify the object of the provisional attachment.[128]

Third, the claimant has to decide how s/he proceeds with enforcing the ruling for the provisional attachment; two options are available under Article 568 of the CCP.

If the claimant opts for enforcement by way of registration of the provisional attachment, s/he shall submit the request to the court that issued the order for provisional attachment of the ship.[129] The request must contain: (1) the name and address of the claimant and his/her representative; (2) description of the title of obligation; (3) the type of judgment execution to be requested at the final stage of proceedings (that is, direct compulsory execution, indirect compulsory execution or execution by a substitute); (4) detail of the property subject to direct compulsory execution; (5) detail of the requested decision on indirect compulsory

[122] ibid, Art 457(4).
[123] ibid, Art 463.
[124] ibid, Art 540.
[125] ibid, Art 541.
[126] ibid, Arts 545, 548.
[127] ibid, Art 545.
[128] ibid, Art 546.
[129] ibid, Art 568(2).

execution or execution by a substitute; (6) the location of the vessel; and (7) the name and current location of the captain.[130] The request then shall be accompanied by an authenticated copy of the title of obligation and an authenticated copy of the certificate of ship registration issued by Cambodian authority, or documents showing that the ship is more than 20 gross tonnage and is possessed by the respondent. If the request is accepted, the tribunal will proceed with ship arrest.[131]

If the claimant opts for enforcement by way of ordering the bailiff to confiscate the certificate of ship registration and other relevant documents, s/he shall file the request to the court of first instance having territorial jurisdiction over the location of the ship.[132] The claimant shall then submit an authenticated copy of the title of obligation attached by an authenticated copy of the certificate of ship registration issued by Cambodian authority, or documents showing that the ship is heavier than 20 gross tonnages and is possessed by the respondent.[133] After receiving the request, the court will order the bailiff to proceed with confiscating the ship registration certificate and other relevant documentation.

IV. Immunities from Jurisdiction

A. Sovereign Immunity

There are two traditional models of state immunity: the absolute doctrine and the restrictive doctrine.[134] The absolute doctrine provides foreign states with absolute immunities from judicial proceedings, excluding a state from addressing, deciding, or enforcing a claim brought in its municipal courts against another state unless otherwise agreed by that state.[135] The restrictive doctrine provides foreign states with limited immunities from judicial proceedings, making 'a distinction between acts performed in [the] exercise of sovereign authority which remain immune and acts of a private or commercial nature in respect of which proceedings in national courts may be brought'.[136] The Cambodian stance on this dichotomy is unclear as it has not yet signed the United Nations Convention on Jurisdictional Immunities of States and Their Property (New York, 2 December 2004)[137] that embraces the restrictive theory of sovereign immunity,[138] and no domestic legislation or regulations exist to deal with this issue. Moreover, there is no discernible discussion of sovereign immunity initiated among legal academics and practitioners in Cambodia.

[130] ibid, Arts 568(4), 455(2).
[131] ibid, Arts 568(4), 455(3).
[132] ibid, Art 568(2).
[133] ibid, Arts 568(4), 455(3).
[134] H Fox and P Webb, *The Law of State Immunity* revised and updated 3rd edn (Oxford, Oxford University Press, 2015) 4.
[135] ibid.
[136] ibid.
[137] treaties.un.org/Pages/ViewDetails.aspx?src=TREATY&mtdsg_no=III-13&chapter=3&clang=_en (accessed 10 December 2024).
[138] DP Stewart, 'The UN Convention on Jurisdictional Immunities of States and Their Property' (2005) 99 *American Journal of International Law* 194.

B. Diplomatic Immunity

Cambodia ratified the Vienna Convention on Diplomatic Relations (Vienna, 18 April 1961) in 1965 with a reservation to Article 37(2).[139] Accordingly, in Cambodia, a diplomatic agent shall enjoy immunity from its civil jurisdiction, except in the case of (in Article 31(1)):

(a) a real action relating to private immovable property situated in the territory of the receiving State, unless he holds it on behalf of the sending State for the purposes of the mission;
(b) an action relating to succession in which the diplomatic agent is involved as executor, administrator, heir or legatee as a private person and not on behalf of the sending State;
(c) an action relating to any professional or commercial activity exercised by the diplomatic agent in the receiving State outside his official functions.

Due to the Article 37(2) reservation, the civil immunity does not extend to members of the administrative and technical staff of the mission and their family.

C. Any Other Immunities

There are several other immunities in Cambodia to varying degrees. Parliamentary immunity is conferred by the Constitution to members of the National Assembly (Parliament) and the Senate, though civil cases are excluded from the scope.[140] Members of the Constitutional Council – the supreme body having the authority to decide constitutional issues – are not subject to any penal or civil sanction for the decisions made while fulfilling their duties.[141] There are no laws or regulations that stipulate immunities of royal family members and state-owned enterprises, but the general practice is that they are liable for any civil liabilities.

V. Conclusions

The lesson from this chapter is clear. Laws and rules on direct jurisdiction in Cambodia are under the strong influence of Japanese law and may, therefore, be regarded as part of a modern choice-of-court system. However, ambiguities persist in the laws and rules, and they might have been preventing Cambodian courts from dealing with transnational cases effectively. This chapter concludes by making three proposals for Cambodia to tackle the persistent problem of uncertainty.

First, further transparency is necessary. In Cambodia, legal research is often understood as a synonym of networking. Lawyers are expected to communicate with contact persons – judges, court clerks, government officials and politicians – to obtain 'allegedly' reliable

[139] https://legal.un.org/ilc/texts/instruments/english/conventions/9_1_1961.pdf (accessed 9 February 2025).
[140] Constitution of Cambodia, Arts 80, 104.
[141] Law on the Organization and the Functioning of the Constitutional Council and Law on the Amendment of the Law on the Organization and the Functioning of the Constitutional Council, Art 11. An unofficial English translation is available at http://ngocedaw.org/wp-content/uploads/2014/10/Law-on-CC.-Eng.pdf (accessed 9 February 2025).

and updated legal information.[142] While judicial proceedings are basically conducted in open court,[143] almost no judicial judgments are made public in a conveniently accessible manner.[144] Such private nature of legal information is unlikely to help legal professionals, especially those outside the special circle, to understand what the law is in Cambodia, much less the law on direct jurisdiction. The Cambodian judicial system should therefore be more open to the public. Improving judicial transparency is the key to sustainable development.[145] It may also assist Cambodian judiciary to rebut the persistent criticisms of corruption (that are often unwarranted) by addressing them with substance.[146]

Second, the doctrine of precedent needs to be further developed. As judgments are not published and often lack adequate judicial reasoning,[147] Cambodian legal practitioners have rarely paid attention to past judgments. This should be changed, since precedence and legal certainty play vital roles in the development of civil law systems even though they have no binding force.[148] In relation to direct jurisdiction, the CCP is based on an old version of the Japanese Code of Civil Procedure whose provisions of direct jurisdiction were supplemented by case law enabling Japanese courts to apply them to cross-border cases.[149] Unfortunately, however, this fact did not gain attention in the drafting process of the CCP, and so the vague provisions were imported into the CCP without any efforts by the drafting committee to ensure clarity. As a result, rules of direct jurisdiction in the CCP remain ambiguous. Further development of case law may be useful for the Cambodian judiciary to deal with the obscurities in the CCP.

Third, there should be increased responsiveness to foreign law reforms. For example, the Japanese Code of Civil Procedure was reformed in 2011, incorporating new rules on international direct jurisdiction.[150] However, the CCP has never been reformed since its promulgation in 2006, and there is no explicit ongoing debate among Cambodian lawyers as to whether Cambodia should revise the somewhat outdated rules on direct jurisdiction in the CCP. A practical option for Cambodia is to enact new international jurisdiction rules based on the current version of the Japanese Code of Civil Procedure.

[142] The author's interview with local practitioners.

[143] For example, CCP, Arts 115, 136, 188.

[144] Y Shinoda, 'Report on the Investigation of Cambodian Court Judgments (1) [in Japanese]' (2019) 79 *ICD News* 60; A Kamiki, 'Report on the Investigation of Cambodian Court Judgements [in Japanese]' (2011) 48 *ICD News* 25.

[145] United Nations Development Programme, *A Transparent and Accountable Judiciary to Deliver Justice for All* (Bangkok, United Nations Development Programme 2016) 10ff.

[146] AM Sassoon and M Dara, 'Kingdom's Judiciary Perceived as Most Corrupt: UNDP', *The Phnom Penh Post*, 11 April 2016, available at www.phnompenhpost.com/national/kingdoms-judiciary-perceived-most-corrupt-undp (accessed 10 December 2024).

[147] Shinoda (n 144); Kamiki (n 144).

[148] C Pejovic, 'Civil Law and Common Law: Two Different Paths Leading to the Same Goal' (2001) 32 *Victorian University of Wellington Law Review* 817, 820–21.

[149] Nishitani (n 4) 252–53.

[150] Takahashi, 'Japan's Newly Enacted Rules' (n 44).

PART III

Choice of Law

5

Choice of Law for Contractual Obligations

I. Introduction

In the context of international business transactions, choice of law has a dual meaning. First, it refers to a choice made by private parties, such as contracting parties, on the law applicable to the legal relationship at issue.[1] Hence, this variant is underpinned by the principle of party autonomy.[2] In the second and broader meaning, choice of law refers to any designation of the governing law, whether by the private parties involved or by a municipal court drawing from case or legislation. This variant of choice of law is sometimes referred to interchangeably with 'conflict of laws'.[3] In either case, the choice of the law governing contractual obligations depends on the forum's conflict rules, which are to be determined by the forum court adjudicating the dispute. When it comes to Cambodia, the courts are required to discern Cambodia's choice of law rules for contractual obligations in identifying the law governing controversies or differences arising out of or in connection with an international contract.

Nevertheless, the Cambodian legal system has no statutory law equivalent to Japan's Act on the General Rules of Application of Laws (AGRAL). It has no explicit choice of law rules on contractual obligations. This is partly due to past Cambodian legal elites' reluctance to elaborate a comprehensive set of conflict rules in the Civil Code (CC).[4] Although Cambodian legal practitioners widely accept that Article 3 of the CC may serve as a basis of parties' rights to choose the governing law of a contract,[5] the Article was originally designed to establish the principle of party autonomy for the whole private law of Cambodia, not just private international law (PIL). Even one of the most fundamental PIL principles lacks direct or clear statutory underpinning, which means that Cambodian judges are required to establish quite a few choice of law rules on contractual obligations based on the broad interpretation of relevant substantive law provisions. If this approach is not sufficient to fill the lacuna of Cambodian PIL, Cambodian jurists will have no practical option but to adopt the principles of Japanese PIL because neither the doctrine of precedent nor legal research based on

[1] J Basedow, 'Choice of Law' in J Basedow and others (eds), *Encyclopedia of Private International Law* (Cheltenham, Edward Elgar Publishing, 2017) 312.

[2] HM Watt, 'Party Autonomy' in J Basedow and others (eds), *Encyclopedia of Private International Law* (Cheltenham, Edward Elgar Publishing, 2017) 1336.

[3] Basedow (n 1) 312.

[4] Industrial Development and Public Policy Department at JICA, *Legal Technical Assistance for Cambodia: The History and Methodology of the Assistance of JICA in Drafting the Civil Code and the Civil Procedure Code* [in Japanese] (2012) 9ff.

[5] Bun & Associates, 'Governing Law and Dispute Resolution [in Japanese]' (2017) *Bun & Associates Newsletter*.

local knowledge is highly regarded by Cambodian legal experts,[6] and because Cambodian private law is built upon Japanese legal doctrines.[7] International legal instruments are not helpful for Cambodian jurists because Cambodia has not ratified major international conventions on contractual obligations, such as the United Nations Convention on Contracts for the International Sale of Goods (Vienna, 1980; CISG).[8]

Choice of law for contractual obligations remains largely untouched by Cambodian jurists, which is unlikely to help Cambodian lawyers deal with the growth of international business transactions and the corresponding rise of cross-border disputes in Cambodia.[9] This chapter intends to address the gap in the Cambodian choice of law rules for contractual obligations. It proceeds as follows. Section II considers what legal norms may apply as the governing (rules of) law of a contract, discussing whether the parties may choose 'soft law' (or 'non-state law') as the (rules of) law applicable to the contract. Section III examines how Cambodian judges decide the applicable law of a contract, taking into account various factors such as intentions of the parties and factual circumstances surrounding the contract. It also addresses the scope of the governing law of a contract, pondering what issues are to be covered by that law. Section IV explores different choice of law rules for specific contracts, such as consumer, employment, insurance and sales contracts, among others. Section V considers trusts and charitable foundations as these can be established by contracts or unilateral conduct that may fall within the scope of the choice of law framework for contracts. Section VI concludes the chapter.

II. Governing Law of a Contract in Cambodia

The Cambodian legal system comprises only a few codified rules to determine the law applicable to contractual obligations involving a foreign element. Article 3 of the CC provides that 'legal relations among private persons, including legal persons, shall be equal and equivalent, respecting the free intentions of such individuals', which is perceived by local legal practitioners as the ground for the parties' right to choose the governing law

[6] N Teramura, 'Cambodia' in A Reyes and W Lui (eds), *Direct Jurisdiction: Asian Perspectives* (Oxford, Hart Publishing, 2021) 202–03; C Seavmey, 'Challenges of Legal Education in Cambodia [in Japanese]' (2020) 85 *ICD News* 16.

[7] J Menzel, 'Cambodian Law: Some Comparative and International Perspectives' in H Peng, K Phallack and J Menzel (eds), *Introduction to Cambodian Law* (Phnom Penh, Konrad-Adenauer-Stiftung Cambodia, 2012) 490; N Teramura, 'Cambodia' in K Nishioka (ed), *Treatment of Foreign Law in Asia* (Oxford, Hart Publishing, 2023); N Teramura, 'Japan as a Source of Legal Ideas: A View from the Mekong Subregion of ASEAN' (2021) 13 *New Voices in Japanese Studies* 19.

[8] UNCITRAL, 'Status: United Nations Convention on Contracts for the International Sale of Goods (Vienna, 1980) (CISG)' (n.d.), available at https://uncitral.un.org/en/texts/salegoods/conventions/sale_of_goods/cisg/status (accessed 10 December 2024). Moreover, Cambodia has not adopted the Hague Principles on Choice of Law in International Commercial Contracts: HCCH, 'Status Tables: Principles on Choice of Law in International Commercial Contracts' (2024), available at www.hcch.net/en/instruments/conventions/publications1/?dtid=41&cid=135 (accessed 10 December 2024).

[9] See generally H Pisel, 'Cambodia's Q1 Trade Volume Hits over $13B', *The Phnom Penh Post*, 16 April 2022, available at www.phnompenhpost.com/business/cambodias-q1-trade-volume-hits-over-13b#:~:text=In%202021%2C%20Cambodia's%20trade%20volume,cent%2C%20according%20to%20the%20GDCE (accessed 10 December 2024); Teramura, 'Japan as a Source of Legal Ideas: A View from the Mekong Subregion of ASEAN' (n 7) 19.

of a contract. Article 36 of the Commercial Arbitration Law also recognises the parties' freedom to choose the rules of law to be applied to the merits of the dispute. Thus, the principle of party autonomy in the choice of law for contractual obligations is codified in Cambodia.

The problem is that no discernible statutory rules explicitly elaborate on the extent to which the courts are required to respect the principle of party autonomy in determining the governing law of a contract. In other words, Cambodian PIL is somewhat obscure regarding the scope and application of the freedom of contract in relation to choice of law. For instance, it does not stipulate expressly what the parties may choose as the "proper law" of a contract. There can be little doubt that the parties may designate a municipal law as the proper law, even if it is a foreign law,[10] but whether they may designate a 'soft law' is not clear from the statutory rules.

The term 'soft law' typically refers to 'instruments of a normative nature with no legally binding force, … which are applied only through voluntary acceptance'.[11] International non-governmental institutions (like the International Institute for the Unification of Private Law – UNIDROIT), global merchants (such as those represented by the International Chamber of Commerce; ICC) and scholars issue such instruments to codify international trade customs and usages, as well as the *lex mercatoria*, as part of their ambitious projects for the harmonisation of international commercial law.[12] Examples of such instruments are the UNIDROIT Principles on International Commercial Contracts 2016 (the UNIDROIT Principles) and the ICC's International Commercial Terms (Incoterms), among many others.[13] Not a few international business persons have found these soft law instruments useful because they believe that 'the [non-binding general principles] reflect their business relationship better than domestic or other international law or they seek a neutral principle that does not give one party an advantage'.[14] Their voluntary acceptance has increased the weight of soft law in international commerce and cross-border dispute resolution.

It is reasonable under Cambodian PIL to construe the principle of party autonomy as providing the parties with the liberty of designating a soft law as the proper law of a contract. The Commercial Arbitration Law allows the parties to select rules of law

[10] A Bhati, 'Choice of Law And Mandatory Provisions', *Lex Kambujadesa Blawg: A Commentary on Cambodian Law and Practice*, 15 December 2018; K Nop, 'Cambodia: What Should Be Included in a Contract?', *Nop Legal: Page of Business Law*, 14 May 2021, available at https://noplegal.com/2021/05/14/what-should-be-included-in-a-contract/ (accessed 9 February 2025); Bun & Associates (n 5) 1.

[11] MJ Bonell, 'Soft Law and Party Autonomy: The Case of the UNIDROIT Principles' (2005) 51 *Loyola Law Review* 229, 229. See also generally AD Robilant, 'Genealogies of Soft Law' (2006) 54 *The American Journal of Comparative Law* 499.

[12] See generally UNIDROIT, 'About UNIDROIT: Overview' (2021), available at www.unidroit.org/about-unidroit/overview/ (accessed 10 December 2024); ICC, 'Business Solutions' (n.d.), available at https://iccwbo.org/business-solutions/ (accessed 10 December 2024). Not a few academics participated in the Working Group for the Preparation of the UNIDROIT Principles of International Commercial Contracts 2016: UNIDROIT, *UNIDROIT Principles of International Commercial Contracts 2016* (Rome, UNIDROIT 2016) x-xi.

[13] See respectively UNIDROIT (n 12); ICC, 'Incoterms® 2020' (n.d.), available at https://iccwbo.org/resources-for-business/incoterms-rules/incoterms-2020/ (accessed 10 December 2024). See also S Jolly and S Khanderia, *Indian Private International Law* (Oxford, Hart Publishing, 2021) 201.

[14] HD Gabriel, 'The Advantages of Soft Law in International Commercial Law: The Role of UNIDROIT, UNCITRAL, and the Hague Conference' (2009) 34 *Brooklyn Journal of International Law* 655, 669.

governing the merits of the dispute.[15] This Law is modelled after the UNCITRAL Model Law on International Commercial Arbitration (the Model Law),[16] which suggests in Article 28(1) that '[t]he arbitral tribunal shall decide the dispute in accordance with such rules of law as are chosen by the parties as applicable to the substance of the dispute'. The drafters of the Model Law intentionally used the term 'rules of law' instead of 'law', to enable parties to agree to apply any rules of law, including quasi-legal instruments that have been prepared by an international organisation but have not yet been incorporated in a national legal system.[17] Thus, 'rules of law' under the Cambodian Arbitration Law provides the parties with the broad freedom to choose the applicable substantive rules from both soft and national laws.

The freedom of parties to choose the proper (rules of) law of a contract also derives from Article 3 of the CC, which may serve as the foundation of the principle of party autonomy and freedom of contract for civil law relationships in general, unless otherwise provided by any special law.[18] Limitations of the parties' authority to choose the governing law of a contract (if any) have to be underpinned by special statutory norms, and no rules in Cambodian law prohibit parties from making their contract subject to soft law instruments. Indeed, the majority of Japanese PIL commentators are against allowing parties to select non-state law as the law governing the contract in litigation.[19] However, this is due to Article 7 of the AGRAL providing that '[t]he formation and effect of a juristic act shall be governed by *the law of the place* which was chosen by the party/parties'.[20] Thus, Japanese choice of law rules explicitly require the parties to choose a national law, unlike Cambodian PIL. Importing the majority opinion to Cambodia is unlikely to be feasible.[21]

Hence, the parties may designate a soft or non-state law as the law governing their contract in arbitration or litigation under Cambodian law. However, further clarification and guidance on the scope and application of the parties' right to choose the proper law of a contract is required.

[15] Commercial Arbitration Law, Art 36(1).

[16] R Weeramantry, 'International Investment Law and Practice in the Kingdom of Cambodia: An Evolving 'Rule Taker'?' in J Chaisse and L Nottage (eds), *International Investment Treaties and Arbitration across Asia* (Leiden, Brill, 2018) 305; L Bosman, 'Note General Editor Cambodia (2017): Supplement No. 93' in L Bosman (ed), *ICCA International Handbook on Commercial Arbitration* (Alphen aan den Rijn, Wolters Kluwer, 2020) i.

[17] UNCITRAL, *UNCITRAL 2012 Digest of Case Law on the Model Law on International Commercial Arbitration* (Vienna, Publishing and Library Section, United Nations Office, 2012) 121.

[18] CC, Art 1. See also K Boren, 'Cambodian Private Law: A Snapshot' in H Peng, K Phallack and J Menzel (eds), *Introduction to Cambodian Law* (Phnom Penh, Konrad-Adenauer-Stiftung Cambodia, 2012) 80–81.

[19] See T Kono, 'Japan' in J Basedow and others (eds), *Encyclopedia of Private International Law* (Cheltenham, Edward Elgar Publishing, 2017) 2224; K Nishioka and Y Nishitani, *Japanese Private International Law* (Oxford, Hart Publishing 2021) 108; Y Nishitani, 'Party Autonomy in Contemporary Private International Law: The Hague Principles on Choice of Law and East Asia' (2016) 59 *Japanese Yearbook of International Law* 300, 338.

[20] (Emphasis added.).

[21] In addition, excluding soft law instruments from options for the proper law of a contract might be against the international-law-friendly nature of the Cambodian Constitution (see Menzel (n 7) 490), since the major international instruments on choice of law for contractual obligations recognise the designation of a soft law instrument by parties as the law governing a contract. See generally UNCITRAL, *UNCITRAL, HCCH and Unidroit Legal Guide to Uniform Instruments in the Area of International Commercial Contracts, with a Focus on Sales* (Vienna, United Nations Publishing and Library Section 2021) 13ff.

III. Determination of the Applicable Law

The proper law of a contract is to be determined by examining (in sequence) whether there is an express choice of law, whether there is an implied choice of law, and, if none of these alternatives exist, which law has the most real and closest connection with the contract.[22] This section considers how the courts in Cambodia may address each of these aspects of the determination of the applicable law under Cambodian PIL, drawing largely on the contract law of Cambodia and Japanese legal principles of choice of law for contractual obligations.

A. Subjective Proper Law: Express and Implied Choice of Law

Parties may agree on the law governing a contract either expressly or impliedly.[23] The CC requires in Article 336 only an offer and acceptance for the formation of a contract, without setting out other conditions.[24] This basic rule of contract formation may extend to the parties' agreement on the governing law of a contract because their right to choose the proper law derives from the freedom of contract provided in the CC, as discussed elsewhere in this chapter. Cambodian law thus basically allows the courts to decide the proper law of a contract based on the meeting of minds between the contracting parties,[25] in accordance with the rules on contractual obligations in the CC.[26]

Cambodian judges are unlikely to face major challenges in identifying the proper law of a contract based on the parties' express choice. In most cases, those businesses which operate in Cambodia designate the proper law of a contract by inserting a governing law clause in the contract.[27] If the contract contained such a choice of law clause, the judges would apply the law designated by the clause in determining differences arose from the contract. However, the judges would be required to regard the choice of law clause as invalid, if it has been obtained by a false manifestation of intention that a party has made in collusion with the other party,[28] or if it has been annulled as the result of a mistake, fraud, duress, misrepresentation, or circumstance abuse.[29]

If there is no express choice of law, the judges would have to examine the parties' implied choice of the law applicable to the contract. No rules indicate what may constitute a tacit choice of law under Cambodian PIL. Japanese law too, provides little guidance, as is evident

[22] A Layton and A Dinelli, 'Proper Law (Doctrine)' in J Basedow and others (eds), *Encyclopedia of Private International Law* (Cheltenham, Edward Elgar Publishing, 2017) 1425.

[23] Regarding the definition of 'contracts', see CC, Art 311.

[24] On the definitions of offer and acceptance, see ibid, Art 337.

[25] Note, however, that special rules apply to specific contracts. See Section IV below.

[26] On the contract law of Cambodia, see generally H Kiyohara, 'Civil Code' in H Peng, K Phallack and J Menzel (eds), *Introduction to Cambodian Law* (Phnom Penh, Konrad-Adenauer-Stiftung Cambodia, 2012) 107ff; L Tayseng, 'Formation of Contract and Third Parties in Cambodia' in M Chen-Wishart, A Loke and S Vogenauer (eds), *Formation and Third Party Beneficiaries* (Oxford, Oxford University Press, 2018) 343ff.

[27] Bhati (n 10); Nop (n 10).

[28] CC, Art 353(1).

[29] ibid, Arts 345–51.

from the AGRAL containing no provisions addressing the issue.[30] Nonetheless, Kono writes that '[i]n the case of a lack of choice-of-law-clause, the governing law of the contract can be identified from the terms of contract or circumstances of the case'.[31] Nishioka and Nishitani attempt to elaborate on the indicators of the tacit choice further (albeit without support from court cases) as follows:

> A tacit choice of law may be inferred, for example, when the parties select only a single place of performance for the entire obligations arising out of a [bilateral] contract. An implicit intent can also be presumed, when the provisions of the contract clearly point to a particular legal system, or when in long-term transactions the individual contracts for delivery of goods do not contain a choice of law clause, but obviously rely on the framework contract governed by a law chosen by the parties.[32]

Regarding forum selection clauses and arbitration agreements (specifying the seat of arbitration), Japanese commentators suggest considering them as factors to determine the applicable law of the contract.[33] In other words, they claim that a choice of forum clause may not on its own indicate the choice of the forum law.[34] Cambodian jurists likely find these discussions by Japanese commentators helpful when they seek for a tacit choice of law in the context of Cambodian PIL.

The problem is whether the law of Cambodia allows the parties to designate a foreign legal system as the proper law even if it bears little or no connection to their contract. The answer to the question is likely to be positive, provided that the parties' intention to refer the contract to the legal system is evident from the terms of the contract or the circumstances surrounding the case. The only limitations to the freedom of the parties to choose any foreign law to govern their contract would be (overriding) mandatory rules of law and provisions on public policy, which are to be discussed in Section III.C below.

B. Objective Proper Law

Parties often have differing views on the proper law of their contract. They are sometimes unable to reach an agreement on the law governing the contract or fail to incorporate a choice of law clause into the contract. Nevertheless, no rules in Cambodian PIL suggest how to objectively determine the applicable law without reference to the parties' explicit or implicit choice of law. Thus, Cambodian jurists are encouraged to refer to the relevant Japanese PIL principles for inspiration. According to Article 8(1) of the AGRAL, '[i]f there

[30] GJ Bouwers, 'Tacit Choice of Law in International Commercial Contracts: An Analysis of Asian Jurisdictions and the Asian Principles of Private International Law' (2021) 26 *Uniform Law Review* 14, 27; J Yokoyama, *Private International Law in Japan* (Alphen aan den Rijn, Wolters Kluwer, 2019) 55. The AGRAL drafters were abstained from establishing a new provision on parties' inferred choice of law, to avoid complicating the legal practice in Japan. See K Koide, *Commentary on the Act on General Rules for Application of Laws* [in Japanese] (Tokyo, Shojihomu Publishing, 2014) 90.

[31] T Kono, 'Comparative Analysis of Recent Developments in Private International Law in Japan and Europe from a Japanese Perspective' (2008) 51 *Japanese Yearbook of International Law* 217, 220.

[32] Nishioka and Nishitani (n 19) 109.

[33] Kono (n 31) 220; Nishioka and Nishitani (n 19) 109.

[34] Bouwers (n 30) 29.

is no applicable law chosen by the party/parties as in the preceding article, the formation and effect of a juristic act shall be governed by the law of the place with which the act was most closely connected at the time the act was made'. The law having the closest connection is to be determined based on all the circumstances surrounding the juristic act, which may lack predictability and certainty.[35] Hence, the AGRAL elaborates further on which place may have the closest connection to a contract. It states in Article 8(2) that 'if the characteristic performance of a juristic act is to be made by one party, the law of his/her habitual residence [or place of business related to the justice act] is presumed to be the law of the place with which the juristic act is most closely connected'.[36] An exception of this rule is Article 8(3) on a contract whose subject matter is a real property, which presumes the location of the real property to be the place having the closest connection to the contract. Another exception is Article 12(3), which provides that '[i]f the parties have not chosen a law to govern the formation and effect of the labour contract …, the law of the place where labour is to be carried out is, …, presumed to be the law with which the labour contract is most closely connected'. These rules are merely presumptive and, therefore, rebuttable based on the surrounding circumstances of the contract. The parties may claim elsewhere as the place having the closest connection to the contract, taking into account all the circumstances of the case, and the court is required to displace the presumption should they find it unpersuasive.[37]

There should be no difficulty for Cambodian PIL to import those rules on the objective proper law test from Japan's AGRAL, provided the test is modified slightly as follows.

The closest connection test enables Cambodian judges to decide the law governing a contract flexibly, based on the objective circumstances surrounding the contract.[38] The flexibility comes with uncertainty due to the difficulty in identifying what circumstances may evidence a place's closest connection to the contract.[39] However, the drafters of the AGRAL attempted to alleviate the unpredictability (for vulnerable parties) by adopting the doctrine of characteristic performance, and by setting out the special rules on real estate and employment contracts.[40] Moreover, the fact that the closest connection test has been adopted by most major common and civil law countries,[41] implies that advantages brought about by the flexibility may carry more weight than the alleged unpredictability in the test.

[35] Koide (n 30) 107.

[36] If the party performing the characteristic obligation has more than one place of business related to the contract in different jurisdictions, the proper law of the contract is to be the law of the place where the party's principal place of business is situated.

[37] There is controversy among Japanese jurists over whether the presumption of closest connection is an *ex officio* matter. The AGRAL contains no provisions addressing this point. However, several judicial decisions suggest parties owe the burden of proof for the presumption of closest connection and rebuttal for the presumption: Koide (n 30) 108.

[38] ibid 107.

[39] Yokoyama (n 30) 58.

[40] ibid.

[41] On the acceptance of the closest connection test in civil law countries, see, e.g., Art 4(3) of the Regulation (EC) No 593/2008 of the European Parliament and of the Council of 17 June 2008 on the Law Applicable to Contractual Obligations (Rome I). On the acceptance in common law countries, see Layton and Dinelli (n 22) 1425; Jolly and Khanderia (n 13) 207ff; R Mortensen, R Garnett and M Keyes, *Private International Law in Australia*, 5th edn, (Chatswood, LexisNexis, 2023) 509–12.

The characteristic performance refers to the 'characteristic' obligation arising from a contract which distinguishes this type of contract from other types by its unique features. For instance, in a contract for the sale of real estate, the conveyance of the real property is perceived as the characteristic performance.[42] In many cases, the doctrine of characteristic performance may serve as a useful standard for the closest connection test.[43] But the characteristic performance doctrine is not always helpful for judges to determine the law having the closest connection to a contract, because it is sometimes unclear which performance is characteristic.[44] In the case of an exchange contract, each party is required to transfer title in property to the other party. This exchange of title is the unique feature of the exchange contract. Determining which transfer of title is more characteristic than the other is likely impractical. Moreover, the parties to a joint venture agreement are jointly responsible for the joint venture's financial decisions and expenditures. Thus, they are required to perform their duties cooperatively, and this joint responsibility distinguishes joint venture agreements from other types of contracts.[45] The drafters of the AGRAL were aware of the ambiguity in the principle of characteristic performance, so that they turned the principle into a presumptive rule which the court may overturn based on its case-by-case assessment of the closest connection. Accordingly, in the absence of the choice of law by the parties, the proper law of the contract is to be the law that has the closest connection to the contract. Jurists in Cambodia are recommended to seek the closest connection objectively, taking into account all the factual circumstances of the case. They may adopt the principle of characteristic performance in Japan's AGRAL, to inform their assessment of the closest connection. But a case-by-case assessment inevitably introduces uncertainty in the end.

Cambodian judges might be able to mitigate the uncertainty in the AGRAL's characteristic performance test by adopting an arguably more advanced approach. According to the drafters of the AGRAL, the closest connection test and the doctrine of characteristic performance under Article 8 were imported from Article 4(2) of the Convention on the Law Applicable to Contractual Obligations Opened for Signature in Rome on 19 June 1980 (the Rome Convention).[46] In 2008, this Convention was replaced by the Regulation (EC) No 593/2008 of the European Parliament and of the Council of 17 June 2008 on the Law Applicable to Contractual Obligations (the Rome I Regulation) except for in Denmark.[47] The Rome Convention thus developed into the Rome I Regulation. The AGRAL does not reflect the law reform in Europe because the AGRAL was promulgated in 2006 and never amended afterwards.

Cambodian jurists might find the Rome I Regulation useful in adopting the closest connection test. The reason for this is that the Regulation redresses the uncertainty of the

[42] Koide (n 30) 108.

[43] ibid.

[44] K Takahashi, 'A Major Reform of Japanese Private International Law' (2006) 2 *Journal of Private International Law* 311, 318.

[45] Takahashi further suggests that the principle of characteristic performance sometimes yields outcomes contrary to the common assumption on the closest connection, in relation to original equipment manufacturing (OEM) contracts and guarantee contracts: ibid 319.

[46] See generally Koide (n 30) 106 and 116.

[47] Rome I Regulation, paragraph 46 of the preamble.

characteristic performance doctrine by incorporating hard-and-fast rules specifying the proper laws of the eight types of contracts:[48]

> (a) a contract for the sale of goods shall be governed by the law of the country where the seller has his habitual residence; (b) a contract for the provision of services shall be governed by the law of the country where the service provider has his habitual residence; (c) a contract relating to a right *in rem* in immovable property or to a tenancy of immovable property shall be governed by the law of the country where the property is situated; (d) notwithstanding point (c), a tenancy of immovable property concluded for temporary private use for a period of no more than six consecutive months shall be governed by the law of the country where the landlord has his habitual residence, provided that the tenant is a natural person and has his habitual residence in the same country; (e) a franchise contract shall be governed by the law of the country where the franchisee has his habitual residence; (f) a distribution contract shall be governed by the law of the country where the distributor has his habitual residence; (g) a contract for the sale of goods by auction shall be governed by the law of the country where the auction takes place, if such a place can be determined; (h) a contract concluded within a multilateral system which brings together or facilitates the bringing together of multiple third-party buying and selling interests in financial instruments, …, in accordance with non-discretionary rules and governed by a single law, shall be governed by that law.[49]

If the contract does not fall within one of the eight contract types, the *lex contractus* may be determined by the doctrine of characteristic performance.[50] However, this last determination of proper law would merely be presumptive in that, if there is a law that is manifestly more closely connected with the contract than the legal system designated by the characteristic performance doctrine, the court should apply that law to the contract.[51] In short, uncertainty remains in the Rome I Regulation's approach to the closest connection test. Nevertheless, Rome I affords greater certainty than the AGRAL's closest connection test. Cambodian judges might thus more usefully apply the hard-and-fast rules of Rome I as an aid to identifying the *lex contractus* for a specific contract efficiently and expeditiously.[52]

C. Limits to the Choice of Proper Law

The freedom to choose the proper law of a contract has limitations as per Article 354 of the CC, which states that the contract (or part of the contract) repugnant to mandatory provisions of law or Cambodia's public orders and good morals shall be void.[53] The parties are not allowed to agree on the application of a foreign law that is contrary to mandatory rules of law or public policy provisions.

[48] Z Tang, 'Law Applicable in the Absence of Choice – The New Article 4 of the Rome I Regulation' (2008) 71 *Modern Law Review* 785, 787.

[49] Rome I Regulation, Art 4.1.

[50] ibid, Art 4.2.

[51] ibid, Art 4.3 (noting that the manifestly close connection is determined in light of all the circumstances of the case).

[52] On choice of law rules for specific contracts, see Section IV.

[53] Bhati (n 10).

i. Mandatory Rules

As discussed in Chapter 1 of this volume, there are two types of mandatory rules – non-derogable rules in the *lex causae* and overriding mandatory rules. The former does not deter the parties from designating foreign law as the governing law of the contract because they merely mean mandatory rules within the proper law of the contract. If the parties chose Japanese law as the law governing the contract, they would not be allowed to contract out certain non-derogable rules in Japanese law, but the rules would not alter the parties' selection of Japanese law. In contrast, overriding mandatory rules restrict the parties' choice of foreign law as the proper law. The forum court is typically required to preclude and to supersede choice of law provisions applying foreign law in favour of the overriding mandatory rules of the forum that embody the forum's social, economic or political interests. In case of a conflict between the overriding mandatory rules of Cambodian law and the foreign law applicable to a contract, the courts in Cambodia would thus give weight to the application of the overriding mandatory rules of law.

Neither the law of Cambodia nor Japanese PIL elaborates on which specific rules deserve overriding mandatory application.[54] However, the Constitution adopts the following doctrines as the foundational principles of the Kingdom of Cambodia: '(1) national sovereignty, (2) democracy, (3) human rights, (4) rule of law, (5) constitutional monarchy system of a parliamentary government, (6) separation of power, and (7) regular process of institutional eternity'.[55] Accordingly, Cambodian judges are likely to perceive the legal norms protecting these core values as the overriding mandatory rules of Cambodian law. For instance, in relation to the national sovereignty of Cambodia, Article 44 of the Constitution provides that only natural persons and legal entities of Cambodian nationality are eligible to own land within the territory of Cambodia. Thus, the courts in Cambodia would not effectuate the sale of land to a foreign entity, even if the *lex contractus* chosen by the parties recognised the purchase of land by foreign entities. Any rules supporting or further elaborating the principle, such as Article 9 of the 2001 Land Law,[56] are likely to be perceived by the court as the overriding mandatory provisions.[57] On human rights, the 1997 Labour Law declares its mandatory nature by stating that '[t]he provisions of this law are of the nature of public order, excepting derogations provided expressly. Consequently, all rules result[ing] from a unilateral decision, a contract or a convention that do not comply with the provisions of this law or any legal text for its enforcement, are null and void'.[58] Accordingly, Khmer judges would vitiate any provision of the proper law of an employment contract, if

[54] Section VII.A of Chapter 2.

[55] H Peng, 'The Modern Era of Cambodian Constitutionalism: Constitutional Analysis of Historical and Contemporary Development' in H Peng, K Phallack and J Menzel (eds), *Introduction to Cambodian Law* (Phnom Penh, Konrad-Adenauer-Stiftung Cambodia, 2012) 39.

[56] Art 9 reads: 'An enterprise registered in Cambodia, in respect of which 51% or more of the shares are held by natural persons of Cambodian nationality or by Cambodian legal entities recognized pursuant to the laws of Cambodia, may be the owner of land. Only percentages stipulated in the articles of incorporation are taken into account. Any private agreement signed by a shareholder that is contrary to this article is null and void. … If percentages stipulated in the articles of incorporation are changed in a way that [the enterprise] ceases to be Cambodian, the enterprise has the obligation to amend the articles of incorporation to comply with the actual circumstances and shall inform … the competent institutions of such amendment according to the laws in force'.

[57] See generally Bhati (n 10).

[58] 1997 Labour Law, Art 13. However, the Law does not prohibit employers from granting workers benefits or rights greater than what is defined in the Law.

it was contrary to the non-derogable rules in the Labour Law. Since listing all overriding mandatory rules of Cambodian law is unlikely to be practical, Cambodian judges would have to determine whether there are any applicable overriding mandatory rules in the case at hand, on a case-by-case basis, taking into account those constitutional principles.

ii. Public Policy

The courts may limit the application of foreign law, invoking the public policy of Cambodia.[59] No noticeable legal norms, judicial precedents and authoritative commentaries elaborate on the adoption of public policy provisions to exclude the application of foreign law in Cambodia. However, Cambodian jurists may overcome this ambiguity by adopting an approach advocated by Japanese PIL commentators. As discussed in Chapter 2 of this volume, the approach makes the application of public policy hinge on the satisfaction of the following two conditions: (1) the application of foreign law to the contract is not acceptable from the standpoint of the forum law, and (2) the contract in dispute manifests sufficient proximity to the forum. There is no concrete threshold for each condition because the two criteria are in an inverse relationship. Thus, if the application of foreign law to the contract was so repulsive to the Cambodian legal system because, for instance, the foreign proper law recognised a transaction which was illegal under Cambodian law,[60] only a reasonably close connection between the contract and Cambodia would fulfil the second condition. If the contract had a very close connection with Cambodia because, for instance, the contract was concluded in the Kingdom, mere minor incompatibility of the foreign proper law with the (non-overriding) mandatory rules of Cambodian law would satisfy the first requirement. Thus, the court will determine whether and how the two conditions are, considering the circumstances surrounding the contract.

D. Scope of Application of the Proper Law

No rules in Cambodian law elaborate on what contractual issues are to be covered by the contract's governing law. In relation to the AGRAL, Japanese commentators suggest that the proper law comprehensively governs matters arising from a contractual relationship, including existence, (material) validity, effects, contents and illegality of the contract, as well as the effects of non-performance of contractual obligations.[61] According to Yokoyama, contractual interpretation is principally governed by the *lex contractus*, but the court is not deterred from taking into consideration any relevant law other than the *lex contractus* and

[59] For details, see Chapter 1, Section VII.B of this volume.

[60] For example, commercial surrogacy is currently illegal in Cambodia, but it is legal in some US states, Russia and Ukraine, among others. See Y Sineat and D Keeton-Olsen, 'A Surrogate Family and the Law That Criminalized Them', *VOD*, 2 November 2020, available at https://vodenglish.news/a-surrogate-family-and-the-law-that-criminalized-them/ (accessed 9 February 2025); V Piersanti and others, 'Surrogacy and "Procreative Tourism": What Does the Future Hold from the Ethical and Legal Perspectives?' (2021) 57 *Medicina (Kaunas)* 47, Tables 1 and 2.

[61] Nishioka and Nishitani (n 19) 110; Yokoyama (n 30) 59–63; Y Sakurada, *Private International Law [in Japanese]*, 7th edn, (Tokyo, Yuhikaku Publishing, 2020) 239; T Sawaki and M Dogauchi, *Introduction to Private International Law* [in Japanese] (Tokyo, Yuhikaku Publishing, 2018) 178.

applicable trade usages.[62] Which law governs the performance of contractual obligations is controversial. The AGRAL does not address this issue explicitly, while some jurists claim that performance is governed principally by the *lex contractus*.[63] The Tokyo High Court once considered the law of the place of performance (the *lex loci solutionis*) in determining the application of public policy to a contract and contents of the public policy.[64] Invoking the judgment, some commentators suggest that Japanese law does not permit the court to apply the *lex loci solutionis* to contractual performance as law, but merely allows the court to take into account the *lex loci solutionis* as data or facts for determining the substance of the performance.[65] To further justify this approach, Yokoyama refers to Article 403 of the Japanese Civil Code, which states, pertaining to payment in foreign currency, that '*the obligor may make the payment in Japanese currency converted with the foreign exchange rate at the place of the performance*'.[66] As the CC of Cambodia contains a rule that is close to and inspired by Article 403 of the Japanese Civil code,[67] extending Yokoyama's thesis to Cambodian PIL is likely to be plausible. Nevertheless, Cambodian PIL is, in principle, encouraged to recognise the broad scope of application of the proper law of the contract because most Cambodian judges are not familiar with handling conflict of laws issues,[68] and because mandating such judges to apply complex PIL theories is likely to cause delays and inefficiencies in litigation.[69]

On contract formation, the AGRAL recognises the formal validity of a contract if it satisfies the formalities imposed by the law applicable to the formation of the contract or the law of the place where the contract was concluded.[70] The law applicable to the formation of the contract is the *lex contractus*.[71] If the contract was concluded between persons in different jurisdictions, the law of the place where the contract was concluded would be either the law of the place where the notice of offer was dispatched or the law of the place where the notice of acceptance was dispatched.[72] In other words, the contract becomes formally valid once its offer and acceptance have satisfied the formal requirements set out in one of those two legal systems.[73] This approach would contribute to raising the probability of establishing the formal validity of cross-border contracts as it gives the parties two optional sets of formal requirements that are closely connected to the formation of the contract, requiring the offer and acceptance to fulfil only one of the two sets of requirements. Thus, the AGRAL offers

[62] Yokoyama (n 30) 61.
[63] Nishioka and Nishitani (n 19) 110; Yokoyama (n 30) 59–60.
[64] *X v Y* [2000] Tokyo High Court Heisei 10(Ne) 2750, 1749 Hanrei Jiho 157.
[65] Nishioka and Nishitani (n 19) 110; Yokoyama (n 30) 59–60.
[66] (Emphasis added).
[67] See CC, Art 317.
[68] See generally Teramura, 'Cambodia' (n 7); Menzel (n 7) 488–91.
[69] Art 4 of the Civil Procedure Code of Cambodia mandates the court to settle civil disputes fairly and expeditiously.
[70] AGRAL, Arts 10(1)–(2).
[71] Yokoyama (n 30) 58.
[72] AGRAL, Art 10(4). In the case of a cross-border unilateral act which is intended to have legal effects on a contract, like a notice of terminating the contract or a declaration of rescinding the contract, the unilateral act's formal validity depends on the law of the formation of the contract or the law of the place where the act was made (that is deemed to be place where the unilateral act was made): ibid, Art 10(3); Takahashi (n 44) 328. Note, however, that Articles 10(2)–(4) do not apply to contracts for the creation or disposal of rights *in rem* to movables or immovables or other rights requiring registration: AGRAL, Article 10(5).
[73] Takahashi (n 44) 328.

the three alternative laws governing contract formation – the *lex contractus*, the law of the place where the notice of offer was dispatched and the law of the place where the notice of acceptance was dispatched. Cambodian judges are likely to find this flexibility helpful in determining the formal validity of contracts as it may prevent contracts and the principle of party autonomy from being invalidated by parochial formalism.

IV. Specific Contracts

This chapter has so far only considered general choice of law rules applicable to multi-state contracts. However, the general rules may be overridden by the special conflict of laws rules of the forum for specific contracts (if any). The ensuing subsections consider such special rules (and also whether the rules can be found in Cambodian law) for consumer contracts, employment contracts, insurance contracts, sales contracts, contracts for the hire of goods, contracts for the carriage of goods by sea, negotiable instruments and agency agreements.

A. Consumer Contracts

The law of Cambodia provides consumers with substantive legislative protections, which may be applied with mandatory effect in international cases. The Law on Consumer Protection (enacted in 2019) states that: '[t]his law shall apply to any person who conducts a business, whether for a profit or non-profit, including the sale of goods or services or real rights over immovable property, to consumers in the Kingdom of Cambodia unless otherwise provided by separate provisions'.[74] Thus, an express choice of foreign law by foreign businesses operating in Cambodia does not necessarily exclude the application of the Consumer Protection Law. Moreover, it is reasonable to regard the provisions of the Consumer Protection Law as overriding mandatory rules because the Law aims to elaborate fundamental consumer rights guaranteed in the Constitution of the Kingdom.[75] In applying the Consumer Protection Law, the courts in Cambodia would possibly be required to invoke the Prakas No 0067 on Unfair Contract Clause as it offers further clarity about unfair contract terms in standard form consumer contracts.

B. Employment Contracts

Substantive rules for labour protections may apply mandatorily to international employment contracts performed in Cambodia. As discussed in Section III.C.i, the 1997 Labour Law expressly states that it is of the nature of public order.[76] Accordingly, provisions of the Labour Law override the law otherwise applicable to the employment contract. The Law applies automatically to any disputes and controversies arising from 'relations between

[74] Law on Consumer Protection, Art 3.
[75] Constitution of Cambodia, Art 64. See also generally Law on Consumer Protection, Arts 1–2.
[76] 1997 Labour Law, Art 13.

employers and workers resulting from employment contracts to be performed within the territory of the Kingdom of Cambodia, regardless of where the contract was made and what the nationality and residences of the contracted parties are'.[77] Thus, Cambodian companies hiring foreign individuals and foreign entities employing Cambodian workers are not allowed to contract out the Labour Law by designating foreign law as the proper law of their employment contract, provided that the place of contract performance is in Cambodia.

Further, parties to international labour contracts are generally bound by the international agreements on employment that Cambodia has ratified.[78] In particular, the following conventions of the International Labour Organisation (ILO) are currently effective in the Kingdom: Forced Labour Convention, 1930 (No 29), Freedom of Association and Protection of the Right to Organise Convention, 1948 (No 87), Right to Organise and Collective Bargaining Convention, 1949 (No 98), Equal Remuneration Convention, 1951 (No 100), Abolition of Forced Labour Convention, 1957 (No 105), Discrimination (Employment and Occupation) Convention, 1958 (No 111), Minimum Age Convention, 1973 (No 138), Worst Forms of Child Labour Convention, 1999 (No 182), Employment Policy Convention, 1964 (No 122), Night Work of Young Persons (Industry) Convention, 1919 (No 6), White Lead (Painting) Convention, 1921 (No 13) and Labour Administration Convention, 1978 (No 150).[79] These international conventions (and relevant domestic legal norms ensuring their enforcement in Cambodia) are likely to have the force of overriding mandatory rules as the Constitution obliges the Kingdom to recognise and respect human rights as stipulated in the covenants and conventions on human rights and women's and children's rights.[80]

C. Insurance Contracts

The Cambodian legal system does not explicitly provide special choice of law rules for insurance contracts. However, any insurance agencies operating in the Kingdom are bound by the 2014 Insurance Law that contains several rules regulating insurance contracts concluded and/or performed in the territory of Cambodia.[81] Although in the Constitution there is no mention of insurance, the Insurance Law clearly states that it has overriding effect over matters arising from an insurance contract concluded or performed in Cambodia.[82] In contrast, no provisions of Cambodian law contain special rules for an insurance contract

[77] ibid, Article 1. However, certain types of workers – such as judges of the Cambodian judiciary, permanent civil servants and police and military officers – are to be excluded from the Labour Law's scope of application. See generally ibid, Paragraph 4.

[78] See generally K Phallack, 'Cambodian Labour and Employment Law' in H Peng, K Phallack and J Menzel (eds), *Introduction to Cambodian Law* (Phnom Penh, Konrad-Adenauer-Stiftung Cambodia, 2012) 289.

[79] ILO, 'NORMLEX (Information System on International Labour Standards): Ratifications for Cambodia' (n.d.), available at www.ilo.org/dyn/normlex/en/f?p=NORMLEXPUB:11200:0::NO::p11200_country_id:103055 (accessed 10 December 2024).

[80] Constitution of Cambodia, Art 31.

[81] 2014 Insurance Law, Arts 3 and 7ff. On the development of insurance laws and regulations in Cambodia, see generally A Fontaine, 'The Insurance and Reinsurance Law Review: Cambodia', *The Law Reviews*, 24 April 2022, available at https://backend.bun-associates.com/attributes/publication/file_1666840442.pdf (accessed 9 February 2025).

[82] Art 3 of the 2014 Insurance Law reads that '[t]his law shall cover and apply to all insurance activities carried out in the Kingdom of Cambodia. Also, Art 114 of the Law states, '[a]ny regulation that is contrary to this law shall be deemed as null and void'.

concluded and performed outside the Kingdom. When it comes to issues pertaining to the proper law of such insurance contract, the court will likely apply general choice of law rules for contracts. If the parties have designated the proper law of the contract, the court will respect the choice of law as per the principle of party autonomy provided in Article 3 of the CC. In the absence of such a choice, the court will seek to apply the law that has the closest connection to the insurance contract.[83] In either case, the court will be required to observe the overriding mandatory rules of the forum, including but not limited to the provisions of the Insurance Law. Hence, if the insured falls within the definition of consumer under the Consumer Protection Law, the court will apply the provisions of the Law to protect the rights of the insured as a consumer.

D. Sales Contracts

Cambodian law has no special choice of law rules for sales contracts. Cambodian judges are therefore most likely to deal with conflict of laws issues arising from a sales contract in accordance with the basic choice of law rules for contracts. The proper law of the sales contract is likely to be the law that the parties intended to apply (either expressly or implicitly), or if their intention cannot be ascertained, the legal system with which the contract is most closely connected. However, how the court adopts the general choice of law rules for contracts will depend on the subject matter of the sales contract.

i. Sale of Immovable Property

When it comes to the law governing the sale of immovable property, the parties are basically free to agree on the proper law of the sales contract. However, they need to bear in mind that the Consumer Protection Law applies (with overriding mandatory effects) to the transfer of rights over real property from a businessperson to a consumer who resides in Cambodia. Another body of law having overriding effects is the 2001 Land Law, which applies to all real properties in Cambodia. The Law is of the nature of public policy as it states that '[t]his law has the objective *to determine the regime of ownership for immovable properties in the Kingdom of Cambodia* to guarantee the rights of ownership and other rights related to immovable property, *according to the provisions of the 1993 Constitution of the Kingdom of Cambodia*'.[84] These overriding mandatory norms restrict the parties' freedom to choose the law governing the sale of real property.

If the parties failed to designate the proper law, the court will likely identify and apply the objective proper law of the contract, adopting the closest connection test derived from Japan's AGRAL. According to Article 8(3) of the AGRAL, the law having the closest connection to a sale of real property is presumed to be the law of the place where the immovable is situated. Cambodian judges may find that adopting this presumptive test conforms with the doctrine of (international) comity – a fundamental principle of PIL that prescribes the recognition and application of foreign law as long as it is not against the forum's public

[83] See Section III.B.
[84] 2001 Land Law, Art 1 (emphasis added).

order.[85] According to Dornis, comity-based adjudication aims to guarantee the avoidance of international policy conflicts, 'particularly with respect to limitations to the state's judicial powers'.[86] As is evident in the 2001 Land Law, Cambodia has a keen interest in applying its law to the transaction of real properties located in the country. It is reasonable for Cambodian judges to assume that foreign states likely have the same interest because the presumption will possibly help Cambodia avoid international policy conflicts with other countries concerning national sovereignty over real properties. Thus, the courts in Cambodia will probably treat the location of real estate as a determinant of the law most closely connected with the contract on the sale of the property, as per Article 8(3) of the AGRAL.

ii. Sale of Goods

As discussed in Section II, parties have a broad liberty to designate the proper law of a contract. They can choose municipal law, soft law and international legal instruments as the law or the rules of law governing a contract for the sale of goods. In the case of a sale of goods agreement between two parties based in Cambodia and China respectively, the parties are free to choose the proper law of the sales contract from Cambodian law, Chinese law and any other municipal law, as well as soft law instruments, such as the UNIDROIT Principles and Incoterms. International conventions can be options, too. Hence, the parties may agree to apply the CISG to their sales contract, and the courts in Cambodia are required to respect the agreement as per the principle of party autonomy, regardless of Cambodia's non-ratification of the convention. Even without an explicit agreement to opt for the CISG, the parties and courts are encouraged to be wary of its applicability because the CISG is still applicable through a choice of law clause designating the law of a signatory to the convention (like the law of China),[87] unless the parties have agreed to exclude the application of the CISG.[88] Note, however, that the parties' freedom to choose the applicable law is not without limitations. Public policy rules of the forum limit the parties' choice of the proper law of the sale of goods contract. Particularly relevant is the Consumer Protection Law, which applies to consumer transactions, including the sale of goods with consumers living in Cambodia.

Suppose the parties have not designated the proper law of the sales contract. In that case, the court will need to identify and apply the law having the closest connection to the contract, turning to the doctrine of characteristic performance inspired by Article 8(2) of the AGRAL. As the characteristic performance of a typical sale of goods contract is the

[85] TW Dornis, 'Comity' in Jürgen Basedow and others (eds), *Encyclopedia of Private International Law* (Cheltenham, Edward Elgar Publishing, 2017) 386.

[86] ibid 389.

[87] Art 1(b) of CISG reads: 'This Convention applies to contracts of sale of goods between parties whose places of business are in different [s]tates … when the rules of private international law lead to the application of the law of a [c]ontracting [s]tate'.

[88] Art 6 of CISG allows the parties to exclude the application of the convention, reflecting the principles of party autonomy and contractual freedom: UNCITRAL, 'Explanatory Note by the UNCITRAL Secretariat on the United Nations Convention on Contracts for the International Sale of Goods' in UNCITRAL (ed), *United Nations Convention on Contracts for the International Sale of Goods* (Vienna, Publishing and Library Section of United Nations Office, 2010) 35–36.

delivery of goods,[89] the proper law of the sales contract is presumed to be the law of the seller's habitual residence or, if the seller has an establishment for the characteristic act, the law of the place where the establishment is located.[90] As the presumption is rebuttable, if a party succeeds in demonstrating a legal system which is more closely connected with the contract than the law of the seller's habitual residence, the court will apply that legal system.[91]

E. Contracts for the Hire of Goods

No noticeable Cambodian PIL norms set out special choice of law rules for hire of goods agreements. Conflict of laws issues on goods hire contracts are therefore subject to the general choice of law rules for contracts as per Article 3 of the CC or, if there is no choice of law by the parties, the principle of closest connection deriving from Article 8 of the AGRAL. Should a party to the hire contract fall within the definition of 'consumer' under the Consumer Protection Law of Cambodia, the provisions of the Law will override the rules of law chosen by the parties or the objective proper law of the contract identified by the court.[92]

F. Contracts for the Carriage of Goods by Sea, Air or Land

Cambodia has not accepted any international regimes for the carriage of goods by sea. The country has yet to ratify the International Convention for the Unification of Certain Rules of Law relating to Bills of Lading (1924; the Hague Rules) and its Protocols (1968 and 1979; the Hague-Visby Rules),[93] as well as the United Nations Convention on the Carriage of Goods by Sea (Hamburg, 31 March 1978; the Hamburg Rules).[94] The proper law of a contract for the carriage of goods by sea is therefore to be determined by the court in accordance with the general choice of law rules for contracts under Article 3 of the CC or the closest connection test inspired by Article 8 of the AGRAL. In adopting the latter, the court might find

[89] Koide (n 30) 108.

[90] Yokoyama (n 30) 63; Nishioka and Nishitani (n 19) 117. If there are several relevant establishments in different jurisdictions, the law of the place of the principal establishment is presumed to be law most closely connected with the contract: AGRAL, Art 8(3). See also Rome I Regulation, Art 4.1(a), which generally leads to the same proper law as under AGRAL, Art 8: Nishioka and Nishitani (n 19) 117.

[91] Takahashi (n 44) 319; Yokoyama (n 30) 63; Nishioka and Nishitani (n 19) 117.

[92] See Section IV.A above.

[93] InforMARE, 'International Conventions: Membership List' (2022), available at www.informare.it/dbase/convuk.htm (accessed 30 May 2022, not accessible as at 12 December 2024).

[94] UNCITRAL, 'Status: United Nations Convention on the Carriage of Goods by Sea (Hamburg, 1978) (the "Hamburg Rules")' (n.d.), available at https://uncitral.un.org/en/texts/transportgoods/conventions/hamburg_rules/status (accessed 10 December 2024). Also, Cambodia has not signed United Nations Convention on Contracts for the International Carriage of Goods Wholly or Partly by Sea (2008; the Rotterdam Rules), although the Convention has not yet entered into force: UNCITRAL, 'Status: United Nations Convention on Contracts for the International Carriage of Goods Wholly or Partly by Sea (New York, 2008) (the "Rotterdam Rules")' (n.d.), available at https://uncitral.un.org/en/texts/transportgoods/conventions/rotterdam_rules/status (accessed 10 December 2024).

Article 5(1) of the Rome I Regulation useful to determine the objective proper law, as it provides an elaborated choice of law rule for contracts of carriage.[95]

On the carriage of goods by air, Cambodia is a member of the Convention for the Unification of Certain Rules Relating to International Carriage by Air (Warsaw, 12 October 1929; the Warsaw Convention) as amended by the Hague Protocol in 1955.[96] The Warsaw Convention applies to 'all international carriage of persons, baggage or cargo performed by aircraft for reward … [and] gratuitous carriage by aircraft performed by an air transport undertaking'.[97] It regulates matters pertaining to an air waybill – a contract of carriage between the shipper and the carrier – and liability of the career in international carriage by air, among others. The courts in Cambodia are expected to deal with issues on international private air law under the Warsaw Convention, although it does not cover carriage of mail and postal packages.[98]

However, the courts should bear in mind that the Warsaw Convention has been replaced by the Convention for the Unification of Certain Rules for International Carriage by Air (Montreal, 28 May 1999; the Montreal Convention) in most contracting parties to the Warsaw Convention.[99] As Cambodia is not a party to the Montreal Convention,[100] Cambodian courts are required to adopt the Warsaw and Montreal Conventions interchangeably, as the situation requires. For instance, they shall adopt the Warsaw Convention to deal with issues arising from an international air carriage between parties to the Warsaw Convention.[101] Likewise, they shall apply the Montreal Convention to an international carriage by air between state parties to the Convention.[102] When it comes to a carriage by air between a party to the Warsaw Convention regime that has not ratified the Montreal Convention (like Cambodia) and a party to the Montreal Convention, the Warsaw Convention is most likely to apply. The reason for this is that the Montreal Convention shall prevail over any rules of the Warsaw Convention or the Hague Protocol only where the international carriage takes place between state parties to the Montreal Convention that are also party to the Warsaw Convention and/or the Hague Protocol,[103] or where the

[95] Art 5(1) of the Rome I Regulation provides: 'To the extent that the law applicable to a contract for the carriage of goods has not been chosen [by the parties], the law applicable shall be the law of the country of habitual residence of the carrier, provided that the place of receipt or the place of delivery or the habitual residence of the consignor is also situated in that country. If those requirements are not met, the law of the country where the place of delivery as agreed by the parties is situated shall apply'. On the relationship between the Rome I Regulation and AGRAL, see Section III.B above.

[96] ICAO, 'Status of Cambodia with Regard to International Air Law Instruments' (n.d.), available at www.icao.int/secretariat/legal/Status%20of%20individual%20States/cambodia_en.pdf (accessed 10 December 2024).

[97] Warsaw Convention, Art 1(1). According to Art 1(2) of the Convention, 'international carriage' means 'any carriage in which, according to the agreement between the parties, the place of departure and the place of destination, whether or not there be a break in the carriage or a transshipment, are situated either within the territories of two High Contracting Parties or within the territory of a single High Contracting Party if there is an agreed stopping place within the territory of another State, even if that State is not a High Contracting Party'.

[98] ibid, Art 2(2).

[99] Compare generally ICAO, 'Contracting Parties to the Convention for the Unification of Certain Rules Relating to International Carriage by Air Signed at Warsaw On 12 October 1929 and the Protocol Modifying the Said Convention Signed at the Hague on 28 September 1955' (n.d.), available at www.icao.int/secretariat/legal/List%20of%20Parties/WC-HP_EN.pdf (accessed 10 December 2024); and ICAO, 'Convention for the Unification of Certain Rules For International Carriage by Air Done at Montreal on 28 May 1999' (n.d.), available at www.icao.int/secretariat/legal/List%20of%20Parties/Mtl99_EN.pdf (accessed 10 December 2024).

[100] Cambodia signed but has not ratified the Warsaw Convention: ICAO (n 96).

[101] Warsaw Convention, Art 1(2).

[102] Montreal Convention, Art 1(2).

[103] ibid, Art 55(1).

international carriage is carried out within the territory of any single state party to the Montreal Convention which is also a party to the Warsaw Convention and/or the Hague Protocol.[104] Another plausible scenario is that an international air carriage is performed between a party to the Warsaw/Montreal Convention and a country that has not adopted either carriage by air convention. In this case, neither the Warsaw Convention nor the Montreal Convention is applicable to the contract for carriage by air in dispute.[105] The court is then highly likely to determine the proper law of the contract by adopting the general choice of law rules for contracts under the Cambodian PIL.[106]

Regarding carriage of goods by land, Cambodia is not a member of the Convention on the Contract for the International Carriage of Goods by Road (Geneva, 19 May 1956; the CMR Convention).[107] However, this does not entirely exclude Cambodian parties from the Convention's scope of application because:

> [The CMR] Convention shall apply to every contract for the carriage of goods by road in vehicles for reward, when the place of taking over of the goods and the place designated for delivery, as specified in the contract, are situated in two different countries, *of which at least one is a contracting country, irrespective of the place of residence and the nationality of the parties.*[108]

Therefore, if a Cambodian party undertakes a delivery of goods by road from a non-member state to a member state of the Convention (or vice-versa), or between member states of the Convention, the contract for the carriage of goods will be governed by the CMR Convention. Otherwise, the proper law of the contract is to be determined based on the general choice of law rules for contracts under Cambodian law.[109]

G. Negotiable Instruments (Including Bills of Exchange and Letters of Credit)

Cambodia has not ratified any choice of law conventions on negotiable instruments such as the Convention Providing a Uniform Law for Bills of Exchange and Promissory Notes and Convention for the Settlement of Certain Conflicts of Laws in Connection with Cheques.[110] Cambodia's non-participation in these international frameworks is highly likely to deter

[104] ibid, Art 55(2).
[105] Warsaw Convention, Art 1(2); Montreal Convention, Art 1(2).
[106] See Section III above.
[107] United Nations, 'United Nations Treaty Collection: Convention on the Contract for the International Carriage of Goods by Road (CMR)' (n.d.), available at https://treaties.un.org/Pages/ViewDetails.aspx?src=IND&mtdsg_no=XI-B-11&chapter=11&clang=_en (accessed 10 December 2024).
[108] CMR Convention, Art 1(1).
[109] See generally Section III above.
[110] See respectively United Nations, 'United Nations Treaty Collection: Convention Providing a Uniform Law for Bills of Exchange and Promissory Notes (Geneva, 7 June 1930)' (n.d.), available at https://treaties.un.org/pages/LONViewDetails.aspx?src=LON&id=559&chapter=30&clang=_en (accessed 10 December 2024); United Nations, 'United Nations Treaty Collection: Convention for the Settlement of Certain Conflicts of Laws in Connection with Cheques (Geneva, 19 March 1931)' (n.d.), available at https://treaties.un.org/pages/LONViewDetails.aspx?src=LON&id=558&chapter=30&clang=_en (accessed 10 December 2024). Moreover, Cambodia has not signed the United Nations Convention on International Bills of Exchange and International Promissory Notes: UNCITRAL, 'Status: United Nations Convention on International Bills of Exchange and International Promissory Notes (New York, 1988)' (n.d.), available at https://uncitral.un.org/en/texts/payments/conventions/bills_of_exchange/status (accessed 10 December 2024).

Cambodian judges from relying on Japanese PIL principles for negotiable instruments. The reason is that Japanese law has special choice of law rules for negotiable instruments in the Bills of Exchange Act (Act No 20 of 15 July 1932; BEA) and the Cheques Act (Act No 57 of 29 July 1933; CHA), which are modelled on those international conventions on negotiable instruments that Cambodia has not ratified.[111] Thus, choice of law issues pertaining to checks, bills of exchange and promissory notes are largely regulated by the general conflict rules for contracts, including those inspired by the AGRAL.

However, Cambodia has the Law on Negotiable Instruments and Payment Transactions (LNIPT) that governs checks, bills of exchange and promissory notes.[112] This Law contains a few special derogable choice of law provisions that are applicable to payment transactions – 'transfers of funds between or from bank accounts' – involved in deals that utilize such instruments.[113] Those provisions apply to payment orders sent by customers from within/outside Cambodia and received by banks located within/outside Cambodia.[114] First, a payment order received by a branch or separate office of a bank located in Cambodia is governed by the law of Cambodia, unless otherwise agreed by the sender and the receiving bank.[115] Second, a payment order received by a branch or separate office of a bank located outside Cambodia is governed by the law of the place of the branch or separate office, unless otherwise the sender and the receiving bank have agreed.[116] Third, rights and obligations between a bank and its customer pertaining to his/her bank account and any incoming/outgoing payment order are governed by the law of the place where the account is maintained, subject to any contrary agreement between the bank and the customer.[117] Further, the timing of payment in a payment transaction is determined by the law of the place where the destination bank of the payment is located.[118] The courts in Cambodia apply these rules to determine choice of law issues pertaining to payment transactions in any currency.[119]

Letters of credit transactions consist of multiple and divergent legal relationships. The court is required to apply different choice of law rules to determine the proper law of each contractual relationship, depending on the nature of the relationship.[120] However, such conflict of laws issues with letters of credit rarely take place in practice because merchants engaged in international trades normally incorporate into their documentary credits the Uniform Customs and Practice for Documentary Credits (UCP),[121] which comprehensively

[111] Yokoyama (n 30) 71; Nishioka and Nishitani (n 19) 118.
[112] LNIPT, Art 1.
[113] ibid, Art 197(3)–(5).
[114] ibid, Art 197(1).
[115] ibid, Art 197(2).
[116] ibid, Art 197(3).
[117] ibid, Art 197(4).
[118] ibid, Art 197(5).
[119] No noticeable provisions in the LNIPT limit the scope of application of the choice of law rules on the payment transactions for negotiable instruments. See also ibid, Art 195 (providing that Arts 195–29 of the LNIPT governs payment transactions in any currency).
[120] See generally Yokoyama (n 30) 72–73; Nishioka and Nishitani (n 19) 119–20.
[121] RK Chhina, 'The Uniform Customs and Practice for Documentary Credit (the UCP): Are They Merely a Set of Contractual Terms?' (2015) 30 *Banking & Finance Law Review* 245, 246 (suggesting that the UCP is accepted and recognised nearly universally). See also RP Buckley, 'The 1993 Revision of the Uniform Customs and Practice for Document Credits' (1995) 28 *George Washington Journal of International Law and Economics* 265 (referring to a comment claiming that virtually 95% of credits worldwide are issued under the UCP).

defines the substantive rights and duties of the parties.[122] Even without agreement by the parties, the UCP is applicable to the letters of credit as a trade custom or usage.[123] Substantive rules on letters of credit are thus virtually unified across jurisdictions, which should significantly reduce the occurrence of conflict of laws issues in practice.

H. Agency Agreements

The term 'agency' typically describes a situation in which one party, the agent, acts on behalf of the other party, the principal, to create or modify rights and obligations against a third party. Agency is characterised by a triangular situation consisting of '(i) the internal relationship between principal and agent, (ii) the external relationship between principal and third party and (iii) the relationship between agent and third party'.[124] The courts in Cambodia need to determine the proper law of each legal relationship in view of its nature, because Cambodian and Japanese PIL rules have no special conflict of laws norms for agency, and because the drafters of the AGRAL agreed that the governing law of each leg of the triangle would be determined by way of interpretation.[125]

Japanese commentators put forward the following arrangements on the proper law of each legal relationship in the triangle. First, the governing law of the internal relationship between principal and agent is determined by the choice of law rules designed for this relationship.[126] For example, if the internal relationship is the product of a contract between the two persons, the choice of law rules for contracts determine the proper law of the relationship.[127] The law governing the underlying relationship between the two persons is basically the proper law of their internal relationship.[128] Second, the proper law of the external relationship between principal and third party can be the law governing the underlying relationship between principal and agent, the law applicable to the legal relationship between agent and third party, or the law of the place where agent and third party have entered into a transaction.[129] Japanese commentators are still divided on which option is the most appropriate as the law applicable to the external relationship.[130] However, the third option – the law of the place where agent and third party have entered into the transaction – has the merit of protecting transactions, and the principal would be in the position to know

[122] D Meynell, 'Documentary Credits: Rules, Guidelines & Terminology', *ICC Academy*, 17 December 2019, available at https://icc.academy/documentary-credits-rules-guidelines-terminology/ (accessed 9 February 2025).

[123] See generally Chhina (n 121).

[124] J Kleinschmidt, 'Agency and Authority of Agents' in Jürgen Basedow and others (eds), *Encyclopedia of Private International Law* (Cheltenham, Edward Elgar Publishing, 2017) 29.

[125] See generally Koide (n 30) 396-405; Nishioka and Nishitani (n 19) 122. Moreover, neither Cambodia nor Japan has signed or ratified the Convention of 14 March 1978 on the Law Applicable to Agency: HCCH, 'Status Table: Convention of 14 March 1978 on the Law Applicable to Agency' (2022), available at www.hcch.net/en/instruments/conventions/status-table/?cid=89 (accessed 10 December 2024).

[126] Nishioka and Nishitani (n 19) 122.

[127] Yokoyama (n 30) 72; Koide (n 30) 402.

[128] Nishioka and Nishitani (n 19) 122; Koide (n 30) 401–02. For example, if the underlying relationship is the parent-child relationship, the choice of law rules for guardianship or custody will determine the proper law of the internal relationship.

[129] Nishioka and Nishitani (n 19) 122–23.

[130] ibid; Sawaki and Dogauchi (n 61) 214.

that law.[131] Third, the relationship between agent and third party is governed by the proper law of the underlying relationship between the two persons.[132] For instance, if an agent is authorised by his/her principal to purchase a movable property from a third party, the proper law of the purchase agreement governs the relationship between the agent and third party. Cambodian jurists will likely find those arrangements helpful in dealing with choice of law issues related to agency agreements.

V. Trusts and Charitable Foundations

A trust is a situation in which property is legally maintained and administered by a trustee forming a separate fund for the benefit of a beneficiary who has an interest in the property.[133] The trust can be created by the original owner of the property to be held in trust – the settlor of the trust – through his/her unilateral declaration, a trust agreement or operation of law.[134] A charitable foundation is a trust established by a settlor for charitable purposes. Although it originated in English law, the trust has been localised into many civil law jurisdictions and is now being used in several countries in Asia, including but not limited to Japan and Cambodia.[135]

Because Cambodia is not a party to the Convention of 1 July 1985 on the Law Applicable to Trusts and on Their Recognition (the 1985 Hague Trusts Convention),[136] a trust is governed by Cambodia's municipal conflict of laws rules. Although Cambodia does not appear to have special choice of law rules for trusts, trusts established in the country are highly likely to be subject to the Law on Trusts promulgated in 2019.[137] The reason for this is that the Trust Law provides in Article 1 that its goal is to manage trust funds established or created in the Kingdom of Cambodia. The Law recognises the following types of trusts: (1) commercial trusts created to make a profit for the trust contributor; (2) public trusts created for the benefit of the Cambodian people; (3) social trusts created through a donation or a will for the cultural, educational, humanitarian, religious or scientific benefit of the general public; and (4) individual (or private) trusts created for the benefit of the beneficiary by a natural person who is either alive or dead.[138] Thus, the Trust Law covers virtually any trust created in Cambodia.

On the other hand, Cambodian law does not have provisions governing choice of law issues on trusts created outside the country. One option for Cambodian jurists to deal

[131] Sakurada (n 61) 192.

[132] Koide (n 30) 402; Nishioka and Nishitani, (n 19) 122.

[133] A Dutta, 'Trust' in J Basedow and others (eds), *Encyclopedia of Private International Law* (Cheltenham, Edward Elgar Publishing, 2017) 1752.

[134] Ibid.

[135] Nishioka and Nishitani (n 19) 133; H Pisei, 'New Trust Law Stabilises Real Estate Sector', *The Phnom Penh Post*, 16 November 2023, available at www.phnompenhpost.com/business/new-trust-law-stabilises-real-estate-sector#:~:text=%E2%80%9CUnder%20the%202019%20trust%20law,in%20property%2C%E2%80%9D%20he%20explained (accessed 9 February 2025).

[136] HCCH, 'Status Table: Convention of 1 July 1985 on the Law Applicable to Trusts and on their Recognition' (2024), available at www.hcch.net/en/instruments/conventions/status-table/?cid=59 (accessed 10 December 2024).

[137] An unofficial translation of the Trust Law prepared by the Trust Regulator of Cambodia is available at: www.trustregulator.gov.kh/storage/lawregulations/January2024/Ko8e0it5UbPMSXND7No2.pdf (accessed 10 December 2024).

[138] Trust Law, Arts 9–14.

with the legal vacuum is to refer to Articles 7-10 of the AGRAL that applies to juristic acts, including not only contracts but also unilateral acts, such as donations and the creation of trusts.[139] This option requires jurists to be wary of the characterisation of a trust and the scope of the law applicable to the trust.[140] On the former, whether a trust is classified as a contractual act or a unilateral act may affect who has the authority to choose the law governing the trust because the parties are free to choose the law governing a juristic act under Articles 7 and 9 of the AGRAL. A settlor alone may choose the applicable law of a trust as a unilateral act, whereas s/he is likely to be required to cooperate with the trustee to choose the law governing a trust classified as a contractual act. On the former, trusts may involve other legal matters, such as real property, succession and consumer contracts. Cambodian jurists will need to elaborate on the boundaries between the laws governing these matters and trusts in due course.

VI. Conclusions

This chapter has examined the principles of Cambodian PIL on the choice of law for contractual obligations and trusts. Cambodian statutes often fall short of provisions governing choice of law issues arising from international contracts, and virtually no judicial precedents on such issues are available to the public. Some commentaries and academic materials on Cambodian law offer guidance on the choice of law for contractual obligations, but their coverage needs to be more comprehensive. Due to this lack of legal sources directly discussing Cambodian conflict of laws rules on contractual obligations, Japanese PIL doctrines are instrumental in shaping the principles of Cambodian law on the subject. Some international legal instruments are crucial, provided that the Kingdom has ratified them, or they are applicable to a dispute via the application of foreign law.[141] As in the case of the Rome I Regulation, the courts in Cambodia are encouraged to take into account some transnational PIL instruments because of Cambodian law's connection with the Japanese legal system.[142] Thus, Cambodian rules on choice of law for contractual obligations are complex mixtures of legal principles derived from Japanese PIL and various international legal instruments. On the other hand, choice of law issues on trusts are likely to be addressed by the combination of the municipal law of Cambodia and the AGRAL of Japan, subject to the discretion of Cambodian courts.

[139] Nishioka and Nishitani (n 19) 134–35; Kono (n 19) 2223.
[140] Nishioka and Nishitani (n 19) 134–35; Yokoyama (n 30) 86.
[141] See Sections IV.D.ii and IV.F above.
[142] See Section III.B above.

6

Choice of Law for Non-Contractual Obligations

I. Introduction

Non-contractual obligations include tortious claims, such as negligence, and claims in respect of unjust enrichment. Choice of law rules for non-contractual obligations (in civil and commercial matters) therefore decide which law the court shall apply to obligation arising from a cross-border tort or unjust enrichment having international elements.[1] Such rules are important for Cambodia: various transnational tort cases in the Kingdom have been featured in both local and international newspapers. For instance, several newspapers reported in August 2022 that hundreds or thousands of young Taiwanese people had been trafficked into Cambodia and forced to work for criminal syndicates in charge of telecom fraud rings.[2] Those victims had been lured to Cambodia by fraudulent job advertisements that promised the provision of high salary, lodging, accommodation and meals, which was never implemented. Those criminal syndicates behind the human trafficking are reportedly connected with foreign-owned casinos whom human rights activists have blamed for suspected corruption, land rights violations and social and environmental damages.[3] Moreover, the number of international product liability claims is projected to rise in the country because of the increase of cross-border e-commerce activities involving Cambodian individuals and the Kingdom's ambition to become a regional manufacturing hub.[4] Thus, the judiciary of Cambodia is required to deal with diverse international tort claims.

[1] A Dickinson, 'Rome II Regulation (Non-contractual Obligations)' in J Basedow and others (eds), *Encyclopedia of Private International Law* (Cheltenham, Edward Elgar Publishing, 2017) 1566; M Wilderspin, 'Contractual Obligations' in Jürgen Basedow and others (eds), *Encyclopedia of Private International Law* (Cheltenham, Edward Elgar Publishing, 2017).

[2] H Davidson and CH Lin, 'Hundreds of Taiwanese Trafficked to Cambodia and Held Captive by Telecom Scam Gangs', *The Guardian*, 23 August 2022, available at www.theguardian.com/world/2022/aug/23/hundreds-of-taiwanese-trafficked-to-cambodia-and-held-captive-by-telecom-scam-gangs (noting that other victims were likely to come from China, Hong Kong, Macau and Vietnam (accessed 10 December 2024)). L Hunt, 'Taiwan Frets for 'Thousands' Trafficked Into Cambodia', *The Diplomat*, 16 August 2022, available at https://thediplomat.com/2022/08/taiwan-frets-for-thousands-trafficked-into-cambodia/ (accessed 10 December 2024); B Hioe, 'Taiwan Grapples with Human Trafficking Spike', *The Diplomat*, 1 September 2022, available at https://thediplomat.com/2022/09/taiwan-grapples-with-human-trafficking-spike/ (accessed 10 December 2024).

[3] D Hutt, 'Should Cambodia Ban Casinos?', *The Diplomat*, 30 August 2022, available at https://thediplomat.com/2022/08/should-cambodia-ban-casinos/ (accessed 10 December 2024).

[4] H Phanet, 'Cambodian E-commerce Surges Nearly a Fifth in 2021', *The Phnom Penh Post*, 3 July 2022, available at www.phnompenhpost.com/business/cambodian-e-commerce-surges-nearly-fifth-2021; S Amarthalingam, 'Cambodia Eyes Key Role in Electronics, Auto Hubs in SEA', *The Phnom Penh Post*, 5 May 2022, available at www.phnompenhpost.com/special-reports/cambodia-eyes-key-role-electronics-auto-hubs-sea (accessed 10 December 2024).

Nevertheless, the Kingdom has yet to commit to developing choice of law rules for non-contractual obligations. For example, the country does not have any statutory law – like Japan's Act on the General Rules of Application of Laws (AGRAL) – that compiles choice of law rules for (non-)contractual obligations and other matters.[5] Moreover, the Kingdom has not adopted international choice of law frameworks for non-contractual obligations, although this is probably because those international frameworks lack global recognition. It has not signed the Convention of 2 October 1973 on the Law Applicable to Products Liability (the 1973 Hague Product Liability Convention) because it came into force in 11 European countries only.[6] Likewise, it has not adopted the Convention of 4 May 1971 on the Law Applicable to Traffic Accidents (the 1971 Hague Traffic Accidents Convention) due to the Euro-centric nature of the legal instrument.[7] Further, no literature suggests Cambodian jurists have interests in Regulation (EC) No 864/2007 of the European Parliament and of the Council of 11 July 2007 on the Law Applicable to Non-contractual Obligations (the Rome II Regulation) as this is a regional choice of law framework for Europe[8] and is not relevant to the legal systems in Southeast Asia. Nor are judgments by the courts helpful for determining Cambodian choice of law rules for non-contractual obligations because the Kingdom's judiciary is not bound by the doctrine of precedent,[9] and because it has published only a limited number of past judgments for reference purposes.[10] Cambodian choice of law rules for non-contractual obligations are therefore at an early stage of development.

Cambodian judges may fill this legal vacuum by referring to the private international law (PIL) of Japan because the development of Cambodian private law drew heavily on Japanese legal principles as shown in the Civil Code and Civil Procedure Code of Cambodia.[11] Accordingly, this chapter discusses whether and how Cambodian PIL may import Japanese choice of law rules for non-contractual obligations in the AGRAL and other legal instruments to deal with cross-border torts (Section II) and international unjust enrichment claims (Section III), taking into account relevant Cambodian statutory norms and international conventions (if any).

[5] See Chapter 5 in this volume; Industrial Development and Public Policy Department at JICA, *Legal Technical Assistance for Cambodia: The History and Methodology of the Assistance of JICA in Drafting the Civil Code and the Civil Procedure Code* [in Japanese] (2012) 9.

[6] HCCH, 'Status Table: Convention of 2 October 1973 on the Law Applicable to Products Liability' (2012), available at www.hcch.net/en/instruments/conventions/status-table/?cid=84 (accessed 10 December 2024).

[7] HCCH, 'Status Table: Convention of 4 May 1971 on the Law Applicable to Traffic Accidents' (2014), available at www.hcch.net/en/instruments/conventions/status-table/?cid=81 (accessed 10 December 2024) (among 21 contracting parties to the Convention, only Morocco is a non-European member).

[8] Dickinson (n 1) 1566; C van Dam, 'Transnational Tort Law' in P Zumbansen (ed), *The Oxford Handbook of Transnational Law* (Oxford, Oxford University Press, 2021). On the relationship between the 1971 Hague Traffic Accidents Convention and the Rome II Regulation and the Euro-centric nature of these instruments, see TK Graziano, 'Traffic Accidents' in Jürgen Basedow and others (eds), *Encyclopedia of Private International Law* (Cheltenham, Edward Elgar Publishing, 2017).

[9] N Teramura, 'Japan as a Source of Legal Ideas: A View from the Mekong Subregion of ASEAN' (2021) 13 *New Voices in Japanese Studies* 19, 34.

[10] N Chheng, 'Courts' Decisions Now Published as Reference Source', *The Phnom Penh Post*, 4 January 2021, available at www.phnompenhpost.com/national/courts-decisions-now-published-reference-source (accessed 10 December 2024).

[11] Teramura (n 9); J Menzel, 'Cambodian Law: Some Comparative and International Perspectives' in H Peng, K Phallack and J Menzel (eds), *Introduction to Cambodian Law* (Phnom Penh, Konrad-Adenauer-Stiftung Cambodia, 2012) 490.

II. Torts

Japanese choice of law rules for torts can be found in Articles 17–22 of the AGRAL. Articles 17 and 20–22 set out general rules on choice of law in cross-border torts, whereas Articles 18 and 19 set out special rules for specific torts, such as product liability and defamation. The following subsections consider how these rules may inspire Cambodian choice of law rules for cross-border torts.

A. Governing Law in Tort Generally

Articles 17 and 20–22 of the AGRAL provide general rules governing different aspects of choice of law in tort. Article 17 is the rule to decide the law applicable to the formation and effect of claims arising from a tort. Article 20 offers an exception of choice of law in tort cases where a manifestly more closely connected place exists for the tort. Article 21 stipulates when parties are allowed to change the governing law of a tort claim. Finally, Article 22 sets out the limitations of public policy on choice of law in tort.

i. General Principles

Adopting the *lex loci delicti* rule that requires the application of the law of the place where the tort was committed,[12] Article 17 of the AGRAL provides that '[t]he formation and effect of claims arising from a tort shall be governed by the law of the place where the results of the [wrongful] act are produced'.[13] The results of the wrongful act connote the direct damages caused by the tortious act, such as physical injury, so that consequential losses, such as costs for medical treatment, are excluded from those results.[14] The law applicable to a personal injury claim is thus the law of the place where the individual sustained injury or death, which means the law of the place where the victim was at the time of injury or death.[15] Likewise, the governing law of a damaged property claim is the law of the place where the destruction or loss to tangible property occurred, which is the law of the place where the property was located at the time of destruction or loss.[16] Hence, the first step for the court to determine the governing law of a tort claim is to identify the place where the direct damage of the tort occurred.

The drafters of the AGRAL provided an exception to the *lex loci delicti* rule with Article 17, to balance legal certainty and case-by-case justice.[17] Accordingly, the second

[12] K Nishioka and Y Nishitani, *Japanese Private International Law* (Oxford, Hart Publishing 2021) 123–24; T Kono, 'Japan' in J Basedow and others (eds), *Encyclopedia of Private International Law* (Cheltenham, Edward Elgar Publishing, 2017) 2224.

[13] The English translation of the AGRAL, prepared by Private International Law Association of Japan, available at: www.pilaj.jp/text/tsusokuho_e.html (accessed 10 December 2024). Unless otherwise specified, this author adopts in this chapter the English translations of AGRAL provisions available on the website.

[14] Kono (n 12) 2224.

[15] K Koide, *Commentary on the Act on General Rules for Application of Laws [in Japanese]* (Tokyo, Shojihomu Publishing 2014) 193.

[16] ibid 193.

[17] Kono (n 12) 2224.

sentence of Article 17 provides that 'if it was not foreseeable under normal circumstances that the results would be produced at that place, the law of the place where the [wrongful] act occurred shall apply'. In determining foreseeability, the court does not take into account the subjective perspective of the wrongdoer. It instead relies on the objective standards, such as the nature of the wrongdoer and tortious act, the situation of damage and other circumstances surrounding the tort claim.[18] For example, if the receiver of gunpowder is injured by an explosion caused by improper packaging, the court would likely decide that the sender of the gunpowder could foresee the sustenance of injury at the place of delivery.[19] In contrast, if someone stole mispackaged gunpowder in transit and delivered it to a third party, and if the third party was injured by the explosion, the court might decide that the original sender could not anticipate injury at the place where the third party received the gunpower (and, thus, the foreseeability requirement in Article 17 of the AGRAL would not be met).[20]

As these examples demonstrate, the decisive factor of the predictability of a result is whether the wrongdoer can foresee the geographical location of the harm or direct damage. It is not whether s/he can foresee the occurrence of damage. For instance, if the receiver of a plant was infected by an unknown virus in the plant, the sender would be able to claim the foreseeability of damage under Article 17 because s/he could still anticipate that damage could occur at the place of delivery.[21] The court decides the foreseeability of damage when it actually applies the governing (i.e., substantive) law of the tort claim.[22]

Cambodian jurists may find the balanced approach under Article 17 of the AGRAL useful in developing their general choice of law rules for tort claims. According to Graziano, the *lex loci delicti* rule has been in force in many jurisdictions around the world thanks to the following rationale:

> First, in situations where the parties had no contact with each other before the damaging event occurred, which is the case e.g., in many road traffic accidents or sports accidents, the place of the accident is the only link between them. Second, the law of the place of the tort or accident is simple …, efficient and … [certain]. Parties know even before a tort is committed which law will apply to potential liability, and they might adapt their insurance cover accordingly. Third, application of the *lex loci delicti* is a neutral solution favouring neither party. Fourth, it is in conformity with the interests of the state in which the damage occurred to have certain victims of accidents compensated, particularly those [who reside] there. Lastly, this solution generally corresponds to the parties' expectations and interests, and is usually fair and recognized as such by the parties.[23]

However, these justifications are probably only sometimes applicable to cross-border tort claims in Cambodia (or elsewhere). In particular, the second point – the law of the place of the tort is simple/efficient/certain – would not be the case if the tort was committed against a bond or intangible asset because the locations of such intangible rights are not always

[18] Koide (n 15) 194.
[19] ibid 194.
[20] ibid 194.
[21] ibid 194–95; Nishioka and Nishitani (n 12) 124.
[22] Koide (n 15) 195.
[23] Graziano, 'Torts' 1712.

clear to the parties.[24] Then, the court would be able to determine the place of the tort (i.e., damage) based on the type and nature of the damaged intangible property, invoking the predictability requirement under Article 17. Moreover, the third justification – application of the *lex loci delicti* is a neutral solution favouring neither party – is not always applicable. For instance, if the *lex loci delicti* was the law of the habitual residence of the victim, and if the wrongdoer unexpectedly visited the place for some reason and caused damage, the victim would have a better knowledge and understanding of the local law and custom than the wrongdoer. Thus, the courts in Cambodia should decide the proper laws of tort claims flexibly, adopting the principle of foreseeability under Article 17 of the AGRAL.

ii. Escape Clause

To add further flexibility to the *lex loci delicti* rule (and the special rules for product liability and defamation under Articles 18 and 19 of the AGRAL),[25] the drafters of the AGRAL included in Article 20 an escape clause enabling the court to deviate from Articles 17–19 to apply another law, provided that such law has a closer connection with the tortious conduct than the *lex loci delicti* and other laws designated by Articles 18 and 19.[26] In determining the law having a closer connection, the court is required to take into account circumstances surrounding the tort, such as (1) whether the parties had their habitual residence in the same jurisdiction when the tort occurred, and (2) whether 'the tort constitutes a breach of obligations under a contract between the parties'.[27] On (1), the drafters of the AGRAL regarded the parties' common habitual residence as the social environment to which the parties belonged, suggesting that the law of such a place reflects the living standard of the parties and therefore offers a more proper standard for damage calculation than the *lex loci delicti* or other laws.[28] On (2), the drafters claimed to align the proper law of the tort claim with the governing law of the underlying contract, pointing out the close connection between the tort and the contract.[29] According to the drafters, it is reasonable for parties to apply the governing law of the contract to the tort claim because the wrongful act constitutes a part of the contractual dispute, and because adopting different laws to the tort claim and contractual dispute might lead to complex conflict of laws problems such as contradictions and concurrent liabilities.[30] In any event, both (1) and (2) are non-exclusive, so that the court may decide which law has a closer connection than other laws through considering other circumstances surrounding the case.

Whether Cambodian jurists find the escape clause in Article 20 of AGRAL useful depends on the purpose of Cambodian PIL. According to Rühl, there are two schools of thought that discuss the objective of choice of law.[31] The classical school, which prevails in most national conflict of laws regimes, suggests that 'choice of law serves to solve conflicts

[24] Koide (n 15) 193.
[25] On these special rules, see Sections 2.2.1 and 2.2.1 below.
[26] J Yokoyama, *Private International Law in Japan* (Alphen aan den Rijn, Wolters Kluwer 2019) 76–77.
[27] AGRAL, Art 20.
[28] Koide (n 15) 234; Nishioka and Nishitani (n 12) 125.
[29] Koide (n 15) 235–36; Yokoyama, (n 26) 77–78.
[30] Koide (n 15) 236; Yokoyama (n 26) 76; Nishioka and Nishitani (n 12) 125.
[31] G Rühl, 'Private International Law, Foundations' in J Basedow and others (eds), *Encyclopedia of Private International Law* (Cheltenham, Edward Elgar Publishing, 2017) 1388.

between private individuals and aims at conflicts justice, notably international uniformity of decisions and legal certainty'.[32] To achieve these aims, this school seeks to identify the law of the closest connection that must always be the same irrespective of the place of a lawsuit, presupposing that every legal relationship has a 'rightful place' or 'seat' which is to be determined by choice of law rules.[33] As a matter of principle, this school considers that the content and function of relevant private laws are immaterial in determining the applicable law, suggesting that territorial aspects as well as legal certainty and predictability are material in assigning a legal relationship to the most appropriate legal order.[34] If Cambodian jurists followed the classical school, the escape clause would be in their interest because its aim was to restore flexibility in applying the law most closely connected to the legal relation in question.[35]

The political school, which is dominant in the United States (US), perceives choice of law as a means to solve conflicts between states and achieve material justice.[36] Rühl suggests that this presupposition differentiates the political school from the classical school as follows:

> Unlike the classical school of thought, the political school does not see private law as a neutral and apolitical legal zone, free of state interests and social functions. Under the influence of American legal realism, it rather emphasizes its socially formative and purposive character, which assists states in realizing their interests and intentions. For choice of law, this understanding of private law means that conflicts between various legal orders are conceived of as conflicts between various states and their interests. The central problem that choice of law must solve is therefore not the finding of the legal order in which the legal relationship has its 'seat'. Rather, the concern is the discovery of the legal order with the largest interest in the application of its substantive norms.[37]

Accordingly, the determination of the applicable law by the political school depends on the intention of the relevant substantive norms, which requires the court to weigh and compare relevant substantive legal norms or governmental interests in each case.[38] Thus, the political school does not aim at searching for the law having the closest connection with a legal relation in dispute.

No literature clarifies the objective of Cambodian PIL. However, Cambodian jurists are unlikely to follow the political school because Cambodian law is not under the influence of US private (international) law. The Cambodian legal system belongs to the civil law tradition, and its modern private law frameworks have been developed based on legal principles of Japan and other civil law countries.[39] The drafters of Cambodia's foundational

[32] ibid.

[33] ibid. See also J Basedow, 'Choice of Law' in Jürgen Basedow and others (eds), *Encyclopedia of Private International Law* (Cheltenham, Edward Elgar Publishing, 2017) 312–13; FC von Savigny, *A Treatise on the Conflict of Laws and the Limits of their Operation in Respect of Place and Time* (William Guthrie tr, Edinburgh, T & T Clark Law Publishers, 1869) 27.

[34] Rühl (n 31) 1388.

[35] Koide (n 15) 233; J Basedow, 'Escape Clauses' in J Basedow and others (eds), *Encyclopedia of Private International Law* (Cheltenham, Edward Elgar Publishing, 2017).

[36] Rühl (n 31) 1388.

[37] ibid 1389.

[38] ibid. See also L Brilmayer, 'Rights, Fairness, and Choice of Law' (1989) 98 *The Yale Law Journal* 1277, 1284.

[39] C Morris, 'Justice Inverted' in K Brickell and S Springer (eds), *The Handbook of Contemporary Cambodia* (Abingdon, Routledge, 2016) 31–33; Teramura (n 9); Y Kaneko, 'Japan's Civil Code Drafting Support for Socialist

law consulted US legal documents in developing the Civil Code (CC).[40] But American legal realism and US common law have little relevance to Cambodian private (international) law.[41] Thus, Cambodian jurists are more likely to import the escape clause from Article 20 of the AGRAL, to enable them to apply flexibly the closest connection test based on the circumstances surrounding the case.

iii. Party Autonomy

Article 21 of the AGRAL is another exception to the *lex loci delicti* rule and the special choice of law rules for product liability and defamation.[42] The provision allows parties to choose (or to change) the governing law of a tort claim, provided that the tortious action has been committed already.[43] It does not explicitly permit the parties to agree on the proper law before the occurrence of the tortious act because the drafters of the AGRAL argued that such an arrangement would lead a dominant party to impose his/her favourable law to a weaker party,[44] although such an imbalance might continue to exist after the occurrence of the wrongful act. In any event, Article 21 does not explicitly prohibit parties from pre-selecting the governing law of a tort claim,[45] and the parties may invoke the designation of applicable law through requesting the court to apply Article 20 of the AGRAL.[46] This provision requires the court to discern the *ex-ante* intention of the parties to determine the applicability of the escape clause.

The second sentence of Article 21 limits parties' *ex-post* designation of the law applicable to a tort claim, prohibiting them from asserting the choice against a third party whose rights may be violated by the selection. Such a third party is a person having a legal interest in damages and compensation arising from the tort action.[47] An example of the third party is an insurer who has entered into an insurance contract with a tortfeasor or a victim. The insurer may claim the violation of his/her rights when the law chosen by the parties (the tortfeasor and the victim) after the occurrence of the incident deters him/her from claiming rights stipulated in the insurance contract.[48] The drafters of the AGRAL excluded a third party having no such legitimate interests from the exception, to honour the autonomy of the parties as much as possible.[49]

There is unlikely to be a strong justification for Cambodian jurists to oppose the introduction of party autonomy to Cambodian choice of law rules for tort cases. In Japan, some

Reform Countries: Diversity of Normative Choice' in Y Kaneko (ed), *Civil Law Reforms in Post-Colonial Asia: Beyond Western Capitalism* (Cham, Springer, 2019).

[40] For instance, Art 742 of the CC of Cambodia was inspired by Arts 8A and 281 of the American Restatement of Torts, Second: JICA, *Commentary on the Civil Code of the Kingdom of Cambodia [in Japanese]* (JICA, 2011) 232.

[41] See Chapter 2 in this volume.

[42] AGRAL, Arts 18 and 19.

[43] Note that 'parties' under Art 21 include only tortfeasors (wrongdoers) and victims. They exclude those who have obtained by succession or insurance victims' rights for claiming compensation: Koide (n 15) 247.

[44] ibid; Nishioka and Nishitani (n 12) 125–26.

[45] K Takeshita, 'Change of Governing Law by the Parties [in Japanese]' in Y Sakurada and M Dogauchi (eds), *Private International Law Annotated*, Vol 1 (Tokyo, Yuhikaku Publishing, 2011) 518.

[46] Koide (n 15) 248; Yokoyama (n 26) 72; Nishioka and Nishitani (n 12) 126.

[47] Koide (n 15) 249.

[48] ibid; Nishioka and Nishitani (n 12) 126.

[49] Koide (n 15) 249–50.

commentators opposed recognising the principle of party autonomy in choosing the law governing a tort claim, insisting that the purpose of tort law was to maintain the social order and public policy of the jurisdiction where the alleged tort was committed.[50] However, Japanese jurists no longer support this view as they regard tort law as an instrument for balancing interests between private parties.[51] Cambodian jurists are likely to follow the suit because the CC of Cambodia provides rules on torts to adjust rights and obligations between wrongdoers and victims.[52]

iv. Double Actionability (Limitation on Torts by Public Policy)

The doctrine of double actionability states that an act which was committed in a foreign land would constitute a tort only if the act was actionable as a tort under both the *lex fori* and the *lex loci delicti*.[53] Article 22 of the AGRAL adopts this doctrine, providing that '(1) [i]f the rights and obligations relating to a tort shall be governed by a foreign law, claims for damages or any other remedies under that law may not be claimed if the actions causing the tort are not unlawful under Japanese law'; and '(2) [i]f the rights and obligations relating to a tort shall be governed by a foreign law, even if the actions causing the tort are unlawful both under that foreign law and Japanese law, the victim may not claim any greater recovery of damages or any other remedies than those available under Japanese law'. Hence, Article 22 mandates courts to prioritise Japanese law (i.e., *lex fori*) over the applicable foreign law – even where the law had the closest connection or was chosen by the parties[54] – in determining the actionability of an unlawful act and calculating damages/remedies for the unlawful act.

However, it is unlikely that Cambodian jurists will import the double actionability rule into Cambodian PIL. First, the rationale behind Article 22 is not applicable to Cambodian PIL. When the drafters of the AGRAL discussed whether to incorporate the double actionability rule into the AGRAL, many Japanese commentators opposed the incorporation.[55] They argued that (1) the rule unreasonably favoured domestic law to foreign law, (2) the cumulative application of Japanese law and foreign law would raise the threshold of tort claims and would undermine the rights of victims and (3) the rule was outdated and had lost support among foreign legislation.[56] Despite these criticisms, the drafters decided to include the double actionability rule in the AGRAL due to requests from the private sector

[50] ibid 246.

[51] ibid; Takeshita (n 45) 510–14.

[52] CC, Arts 742ff; JICA (n 40) 231–32.

[53] S Jolly and S Khanderia, *Indian Private International Law* (Oxford, Hart Publishing, 2021) 229; Basedow, (n 33) 320.

[54] Yokoyama (n 26) 77.

[55] Koide (n 15) 258; Nishioka and Nishitani (n 12) 126; T Kanzaki, 'Limitation on Torts by Public Policy [in Japanese]' in Y Sakurada and M Dogauchi (eds), *Private International Law Annotated, Vol 1* (Tokyo, Yuhikaku Publishing, 2011) 526.

[56] However, not a few jurisdictions still maintain the doctrine of double actionability as a rule for specific torts, such as defamation and product liability: KF Tsang, 'Double Actionability: An Outdated Rule in Modern Times?' (2017) 86 *UMKC Law Review* 73; Koide (n 15) 268; TM Ren, 'Revisiting the Double Actionability Rule in Singapore: Time for a Change' (2021) 2021 *Singapore Journal of Legal Studies* 155, 162 (claiming that the double actionability rule applies to all torts in Singapore); EKH Ng, 'Revisiting International Tort Actions in Hong Kong' (2019) 13 *Hong Kong Journal of Legal Studies* 19 (suggesting that Hong Kong courts should stop using the double actionability rule to determine the applicable laws of international tort claims).

that emphasised Japanese practitioners' long-term familiarity with the rule since the promulgation of the old AGRAL in 1898.[57] However, no evidence suggests that Cambodian PIL has been influenced by the old AGRAL, or that Cambodian lawyers have become used to the double actionability rule in the same way as Japanese practitioners.

Second, the drafters of the AGRAL left the unlawfulness requirement under Article 22 open for interpretation, which would complicate Cambodian choice of law in torts if the double actionability rule was imported into the Kingdom. This is because the meaning of 'unlawfulness' is still being discussed among Japanese commentators. Some suggest that the term connotes the elements of torts under Japanese law, whereas others claim that the word implies the subjective elements of torts only, such as wilful misconduct and negligence.[58] To mandate Cambodian jurists to deal with this task of legal interpretation on a case-by-case basis would exacerbate the unpredictability of Cambodian PIL.

Third, Article 22 is a hidden contradiction in the system of Japanese PIL. Article 20 of the AGRAL allows courts to treat the governing law of an underlying contract as the law applicable to a relevant tort claim, whereas Article 21 recognises the principle of party autonomy for choice of law in tort cases. Accordingly, parties under Articles 20 and 21 may designate a foreign law as the law applicable to their tort claim, but the cumulative application of Japanese law under Article 22 violates those parties' express intention.[59] Cambodian jurists should not import this cause of contradictions from the AGRAL, as they are encouraged to adopt the principles of party autonomy under Articles 20 and 21. Therefore, Article 22 of the AGRAL is unlikely to contribute to developing Cambodian choice of law rules.[60] If imported, the provision will do more harm than good for Cambodian PIL.

B. Governing Law in Specific Torts

No accessible material suggests that the Kingdom of Cambodia has choice of law rules for specific tort claims. Thus, it is advisable for Cambodian jurists to examine Japan's AGRAL in deciding the law applicable to a specific tort, although the AGRAL contains only two special rules for specific torts: Article 18 for product liability and Article 19 for defamation.[61] In the subsections that follow, this chapter considers how these provisions are likely to inform the way in which Cambodian courts decide the governing laws of specific torts. The subsections further discuss how the courts should address choice of law for other specific torts, such as private nuisance, wrongful interference with goods and environmental damage and pollution.

[57] Koide (n 15) 259; Nishioka and Nishitani (n 12) 127.

[58] Koide (n 15) 255–56.

[59] Y Okuda, 'Reform of Japan's Private International Law: Act on the General Rules of the Application of Laws' (2006) 8 *Yearbook of Private International Law* 145, 164; Nishioka and Nishitani (n 12) 126–27; P Mankowski, 'The New Japanese Private International Law Act from a European Perspective' (2008) 51 *Japanese Yearbook of International Law* 241, 279.

[60] Mankowski criticises Art 22 of the AGRAL as follows: 'The by far most odious and questionable part of the … PIL of torts definitely is the double actionability rule in torts as to be found in Art. 22 of [the AGRAL]. … Japan still adheres to one of the most incriminating and discriminating rules PIL has ever generated worldwide, and thus qualifies as some kind of outcast … [T]he double actionability rule … makes Japan an unattractive forum for actions in tort': Mankowski (n 59) 278.

[61] Arts 18 and 19 have priority over Art 17 of the AGRAL.

i. Product Liability

Product liability is the area of law that deals with the non-contractual liability of manufacturers, distributors, suppliers, retailers and other persons for damage caused by products they have offered to the public (or consumers).[62] Article 18 of the AGRAL sets out a special choice of law rule for product liability, providing that:

> [T]he formation and effect of claims arising from torts which are detrimental to life, body or property of other persons caused by a defect in a delivered product … against a producer … or any person who identifies himself/herself as a producer by indicating on the product to the effect that he/she is presumed to be a producer … shall be governed by the law of the place where the product is delivered to the victim.

The technical terms in the Article are defined by the Article itself and its commentaries. The term 'product' means any goods that have been produced or processed (by anyone), including but not limited to produced or processed movable property, unprocessed natural products (such as agricultural and fishery products) and immovable property (e.g., buildings and developed residential lands).[63] The word 'producer' connotes 'any person who produces, processes, imports, exports, distributes or sells the product in the course of his/her business',[64] for instance a wholesale distributor, retailer, forwarder or warehouse keeper.[65] 'Defect' refers to any situation in which a product lacks the quality normally required after its delivery.[66] The definitions of 'product', 'producer' and 'defect' under Article 18 of the AGRAL are therefore more comprehensive than those under Japan's substantive legislation, such as the Product Liability Act.

The term 'victim' in Article 18 means the person to whom the defective product has been delivered. The drafters of the AGRAL justified this construction by referring to the fact that Article 18 provides the place of delivery as the principal connecting factor for product liability claims.[67] Accordingly, Article 18 excludes from 'victims', bystanders who sustain personal injury from an alleged product defect despite not having received, used or purchased the product. Product liability claims filed by bystanders are therefore to be dealt with by the court under Article 17 of the AGRAL.[68] However, Koide suggests that Article 18 is applicable by analogy to the family members of the victim, if they were injured by a defective product while living with the victim.[69] Thus, the court may exceptionally regard family bystanders as victims under Article 18.

Furthermore, 'the place where the product is delivered to the victim' is the place where the victim has acquired the right to possess movable or immovable property.[70] For example, if a company in Japan purchased a machine from a factory in Malaysia and then made

[62] TK Graziano, 'Products liability' in J Basedow and others (eds), *Encyclopedia of Private International Law* (Cheltenham, Edward Elgar Publishing, 2017) 1414.

[63] AGRAL, Art 18; Nishioka and Nishitani (n 12) 128; Koide (n 15) 204.

[64] AGRAL, Art 18.

[65] Nishioka and Nishitani (n 12) 128.

[66] Koide (n 15) 204 and 206.

[67] ibid 206.

[68] Kono (n 12) 2225.

[69] Koide (n 15) 206; K Takahashi, 'A Major Reform of Japanese Private International Law' (2006) 2 *Journal of Private International Law* 311, 330. See also Okuda (n 59) 159 (curiously suggesting that 'Article 18 covers all aspects of product liability, even though it refers to a nonexistent law in the case of [a] bystander').

[70] Koide (n 15) 205.

its agent bring the product back from Malaysia to Japan, the place of delivery would be Malaysia.[71] Likewise, if the factory in Malaysia agreed to transfer the company in Japan the right of possession in Malaysia, the place of delivery would be Malaysia.[72] Accordingly, the place of delivery under Article 18 is not the location where the victim brought the product under his/her control, but the place where s/he obtained the legal right to claim the possession of the product.

For the sake of ensuring equilibrium between a producer and a victim, Article 18 provides that 'if the delivery of the product at that place [of the delivery] is not foreseeable under normal circumstances, the law of the place of the principal establishment of the producer etc. (if he/she has no establishment, the law of the place of his/her habitual residence) shall apply'. As in the case of Article 17, the foreseeability requirement under Article 18 requires the court to consider if it is reasonable for the producer to anticipate the delivery of the product at the place of the delivery.[73] Reasonableness needs to be based on objective circumstances, such as the nature and background of the producer and product, the extent of the product's dissemination and the state of the product's market.[74] For instance, suppose a manufacturer in Malaysia who exported a product to Indonesia that complied with safety regulations effective in Indonesia. If someone stole the product along the way, to sell the product in the Japanese market, and if a person in Japan purchased the item and was injured by harmful features of the product prohibited under Japanese law but not under Indonesian law, the court would find that the manufacturer would not be able to foresee the delivery of the product taking place in Japan.[75] The court would then not take into account the manufacturer's subjective circumstances in determining the foreseeability of the delivery in Japan.

Article 18 of the AGRAL is likely have a positive impact on Cambodia's choice of law rules for product liability. First, there is an increasing awareness of the need for consumer protection among Cambodian citizens and businesses,[76] and it would be along the lines of this trend to import Japan's choice of law rule for product liability. Responding to international criticism of Cambodia's lack of comprehensive legislation for product safety and consumer protection,[77] the government of Cambodia enacted in 2019 the Law on Consumer Protection (LCP). Further, the Law on Management of Quality and Safety of Products, Goods and Services (LMQSPGS) has been in force since 2000. However, both legal instruments fall short of provisions guiding the courts in Cambodia in determining

[71] ibid.

[72] ibid.

[73] ibid 206. On criticisms of the foreseeability requirement following the model of Art 18, see Okuda (n 59) 158.

[74] H Sano, 'Special Rule for Product Liability [in Japanese]' in Y Sakurada and M Dogauchi (eds), *Private International Law Annotated*, Vol 1 (Tokyo, Yuhikaku Publishing, 2011) 474.

[75] Koide (n 15) 206.

[76] Khmer Times Writer, 'Ministry of Commerce Urges Implementation of Consumer Protection Laws', *Khmer Times*, 13 July 2022, available at www.khmertimeskh.com/501111823/ministry-of-commerce-urges-implementation-of-consumer-protection-laws/ (accessed 10 December 2024). S Sithika, 'CCF Holds Workshop on Consumer Protection Programmes', *Khmer Times*, 14 July 2022, available at www.khmertimeskh.com/501112262/ccf-holds-workshop-on-consumer-protection-programmes/ (accessed 10 December 2024).

[77] ASEAN Secretariat, *Handbook on ASEAN Consumer Protection Laws and Regulation* (Jakarta, ASEAN Secretariat 2018) 22–24; L Nottage and others, *ASEAN Consumer Law Harmonisation and Cooperation: Achievements and Challenges* (Cambridge, Cambridge University Press, 2019) 122ff.

the governing law of a product liability claim. This gap needs to be addressed, to enhance consumer protection in the sphere of PIL.

Second, Cambodian jurists are likely to find the simplicity of the connecting factor in Article 18 of the AGRAL convenient, compared with that in European choice of law rules for product liability. The drafters of the AGRAL decided to adopt the law of 'the place where the product is delivered to the victim' as the law applicable to product liability claims because they considered that the venue of delivery is the place closest to the victim in the product's stream of distribution.[78] They avoided relying on the ambiguous concept of 'marketplace' that implies either the first place of the stream of commerce or the place of the delivery to the victim,[79] although they understood that the law of a marketplace is neutral to and closely connected with producers and victims.[80] In contrast, the Rome II Regulation provides in Article 5 choice of law rules for product liability which designates (1) the law of the country where the victim had his/her habitual residence, (2) the law of the country where the victim acquired the product or (3) the law of the country where the damage occurred. These laws apply only where they are the law of the product's marketplace, which is difficult to determine. The European approach is thus more complicated than the Japanese approach.[81] Cambodian judges will likely prefer the latter to the former due to their unfamiliarity with PIL and foreign legal systems.[82]

ii. Defamation

The drafters of the AGRAL set out a special choice of law rule for defamation, reflecting difficulties in identifying the place of damage in defamation cases.[83] The causes of such difficulties are complexities in deciding the country/jurisdiction where the victim maintains his/her reputation and the development of info-communication technologies, such as the internet, that transmit defamatory information spontaneously across the globe.[84] Thus, Article 19 of the AGRAL designates the law of the victim's habitual residence (or the principal place of business in case of a corporation or other association) as the governing law of his/her defamation claim.[85] The justification for using the victim's habitual residence (and principal place of business) as the connecting factor is explained by Takahashi as follows:

> [A] single governing law will be specified even if the victim's reputation is harmed in more than one jurisdiction. This special rule avoids the complexity of applying different governing laws to what is from the offender's point of view a single incident of defamation. Its choice of

[78] T Kono, 'Comparative Analysis of Recent Developments in Private International Law in Japan and Europe from a Japanese Perspective' (2008) 51 *Japanese Yearbook of International Law* 217, 232.

[79] ibid; Takahashi (n 69) 330.

[80] Koide (n 15) 203.

[81] Mankowski (n 59) 275.

[82] Menzel (n 11) 491; N Teramura, 'Cambodia' in Kazuaki Nishioka (ed), *Treatment of Foreign Law in Asia* (Oxford, Hart Publishing, 2023).

[83] Takahashi (n 69) 331.

[84] Koide (n 15) 222; Kono (n 78) 234.

[85] 'Defamation' under Art 18 does not incorporate the infringement of other personality rights, such as the right to privacy, the right of publicity and the right to be forgotten. The reason for this exclusion by the drafters of the AGRAL is due to the diversity of definitions of various personality rights among different jurisdictions: Koide (n 15) 224.

> the victim's habitual residence as the connecting factor was considered by the drafters to be defensible since it is conducive to protecting the victims' interest [as the law of the habitual residence has the closest connection with the victim's daily life] while at the same time providing the offenders with a degree of predictability [as they are expected to know the victim's habitual residence], and since it is usually in that place where his reputation is harmed most.[86]

Accordingly, Article 19 aims to strike a balance between victims and tortfeasors in choosing the law applicable to defamation claims, considering the intangible nature of reputation and the transmissibility of defamatory information in the age of information communication technologies. Following Article 19 of the AGRAL, Cambodian PIL should adopt the victim's habitual residence as a connecting factor in cross-border defamation cases because the rationale behind the rule as demonstrated by Takahashi would also be valid in Cambodia.

The appropriateness of the habitual residence rule can be assessed by reference to the legislative history of the Rome II Regulation. The European Commission attempted and then failed to use the victim's habitual residence as a connecting factor for defamation claims despite its fairness, simplicity, convenience and predictability.[87] The cause of the failure was opposition from media associations that perceived that (1) the law of the habitual residence of the harmed person is too favourable to the victim, (2) celebrities' (i.e., victims') habitual residence is difficult to identify, (3) application of the law would endanger freedom of speech by making a media provider liable for behaviour that is legal in the place of publication and (4) defamation involves two fundamental rights – freedom of speech and privacy rights – so that each nation should remain in charge of maintaining the balance between those rights in its own territory.[88] However, these criticisms would not be relevant to Cambodian PIL. On (1), the law of the victim's habitual residence is not necessarily in favour of his/her claims as s/he is not always more knowledgeable of the law than the tortfeasor. On (2), the wrongdoer normally knows or can easily tell the location of the victim's habitual residence.[89] On (3), some take the example of a foreign dictator who adopts a law

[86] Takahashi (n 69) 331. See also Koide (n 15) 223.

[87] FM Meier, 'Unification of Choice-of-law Rules for Defamation' (2016) 12 *Journal of Private International Law* 492, 496, 514–15; P Huber, *Rome II Regulation: Pocket Commentary* (Munich, Sellier European Law Publishers 2011) 456–57; J von Hein, 'Von Hein on Rome II and Defamation', *Conflict of Laws.net*, 19 July 2010, available at https://conflictoflaws.net/2010/von-hein-on-rome-ii-and-defamation/ (noting that the victim's habitual residence as a connecting factor has the virtue of simplicity (accessed 10 December 2024)). On the advantages of adopting the victim's habitual residence as a connecting factor for defamation claims in Europe and beyond, see also PE Nygh, 'The Reasonable Expectations of the Parties as a Guide to the Choice of Law in Contract and in Tort' (1995) 251 *Collected Courses of the Hague Academy of International Law* 269, 374–75.

[88] O Boskovic, 'Boskovic on Rome II and Defamation', *Conflict of Laws net*, 20 July 2010, available at https://conflictoflaws.net/2010/boskovic-on-rome-ii-and-defamation/; M van Eechoud, 'The Position of Broadcasters and Other Media under 'Rome II' Proposed EC Regulation on the Law Applicable to Non-contractual Obligations' (2006) IRIS Plus (Supplement to IRIS – Legal Observations of the European Audiovisual Observatory) 14, available at www.obs.coe.int/; https://papers.ssrn.com/sol3/papers.cfm?abstract_id=973774 (accessed 10 December 2024); A Warshaw, 'Uncertainty from Abroad: Rome II and the Choice of Law for Defamation Claims' (2006) 32 *Brooklyn Journal of International Law* 269, 293.

[89] Boskovic (n 88). In contrast, Dickinson insists that the victim's habitual residence as a connecting factor is an unworkable solution. Having regard to the situation in which a regional newspaper published an article on a locally born celebrity who had relocated his habitual residence to Monaco for tax reasons, he claims that 'the newspaper editor would need to take advice as to Monegasque law on defamation and similar issues': A Dickinson, 'Cross-Border Torts in EC Courts – A Response to the Proposed "Rome II" Regulation' (2002) 13 *European Business Law Review* 369, 377. However, Dickinson's view is too benign to the regional newspaper because the editor should be aware of the potentially widespread consequence of his/her article in the age of information technologies.

that characterises any criticism as *ipso facto* defamatory, so that to require publishers to abide by such foreign law would endanger freedom of speech and expression.[90] However, the public order exception of Article 26 Rome II Regulation would be a sufficient barrier for this 'excessive example' in European countries.[91] Similarly, the extreme situation can be dealt with under Cambodian PIL by applying the public policy exception that follows Article 42 of the AGRAL. Therefore, (1)–(3) are not convincing in the contexts of European, Japanese and Cambodian PIL. Point (4) is the justification used by influential media moguls to prevent European countries from establishing a uniform choice of law rule for defamation.[92] It should not prevent Cambodia from adopting the victim's habitual residence as a connecting factor in defamation cases. Therefore, (1)–(4) do not present grounds that prevent Cambodian jurists from following Article 19 of the AGRAL in Cambodia in dealing with cross-border defamation cases.

iii. Private Nuisance

Private nuisance is '[a]n activity or state of affairs that [unreasonably] interferes with the use or enjoyment of land or rights over land'.[93] The aim of the law of private nuisance is to protect occupiers of land – persons who have the property rights or exclusive occupation of the land – from damage to the land, buildings or plants or from unreasonable interference with their comfort or convenience, such as excessive noise, dust, fumes and smells.[94] Jurists in Cambodia are likely to be familiar with this type of tort as the CC provides rules governing claims arising from private nuisances.[95]

Nonetheless, no evidence suggests that Cambodian PIL has choice of law rules for private nuisance. Thus, Cambodian judges could decide the law applicable to private nuisance claims in accordance with Japan's approach to the governing law, which is to decide the law by applying the general choice of law rules in torts (i.e., Articles 17, 20–22 of the AGRAL) because the AGRAL has no special rule for private nuisance.[96] Accordingly, a private nuisance claim is to be governed by the law of the place where the consequence of unreasonable interference with the use of land took place, provided that the occurrence

[90] Boskovic (n 88); T Hartley, 'Hartley on The Problem of "Libel Tourism"', *Conflict of Laws.net*, 19 July 2010, available at https://conflictoflaws.net/2010/hartley-on-the-problem-of-libel-tourism/ (accessed 10 December 2024).

[91] Meier (n 87) 515; Boskovic (n 88).

[92] Mankowski (n 59) 274 (stating that '[t]he European compromise bowing to Mr Rupert Murdoch's insistence and the British prime minister's obedience to his yellow press at home and Fleet Street in general was to expressly exclude defamation from the scope of the Rome II Regulation. The resulting oddity is the continuous application of old national, not unified conflict rules in this sensitive area).

[93] J Law (ed) *A Dictionary of Law* (Oxford, Oxford University Press, 2018).

[94] ibid. See also generally A Beever, *The Law of Private Nuisance* (Oxford, Hart Publishing, 2013).

[95] For instance, Art 139 of the CC prohibits landowners from using their land to disturb activities of others or cause private nuisances. Moreover, Art 140(1) of the CC provides that '[if] a[n] [alleged] nuisance … incurred by the land of another due to activities involving gas, steam, odor, smoke, soot, heat, sound, vibration or other disturbances, be within the … scope of normal use of the land …, and is not otherwise prohibited by law or regulation, the owner of the affected land may not seek an injunction against such activities'. In addition to injunction, the landowners affected by a private nuisance may seek for damages for the loss of enjoyment of his/her property rights under Art 140(2) of the CC. See also K Boren, 'Cambodian Private Law: A Snapshot' in H Peng, K Phallack and J Menzel (eds), *Introduction to Cambodian Law* (Phnom Penh, Konrad-Adenauer-Stiftung Cambodia, 2012) 83–84.

[96] Nishioka and Nishitani (n 12) 130.

of the consequence in that place was usually predictable based on objective circumstances surrounding the wrongdoer and the nuisance.[97] Should the consequence be unforeseeable, the court would apply the law of the place of the harmful act. With or without the application of this exception, the applicable law would likely be the law of the place where the affected land is situated because the nature of private nuisance is that it cannot be separated from the location of the targeted land.

iv. Wrongful Interference with Goods

Wrongful interference with goods means any torts to goods, including conversion, trespass to goods, negligence causing damage to goods or interests in goods, and any other torts that result in damage to goods or interests in goods.[98] Cambodian PIL has no choice of law rules for this category of torts, so Cambodian jurists may fill this legal vacuum by referring to the relevant Japanese choice of law rules. As the AGRAL has no special rules for torts to goods,[99] those who deal with wrongful interference with goods are recommended to consult the general choice of law rules for tort claims (i.e., Articles 17, 20–22 of the AGRAL). As per Article 17, the basic rule is that a claim pertaining to a tort to goods is to be governed by the law of the place where the goods or interests in the goods have been damaged. Then, the place of the harmful act and the place of the damage are highly likely to correspond because physical interference is the cause of damage to the goods. However, damage to interests in goods may happen in places other than the locations of the goods. For instance, a person can be prevented from receiving income from a house rental in a place away from the house if, for example, one's online bank account is hacked. In that case, the foreseeability exception in Article 17 is likely to come into play.

v. Environmental Damage and Pollution

Cambodian PIL has no rules for determining the law applicable to cross-border environmental damage. The courts in the Kingdom might therefore refer to the AGRAL in dealing with choice of law issues concerning environmental pollution claims. Such issues are to be determined in light of Article 17 of the AGRAL and other general rules, as the statute has no special rules for cross-border environmental damage.[100] Accordingly, the connecting factor for the choice of law issues shall be the place where environmental damage occurred, and, if it was unforeseeable that the damage would occur in the place, the connecting factor would be the place in which the event giving rise to the damage happened. In the case of an air pollution incident in which smog produced by a Lao company caused health problems among Cambodian citizens, the individuals would be able to claim compensation against the company based on Cambodian law because the pollution triggered negative consequences in the Kingdom. Should the company invoke the foreseeability exception under Article 17, the applicability of the provision would be determined based on the objective circumstances surrounding the case.

[97] AGRAL, Art 17.
[98] Law (n 93).
[99] Nishioka and Nishitani (n 12) 130–31.
[100] ibid 131; Takahashi (n 69) 329.

On international frameworks of environmental tort claims, Cambodia is a member of the International Convention on Civil Liability for Oil Pollution Damage of 1992 (London, 27 November 1992; the 1992 Civil Liability Convention),[101] which governs the liability of shipowners for any oil pollution damage caused by their ship in the territory and exclusive economic zone of a contracting state. However, the country has yet to adopt the following nuclear liability conventions under the auspices of the International Atomic Energy Agency (IAEA): Convention on Supplementary Compensation for Nuclear Damage (Vienna, 12 September 1997),[102] the Vienna Convention on Civil Liability for Nuclear Damage (Vienna, 21 May 1963)[103] and the Convention on Third Party Liability in the Field of Nuclear Energy (Paris, 29 July 1960).[104] Thus, the courts in Cambodia may well decide nuclear pollution claims as per applicable national laws designated by the general choice of law rules based on the AGRAL. Moreover, there is no regional framework governing tort claims arising from cross-border environmental harms in the Mekong despite serious plastic pollution and hazardous construction projects that have been plaguing in the transboundary river.[105] No discernible evidence suggests that the Mekong River Commission plans to address this issue in the foreseeable future.[106]

III. *Negotiorum Gestio* and Unjust Enrichment

Article 14 of the AGRAL makes a claim arising from *negotiorum gestio* – agency by necessity without mandate[107] – and unjust enrichment subject to the law of the place where the cause of the claim occurred. Khmer jurists may find the provision convenient in addressing the absence of Cambodian choice of law rules for the non-contractual claims as they might have been exposed to cases involving *negotiorum gestio* and unjust enrichment since the promulgation of the CC.[108] However, the Article does not define the place of the cause.[109] For instance, in the case of *negotiorum gestio*, the place of an authorised agency

[101] IMO, 'Status of Conventions: Ratifications by State' (n.d.), available at https://wwwcdn.imo.org/localresources/en/About/Conventions/StatusOfConventions/x-Status.xlsx (accessed 10 December 2024).

[102] See respectively, IAEA, 'Convention on Supplementary Compensation for Nuclear Damage: Latest Status' (2020), available at www.iaea.org/sites/default/files/22/06/supcomp_status.pdf (accessed 10 December 2024).

[103] IAEA, 'Vienna Convention on Civil Liability for Nuclear Damage: Latest Status' (2024), available at www.iaea.org/sites/default/files/24/03/63_vc_status.pdf (accessed 10 December 2024).

[104] OECD, 'Paris Convention: Latest Status of Ratifications or Accessions' (2024), available at www.oecd-nea.org/jcms/pl_31798/paris-convention-latest-status-of-ratifications-or-accession (accessed 10 December 2024).

[105] S Lovgren, 'Southeast Asia's Most Critical River Is Entering Uncharted Waters', *National Geographic*, 31 January 2020, available at www.nationalgeographic.com/science/article/southeast-asia-most-critical-river-enters-uncharted-waters (accessed 10 December 2024); M Sreypich and M Dickinson, 'Fishing for Plastic', *VOD*, 17 September 2021, available at https://vodenglish.news/trash-on-the-surface-microplastics-below-hundreds-of-tons-of-plastic-carried-daily-by-phnom-penh-rivers-research-finds/ (accessed 10 December 2024).

[106] The Mekong River Commission is an intergovernmental organisation for regional dialogue and cooperation in the Lower Mekong River Basin, established in 1995 by Cambodia, Laos, Thailand and Vietnam: www.mrcmekong.org/about/ (accessed 10 December 2024).

[107] *Negotiorum gestio* typically concerns the situation in which a person voluntarily handles the affairs of another person (e.g., a neighbour) who is temporarily absent. Takahashi defines *negotiorum gestio* as management of another person's affairs without mandate, pointing out that the Roman law concept has no equivalent in the common law, albeit its similarity to agency by necessity: Takahashi (n 69) 334–35.

[108] See CC, Articles 729–41; JICA (n 40) 226–31.

[109] Takahashi (n 69) 335.

act may be different from the place where the object of the act is situated. Likewise, the place of the cause of an unjust enrichment claim may diverge from the place of the loss caused by the enrichment. Thus, Cambodian jurists need to determine the place of cause by relying on the facts of each case.[110] However, this connecting factor may be replaced with a place manifestly more closely connected with the case under Article 15 or an *ex-post* choice of law agreement by the parties as per Article 16 of the AGRAL.[111]

IV. Conclusions

This chapter has considered the methods that Cambodian PIL may employ to identify the law applicable to cross-border non-contractual obligations. In the absence of black letter law on the subject in Cambodia, it is open to Cambodian jurists to develop choice of law methods inspired by the AGRAL because of the close ties between the legal systems of Cambodia and Japan. As mentioned in Chapters 1 and 2, Japanese legal ideas are integral to Cambodia's private law. However, it is not advisable for Cambodian PIL to adopt Japanese choice of law rules for non-contractual obligations without any revision. As this chapter has demonstrated, the general and special choice of law rules of Articles 17–21 for tort claims are generally compatible with the legal environment of Cambodia. Nonetheless, the double actionability rule in Article 22 of the AGRAL has been criticised by both Japanese and international commentators for its anti-reciprocity nature, inadequate protection of victim's rights and lack of international support. Thus, Cambodian jurists should refrain from importing this controversial doctrine into the Kingdom. In contrast, there are likely to be no challenges to adopting Japanese choice of law rules for *negotiorum gestio* and unjust enrichment in Articles 14–16 of the AGRAL because they do not contain any double actionability rule. Moreover, gaps in the AGRAL can be covered by the general choice of law rules for tort claims. The AGRAL does not contain special rules for certain specific torts, such as private nuisance, wrongful interference with goods and environment damage,[112] as well as the infringement of intellectual property rights.[113] In the interim period, Cambodian jurists may decide governing laws in these specific torts by applying Articles 17 and 20–22 of the AGRAL because there are no Cambodian statutory provisions that may serve as the basis of choice of law rules for such non-contractual liabilities. To conclude, Articles 14–21 of the AGRAL can serve as a sound foundation for Cambodian choice of law rules for torts, *negotiorum gestio* and unjust enrichment, whereas Article 22 would probably do more harm than good to the PIL of Cambodia.

[110] On *negotiorum gestio*, Yokoyama claims that the majority of Japanese commentators favour the application of the law where the direct consequence of an unauthorised act took place: Yokoyama (n 26) 79.

[111] Kono (n 12) 2225; Kono (n 78) 239.

[112] See Sections II.B.iii–II.B.v above.

[113] Koide (n 15) 229.

7

Choice of Law for Property Issues

I. Introduction

This chapter considers choice of law issues pertaining to tangible and intangible property. 'Tangible property' means any property with physical substance, including real and movable property. On the other hand, 'intangible property' refers to any property without physical existence, such as debts, intellectual property rights (IP rights), shares, negotiable and other registered rights.[1] Among these different types of intangible property, this chapter focuses on IP rights, such as patents, trademarks and copyrights, because of growing international interest in IP rights protection in Cambodia.[2] This chapter discusses the ways in which Cambodian judges (and other legal officers) might determine the governing laws of tangible property and IP rights in Cambodia.

It is anticipated that the number of cross-border disputes on tangible property and IP rights will increase in Cambodia as a result of the Kingdom's reliance on foreign direct investment (FDI) for economic growth.[3] For example, foreign investors are key players in the domestic property market despite the global impacts on their financial activities because of the COVID-19 pandemic.[4] It was reported in late 2022 that only 20 per cent of real estate buyers in Cambodia were locals, whereas 80 per cent were from foreign countries: the United States (20 per cent), China (15 per cent), France (11 per cent), Singapore (10 per cent), Japan (10 per cent), the United Kingdom and Italy (10 per cent) and other European countries (4 per cent).[5] If these foreign investors are involved in any dispute arising from, for example, the title of their real property (e.g., condominiums), they will probably ask a local

[1] L d'Avout, 'Property and Proprietary Rights' in Jürgen Basedow and others (eds), *Encyclopedia of Private International Law* (Cheltenham, Edward Elgar Publishing, 2017) 1428–36.

[2] R Sochan, 'Commerce Ministry Official Addresses Intellectual Property Conference', *The Phnom Penh Post*, 16 July 2022, available at www.phnompenhpost.com/business/commerce-ministry-official-addresses-intellectual-property-conference (accessed 10 December 2024); T Vireak, 'Cambodia Continues Intellectual Property Cooperation with EU', *The Phnom Penh Post*, 28 January 2020, available at www.phnompenhpost.com/business/cambodia-continues-intellectual-property-cooperation-eu (accessed 10 December 2024).

[3] World Bank, 'Data: Foreign Direct Investment, Net Inflows (% of GDP) – Cambodia' (2024), available at https://data.worldbank.org/indicator/BX.KLT.DINV.WD.GD.ZS?locations=KH (accessed 10 December 2024). See also N Teramura, 'Japan as a Source of Legal Ideas: A View from the Mekong Subregion of ASEAN' (2021) 13 *New Voices in Japanese Studies* 19, 24–25.

[4] Morning Studio Editors, 'Cambodia's Property Investment Market Well-Positioned for Post-Pandemic Recovery ahead of Next Year's Southeast Asian Games', *South China Morning Post*, 3 August 2022, available at www.scmp.com/presented/property/international/topics/cambodias-emerging-property-market/article/3186913/recovery (accessed 10 December 2024).

[5] Khmer Times, 'Cambodia Property Growth Well Poised by the End of 2022', *Khmer Times*, 2 November 2022, available at www.khmertimeskh.com/501179287/cambodia-property-growth-well-poised-by-the-end-of-2022-2/ (noting that 'foreigners are still the main force of real estate investment in Cambodia' (accessed 10 December 2024)).

court to determine the governing law of that property to confirm their ownership right. Many foreign businesses now operate and sell their products in Cambodia. Nevertheless, the number of counterfeit products circulating on the market is unlikely to decrease soon, despite the rigorous efforts of the Counter Counterfeit Committee of Cambodia (CCCC) to curb counterfeit goods and international companies' efforts to reduce such goods in the Kingdom through various educational programmes.[6]

Accordingly, if international corporations request a local court and/or concerned government agency to protect their IP rights, they will have to identify the law governing those rights. The economic development of the Kingdom is inseparable from the increase of choice of law issues on immovable and movable property and IP rights.

However, there is a paucity of literature and (often) statutory norms providing Cambodian choice of law rules for property issues.[7] For instance, no statutes set out the rules to determine the law applicable to immovable or movable property. Section II of this chapter therefore discusses how Cambodia jurists may fill the legal vacuum based not only on Cambodian legal principles but also on relevant Japanese private international law (PIL) rules.[8] On choice of law rules for IP rights, Cambodia has ratified several international conventions, some of which arguably contain PIL rules. Accordingly, Section III analyses Cambodian PIL rules for IP rights, considering applicable international agreements. Section IV concludes the chapter.

II. Law of Property

Under the Civil Code (CC) of Cambodia, immovables (i.e., real property) are land and fixtures. The latter includes buildings, structures, crops, woods and any other objects that are fixed permanently to land.[9] Movables (i.e., movable property) are any objects other than real property.[10] This chapter broadly follows those definitions of real property and movable property in discussing the choice of law for tangible property under Cambodian law. It considers the rules for the courts in the Kingdom to decide the law applicable to rights *in rem* in immovable and movable property.

[6] A Nortajuddin, 'Cambodia's Fight Against Counterfeit Goods', *The ASEAN Post*, 25 September 2020, available at https://theaseanpost.com/article/cambodias-fight-against-counterfeit-goods (reporting that 'the Kingdom's Interior Ministry destroyed more than 100 tonnes of seized counterfeit goods' in 2019, including medical products, cosmetics, cigarettes and alcohol (accessed 10 December 2024)); T Kongnov, 'CCCC Handled 140 Cases of Counterfeit Products Last Year', *Khmer Times*, 24 January 2022, available at www.khmertimeskh.com/501011959/cccc-handled-140-cases-of-counterfeit-products-last-year/ (reporting that 'a total of 140 cases of illegal medicine, medical products, cosmetics and general counterfeit products, equivalent to more than 4.7 tonnes, 77 packs of tobacco and medical equipment including (77,770 litres of alcohol and 59 cases of face masks) were confiscated [in 2021]' (accessed 10 December 2024)); R Spiess, 'Investors, Governmant Talk Intellectual Property', *The Phnom Penh Post*, 12 February 2018, available at www.phnompenhpost.com/business/investors-government-talk-intellectual-property (accessed 10 December 2024).

[7] See generally Chapter 2 in this volume.

[8] This approach is justified by J Menzel, 'Cambodian Law: Some Comparative and International Perspectives' in H Peng, K Phallack and J Menzel (eds), *Introduction to Cambodian Law* (Phnom Penh, Konrad-Adenauer-Stiftung Cambodia, 2012).

[9] CC, Art 120(2).

[10] ibid, Art 120(3).

A. Immovable Property

The Cambodian legal system has no statutory rules to determine the governing law of real property. In contrast, the Japanese legal system provides in the Act on General Rules for Application of Law (AGRAL) that '[r]ights *in rem* and other rights requiring registration with regard to … immovables shall be governed by the law of the place where the subject property is located'.[11] One may find the origin of this *lex situs* rule in the feudal system of Europe that was largely based on the regime of immovable property and hence made the acquisition by citizens and foreigners of an individual interest in an immovable property subject to local law (i.e., the *lex situs*).[12] Cambodia is not a country of feudalism, but its legal system contains several rules that conform with the *lex situs* rule. For instance, Article 44 of the Constitution of the Kingdom of Cambodia provides that '[o]nly [Cambodian] legal entities and citizens of [Cambodian] nationality shall have the right to own land'. Likewise, Article 1155 of the CC prohibits the acquisition of land through succession by foreigners without Cambodian nationality. That Cambodian land transactions may occur only among Cambodian citizens means that foreign law is unlikely to be applicable to those transactions, along the lines of the *lex situs* rule.

In principle, justifications for the *lex situs* rule are maintainable under the Cambodian legal system. According to Yokoyama, the AGRAL adopts the *lex situs* rule for four reasons.[13] First, the place of real property is a clear connecting factor for those with interests in property, such as creditors and purchasers. This idea is applicable to real property in Cambodia as those who have interests in immovables in the Kingdom may identify their location through the Ministry of Land Management, Urban Planning and Construction (MLMUPC).[14] Second, 'the principle of *numerus clausus* would not allow such rights over things situated in a country to be created under the law of another country, in the interests of clarity and legal certainty'.[15] Yokoyama does not clarify the logic behind this statement. However, enabling foreign legal systems to govern Cambodian real property may indeed confuse the property market of the Kingdom because foreign laws are unlikely to be compatible with circumstances surrounding Cambodian real property.[16] Third, the *lex situs* rule may arguably lead to the application of the *lex fori* to immovable property, which is convenient for registrars and execution officers who oversee real property registration. Because Yokoyama does not explain the rationale of this argument,[17] it is not possible fully to examine the statement's

[11] AGRAL, Art 13(1). Note that 'rights *in rem*' under the Article refers to all rights *in rem*, including ownership possessory rights, usufruct and leasehold: K Nishioka and Y Nishitani, *Japanese Private International Law* (Oxford, Hart Publishing, 2021) 145.

[12] d'Avout (n 1) 1428.

[13] J Yokoyama, *Private International Law in Japan* (Alphen aan den Rijn, Wolters Kluwer, 2019) 82.

[14] I Sakano, 'Registration of Land-Ownership in Cambodia: Protection of Private Rights in Development' in Y Kaneko, N Kadomatsu and BZ Tamanaha (eds), *Land Law and Disputes in Asia In Search of an Alternative for Development* (Abingdon, Routledge, 2021) 37ff (noting, however, in footnote 27 that '83.1 percent of the total estimated land parcels have been registered [with MLMUPC]'. See also generally E Kanetake, 'Real Property Registration in Cambodia [in Japanese]' (2017) 73 *ICD News* 41; A Uchiyama, 'Cambodian Justice System: Disputes over Non-registered Land' (2018) 75 *ICD News* 39.

[15] Yokoyama (n 13) 82.

[16] See K Koide, *Commentary on the Act on General Rules for Application of Laws [in Japanese]* (Tokyo, Shojihomu Publishing, 2014) 171 (pointing out technical difficulties in applying the law other than the *lex situs* to property rights).

[17] Yokoyama (n 13) 82.

applicability to Cambodian PIL. At least, the *lex situs* does not always correspond with the *lex fori* under the Cambodian legal system unless Cambodian courts are conferred exclusive jurisdiction over the real property in the Kingdom.[18] Fourth, as land is a state's national resource and is linked closely with economic and political interests, it should be governed by the law of its situs.[19] This idea is in line with the principle of territoriality that aims to mandate 'all individuals and institutions in a particular state [to be] subject to the regulations applicable in the territory of that state'.[20] As discussed in this section, Cambodia has expressed in the Constitution and other law codes its strong interest in land, and therefore its legal system is largely in conformity with the territoriality principle. Thus, Cambodian jurists and government officers could determine the law of real property by adopting Japan's approach – Article 13(1) of the AGRAL.

B. Movable Property

No obvious rule in Cambodian statutes offers guidance on the choice of law for movable properties, whereas Japan's AGRAL adopts the *lex situs* rule for such properties, as in the case of real properties.[21] One may find Japan's unified reference of movable and immovable property to the *lex situs* convenient as it avoids dealing with the complex choice of law issues – the characterisations of real property and movable property.[22] Such convenience is likely to be useful for Cambodia, where many jurists are unfamiliar with PIL and comparative law.[23] It is thus recommended that, as a matter of principle, Cambodian PIL apply the *lex situs* as the governing law of movable property.

i. Res in Transitu

However, the *lex situs* rule has triggered debates pertaining to movable properties in transit (*res in transitu*) – objects being transported on trains or ships across borders. Some Japanese commentators are against the application of the *lex situs* to rights *in rem* while in transit, because the connection between the object being transported and its situs is often accidental and temporal,[24] and because it is difficult to identify the location of the property as it moves

[18] N Teramura, 'Cambodia' in A Reyes and W Lui (eds), *Direct Jurisdiction: Asian Perspectives* (Oxford, Hart Publishing, 2021) 209–10; Chapter 4 in this volume.

[19] See also Koide (n 16) 165 (noting that a property right is an exclusive authority to determine the usage and ownership of an im/movable and thus has a close connection with the situs of the property).

[20] T Kono, 'Territoriality' in J Basedow and others (eds), *Encyclopedia of Private International Law* (Cheltenham, Edward Elgar Publishing, 2017) 1702.

[21] AGRAL, Art 13(1). Moreover, Art 13(2) provides that '[n]otwithstanding [Article 13(1)], the acquisition and loss of the rights provided for in [Article 13(1)] shall be governed by the law of the place where the subject property is located at the time when the events causing the acquisition or loss were completed'. On the implication of this rule on movable property, see Yokoyama (n 13) 83.

[22] Nishioka and Nishitani (n 11) 142; Yokoyama (n 13) 81.

[23] V Phun, 'Country Factsheet 2: Judicial Training in Cambodia' in A Nababan and others (eds), *Judicial Training in ASEAN: A Comparative Overview of Systems and Programs* (Phnom Penh, Konrad-Adenauer-Stiftung Cambodia, 2014) 34. See also N Teramura, 'Cambodia' in K Nishioka (ed), *Treatment of Foreign Law in Asia* (Oxford, Hart Publishing, 2023) and Chapter 3 in this volume.

[24] Koide (n 16) 165. Note, however, the AGRAL does not necessarily require a close connection between the object and its *lex situs*: K Takahashi, 'A Major Reform of Japanese Private International Law' (2006) 2 *Journal of*

towards its destination across national boundaries.[25] The commentators instead suggest the law of the destination to be the governing law of the *res in transitu* because of its stability – the destination of transport is pre-determined by the parties and is not changed easily – and its material connection compared to the situs and place of dispatch.[26] They do, nonetheless, recognise the application of the *lex situs* rule for transactions that have taken place at a temporal stoppage during transportation.[27]

However, the AGRAL does not expressly endorse transport destination as the connecting factor for movables in transit due to opposition by some drafters of that legal instrument. According to them, the application of the law of destination may rarely take place in practice as long as the *lex situs* applies to the *res in transitu* at a temporal stoppage during transportation.[28] On the other hand, the law of destination should not be applied to such a property at a temporal stoppage because the application of that law would undermine the expectation of third parties who were not aware that the property had been in transportation.[29] Those drafters further argued that complex choice of law issues might arise if the parties have failed to designate the destination of transportation, or if they have provided optional destinations of transportation.[30] In light of those criticisms on the law of destination, the drafting committee of the AGRAL decided not to establish any special choice of law rule for *res in transitu*, leaving the matter to interpretation by courts.

In Cambodia, the governing law of rights *in rem* in a property in transit is, in any event, to be determined by the courts' interpretation because the Kingdom's legal system has no obvious statutory rules or cases addressing the matter. The pragmatic approach to the interpretive task is likely to identify the law applicable to the *res in transitu* on a case-by-case basis, considering the circumstances of the transport, especially, foreseeability by the parties (including third parties) involved. This is because neither the *lex situs* nor the law of destination always has the closest connection with the property in transit, as pointed out by the Japanese commentators above. The *res in transitu* often only has a trivial connection with the *lex situs*, but nevertheless, the application of the *lex situs* may be justified where the transport destination is uncertain or undetermined (although such a situation is likely to be rare).[31] The law of the uncertain transport destination is unlikely to be the law having the closest connection with the *res in transitu*. Moreover, applying such a law would undermine the foreseeability of a third party who has acquired the object while it is in transit or at a temporal stoppage.

Private International Law 311, footnote 8 (noting that '[t]he March 2005 proposal [of the AGRAL] contained an option to create an exception to the *lex situs* rule … where there is another place clearly more closely connected in the circumstances of the case. However, the public consultation [for the proposal] … produced an unenthusiastic response, some pointing out the risk of undermining legal certainty and the possibility of flexibly interpreting the existing *lex situs* rule where necessary').

[25] Koide (n 16) 165; Nishioka and Nishitani (n 11) 142.

[26] Koide (n 16) 165; Nishioka and Nishitani (n 11) 142; Y Sakurada, *Private International Law [in Japanese]*, 7th edn, (Tokyo, Yuhikaku Publishing, 2020) 204–05; T Sawaki and M Dogauchi, *Introduction to Private International Law [in Japanese]* (Tokyo, Yuhikaku Publishing, 2018) 248. See also d'Avout (n 1) 1433.

[27] Koide (n 16) 166.

[28] ibid.

[29] ibid.

[30] ibid.

[31] d'Avout (n 1) 1432.

ii. Means of Transportation

As in the case of *res in transitu*, Cambodian jurists should exercise caution in using the *lex situs* as the law applicable to rights *in rem* in transport vessels, such as ships, planes, vehicles and trains because these vessels continually move and change their location, sometimes without deciding the final destination.[32] In Japan, the governing laws of such property rights are subject to discussions by jurists and commentators as the country has no explicit special choice of law rules for transport by vessels.[33]

First, the courts in Japan have traditionally referred rights *in rem* in ships to the law of the flag – the law of the state under whose flag the ship flies[34] – or the law of the state of registration.[35] Assuming that the state of the flag is identical to the state of registration, many Japanese commentators support the application of the law of the flag to rights *in rem* in ships because the law is arguably more predictable than the *lex situs*, especially where the ship is sailing in the high seas.[36] However, some commentators point out that the state of the flag and that of registration sometimes do not correspond where, for example, the ship is under a demise charter, flying the flag of a state different from the state of registration (albeit temporarily).[37] The governing law of the rights will then likely be the law of the place of registration,[38] based on the presumption that 'the registration reflects the legal relationship *in rem* and is more permanent than the flag'.[39] Cambodia is encouraged to follow suit, provided at least that the state of registration means the state of the primary registration that contains 'all the entries regarding rights *in rem* for the purposes of conflict of laws'.[40]

Second, there is a paucity of discussion in Japan pertaining to the conflict of laws for rights *in rem* in aircraft.[41] Some commentators suggest adopting the law of the place of registration as the governing law of the rights in aircraft, as in the case of choice of law for ships.[42] This approach was reportedly supported by the drafters of the AGRAL.[43] However, the drafters did not incorporate it into the AGRAL due to their interest in first observing the development of the international electronic registration system for high-value aviation assets,[44] which was established by the Convention on International Interests in Mobile Equipment and the Protocol on Matters Specific to Aircraft Equipment (Cape

[32] Nishioka and Nishitani (n 11) 144.

[33] AGRAL, Art 13.

[34] D Damar, 'Flag' in Jürgen Basedow and others (eds), *Encyclopedia of Private International Law* (Cheltenham, Edward Elgar Publishing, 2017).

[35] Nishioka and Nishitani (n 11) 144; Sakurada (n 26) 205; M Narasaki, 'Rights in Rem in Ships [in Japanese]' in M Dogauchi and Y Nakanishi (eds), *Leading Cases in Private International Law*, 3rd edn, (Tokyo, Yuhikaku Publishing, 2021) 50–51.

[36] Koide (n 16) 423.

[37] Ibid 423, 430; Nishioka and Nishitani (n 11) 144; Damar (n 34) 759.

[38] Koide (n 16) 423.

[39] Nishioka and Nishitani (n 11) 144. However, Yokoyama suggests that: 'the place of registration of the ship appeared to be dubious as a connecting factor … [as] ships were sometimes registered in more than one country and that places of registration might have almost nothing to do with their ownerships and managements': Yokoyama (n 13) 82.

[40] Damar (n 34) 764.

[41] Koide (n 16) 425.

[42] ibid; Nishioka and Nishitani (n 11) 144.

[43] Yokoyama (n 13) 82.

[44] Koide (n 16) 425.

Town, 16 November 2001). As Cambodia is not a party to these international frameworks,[45] Cambodian jurists are unlikely to be deterred from applying the law of the country of registration to property rights in aircraft.

Third, Japanese commentators were hesitant to maintain the *lex situs* rule in determining the law governing rights *in rem* in means of land transportation, such as vehicles and trains, due to the lack of close connection between those means and their situs.[46] Thus, such rights were traditionally made subject to the law of the state of registration.[47] However, the Supreme Court of Japan held in 2002 that:

> [T]he applicable law to the acquisition of title to a car is the law of the place of its primary use in cases where the car is in a state ready for use, and in cases where it is not ready for use, unless there are special circumstances such as where it is in the process of transportation to another country, the law of the place where it physically exists.[48]

On the advantage of this approach, the Supreme Court reasoned as follows.

> In cases where cars which are ready to be placed in use are traded, the buyer may easily obtain information for finding out the place of primary use by inspecting documents such as the car registration or the state of the car maintenance. By acknowledging the law of the place of its primary use rather than the law of the country in which the car physically happened to be as the applicable law, there is greater legal transparency for the seller and this will contribute to the safety of trading.[49]

According to this judgment, the court may therefore decide the place of primary use flexibly, taking account of the vehicle's places of registration and maintenance.

Recently, some Japanese commentators have criticised the approach adopted by the Supreme Court.[50] According to them, the car's readiness for use (i.e., roadworthiness) can be decided only by the applicable substantive law, and no uniform criteria of roadworthiness is provided at the choice of law level. They further claim that the place of registration is not always closely connected with the parties or transaction of the vehicle because ordinary people (in Europe) may freely cross borders in their cars and sell or purchase the cars, regardless of whether and where the vehicles are registered. To ensure legal certainty and predictability, they allege that rights *in rem* in vehicles should be generally governed by the *lex situs*, whereas such rights in vehicles in the process of transportation should be regulated by the law of the place of primary use.

The recent criticism of the Supreme Court's approach is maintainable under the legal system of Cambodia. Using a car's roadworthiness as the threshold to decide applicable law

[45] UNIDROIT, 'Convention on International Interests in Mobile Equipment (Cape Town, 2001) – States Parties' (2021), available at www.unidroit.org/instruments/security-interests/cape-town-convention/states-parties/ (accessed 10 December 2024); UNIDROIT, 'Protocol to the Convention on International Interests in Mobile Equipment on Matters Specific to Aircraft Equipment – States Parties' (2021), available at www.unidroit.org/instruments/security-interests/aircraft-protocol/states-parties/ (accessed 10 December 2024).

[46] Koide (n 16) 166.

[47] Nishioka and Nishitani (n 11) 144.

[48] *A v B* [2002] Supreme Court (The Third Petty Bench) 2000 (Ju) 612, 56(8) Minshu (Supreme Court Reports (civil cases)) 1964. The English translation of this judgment is available at www.courts.go.jp/app/hanrei_en/detail?id=604 (accessed 10 May 2025).

[49] Ibid.

[50] Nishioka and Nishitani (n 11) 145; T Kanzaki, 'Rights in Rem in Vehicles [in Japanese]' in M Dogauchi and Y Nakanishi (eds), *Leading Cases in Private International Law*, 3rd edn, (Tokyo, Yuhikaku Publishing, 2021) 48–49.

is mixing up choice of law issues with substantive law issues. This may dilute the significance of conflict of laws and may undermine the development of PIL in the Kingdom, although the choice of law is inevitably influenced by relevant substantive legal norms, such as the substantive law of the forum.[51] Nonetheless, it might be difficult for Cambodian jurists to adopt the more recent Japanese commentators' suggested approach because, as pointed out by traditional Japanese commentators, a vehicle does not always have a close connection with the *lex situs*. In addition, the relatively strict border controls between Cambodia and its neighbouring countries (unlike that of Europe) prevents ordinary consumers in the region from driving and selling their cars freely beyond the borders of their home country.[52] Consumers capable of moving freely through Cambodia and its neighbours are likely to be rare. Thus, Cambodian jurists should probably apply the law of the state of registration to property rights in vehicles, and, in exceptional circumstances, for example, when the vehicle is in transportation for the purposes of sale, they may rely on the *lex situs* rule.

C. Expropriation

The general rule of PIL is that '[t]he law applicable to expropriations is the law of the state on whose territory the expropriation takes place, since by definition an expropriation must be carried out by a state …, and can only be effective in relation to property … situated within the territory of that state'.[53] No obvious provisions in Cambodian law prevents the application of this general rule at the courts in the Kingdom.[54] Japan follows this general approach, as demonstrated by the Tokyo High Court's dealing with a dispute that arose from a Japanese company's purchase of oil from an Iranian state-owned company.[55] In this case, Idemitsu Kosan, a Japanese petroleum refineries company, imported oil from the National Iranian Oil Company (NIOC), which was established by Iran's 1951 oil nationalisation legislation confiscating the oil installation and resources of the Anglo-Persian Oil Company (APOC). As the oil that Idemitsu purchased was stored in Yokohama, Japan, the APOC requested the Tokyo District Court to issue a provisional injunction order to suspend Idemitsu from selling that oil, insisting its ownership over it. Upon appeal, the Tokyo High Court determined the effects of the nationalisation legislation and title to that oil as per Iranian law, in light of the

[51] Yokoyama (n 13) 33. See also Chapter 2 in this volume.

[52] Tensions over states' jurisdictional and sovereign limits at land still persist in Mainland Southeast Asia: S Koemsoeun, 'Cambodia, Thailand Discuss Border Posts', *Khmer Times*, 23 January 2023, available at www.khmertimeskh.com/501224027/cambodiathailand-discuss-border-posts/ (accessed 10 December 2024); T Kang, 'Are Cambodia and Laos Really Any Closer to Resolving Their Border Dispute?', *The Diplomat*, 21 May 2018, available at https://thediplomat.com/2018/05/are-cambodia-and-laos-really-any-closer-to-resolving-their-border-dispute/ (accessed 10 December 2024).

[53] E-M Kieninger, 'Expropriation' in J Basedow and others (eds), *Encyclopedia of Private International Law* (Cheltenham, Edward Elgar Publishing, 2017) 726.

[54] Article 44 of the Constitution of Cambodia provides that '[t]he right to confiscate properties from any person shall be exercised only in the public interest as provided for *under the law* …' (emphasis added). 'The law' is highly likely to refer to the law of the Kingdom of Cambodia. See also K Boren, 'Cambodian Private Law: A Snapshot' in H Peng, K Phallack and J Menzel (eds), *Introduction to Cambodian Law* (Phnom Penh, Konrad-Adenauer-Stiftung Cambodia, 2012) 79.

[55] *Anglo-Persian Oil Company v Idemitsu Kosan Co, Ltd* [1953] Tokyo High Court Showa 28 (Ne) 899, 6(11) Koto Saibansho Minji Hanrei Shu (High Courts Reports (civil cases)) [in Japanese] 702. See also Yokoyama (n 13) 86; Nishioka and Nishitani (n 11) 148.

lex situs rule under Article 13 of the AGRAL. Thus, the Court applied the general PIL rule to expropriations, and the courts in Cambodia are recommended to follow the same path.

D. Succession to Property

Much has been written on succession to property in Cambodia.[56] However, less is known about the conflict of laws for international succession in the Kingdom. This is somewhat inevitable because the Cambodian legal system contains no clear choice of law rules for cross-border succession to property. Cambodia is not a party to PIL instruments on succession, such as the Convention of 5 October 1961 on the Conflicts of Laws Relating to the Form of Testamentary Dispositions (the 1961 Hague Testamentary Dispositions Convention),[57] the Convention of 2 October 1973 Concerning the International Administration of the Estates of Deceased Persons (the 1973 Hague Estates Administration Convention)[58] or the Convention of 1 August 1989 on the Law Applicable to Succession to the Estates of Deceased Persons (the 1989 Hague Succession Convention).[59] By itself, this is hardly surprising as these international instruments have not been very successful in gaining international support.[60] This section therefore discusses Cambodian choice of law rules for succession, based on those of Japan's AGRAL.

i. Succession in General

Article 36 of the AGRAL provides that '[s]uccession shall be governed by the national law of the decedent'. Thus, the AGRAL adopts the unitary approach in which one single law – the law of the deceased's nationality at the time of death – governs all assets belonging to the deceased's estate, regardless of whether they are in a single state or several states.[61] The unitary approach refers all aspects of the succession, including matters pertaining to the administration of the estate, to the national law of the deceased.[62] Therefore, 'the unitary

[56] R Samnang, 'Succession in Cambodia: Background, Disqualification and Types' (2019) 2 *UC Working Paper Series* 74; H Kiyohara, 'Civil Code' in H Peng, K Phallack and J Menzel (eds), *Introduction to Cambodian Law* (Phnom Penh, Konrad-Adenauer-Stiftung Cambodia, 2012) 130ff; S Serena, 'Cambodian Family Law: Development and Challenges Ahead' in H Peng, K Phallack and J Menzel (eds), *Introduction to Cambodian Law* (Phnom Penh, Konrad-Adenauer-Stiftung Cambodia, 2012) 147–49.

[57] HCCH, 'Status Table: Convention of 5 October 1961 on the Conflicts of Laws Relating to the Form of Testamentary Dispositions' (2017), available at www.hcch.net/en/instruments/conventions/status-table/?cid=40 (accessed 10 December 2024).

[58] HCCH, 'Status Table: Convention of 2 October 1973 Concerning the International Administration of the Estates of Deceased Persons' (2014), available at www.hcch.net/en/instruments/conventions/status-table/?cid=83 (accessed 10 December 2024).

[59] HCCH, 'Status Table: Convention of 1 August 1989 on the Law Applicable to Succession to the Estates of Deceased Persons' (2015), available at www.hcch.net/en/instruments/conventions/status-table/?cid=62 (accessed 10 December 2024).

[60] A Bonomi, 'Succession' in J Basedow and others (eds), *Encyclopedia of Private International Law* (Cheltenham, Edward Elgar Publishing, 2017) 1683. In fact, the Hague Testamentary Dispositions Convention has been ratified by 41 (non-)European States, the Hague Estates Administration Convention is in force in only three states and the Hague Succession Convention has yet entered into force: HCCH (n 57); HCCH (n 58); HCCH (n 59).

[61] Nishioka and Nishitani (n 11) 195; Bonomi (n 60) 1683.

[62] Nishioka and Nishitani (n 11) 195 (noting that other matters governed by the applicable law include: '(i) when, how and where the inheritance commences; (ii) who are heirs; (iii) portion of inheritance; (iv) range of estates; and (v) the availability of qualified acceptance or renunciation' (footnotes omitted)). See also Sakurada, (n 26) 339ff.

approach … avoids a scission of the succession and the complicated problems related to the simultaneous application of different laws to separate parts and distinct aspects of one single estate'.[63] This simplicity, which is supported by most civil law countries,[64] is advantageous to the Cambodian justice system that is mostly run by judges currently lacking profound expertise in PIL.[65]

The drafters of the AGRAL once considered whether they should elaborate Article 36 further on (1) the main connecting factor and (2) party autonomy.[66] However, they eventually concluded that such elaboration was unnecessary under Japanese law. It is worth examining whether Cambodian PIL should follow the AGRAL's approach to succession in this respect.

On (1), the main connecting factor, some commentators suggest that the deceased's last domicile or habitual residence is more appropriate as a connecting factor than nationality because the deceased's last principal place of daily activity is closely connected with succession that involves both personal status law and property law matters.[67] The drafters of the AGRAL did not adopt this proposal as they considered that: (i) habitual residence was more discrete than nationality; (ii) if the deceased was a Japanese living abroad, Japanese law would be the most suitable governing law of the succession as his/her estate and heirs would highly likely to be in Japan; and (iii) nationality is the main connecting factor for other choice of law issues on personal status and domestic relations under Japanese PIL.[68]

These arguments are maintainable in Cambodia to some extent but are unlikely to justify using nationality as the sole connecting factor for international succession under Cambodian PIL. For instance, the Cambodian concept of habitual residence is vague and needs further development, as no statutes in Cambodia adopt that connecting factor clearly.[69] However, the use of domicile is prevalent in Cambodian law,[70] and the deceased's last domicile is highly likely to have close proximity with his/her estate especially where s/he left the home country a long time ago and has been working in a foreign country for many years.[71] Complications may arise in which the deceased has multiple domiciles,[72] but they are unlikely to turn 'domicile' into a significantly more complex connecting factor than 'nationality' because the number of people having dual or multiple citizenships keeps increasing.[73] Some persons are stateless. The fact that nationality is the primary connecting

[63] Bonomi (n 60) 1683.

[64] Koide (n 16) 350.

[65] See Chapter 3 in this volume; Teramura (n 23). Note, however, that the doctrine of *renvoi* is not applicable to the succession governed by the deceased's national law as the Cambodian legal system is unlikely to be supportive of that doctrine: Chapter 2 in this volume.

[66] Sawaki and Dogauchi (n 26) 140.

[67] Koide (n 16) 350; S Hayakawa, 'International Aspects of Succession [in Japanese]' (1999) 1 *Yearbook of Japanese Private International Law* 79.

[68] Koide (n 16) 350.

[69] See Chapter 2 in this volume.

[70] ibid; CC, Art 34.

[71] K Um, 'The Cambodian Diaspora: Community Building in America', *Asia Society*, n.d., available at https://asiasociety.org/cambodian-diaspora (noting that '[d]uring the Khmer Rouge reign in Cambodia … [a]n estimated one million others fled Cambodia' (accessed 10 December 2024)).

[72] Bonomi (n 60) 1684.

[73] H-P Mansel, 'Nationality' in J Basedow and others (eds), *Encyclopedia of Private International Law* (Cheltenham, Edward Elgar Publishing, 2017) 1299.

factor for Cambodian choice of law rules on personal status and domestic relations,[74] does not necessitate that all such rules use nationality as the only connecting factor unanimously. Cambodian jurists should be able to rely on both connecting factors – the deceased's last domicile and nationality – in international succession cases.

On (2), party autonomy, some Japanese scholars recommended that the AGRAL include a rule that allows the deceased to choose the law governing succession to his/her estate.[75] They suggested that such a rule would be convenient if, for example, the deceased had multiple nationalities, or s/he did not maintain a close connection with his/her home state. However, the drafters of AGRAL refused to incorporate that rule into Japanese PIL for various reasons, such as (a) the deceased's fundamental freedom to decide by will on the disposition of his/her estate that would make the deceased's choice of law unnecessary, (b) potential uncertainty as to whether the deceased's choice of law would include stakeholders in the home country, and (c) potential disputes among succession stakeholders on the validity and interpretation of the deceased's choice of law.

However, awareness has grown among those people working in international initiatives and domestic legislation regarding the advantages of a limited recognition of party autonomy in international succession.[76] In fact, the Hague Succession Convention provides in Article 5(1) that the deceased may designate the law of his/her nationality or that of last habitual residence to govern the succession to the whole of his/her estate. Cambodian jurists can follow a different approach as the Kingdom is not a party to the Hague Succession Convention, and habitual residence is little used in Cambodian PIL. However, they may allow the deceased to choose the governing law of succession from his/her national law and the law of his/her last domicile, in light of the deceased's liberty to decide on his/her private property rights.[77]

ii. Wills

Along the lines of Article 36 of the AGRAL that designates the deceased's national law as the governing law of succession to his/her estate,[78] Article 37(1) of the AGRAL makes the formation and effect of a will subject to the national law of a testator at the time of the will's creation. The majority of Japanese commentators agree that the law chosen by Article 37(1) applies to the will's (substantive) validity and effects, such as the testator's capacity and vitiated intention, as well as the will's date of commencement.[79] On the other hand, they claim that Article 37(1) does not apply to the testator's individual juristic acts through the will because such acts are subject to their individual *lex causae*.[80] Thus, the creation of legacy and testamentary trusts is governed by the law of succession, the acknowledgement of an

[74] Law on Marriage and Family, Art 79; Civil -Status Sub-Decree, Art 34; Chapter 1 in this volume.

[75] Koide (n 16) 351.

[76] Bonomi (n 60) 1686 (noting that 'when the deceased had designated the law governing his succession, the chosen law remains applicable notwithstanding a subsequent change of domicile, habitual residence or nationality, thus granting the stability and predictability required for efficient estate planning').

[77] Constitution of Cambodia, Art 50; CC, Arts 2 and 3. However, see also Art 1155 of the CC prohibiting succession by a foreigner to land in Cambodia.

[78] Koide (n 16) 354–55.

[79] Yokoyama (n 13) 119; Nishioka and Nishitani (n 11) 199; Sawaki and Dogauchi (n 26) 141.

[80] Yokoyama (n 13) 119; Nishioka and Nishitani (n 11) 199.

illegitimate child is subject to the law governing illegitimate parentage, and the appointment of a guardian for the testator's child follows the law applicable to guardianship.

Cambodian PIL may adopt Article 37(1)'s approach,[81] provided that it gives the courts an option to apply the law of the testator's domicile at the time of the will's creation. As discussed in Section II.D.i, nationality is not the most convenient connecting factor in identifying the place with the closest connection with the testator's will, if s/he left his/her home country many years ago. Then, the testator's domicile at the time of the creation of the will may be the most useful connecting factor for deciding the will's governing law, depending on the circumstances of the case. For example, if the testator changed domicile from his/her country of nationality after preparing the will, the law of his/her nationality would be the most suitable governing law. Moreover, Cambodian PIL should confer on the testator a liberty to choose the will's applicable law from the laws of the testator's nationality and domicile at the time of the will's creation, because some recognition of party autonomy in international succession would be advantageous for Cambodian law.[82] In any event, it is unreasonable to make wills' choice of law rules significantly deviate from that for succession because individuals prepare a will to direct how their inheritance and succession will take place after their demise.[83]

On revocation of a will, Article 37(2) requires the will's revocation (if any) to follow the testator's national law at the time of that act. This law determines the capacity of the testator to revoke a will, the vitiated intention of the testator to revoke a will, and the timing of the will's commencement.[84] Under Cambodian PIL, however, these matters are unlikely to be subject to the exclusive application of the testator's national law (as in the cases of choice of law rules for succession and wills) because nationality does not always indicate the law most closely connected with the testator and the revocation of his/her will, as discussed above.

Under Japanese PIL, formal requirements of a will are subject to the Act on the Law Applicable to the Form of Wills (ALAFW),[85] which was established to enact the Hague Testamentary Dispositions Convention.[86] As Cambodia is not a member of this Convention, Cambodian jurists need not rely on the ALAFW in determining the law governing formalities of a will. They are instead likely to recognise the formal validity of a will if it complies with the formalities specified by the law most closely connected with that will, which is the law of the testator's domicile or that of his/her nationality at the time of the will's creation.

III. Law of Intellectual Property

Cambodia's keen interest in the protection of IP rights is evident not only from its comprehensive IP legislation, but also from its membership in international institutions

[81] Note, however, that the doctrine of *renvoi* is not applicable even if the governing law of the will is the testator's national law: Chapter 2 in this volume.

[82] Section II.D.i.

[83] See Koide (n 16) 355–56.

[84] Nishioka and Nishitani (n 11) 199.

[85] (Act No 100 of 10 June 1964).

[86] Supplementary Provisions in ALAFW, Article 1; Sawaki and Dogauchi (n 26) 142; Sakurada (n 26) 345–47.

and instruments for IP rights protection.[87] It became a member of the World Intellectual Property Organisation (WIPO) in 1995,[88] the Paris Convention for the Protection of Industrial Property (Paris, 20 March 1883; the Paris Convention) in 1998,[89] the Agreement of Trade-Related Aspects of Intellectual Property Rights (Marrakesh, 1994; the TRIPS Agreement) in 2004,[90] the Protocol Relating to the Madrid Agreement Concerning the International Registration of Marks (Madrid, 27 June 1989; the Madrid Protocol) in 2016,[91] and the Lisbon Agreement on Appellations of Origin and Geographical Indications (Lisbon, 31 October 1958; the Lisbon Agreement) in 2018.[92] It also signed memoranda of understanding for patent grant and recognition with Singapore in 2016, Japan in 2016, the EU in 2017, China in 2018 and the United States in 2020, among others.[93] More recently, the Kingdom became the 180th contracting party to the Berne Convention for the Protection of Literary and Artistic Works (Berne, 1886; the Berne Convention) in 2021.[94] Because Cambodia has no clear legislation or case law on the conflict of laws in IP, those international legal instruments may provide a basis for Cambodian choice of law rules for the protection of IP rights, although they do not always contain conflict of laws rules for IP rights protection.

A. Copyright and Other Non-Registered Rights

Cambodian jurists may rely on the Berne Convention to identify Cambodian choice of law rules for copyright protection. Article 5(2) of the Convention provides that 'apart from the provisions of this Convention, the extent of protection, as well as the means of redress afforded to the author to protect his rights, shall be governed exclusively by the laws of the country where protection is claimed'. There is a controversy over the meaning of 'the laws of the country where protection is claimed' as it appears to be directing the application of either the law of the place where the alleged infringement occurred or the *lex fori*.[95] Since

[87] The overview of Cambodian IP law is available in P Sovath, 'Economic Law: Intellectual Property Rights' in H Peng, K Phallack and J Menzel (eds), *Introduction to Cambodian Law* (Phnom Penh, Konrad-Adenauer-Stiftung Cambodia, 2012); ASEAN, 'ASEAN Intellectual Property Portal: Cambodia' (2024), available at www.aseanip.org/Resources/ASEAN-IP-Offices-Details/Cambodia (accessed 10 December 2024).

[88] WIPO, 'Members: Cambodia' (n.d.), available at www.wipo.int/members/en/details.jsp?country_code=KH (accessed 10 December 2024).

[89] WIPO, 'Contracting Parties: Paris Convention (Total Members: 180)' (n.d.), available at www.wipo.int/wipolex/en/treaties/ShowResults?search_what=C&treaty_id=2 (accessed 10 December 2024).

[90] WTO, 'Member Information: Cambodia and the WTO' (n.d.), available at www.wto.org/english/thewto_e/countries_e/cambodia_e.htm (accessed 10 December 2024).

[91] WIPO, 'Madrid Agreement Concerning the International Registration of Marks and Protocol Relating to the Madrid Agreement Concerning the International Registration of Marks: Status on May 3, 2024' (2024) available at www.wipo.int/export/sites/www/treaties/en/docs/pdf/madrid_marks.pdf (accessed 10 December 2024).

[92] WIPO, 'Lisbon Agreement for the Protection of Appellations of Origin and their International Registration: Status on July 11, 2024' (2024) available at www.wipo.int/export/sites/www/treaties/en/docs/pdf/lisbon.pdf (accessed 10 December 2024).

[93] D Haskel, 'Guest Article from Abacus IP – 20 Years of Patent Law in Cambodia: Milestones and Future Outlook', *European Commission IP Helpdesk: News Article*, 3 April 2023, available at https://intellectual-property-helpdesk.ec.europa.eu/news-events/news/guest-article-abacus-ip-20-years-patent-law-cambodia-milestones-and-future-outlook-2023-03-25_en (accessed 10 December 2024).

[94] WIPO, 'Cambodia Joins Berne Convention', *News*, 3 April 2023, available at www.wipo.int/about-wipo/en/dg_tang/news/2021/news_0069.html (accessed 10 December 2024).

[95] S Ricketson and J Ginsburg, *International Copyright and Neighbouring Rights: The Berne Convention and Beyond*, 3rd edn, (Oxford, Oxford University Press, 2023) 1322.

the forum is not necessarily the place of copyright infringement, applying the *lex fori* to the infringement may lead to 'a disjunction between the law applied to the claim and the law that governs in the place where the infringement occurred; that in turn may mean that the author does not receive the same level of protection as do authors in the country of infringement'.[96] Thus, many commentators have interpreted 'the country where protection is claimed' to mean 'country, or countries, *for which* [copyright] protection is claimed'.[97] They suggest that Article 5(2) embodies the long-standing PIL principle of *lex loci protectionis* that makes the protection of IP rights subject to the law of the country in which the alleged infringements occurred,[98] although the Article arguably excludes questions of authorship, initial ownership of copyright and transfers of ownership of copyright from the scope of application.[99]

i. Authorship

Some commentators point out that Article 5(2) of the Berne Convention may be construed to cover choice of law issues on authorship.[100] According to them, the Berne Convention does not define authorship and does not have any special choice of law rules for determining authorship issues such as authorship status, and this uncertainty may be overcome by extending the application of Article 5(2) to authorship.[101] This approach is compatible with the territorial view of international copyright protection. It also conforms to the national treatment provision of Article 5(1) that protects 'the rights [of foreign authors from Berne member states] which their respective laws [of the countries of protection] do now or may hereafter grant to their nationals' because 'the rights' may cover the determination of authorship.[102] Although the Berne Convention does not necessarily follow the strict territoriality principle,[103] it is impractical to remit issues of authorship to the choice of law rules of Cambodia as the Kingdom does not have the choice of law rule applicable to such issues, and Japanese PIL does not address the issues explicitly.[104] Thus, it would be more practical for Cambodian jurists to apply the *lex loci protectionis* to authorship issues.

ii. Initial Ownership of Copyright

On the initial ownership of copyright, the Berne Convention only provides in Article 14bis(2)(a) the application of the *lex loci protectionis* to the initial allocation of copyright ownership

[96] ibid 1321.
[97] ibid.
[98] DM Vicente, 'Intellectual Property, Applicable Law' in J Basedow and others (eds), *Encyclopedia of Private International Law* (Cheltenham, Edward Elgar Publishing, 2017) 964. The principle of *lex loci protectionis* is adopted by other provisions of the Berne Convention, including Arts 7(8), 10bis(1) and 14bis(2)(a). Thus, the principle is likely to be a foundational rule for determining the law applicable to copyright protection under Cambodian law. Note, however, that the *lex loci protectionis* does not extend to remedies for copyright infringement as they are characterised as issues of torts: ibid 965; Nishioka and Nishitani (n 11) 156–57. See also Section III.B.ii below.
[99] Ricketson and Ginsburg (n 95) 1322, 1339; WIPO, *Guide to the Berne Convention for the Protection of Literary and Artistic Works (Paris Act, 1971)* (Paris, WIPO 1978) 33–34.
[100] Ricketson and Ginsburg (n 95) 1341.
[101] ibid 1342.
[102] ibid 1342.
[103] ibid 1322, 1342. Cf, Vicente (n 98) 965.
[104] Yokoyama (n 13) 89; Nishioka and Nishitani (n 11) 148ff; Koide (n 16) 457.

of cinematographic works. Thus, each member state is free to apply its choice of law rules to determine initial copyright ownership of works other than cinematographic works.[105] Several Japanese commentators suggest that the law applicable to ownership is to be determined through the application of the general principle of PIL – the principle of the closest connection.[106] However, they are divided on whether the applicable law is the *lex loci protectionis* or the law of the country of origin (*lex originis*) within the meaning of Article 5(4) of the Berne Convention, i.e., the law of the country where the work was first published, or, for an unpublished work, the author's national law or the law of the country where the author has a domicile.[107] According to the proponents of applying the *lex originis*, the initial ownership of copyright has to be determined uniformly across states because copyright arises automatically once an original work is created, without the involvement of any act of state.[108] In this regard, the *lex originis* is arguably more appropriate than the *lex loci protectionis* because the application of the former may avoid 'limping legal relations among different protecting countries'.[109] The proponents suggest that applying the *lex originis* is in line with the negative inference of Article 14bis(2)(a) – the *lex loci protectionis* would determine initial copyright ownership of 'cinematographic works' only and would not determine such ownership of other works.[110] Aside from these arguments by Japanese commentators, Cambodian jurists may be attracted to the *lex originis* because the reference to the *lex* is simple and just for determining the initial copyright ownership. Ricketson and Ginsburg suggest as follows:

> But why is it 'simpler and more just' to adopt the law of the country of origin to govern initial copyright ownership? Because that choice of law rule ensures that the work will not change owners by operation of law each time the work crosses an international boundary. By the same token, licensees in all countries will know that they have acquired rights from their owner. … [L]ocal law will determine what rights can be acquired for each territory. Nonetheless, in principle, resort to the law of the source country to determine initial ownership reinforces the security of international contracts, and therefore would seem to promote the international exchange of copyrighted works.[111]

Different considerations are arguably required to decide the law applicable to the initial allocation of copyright ownership for a work created by an employee in the course of his/her duties. The laws potentially applicable to that initial allocation are (1) the personal law of the creator(s) (i.e., the law of the creator's residence, nationality or domicile), (2) the personal law of the employer (i.e., the law of the employer's residence, nationality, domicile, or principal place of business (if the employer is a company)), (3) the law governing the employment contract, (4) the *lex originis* (i.e., the law of the country of first publication), (5) the law of the place of the work if it is immovable or (6) the *lex fori*.[112] Referring to Article 15 of the Copyright Act of Japan that confers the initial copyright ownership to the employer unless otherwise specified by the employment contract, some Japanese commentators and jurists suggest applying (3) the governing law of the employment contract, to the

[105] Ricketson and Ginsburg (n 95) 1341.
[106] Nishioka and Nishitani (n 11) 151; Yokoyama (n 13) 18.
[107] Y Nishitani, 'Intellectual Property in Japanese Private International Law' (2005) 48 *Japanese Annual of International Law* 87, 96; Nishioka and Nishitani (n 11) 151; Yokoyama (n 13) 89.
[108] Nishitani (n 107) 96.
[109] ibid; Nishioka and Nishitani (n 11) 151.
[110] Nishitani (n 107) 96.
[111] Ricketson and Ginsburg (n 95) 1345.
[112] ibid 1343.

question of initial ownership because this issue is embedded in the employment relationship, and the parties may decide in the contract who shall acquire the initial ownership.[113] However, this approach is unlikely to be ideal for Cambodia because it could enlarge pre-existing asymmetries between the employer and employee.[114] In particular, the admission of party autonomy in this field will probably expose vulnerable parties (i.e., employees under international employment contracts) to foreign laws, depriving them of the benefits of their authorship that are normally available under their own personal laws.[115] Cambodian PIL has no discernible choice of law rules that may adjust the imbalance between the employer and employee unlike Japan's AGRAL,[116] although provisions of the 1997 Labour Law are overriding mandatory rules that apply to employment contracts to be performed in the Kingdom.[117] Concern has been expressed that 'free choice of law, where applied to initial ownership, would broaden the brain drain from developing and threshold countries to the industrialised world'.[118] Unfortunately, this possibility has to be taken seriously in Cambodia, which has been suffering from a brain drain for a long time.[119] Accordingly, Cambodian PIL might apply the *lex originis* to determine initial ownership because the law has the 'most significant relationship' to the work, thanks to the place of first publication's generally frequent correspondence to the country where the employer/publisher has its principal place of business and the place of residence or nationality of the employees.[120]

iii. Transfer of Copyright Ownership

On the transfer of copyright ownership, commentators and courts in Japan suggest in general that different characterisations should be applied to the underlying act – the transfer or licence agreement – and the attribution of copyright.[121] They claim that the former is to be classified as an issue of contract and thus is to be governed by the doctrine of party autonomy under Articles 7–10 of the AGRAL, whereas the latter should be categorised as a matter of proprietary right and therefore governed by the *lex loci protectionis* in line with Article 13 of the AGRAL.[122] On the application of the *lex loci protectionis* to the attribution of copyright, the Intellectual Property High Court in Tokyo held:

[113] Nishioka and Nishitani (n 11) 151; Nishitani (n 107) 97; *A v Industrial Bank of Japan, Ltd* [2001] Tokyo High Court Heisei 12(Ne)7, Intellectual Property Cases Reports, Section 3.4.

[114] J Basedow, 'Foundations of Private International Law in Intellectual Property' in J Basedow, T Kono and A Metzger (eds), *Intellectual Property in the Global Arena: Jurisdiction, Applicable Law, and the Recognition of Judgments in Europe, Japan and the US* (Heidelberg, Mohr Siebeck GmbH & Co. KG, 2010) 22.

[115] ibid.

[116] See AGRAL, Art 12.

[117] 1997 Labour Law, Art 1; Chapter 5 in this volume.

[118] Basedow (n 114) 22.

[119] F Docquier and A Marfouk, 'International Migration by Education Attainment, 1990-2000' in C Ozden and M Schiff (eds), *International Migration, Remittances and the Brain Drain* (London, Palgrave Macmillan, 2006); J Wilwohl, '40 Years After KR Victory, Has Cambodia Dealt With Its Past?', *The Cambodia Daily*, 18 April 2015, available at https://english.cambodiadaily.com/news/40-years-after-kr-victory-has-cambodia-dealt-with-its-past-82106/ (accessed 10 December 2024).

[120] Ricketson and Ginsburg (n 95) 1345.

[121] Nishioka and Nishitani (n 11) 150–51; Yokoyama (n 13) 89–90. Cf D Yokomizo, 'Japan' in T Kono (ed), *Intellectual Property and Private International Law: Comparative Perspectives* (Oxford, Hart Publishing, 2012) 787.

[122] *A v Industrial Bank of Japan, Ltd*, Section 3.6; *Dalí Foundation & others v Demart Pro Atte BV* [2003] Tokyo High Court Heisei 12(Ne) 4720, 47 Japanese Annual of International Law, 218, 224; *Von Dutch Originals LLC v Y* [2008] Intellectual Property High Court Heisei 19(Ne)10095, Intellectual Property Cases Reports.

> As for copyright, the content and effect of the right are provided for by the law of the country protecting it .... Since copyright has exclusive effect against third parties in relation to use of the copyrighted item, for the same reason that the [law of the location of the object] is applied in relation to the loss and gain of property rights [under Article 13 of the AGRAL], in relation to alterations in the ownership relationship of a quasi-property right such as copyright, it is appropriate to construe the law of the protecting country as the governing law.[123]

The distinction between the underlying act for the transfer of copyright ownership and the actual attribution of copyright is maintained under the Berne Convention regime (without excluding such transfer in employment relationships) and is thus applicable to the Cambodian legal system.[124] Applying the *lex contractus* to the transfer agreement and the *lex loci protectionis* to the attribution of copyright in principle would be compatible with the doctrine of closest connection under Cambodian PIL.[125]

B. Registered Rights

On registered IP rights, such as patents and trademarks, Article 2(1) of the Paris Convention provides national treatment for nationals of parties to the Convention, which requires each party to grant the protection of industrial property rights under its law to nationals and foreigners without distinction. The Convention provides in Article 4bis(1) that patents applied in some member states of the Convention shall be independent of patents obtained for the same invention in other countries, including non-member states of the Convention. Article 6(3) also states '[a] mark duly registered in a [member] of the [Convention] shall be regarded as independent of marks registered in the other [members] of the [Convention], including the country of origin'. Commentators suggest that these provisions of the Convention entail the application of local law to the protection accorded to registered IP rights in the territory of each party.[126] In other words, they claim that those provisions of the Convention are choice of law rules that apply the *lex loci protectionis* – the law of the country of registration – to the existence, validity and effects of registered IP rights.[127] This interpretation is supported not only by Japanese commentators[128] but also by a decision of the Supreme Court of Japan that held, '[i]n regard to the applicable law regarding the effect of patents, as there is no direct provision in the [AGRAL], it is proper to determine this based on general principles in accordance with the law of the country in which the relevant patent was registered, which is the country with the closest relationship with the relevant

[123] *Dalí Foundation & others v Demart Pro Atte BV* 224.

[124] Ricketson and Ginsburg (n 95) 1343 (suggesting in the context of the Berne Convention that '[c]oncerning transfers of copyright ownership, it is necessary to distinguish between matters of substantive copyright law, going to whether, and the extent to which a right may be transferred, on the one hand, and matters of contract law, going to whether and the extent to which the contract in fact purports to effect the transfer, on the other').

[125] However, Ricketson and Ginsburg suggest that a copyright licensor's grant of rights for a foreign territory shall be governed primarily by the *lex contractus* and secondarily by the *lex protectionis*: ibid 1347–48.

[126] Vicente (n 98) 966.

[127] SJ Schaafsma, *Intellectual Property in the Conflict of Laws: The Hidden Conflict-of-law Rule in the Principle of National Treatment* (Cheltenham, Edward Elgar Publishing, 2022) 168ff; S Ricketson, 'The Trademark Provisions in the Paris Convention for the Protection of Industrial Property' in I Calboli and JC Ginsburg (eds), *The Cambridge Handbook of International and Comparative Trademark Law* (Cambridge, Cambridge University Press, 2020) 10; Nishioka and Nishitani (n 11) 150.

[128] Yokoyama (n 13) 87–91; Nishioka and Nishitani (n 11) 150; Nishitani (n 107) 95.

patent'.[129] Thus, neither reference to the Paris Convention nor to Japanese PIL would bar Cambodian PIL from adopting the *lex loci protectionis* doctrine to decide the law applicable to the protection of registered IP rights. However, special considerations are required to discern choice of law rules for employees' inventions and the infringement of patents and trademarks.

i. Employee's Inventions

As per the *lex loci protectionis* doctrine under the Paris Convention, the issue of initial patent ownership of the employee's invention is governed by the law of the country of patent registration.[130] On the other hand, the Paris Convention is silent on the law applicable to patent transfer/licence from the employee to employer. Thus, Cambodian jurists might deal with the gap by taking Japanese PIL into consideration. However, Japanese commentators are divided on whether the governing law of the patent transfer/licence is the law of the place of registration (i.e., the *lex loci protectionis*), the law applicable to the employment relation, or the law governing the patent transfer/licence agreement.[131] The Supreme Court of Japan adopted the third option, suggesting that the amount of remuneration for the employee's invention is characterised as an issue of obligation that arises from the patent transfer/licence contract between the parties.[132] Nonetheless, this approach is unlikely to be suitable for Cambodian PIL due to the asymmetric bargaining power between the employee and employer in concluding a patent transfer/licence contract, and because Cambodian PIL lacks choice of law rules for patents that may address such an imbalance. Thus, it is advisable for Cambodian PIL to apply the governing law of employment relation to the patent transfer/licence. There is likely to be no strong ground for applying the *lex loci protectionis* to the transfer/licence because patents and other registered IP rights are, somewhat like commodities, subjects of international transactions under the principle of party autonomy.[133]

ii. Patent and Trademark Infringement

When it comes to the choice of law for international patent infringement, a core issue is the characterisation of remedies for the infringement. Some commentators and legal systems suggest that international patent infringement is an issue of torts and not IP rights protection, and thus ought to be governed by choice of law rules for torts instead of the *lex loci protectionis*.[134] Nonetheless, the Japanese Supreme Court refused to characterise such remedies in a uniform way, stating that the law applicable to an injunction against patent infringement and the destruction of patent infringing products is the *lex loci protectionis* (i.e., the law of the country of registration) as these requests are issues of the effect of patents, whereas the

[129] *Fujimoto v Neuron Corporation* [2002] Supreme Court Heisei 12(Ju)580, 46 Japanese Annual of International Law 168, 174.

[130] Yokoyama (n 13) 88; Nishioka and Nishitani (n 11) 152.

[131] H Yokoyama, 'The Employee's Invention for Patent [in Japanese]' in M Dogauchi and Y Nakanishi (eds), *Leading Cases in Private International Law*, 3rd edn, (Tokyo, Yuhikaku Publishing, 2021) 87.

[132] *X v Y* [2006] Supreme Court Heisei 16(Ju)781, 60 Supreme Court Decision for Civil Actions 2853.

[133] AD Marco and others, 'Global Markets for Technology: Evidence from Patent Transactions' (2017) 46 *Research Policy* 1644.

[134] Vicente (n 98) 965.

governing law of damages for patent infringement is the *lex loci delicti* as per the applicable choice of law rule for torts.[135] Cambodian jurists are unlikely to be keen to import this characterisation approach to Cambodian PIL, which is criticised by Japanese commentators as overly influenced by Japanese substantive law. The characterisation approach has a dubious theoretical foundation and is incompatible with the AGRAL's choice of law rules for tort claims.[136] Remedies for patent infringement should be uniformly classified as issues of torts under Cambodian law,[137] although the search for an applicable law is likely to start from the *lex loci protectionis* because patent infringement normally takes place in the country of patent registration.

The above discussion on the choice of law for patent infringement likewise applies to trademark infringement. Trademarks are registered IP rights. Accordingly, trademark infringement should be classified as a tort issue and its governing law is to be determined as per the applicable choice of law rules for torts.[138] Remedies for trademark infringement should be uniformly classified as issues of torts under Cambodian PIL.

IV. Conclusions

Although Cambodia appears to have strong interests in developing laws and regulations on tangible and intangible property, it has only very limited experience in adopting choice of law rules on such properties. The Constitution of Cambodia expresses the country's firm intention to recognise exclusive land ownership by Cambodian citizens. However, Cambodian law does not generally elaborate on how Cambodian courts determine the law governing a transaction of real property. Likewise, it does not offer guidance on choice of law issues for movable property. It has not adopted key international legal instruments in this area of law – the Convention on International Interests in Mobile Equipment and the Protocol on Matters Specific to Aircraft Equipment. These legal vacuums can be filled by adopting relevant PIL principles of Japanese law. Taking advantage of relevant Japanese legal principles is also helpful in dealing with the Cambodian law's gaps in choice of law rules for the expropriation of property and for succession to property, although fundamental differences between the Japanese and Cambodian legal frameworks on these issues must not be overlooked. Unlike Japan, Cambodia has not ratified the Hague Succession Convention and the Hague Testamentary Dispositions Convention.

On the other hand, Cambodia has ambitions to regulate conflict of law issues of intellectual property along the lines of key international frameworks. The country is a member of the WIPO, the Paris Convention, the Madrid Protocol and the Berne Convention. Choice of law issues pertaining to copyright and other non-registered rights, patents and trademarks can be solved before Cambodian courts under those international frameworks.

[135] *Fujimoto v Neuron Corporation.*

[136] R Shimanami, 'Patent Right Infringement [in Japanese]' in M Dogauchi and Y Nakanishi (eds), *Leading Cases in Private International Law*, 3rd edn, (Tokyo, Yuhikaku Publishing, 2021) 84; Nishioka and Nishitani (n 11) 155; Yokoyama (n 13) 89; S Kidane, 'Private International Law Principles on Intellectual Property: Recent Development of Court Precedents in Japan and Current Characteristics' (2009) 52 *Japanese Yearbook of International Law* 454, 472.

[137] On choice of law rules for torts, see Chapter 6 in this volume.

[138] Nishioka and Nishitani (n 11) 156.

The international agreements on IP rights are not free from ambiguities and uncertainties (like other international treaties). Cambodian jurists might address the gaps based on relevant international commentators' opinions on those international frameworks and the AGRAL (but always bearing in mind that Cambodia's law and society are different from Japan's).

To summarise, the gaps in Cambodian choice of law rules for property are not as yawning as they might initially seem. Cambodian law is equipped with basic rules governing conflict of law issues on immovable property and intellectual property. Gaps in such rules on movable property may be covered by importing PIL doctrines from Japanese law until Cambodia develops a comprehensive statute on choice of law for property issues.

8

Family Law*

I. Introduction

Like other Asian states, Cambodia is not immune to the emergence of cross-border family law issues triggered by globalisation. For instance, until its total ban in 2016,[1] the Kingdom had been a major destination for commercial surrogacy. Couples who were happy to compensate surrogate mothers beyond their medical expenses often travelled to Cambodia to have babies borrowing the wombs of economically disadvantaged Cambodian women.[2] The crackdown by the Government has not been effective. Commercial surrogacy persists in the country despite its illegality, in part because demand from Chinese couples soared after the easing of China's one-child policy in 2015.[3]

Before commercial surrogacy became technologically easier, many American couples travelled to Cambodia to adopt Cambodian children from local orphanages and agents that reportedly turned out to be fraudulent.[4] The so-called 'facilitators' tricked desperately poor parents and single mothers into temporarily handing over their children for meals and medical treatment, intending to sell the children for international adoption after forging the children's identity documents.[5] The trend formally came to an end in 2001 when the US suspended the new orphan visa petition processing in Cambodia 'due to the inability to verify that any particular Cambodian child is an orphan as defined in US immigration law'.[6] Other western governments followed suit.[7]

* A version of this chapter is available as N Teramura, 'Cambodia' in A Reyes, W Lui and K Nishioka (eds), *Choice of Law and Recognition in Asian Family Law* (Oxford, Hart Publishing, 2023) 219–40.

[1] L Murdoch, 'Australian Couples' Baby Plans in Limbo as Cambodia Bans Commercial Surrogacy' *The Sydney Morning Herald*, 2 February 2022, available at www.smh.com.au/world/australian-couples-baby-plans-in-limbo-as-cambodia-bans-commercial-surrogacy-20161104-gshx2x.html (accessed 10 December 2024).

[2] M Blomberg, 'Surrogate Mothers from Cambodia Given Suspended Jail Terms in Landmark Case' *Reuters*, 31 March 2020, available at www.reuters.com/article/us-cambodia-surrogacy-women-idUSKBN21I1NS (accessed 10 December 2024).

[3] E Handley and K Meta, '"I Will Not Give Them the Baby": the Plight of Cambodia's Detained Surrogates', *The Guardian*, 2 October 2018, available at www.theguardian.com/global-development/2018/oct/02/i-will-not-give-them-the-baby-plight-cambodia-detained-surrogates (accessed 10 December 2024).

[4] R McDowell, 'Rush Is On To Adopt Cambodia Babies' *AP News*, 25 July 1998, available at apnews.com/article/b21178898d6e12e01469a9135ca3356a (accessed 10 December 2024).

[5] 'Babies for Sale: No Warranty' *The Sydney Morning Herald*, 16 December 2003, available at www.smh.com.au/national/babies-for-sale-no-warranty-20031216-gdhzp5.html (accessed 10 December 2024); S Corbett, 'Where Do Babies Come From?' *The New York Times Magazines*, 16 June 2002, available at www.nytimes.com/2002/06/16/magazine/where-do-babies-come-from.html (accessed 10 December 2024); DM Smolin, 'Child Laundering: How the Intercountry Adoption System Legitimizes and Incentivizes the Practices of Buying, Trafficking, Kidnapping, and Stealing Children' (2006) 52 *The Wayne Law Review* 113, 136ff.

[6] US Citizenship and Immigration Services, 'Adoption Information: Cambodia' (2013), available at www.uscis.gov/adoption/uscis-country-specific-processing/adoption-information-cambodia (accessed 10 December 2024); B Bainbridge, 'US Adoption Agent Guilty of Visa Fraud' *The Phnom Penh Post*, 19 December 2003, available at www.phnompenhpost.com/national/us-adoption-agent-guilty-visa-fraud (accessed 10 December 2024).

[7] AE Kubo, 'Cambodia to Lift Ban on International Adoptions: The Resumption of Intercountry Adoptions Comes Four Years after Reports of Child Abuse and Trafficking' *The Diplomat*, 10 December 2013, available at thediplomat.com/2013/12/cambodia-to-lift-ban-on-international-adoptions (accessed 10 December 2024).

However, the practice continued under the radar.[8] Thus, in 2007, the country ratified the Convention of 29 May 1993 on Protection of Children and Co-operation in Respect of Intercountry Adoption (1993 Hague Adoption Convention), and prohibited foreign couples from adopting Cambodian children in 2009.[9] Since then, the Government of the Kingdom has declared the intention to resume intercountry adoption of Cambodian children several times,[10] but the schedule for the resumption has yet to be published because of western counterparts' continuing suspension of child adoptions from Cambodia.[11] Accordingly, international adoption and commercial surrogacy are examples of the various complicated cross-border family issues that the Cambodian Government is expected to deal with to improve the welfare of its citizens.

Nonetheless, private international law (PIL) for family issues has not yet fully developed in Cambodia. Cambodian private law does not have a comprehensive set of modern choice of laws rules,[12] unlike the Japanese civil law which has the Act on General Rules for Application of Laws (AGRAL),[13] to which Cambodian private law traces its roots.[14] Instead, sources of PIL can be found in different statutes of Cambodian law.[15] For example, the Law on Marriage and Family of Cambodia (the Marriage and Family Law) contains a few provisions governing conflict of law issues in cross-border marriages, although these rules are somewhat restrictive in scope and coverage for addressing diverse aspects of such matrimonial relationships. Furthermore, the Law on the Inter-country Adoption 2009, sets out 'the principles, conditions, procedures, formalities and effects of inter-country adoption',[16] including legal doctrines covering PIL issues that may arise from the process. Other statutes such as the Code of Civil Procedure 2006 (CCP) and the Civil Code 2007 (CC) also contain a couple of provisions that regulate some dimensions of conflict of laws in international family relationships.[17] These examples imply that both Cambodian and foreign individuals who come across international family problems related to Cambodia will have to spot applicable PIL rules from various statutory norms in the Cambodian legal system. The situation

[8] J Welsh, 'Int'l Adoptions of Local Children Double in 2006' *The Cambodian Daily*, 5 March 2007, available at https://english.cambodiadaily.com/news/intl-adoptions-of-local-children-double-in-2006-73458/ (accessed 10 December 2024).

[9] Kubo (n 7).

[10] A Woodside and S David, 'Gov't Looks to 2014 for Adoptions' *The Phnom Penh Post*, 5 December 2013, available at www.phnompenhpost.com/national/gov%E2%80%99t-looks-2014-adoptions; US Department of State–Bureau of Consular Affairs, 'Intercountry Adoption News and Notices: Government of Cambodia Announcement on Intercountry Adoptions' (2021), available at travel.state.gov/content/travel/en/News/Intercountry-Adoption-News/government-of-cambodia-announcement-on-intercountry-adoptions-.html (accessed 10 December 2024).

[11] Kubo (n 7); US Department of State–Bureau of Consular Affairs (n 10).

[12] Industrial Development and Public Policy Department at JICA, 'Legal Technical Assistance for Cambodia: The History and Methodology of the Assistance of JICA in Drafting the Civil Code and the Civil Procedure Code' [in Japanese] (2012) 9.

[13] (Act No 78 of 21 June 2006), available at www.japaneselawtranslation.go.jp/ja/laws/view/3783#je_ch3sc5at12 (accessed 10 December 2024).

[14] The private law of Cambodia is built upon Japanese civil law because of the Legal and Technical Assistance Project by the Japan International Cooperation Agency (JICA). See, e.g., N Teramura, 'Cambodia' in Anselmo Reyes and Wilson Lui (eds), *Direct Jurisdiction* (Oxford, Hart Publishing, 2021); N Teramura, 'Japan as a Source of Legal Ideas: A View from the Mekong Subregion of ASEAN' (2021) 13 *New Voices in Japanese Studies* 19; Y Kaneko, 'Japan's Civil Code Drafting Support for Socialist Reform Countries: Diversity of Normative Choice' in Y Kaneko (ed), *Civil Law Reforms in Post-Colonial Asia: Beyond Western Capitalism* (Cham, Springer, 2019).

[15] See Chapter 2 in this volume.

[16] Art 1.

[17] See, e.g., Art 36 of the CC and Art 199 of the CCP. The English translation of the CC is available at www.jica.go.jp/project/english/cambodia/0701047/materials/c8h0vm000000zsb2-att/01_02e_1.pdf (accessed 10 December 2024), and that of the CCP is available at, available at www.jica.go.jp/project/english/cambodia/0701047/materials/c8h0vm000000zsb2-att/01_01e.pdf (accessed 10 December 2024). Unless otherwise stated, this chapter relies on these materials.

is unlikely to reduce the burden of legal practitioners who are under increasing pressure to pursue efficiency and quality in their service.[18] This chapter attempts to offer structured guidance on choice of law under Cambodian family law.

The lack of comprehensive statutes on conflict of laws means that gaps inevitably exist in the statutory norms of Cambodian international family law.[19] The remedy for the gaps under Cambodian law is somewhat tricky. One may not expect case law to play a gap-filler role because the Cambodian judiciary may not respect precedent[20] – the courts only occasionally publish past judgments as 'points of reference', not as sources of law.[21] Thus, one may need to address ambiguities in PIL statutes by relying on official commentaries, textbooks and reports on Cambodian private law that are written in Khmer and Japanese (or sometimes in the latter language only),[22] since Cambodian and Japanese legal experts drafted major statutes and relevant rules of Cambodian private law through the Japan International Cooperation Agency's (JICA's) legal technical assistance projects (JICA projects).[23] If such materials are not helpful, one may find PIL discussion pertaining to Japanese international family law useful because the current Cambodian private law has its origin in Japanese civil law, thanks to the JICA projects.[24] Jörg Menzel, former legal adviser to the Senate of the Kingdom of Cambodia, suggests that 'the new Civil Code and Civil Procedure Code are not influenced by France but by Japanese legal concepts, thus it might be appropriate to draft legislation largely inspired by Japanese private international law and *apply those [Japanese private international law] principles as much as appropriate for the interim period*'.[25] This chapter will largely follow his view for filling the lacuna of choice of law in Cambodian family law.

II. Choice of Law

A. Marriage

The Marriage and Family Law is the main body of law regulating choice of law for international marriage. Its drafters were compelled to work on it expeditiously with limited

[18] N Teramura, *Ex Aequo et Bono as a Response to the 'Over-Judicialisation' of International Commercial Arbitration* (Alphen aan den Rijn, Wolters Kluwer, 2020) ch 1.

[19] World Intelligence Partners Japan Co Ltd, *Research Report on Personal Status Law in the Kingdom of Cambodia* [in Japanese] (The Ministry of Justice of Japan, 2018) 24.

[20] Teramura, 'Cambodia' (2021) 201–03.

[21] N Chheng, 'Courts' Decisions Now Published as Reference Source' *The Phnom Penh Post*, 4 January 2021, available at www.phnompenhpost.com/national/courts-decisions-now-published-reference-source (accessed 10 December 2024).

[22] JICA, 'The Legal and Judicial Development Project (Phase 3): Materials', available at www.jica.go.jp/project/english/cambodia/0701047/materials/index.html (accessed 10 December 2024); Ministry of Justice of Japan, 'Legal Technical Assistance Activities by the International Cooperation Department ~Contributing to the World is Japan's Strength!~: Cambodia' [in Japanese], available at www.moj.go.jp/housouken/houso_houkoku_cambo.html (accessed 10 December 2024).

[23] Teramura, 'Japan as a Source of Legal Ideas' (n 14) 26–27.

[24] A Morishima, 'Reflection on the Legal and Judicial Development Project for Drafting the Civil Code of Cambodia [in Japanese]' (2003) 11 *ICD News* 4, 7; I Sakano, 'Reflection on the Legal and Judicial Development Project for Drafting the Civil and Civil Procedure Codes of Cambodia [in Japanese]' (2003) 7 *ICD News* 91; I Sakano, 'Reflection on Diverse Issues in Legal Technical Assistance for Cambodia [in Japanese]' (2021) 87 *ICD News* 57.

[25] J Menzel, 'Cambodian Law: Some Comparative and International Perspectives' in H Peng, K Phallack and J Menzel (eds), *Introduction to Cambodian Law* (Phnom Penh, Konrad-Adenauer-Stiftung Cambodia, 2012) 490–91 (emphasis added).

preparation time provided, because in the 1980s the Kingdom faced a pressing need to fill the legal vacuum in family matters in the aftermath of the (near) total abolition of rule of law by the Khmer Rouge regime in the 1970s.[26] Being aware of the vagueness and insufficiency within emergency legislation,[27] Cambodian lawyers and Japanese legal experts involved in the JICA projects decided to deal with family law issues in the CC.[28] The result of this new codification was the repeal of the Marriage and Family Law except for a few provisions governing PIL issues pertaining to cross-border marriage.[29] These remaining provisions are not based on Japanese law because they were established before the commencement of JICA's legal technical assistance for Cambodia in 1996.[30] Nevertheless, filling their gaps by applying Japanese legal principles is not an unreasonable option since most parts of Cambodian family law are regulated by the CC under the influence of Japanese legal ideas.[31] Such an approach will likely assist Cambodian family law in achieving legal certainty and consistency.

i. Formal Validity

The basic rule under Cambodian family law is that the formal validity of a marriage is determined by the law of the place where the marriage has taken place. For example, Article 80 of the Marriage and Family Law requires that a marriage between a Cambodian citizen and a foreigner in Cambodia is to be held in accordance with laws of Cambodia, while Article 79(2) provides that:

> Marriage between [Cambodians] or [a] Cambodian citizen and [a] foreigner, which is *formally held according to marriage procedure described by the law of the marriage*, shall be recognised as being valid in the State of Cambodia as long as such marriage is not against the provisions of the laws of the State of Cambodia.[32]

On a wedding taking place between Cambodian nationals or between a Cambodian national and a foreign citizen, Article 79(1) requires it to be held before the registrar of the embassy or consulate of Cambodia located in the country where the couple reside. However, failing to do so is unlikely to lead to the foreign marriage being voided or refused recognition under Cambodian law, as long as the formalities of the marriage comply with the local marriage law. The reason for this is that Article 79(2) of the Marriage and Family Law

[26] S Serena, 'Cambodian Family Law: Development and Challenges Ahead' in H Peng, K Phallack and J Menzel (eds), *Introduction to Cambodian Law* (Phnom Penh, Konrad-Adenauer-Stiftung Cambodia, 2012) 139. See also K Phallack, 'Overview of the Cambodian Legal and Judicial System and Recent Efforts at Legal and Judicial Reform' in H Peng, K Phallack and J Menzel (eds), *Introduction to Cambodian Law* (Phnom Penh, Konrad-Adenauer-Stiftung Cambodia, 2012) 7; M Vickery, *Kampuchea: Politics, Economy and Society* (London, Frances Pinter, 1986) 120.

[27] Serena (n 26).

[28] First Asia Division at JICA, *Evaluation Report on Japanese Cooperation to Support the Formulation of Key Government Policies on the Legal and Judicial System in the Kingdom of Cambodia [in Japanese]* (JICA, 2002). See also Art 1 of the CC.

[29] Art 78 of the Law on Implementation of the Civil Code provides that: 'Law on Family and Marriage shall become ineffective from the Date of Application, except the provisions of Article 76 and 77 and provisions from Article 79 to 81 of that law which shall remain effective after the Date of Application until otherwise provided by other laws', available at cdc.gov.kh/wp-content/uploads/2022/04/Law-on-Implementation-of-CC_Eng_FINAL_110531.pdf (accessed 10 December 2024).

[30] JICA (n 22).

[31] Teramura, 'Japan as a Source of Legal Ideas' (n 14) 26–27.

[32] Emphasis added: www.ilo.org/dyn/natlex/docs/ELECTRONIC/86095/96933/F1861658608/KHM86095.pdf (accessed 10 December 2024).

requires the courts in Cambodia to recognise a marriage held abroad following the formal procedures specified by the law of the place where the marriage took place, and Article 957 of the CC provides for registration at the competent embassy (or consulate) as an option for Cambodian couples residing abroad to effectuate their marriage formally in the Kingdom.[33] Thus, the courts in Cambodia decide the formal validity of marriage in light of the applicable *lex loci celebrationis.*

ii. Capacity to Marry

There are no laws or regulations that stipulate what conflict of law principles Cambodian judges should apply in judging the capacity of a couple to get married. Nonetheless, one may find implied principles in the rules on the recognition of foreign decrees. Article 79(2) of the Marriage and Family Law mandates Cambodian courts to recognise the validity of foreign marriage provided that such marriage is not unlawful in the Kingdom. A plausible interpretation of this rule is that the courts ultimately decide the substantive validity of marriage in accordance with the *lex fori*, i.e., the matrimonial law of Cambodia. The CC defines the substantive requirements of marriage as follows:

(1) A person under the age of 18 may not enter into marriage.[34] However, if a partner in a couple is over age 18, and the other partner is 16 years old or above, and if the parent or guardian of the minor permits, the couple may marry.[35]
(2) Bigamy is prohibited, i.e., a person who already has a spouse shall not enter into another marital relationship.[36]
(3) A woman may not remarry unless 120 days have elapsed since the day of dissolution or rescission of her previous marriage.[37] This rule does not apply where the woman was pregnant before the dissolution or rescission of the previous marriage and has given birth already, or where she has a medical certificate showing her non-pregnancy.[38]
(4) On marriage between close relatives, first, neither lineal nor collateral relatives by blood within the third degree of kinship may marry.[39] This rule is applicable notwithstanding the termination of the relationship with natural parents,[40] the dissolution of full adoption[41] and the dissolution of simple adoption.[42] Second, lineal relatives by affinity may not marry regardless of the termination of the affinity,[43] the dissolution of full adoption[44] and the dissolution of simple adoption.[45] Third, collateral relatives

[33] World Intelligence Partners Japan Co Ltd (n 19) 25.
[34] CC, Art 948, available at www.moj.go.jp/content/000122395.pdf (accessed 10 May 2025).
[35] ibid, Arts 948 and 953.
[36] ibid, Art 949.
[37] ibid, Art 950(1).
[38] ibid, Art 950(2).
[39] ibid, Art 951(1).
[40] ibid, Arts 951(2) and 1014.
[41] ibid, Arts 951 (2) and 1016.
[42] ibid, Arts 951(2) and 1032.
[43] ibid, Arts 952(1) and 941.
[44] ibid, Arts 952(1) and 1016.
[45] Ibid, Arts 952(1) and 1032.

by affinity within the third degree of kinship may not marry in spite of the affinity's termination.[46]

(5) A general ward – i.e., a person who is under general guardianship declared by a court due to his or her mental disorder and associated disability to comprehend the consequence of his or her legal actions[47] – may enter into a matrimonial relationship without his or her guardian's consent to the marriage, provided that he or she has the minimum capacity to effectuate the marriage.[48]

In addition, Article 45 of the Constitution states that: 'Marriage shall be conducted according to law, based on the principle of mutual consent between one husband and one wife'. Thus, same-gender couples are unable to marry legally under the law of Cambodia.[49]

iii. Consent of Parties

The Marriage and Family Law does not contain rules to determine the validity of parties' consent to marriage. However, they may apply Cambodian law as a minimum threshold.[50] Since the law treats matrimonial consent as a normal contractual relationship, the courts in Cambodia adopt principles of contract law in judging the validity of a marriage agreement.[51] A matrimonial contract would therefore come into effect when a partner in a couple makes an offer of marriage, and the other partner accepts the offer.[52] The couple then would have to satisfy the substantive conditions of marriage listed in section II.A.ii above. Under the old Civil Code, couples were not allowed to marry without permission from their parents.[53] However, this requirement was abolished upon the enactment of the Marriage and Family Law in 1989. Hence, heterosexual couples may marry at their free will under Cambodian law.

B. Matrimonial Causes

i. Divorce, Nullity and Separation

According to the Marriage and Family Law, the place of divorce determines the law applicable to the validity of divorce. For instance, Article 81 of the Law provides that the dissolution of marriage held in the Kingdom between a Cambodian citizen and a foreigner or between foreign nationals shall follow Cambodian law. Accordingly, the applicable law

[46] ibid, Arts 952(2) and 941.

[47] ibid, Art 24.

[48] ibid, Art 954. 'The minimum ability to effectuate the marriage' means the capacity adequate to express the person's intention to marry: JICA, *Commentary on the Civil Code of the Kingdom of Cambodia [in Japanese]* (JICA, 2011).

[49] See Section III.A. below.

[50] Marriage and Family Law, Art 79(2).

[51] T Kuong, 'Development of Legal Norms on Marriage and Divorce in Cambodia – The Civil Code Between Foreign Inputs and Local Growth (I)' (2016) 1 *Nagoya University Asian Law Bulletin* 69, 74.

[52] CC, Art 336. Note that Art 944 of the CC sets out a rule on engagement, stipulating that '[a]n engagement shall be formed through a promise to marry in the future between a man and a woman, and the performing of a ceremony of engagement'. Such a ceremony is unlikely required when a couple conclude a marriage contract.

[53] Kuong (n 51) 74.

of a divorce will be Cambodian family law if the divorce is held in the Kingdom. However, the Article does not clearly explain how Cambodian courts decide the validity of divorce held abroad. It provides that the dissolution of a marriage between Cambodian citizens or a Cambodian citizen and a foreigner residing in a foreign country is recognised as being valid in Cambodia,[54] without clarifying whether the recognition requires the compliance of the divorce with the marriage law of the foreign country or that of Cambodia. Conformity with the former law should possibly suffice. Otherwise, drafters of the Marriage and Family Law would have explicitly demanded the divorce to follow Cambodian marriage law, as they did when drafting Article 79(2) of the Law on the recognition of foreign marriage.[55] Thus, the law of the place of divorce decides the validity of divorce under Cambodian law.[56]

However, the Marriage and Family Law and the CC do not address how Cambodian judges deal with PIL issues in adjudicating the nullity of marriage. The matter is likely to be determined based on the choice of law rules on the validity of marriage. The reason for this presumption is that a person who claims the nullity of his or her marriage may typically invoke a failure to satisfy the requirements of a valid marriage. Hence, if the person insists on procedural errors in his or her marriage, the competent court will apply the *lex loci celebrationis* to decide the matter.[57] On the other hand, if the person claims his or her marriage's non-compliance with its substantive requirements, the court will adopt principles of Cambodian marriage law.[58] Then, the court will treat the marriage as void if one of the parties has no intention to marry due to mistaken identity, coercion or other causes.[59] Moreover, the court will annul the marriage on the grounds of fraud and duress,[60] as well as incapacity.[61] In any event, Cambodian judges will likely not treat the nullity and annulment of marriage as a type of divorce in the context of PIL.

A complicated issue may arise when a partner in a couple requests a Cambodian court to decide matters pertaining to separation. Since separation is a ground of divorce under Cambodian law,[62] the court will likely decide the proper law of separation following choice of law rules in the law of the place of divorce.[63] However, the law is obscure about the treatment by Cambodian courts of legal separation, which is often admissible in Christian countries like the Philippines, but is unlikely to be recognised in Cambodia, which designates Buddhism as the national religion.[64]

[54] Marriage and Family Law, Art 81(1).

[55] See also World Intelligence Partners Japan Co Ltd (n 19) 24.

[56] However, no noticeable rules in Cambodian law clarify the law applicable to the effect of divorce, such as the division of property between divorced partners. In the context of Japanese law, commentators suggest that the governing law of divorce basically determines the division of property, allowing exceptionally the divorced couple to designate the law applicable to the distribution of joint assets. The couple need to choose in writing the law of the country where the husband/wife has his or her nationality, the law of the habitual residence of the wife/husband or, in case the subject of the dispute is real property, the law of the place where the real property is situated: S Iriinafuku, 'Lecture Note on Private International Law: Divorce' [in Japanese] (2021), available at eu-info.jp/IPR/dev.html (accessed 10 December 2024); AGRAL, Arts 25–27.

[57] Marriage and Family Law, Arts 79(2) and 80; section II.A.i above.

[58] Marriage and Family Law, Art 79(2); section II.A.ii–iii above.

[59] CC, Art 958.

[60] ibid, Art 963.

[61] ibid, Arts 959–62.

[62] ibid, Art 978.

[63] Marriage and Family Law, Art 81.

[64] Family Code of the Philippines (6 July 1987), Art 55ff; Constitution of Cambodia, Art 43.

ii. Presumption of Death

No choice of law rules on the presumption of death exists in Cambodian law. In contrast, the AGRAL of Japanese law provides in Article 6(1) that:

> The court may make an adjudication of [an absentee's] disappearance [to presume his/her death] under Japanese law where [the] absentee had [a] domicile in Japan or had Japanese nationality, at the latest point of time when [the absentee was] found to be alive.

Even where the absentee did not have a Japanese domicile or nationality, the court will still apply Japanese law to declare the absentee's disappearance in relation to his or her property or legal relationship,

> if [the] property is situated in Japan, or if [the] legal relationship should be governed by Japanese law or is connected with Japan in light of the nature of the legal relationship, the domicile or nationality of the part[ies] and any other circumstances concerned.[65]

Accordingly, the drafters of the AGRAL prioritised the application of Japanese law. They argued that a non-contentious matter, such as a request for disappearance declaration, requires judicial procedures to be closely supervised by a Japanese court, pointing out that mandating the court in such procedures to follow foreign procedural rules is impractical.[66] This suggestion is applicable to the Cambodian judiciary which has limited capacity to investigate foreign law.[67] Accordingly, Cambodian judges are unlikely to be equipped with sufficient resources to declare someone's disappearance as per an applicable foreign law, even where some foreign elements are involved in the case. It is therefore reasonable for Cambodian judges to follow Cambodian procedures in declaring an absentee's disappearance. This is provided that the procedural law does not apply to indirect effects of the declaration, such as the commencement of succession and the dissolution of marriage.[68] The law may only cover the direct effect of the declaration, i.e., the presumption of an absentee's death.[69]

According to the CC, upon a petition by any individual who has an important legal interest in the declaration the court may declare the disappearance of a person who has been missing for more than five years.[70] In issuing such a declaration, the court shall observe the procedures for public notification as per Article 54 of the Non-Suit Civil Case Procedural Law.[71] Accordingly, the court is required to post the public notification of disappearance

[65] AGRAL, Art 6(2).

[66] K Koide, *Commentary on the Act on General Rules for Application of Laws* [in Japanese] (Tokyo, Shojihomu Publishing, 2014) 70.

[67] Cambodian judges rarely have opportunities to learn about foreign legal systems: A Misawa, 'Supporting the Training of Judges and Prosecutors in Cambodia' [in Japanese] (2004) 18 *ICD News* 1; V Phun, 'Country Factsheet 2: Judicial Training in Cambodia' in A Nababan et al (eds), *Judicial Training in ASEAN: A Comparative Overview of Systems and Programs* (Phnom Penh, Konrad-Adenauer-Stiftung Cambodia, 2014). See also Y Shinoda, 'Report on the Investigation of Cambodian Court Judgments (1)' [in Japanese] (2019) 79 *ICD News* 60 (suggesting that the primary task for Cambodian judges is to improve their ability to apply domestic law and write judgments properly).

[68] Koide (n 66) 71 (suggesting that the governing law of the declaration of disappearance under Japanese PIL may apply only to the direct effect of the declaration).

[69] ibid.

[70] CC, Art 41(1) (defining such an individual as 'his/her spouse, heir, legatee, … designated insurance beneficiary, … parental authority holder, guardian, father, mother or any other person').

[71] ibid, Art 42.

on the bulletin board of the court and to publish the notification in the official gazette of the Ministry of Justice.[72] If appropriate, the court may publish the notification in other media, such as in daily newspapers.[73] The public notification must contain: (1) the name and address of the petitioner; (2) the absentee's name, last known domicile and birthday; (3) a note stating that the absentee is required to inform the court of his or her life within the period of public notification – not less than six months,[74] and that failing to do so will result in the declaration of his or her disappearance; (4) a note stating that anyone who knows about the absentee's life and death shall report the fact to the court within the public notification period; and (5) the expiry date of the public notification period.[75] The effect of the declaration of disappearance is the absentee's deemed death from the time the five years period has passed, 'in respect to any legal relationship existing at or around the [domicile] or the place of [residence]'.[76]

Different rules apply to a person who has encountered any danger that may cause death, such as military engagement in combat zones and shipwrecking.[77] If that is the case, and if the person has been missing for one year, the court may declare the disappearance of the absentee, upon a petition by any individual having important legal interests in such a declaration.[78] Once the court has issued the declaration as per the procedures provided in Article 54 of the Non-Suit Civil Case Procedural Law,[79] it shall deem the absentee dead from the point where the fatal risk ceased to exist, concerning any legal relationship existing at or around the absentee's domicile or residence.[80]

C. Children

The Kingdom of Cambodia has a constitutional obligation to protect the rights of children as per the United Nations Convention on the Rights of the Child (New York, 1989; the 1989 Convention on the Rights of the Child).[81] The Convention attempts to establish a complete statement of children's rights under international law, expanding the scope of study of international children's rights to the private and family spheres.[82] In fact, Article 18(1) of the Convention provides that:

> States Parties shall use their best efforts to ensure recognition of the principle that both parents have common responsibilities for the upbringing and development of the child. Parents or, as the case may be, legal guardians, have the primary responsibility for the upbringing and development of the child. The best interests of the child will be their basic concern.

[72] Non-Suit Civil Case Procedural Law, Art 54(1)–(2), available at www.moj.go.jp/content/001182879.pdf [in Japanese] (accessed 10 December 2024).

[73] ibid, Art 54(3).

[74] ibid, Art 54(5).

[75] ibid, Art 54(4).

[76] CC, Art 43.

[77] ibid, Art 41(2).

[78] ibid.

[79] Note that the public notification period for an absentee who encountered a fatal risk shall not be less than two months: Non-Suit Civil Case Procedural Law, Art 54(5).

[80] CC, Art 43.

[81] Constitution of Cambodia, Art 48.

[82] S Jolly and S Khanderia, *Indian Private International Law* (Oxford, Hart Publishing, 2021) 153.

However, the Kingdom's best efforts have yet to extend to rules designating the law applicable to matters relating to the protection of children's rights. For instance, apart from the 1993 Hague Adoption Convention, Cambodia has not ratified any major PIL instruments established by the Hague Conference on Private International Law (HCCH) to enhance the well-being and best interests of the child. It has yet to adopt the Convention of 25 October 1980 on the Civil Aspects of International Child Abduction (the 1980 Hague Abduction Convention),[83] the Convention of 2 October 1973 on the Law Applicable to Maintenance Obligations (the 1973 Hague Maintenance Convention),[84] the Convention of 19 October 1996 on Jurisdiction, Applicable Law, Recognition, Enforcement and Co-operation in Respect of Parental Responsibility and Measures for the Protection of Children (the 1996 Hague Parental Responsibility and Protection of Children Convention),[85] the Convention of 23 November 2007 on the International Recovery of Child Support and Other Forms of Family Maintenance (the 2007 Hague Child Support Convention),[86] and the Protocol of 23 November 2007 on the Law Applicable to Maintenance Obligations (the 2007 Hague Maintenance Protocol).[87]

The Kingdom's non-participation in these multilateral legal frameworks might be legitimate because of the ambiguities inherent in those PIL instruments. As rightly pointed out by some commentators, despite putting the best interests and/or welfare of the child as determinative safeguards for children's rights, those conventions do not always clarify the key elements constituting such interests and/or welfare.[88] When international syndicates' operations in Cambodia on fake child adoption became apparent and caught global attention in the early 2000s,[89] the Kingdom quickly moved to protect Cambodian infants by ratifying the 1993 Hague Adoption Convention.[90] Cambodia's general hesitancy in acceding HCCH frameworks therefore does not necessarily equate to the country's reluctance to protect children's rights in the dimension of PIL. Nonetheless, as the Adoption Convention appears to be the only international choice of law scheme on children's affairs that Cambodia has adopted, Cambodian judges are normally expected to apply the domestic law of

[83] HCCH, 'Status Table: Convention of 25 October 1980 on the Civil Aspects of International Child Abduction' (2022), available at www.hcch.net/en/instruments/conventions/status-table/?cid=24 (accessed 10 December 2024).

[84] HCCH, 'Status Table: Convention of 2 October 1973 on the Law Applicable to Maintenance Obligations' (2013), available at www.hcch.net/en/instruments/conventions/status-table/?cid=86 (accessed 10 December 2024).

[85] HCCH, 'Status Table: Convention of 19 October 1996 on Jurisdiction, Applicable Law, Recognition, Enforcement and Co-operation in Respect of Parental Responsibility and Measures for the Protection of Children' (2024), available at www.hcch.net/en/instruments/conventions/status-table/?cid=70 (accessed 10 December 2024).

[86] HCCH, 'Status Table: Convention of 23 November 2007 on the International Recovery of Child Support and Other Forms of Family Maintenance' (2024), available at www.hcch.net/en/instruments/conventions/status-table/?cid=131 (accessed 10 December 2024).

[87] HCCH, 'Status Table: Protocol of 23 November 2007 on the Law Applicable to Maintenance Obligations' (2022), available at www.hcch.net/en/instruments/conventions/status-table/?cid=133 (accessed 10 December 2024).

[88] H Loo, 'In the Child's Best Interests: Examining International Child Abduction, Adoption, and Asylum' (2016) 17 *Chicago Journal of International Law* 609; M Leto, 'Whose Best Interest? International Child Abduction Under the Hague Convention' (2002) 3 *Chicago Journal of International Law* 247; S Parker, 'The Best Interests of the Child – Principles and Problems' (1994) 8 *International Journal of Law, Policy and the Family* 26; Jolly and Khanderia, (n 82) 153.

[89] 'Adoption Scammer Gets 18 Months in Jail' *ABC News*, 8 January 2006, available at abcnews.go.com/WNT/story?id=267559&page=1; AB Goldberg and D Apton, 'U.S. Families Learn Truth About Adopted Cambodian Children' *ABC News*, 12 January 2007, available at abcnews.go.com/2020/International/story?id=611826&page=1 (accessed 10 December 2024).

[90] Cambodia ratified the Convention in 2007: www.hcch.net/en/instruments/conventions/status-table/?cid=69 (accessed 10 December 2024).

Cambodia to PIL issues on children's affairs. This section discusses how the judges might handle child-related PIL disputes, overcoming the deficiencies of applicable legal norms in Cambodian law.

i. Parental Responsibility

The CC and the Marriage and Family Law do not have clear rules to determine the applicable law of parental responsibility. Accordingly, Cambodian judges might find the PIL of Japan useful for filling the gap in Cambodian law, as Japan has the Act on the Law Governing Duty to Support,[91] which builds upon the 1973 Hague Maintenance Convention. The Act decides the governing laws of obligations arising from family relationships, including parentage.[92] It therefore may provide Cambodian judges with guidance for designating the law applicable to parental responsibility. According to Article 2(1) of the Act, the duty to support (i.e., maintenance obligation) is governed by the law of the habitual residence of the support obligee. If the support obligee is unable to receive any support from the support obligor under the law of his or her habitual residence, the duty is governed by the common national law of the support obligee and obligor. If either the law of the obligee's habitual residence or the common national law of the obligee and obligor do not admit the obligee to be granted maintenance from the obligor, Japanese law will govern the maintenance obligation.[93] Hence, the Act intends to apply the law that is most likely to require the parent to offer support to the child. It confers the law of the child's habitual residence priority in choosing the law applicable to parental responsibility, giving the common national law of the child and parent and Japanese law (i.e., the law of the forum) second and third priorities, respectively.

Such PIL norms in the Act on the Law Governing Duty to Support are compatible with the Cambodian legal system that emphasises the protection of children's rights.[94] According to Torii, justifications for the 1973 Hague Maintenance Convention (and the Act on the Law Governing Duty to Support) to prioritise the law of the child's habitual residence are that: (1) the maintenance of a child is closely connected to the economic and social situation of the place where the child resides; and (2) the application of the law of the child's habitual residence may help to offer the child support that accords with the system of public welfare provided in the place.[95] The prioritisation of the child's habitual residence and its justifications have also been maintained in other Hague Conventions.[96] In the author's opinion, Cambodian judges probably have no solid basis for rejecting the choice of law scheme for child protection adopted by the Act and 1973 Hague Maintenance Convention for the following reasons:

(1) Article 7 of the 1989 Convention on the Rights of the Child provides that the child shall have the right to be cared for by his or her parents among other rights, and that '*States Parties shall ensure the implementation of these rights in accordance with their national*

[91] (Act No 84 of 12 June 1986), www.japaneselawtranslation.go.jp/en/laws/view/3919/en (accessed 10 December 2024).

[92] Act on the Law Governing Duty to Support, Art 1.

[93] ibid, Art 2(2).

[94] See section II.C above.

[95] J Torii, 'The Response of Hague Child Protection Conventions to the Globalisation of Family Life [in Japanese]' (2011) 607 *International Issues* 1, 2.

[96] ibid 1–4.

law'.[97] Certainly, Cambodian private law contains no PIL rules on parental responsibility. However, as the law is based on Japanese civil law, importing Japanese PIL principles to fill the legal vacuum is likely to be a reasonable option for Cambodian judges.[98] The judges may therefore elect to apply the law of the child's habitual residence in choosing the law applicable to parental responsibility, as practised under Japanese law.

(2) The fact that the international instruments of the HCCH have adopted the approach in general[99] may further underpin the option to apply the law of the child's habitual residence because the 1989 Convention obliges Member States to ensure the implementation of parental responsibility in accordance with relevant international instruments.[100]

ii. Guardianship and Custody

As in the case of parental responsibility, Cambodian judges dealing with choice of law issues on guardianship and custody may rely on Japanese PIL due to the lack of noticeable rules on such matters in Cambodian private law. The AGRAL has a few provisions regulating choice of law concerning guardianship. Article 35(1) provides that 'Guardianship, curatorship or assistance … is governed by the national law of a ward, person under curatorship or person under assistance'. Further, Article 35(2) exceptionally recognises the court's ability to apply Japanese law in ruling the guardianship, curatorship or assistance of foreign nationals in the following circumstances:

> (i) where the grounds for commencement of [g]uardianship, [curatorship or assistance] of the foreign national exist under their national law, and there is no person to conduct the affairs of [g]uardianship, [curatorship or assistance] in Japan; or
>
> (ii) where a [r]uling for [c]ommencement of [g]uardianship, [curatorship or assistance] of the foreign national is made in Japan.

The aim of Article 35 is to decide the law applicable to the commencement of guardianship and the effect of guardianship, among others.[101] When deciding the governing laws of these issues, Cambodian judges will likely find the Article as a useful reference point.

iii. Legitimacy and Legitimation

Cambodian judges might not be familiar with legitimacy and legitimation because the family law of Cambodia does not have rules that refer to such legal concepts. In fact, the CC does not use the phrase 'illegitimate child' in its texts.[102] Nor does it establish any distinction between 'legitimate child' and 'illegitimate child' even in the context of succession.[103] Should the judges nevertheless face legitimacy issues concerning international family law, they may gain insights from the AGRAL. The AGRAL states that a child becomes a legitimate child

[97] Emphasis added.
[98] Menzel (n 25).
[99] Torii (n 95) 1–4.
[100] 1989 Convention on the Rights of the Child, Art 7(2).
[101] Koide (n 66) 335.
[102] World Intelligence Partners Co Ltd (n 19) 16.
[103] ibid.

when he or she has been legitimated under the national law of his or her father or mother, or of him or herself, at the time that the facts constituting the requirements for legitimation under the law were established.[104] Because some countries treat illegitimate children differently from legitimate ones on various occasions,[105] Cambodian judges and legal practitioners might find the lacuna in Cambodian PIL inconvenient.

iv. Adoption

Cambodia is a party to the 1993 Hague Adoption Convention. Its Government is therefore required to ensure that intercountry adoptions take place in the best interests of the child and protects his or her fundamental rights.[106] The Convention defines intercountry adoption as adoption to create a permanent parent–child relationship that involves the movement of a child from his or her habitual residence in a contracting state of the Convention ('the state of origin') to another contracting state ('the receiving state').[107] Spouses or persons habitually resident in the receiving state may undertake such cross-border adoptions.[108] Also, the Convention sets out in Article 4 requirements for intercountry adoptions, conferring the competent authority of the state of origin the substantial power to determine the feasibility of intercountry adoptions. The Article requires the authority – the Ministry of Social Affairs, Veterans and Youth Rehabilitation (MOSVY), in the case of Cambodia[109] – to carefully discern the possibilities for the intra-country adoption of the child before endorsing the child's intercountry adoption for his or her best interests. Hence, the Convention perceives intercountry adoptions as secondary options, giving priority to intra-country adoptions.[110]

To align Cambodian law with the requirements and principles of the 1993 Hague Adoption Convention, the National Assembly of the Kingdom approved the Law on Intercountry Adoption in 2009.[111] The Law governs the intercountry adoption by a foreign

[104] AGRAL, Art 30(1). See also Art 30(2) stating that if a person (i.e., the mother, father or child) under Art 30(1) 'has died before the facts constituting the requirements for legitimation are completed, the person's national law at the time of this person's death is deemed to be the person's national law'.

[105] V Vatsa, 'Rights of an Illegitimate Child' *Jus Corpus Law Journal* (24 June 2021), available at www.juscorpus.com/rights-of-an-illegitimate-child (accessed 10 December 2024).

[106] 1993 Hague Adoption Convention, Art 1(a).

[107] ibid, Art 2.

[108] ibid.

[109] HCCH, 'Country Profile 1993 Hague Intercountry Adoption Convention: State of Origin (the Kingdom of Cambodia)' (2021), available at assets.hcch.net/docs/cb910351-cb41-4832-8a9a-8fbd8e680122.pdf (noting that the Kingdom also has concluded bilateral agreements on intercountry adoptions with Italy, Spain (Catalonia) and Malta (accessed 10 December 2024)).

[110] This approach is called for by the HCCH recommending the Subsidiarity Principle that treats intercountry adoption as a last resort: G Parra-Aranguren, 'Explanatory Report on the Convention on Protection of Children and Co-Operation in Respect of Intercountry Adoption' (1994), para 108, available at assets.hcch.net/upload/expl33e.pdf (accessed 10 December 2024); HCCH, *The Implementation and Operation of the 1993 Hague Intercountry Adoption Convention: Guide to Good Practice* (Bristol, Family Law, 2008) 29. See also S-V Brakman, 'The Principle of Subsidiarity in the Hague Convention on Intercountry Adoption: A Philosophical Analysis' (2019) 33 *Ethics & International Affairs* 207.

[111] Cambodian League for the Promotion and Defense of Human Rights (LICADHO), 'Cambodia's Stolen Children: Fraud and Corruption in the Inter-country Adoption System' (2018) 6, available at www.licadho-cambodia.org/reports/files/226LICADHOAdoptionReport30March2018_ENG.pdf (accessed 10 December 2024).

married couple of a Cambodian child who has permanent residence in Cambodia.[112] It lists detailed conditions for the intercountry adoption.[113]

For example, the Law provides that a child shall meet the following conditions to be an adoptable one:

(1) having Cambodian nationality and permanent residence in Cambodia;[114]
(2) being less than eight years old at the date of receipt of the application for adoption;[115]
(3) living in an orphanage or other appropriate placement supervised by the MOSVY;[116]
(4) being under guardianship or living in extreme poverty under the custody of the child's parent(s);[117] and
(5) having been declared by the MOSVY eligible for intercountry adoption after all its reasonable efforts to return the child to his or her birth family and, if this is not plausible, all reasonable efforts to place the child for domestic adoption within Cambodia.[118]

On eligibility for becoming adoptive parents, the Law sets out many requirements as follows:

(1) in the case of adoptive parents who are married, the couple must be 30 years old or above and 22–45 years older than the adopted child on the date of the submission of the adoption application;[119]
(2) if an adopter does not satisfy the first condition, and if the intercountry adoption nevertheless fulfils the best interests of the child, he or she may still undertake the adoption, provided that: (a) the adopter is of Cambodian origin and seeks to adopt his or her relative; (b) the adopter seeks to adopt the child of his or her spouse; or (c) the adopter seeks to adopt a child who needs special care or who is in special circumstances, and the adoption serves the best interests of the child;[120]
(3) if the adopter is married, he or she shall adopt the child jointly with his or her spouse, unless he or she intends to adopt the biological child of his or her spouse;[121]
(4) the national law of the adopter and the law of his or her permanent residency recognise and permit full adoption;[122]
(5) the adopter's country of nationality or permanent residence has diplomatic relations with Cambodia;[123]
(6) the adopter satisfies the eligibility and essential conditions for adoption under the laws of his or her permanent residency;[124]

[112] Law on Inter-country Adoption, Art 3.

[113] The Law also provides in Art 5 the general principles of inter-country adoption that are in line with those in the 1993 Hague Adoption Convention.

[114] Law on Inter-country Adoption, Art 10(1).

[115] ibid, Art 10(2) (noting that the adoption of a child who needs special care may be authorised at an age below 18 years old. According to Art 4, such a child refers to 'a child who has a serious physical disability or mental disability, or who has a chronic illness').

[116] ibid, Art 10(3).

[117] ibid, Art 10(4).

[118] ibid, Arts 10(5) and 13.

[119] ibid, Art 21(1).

[120] ibid, Art 21(2).

[121] ibid, Art 21(3).

[122] ibid, Art 21(4).

[123] ibid, Art 21(5).

[124] ibid, Art 21(6).

(7) the adopter is not subject to any criminal prosecution or penalty for a felony or misdemeanour at the court in his or her country of nationality, permanent residence or last residence;[125]
(8) the adopter has the capacity to provide the adopted child with appropriate care and needed support;[126] and
(9) the adopter has no more than one child and applies to adopt one child only. However, if the adopter intends to adopt a child who has siblings, he or she may be authorised to adopt the siblings, too.[127]

When a couple (or a parent) who intend to adopt a Cambodian child file an application to the MOSVY,[128] the Inter-country Adoption Administration (ICAA) attached to the MOSVY[129] will review the application and discern whether the couple have satisfied the requirements for being adoptive parents.[130] If the ICAA finds that the application is complete and the couple are qualified to be adoptive parents under the law, it shall examine the list of Cambodian children who are eligible for intercountry adoption, to match the adopters with the child who has the best suitable profile.[131] In doing so, the ICAA takes into account the best interests of the child, including the continuity of the child's upbringing and his or her social, ethnic, religious and cultural background.[132] If the adopters agree to accept the matching,[133] and if the ICAA finds that the criteria and conditions for intercountry adoption have been satisfied by the adopters and the adoptable child, the ICAA shall forward the application to the minister of the MOSVY for his or her examination and recommendation on the adoption.[134] Upon the receipt of the recommendation, the adopters shall file a petition via the ICAA for the adoption to the Court of First Instance in Phnom Penh.[135] The Court then examines whether the adoption is in compliance with the Law on Inter-country Adoption and other requirements before issuing its writ of decision.[136] Once the writ has been finalised, the intercountry adoption creates a permanent parent–child relationship, providing the adopted child with the same status, rights and obligations as the adopters' biological children.[137] Any other effect of the intercountry adoption shall be governed by the adopters' common national law or, if the adopters have no such law, the law of their permanent residence.[138]

However, the Cambodian civil law has no rules that regulate conflict of laws pertaining to a national adoption involving foreign elements. Such an intra-country adoption may occur when an expatriate couple permanently living in Cambodia intend to adopt a Cambodian

[125] ibid, Art 21(7).
[126] ibid, Art 21(8).
[127] ibid, Art 21(9). The Law also sets out in Arts 14–20 the requirements for consent to adoption.
[128] Requirements for the application are provided in Art 23ff of the Law on Inter-country Adoption.
[129] ibid, Art 8.
[130] ibid, Arts 26–27.
[131] ibid, Art 27.
[132] ibid.
[133] ibid, Art 29.
[134] ibid, Art 32.
[135] ibid, Art 33.
[136] ibid, Arts 37 and 39.
[137] ibid, Art 41.
[138] ibid, Art 42.

infant whose habitual residence is also in the Kingdom.[139] Cambodian lawyers might therefore find Article 31(1) of the AGRAL useful as a reference point. It provides that:

> Adoption is governed by the national law of an adoptive parent at the time of the adoption. … [I]f obtaining the acceptance or consent from the person to be adopted or a third party, or obtaining permission or any other disposition from a public authority is required for adoption under the national law of the person to be adopted, that requirement [must] also [be] satisfied.

In other words, Article 31(1) requires the court to cumulatively apply the law of the parent and that of the child (albeit partially) in examining the validity of the adoption. The governing laws designated by this provision are also applicable to the dissolution of adoptive relations and the termination of relationships between the adopted child and his or her kin.[140] They also apply to formal requirements of adoption, but notwithstanding that, the court may require that the formalities comply with the law of the place where the adoption takes place.[141] Thus, the courts in Cambodia may apply Cambodian law to discern the formal validity of the adoption.

v. Child Surrogacy

Some Cambodian judges might be reluctant to handle PIL issues on child surrogacy because the latter is effectively illegal under the current legal system of Cambodia.[142] In October 2016, the Ministry of Health (MOH) of Cambodia issued a ministry directive (i.e., *prakas*) that states in Article 12 that 'Surrogacy, one of a set of services to have a baby by Assisted Reproductive Technology, is banned completely'.[143] This global statement quickly altered the status of surrogacy services from legal (or at least non-illegal as there were no laws prohibiting practice) to dubious legal ground.[144] Within a month of the issuance of the directive, an Australian lady running a surrogacy clinic and two Cambodian associates were arrested and charged with human trafficking offences and other grounds.[145] Surrogate mothers – typically poor Cambodian women – also faced difficult circumstances. They were required to choose between forced motherhood for their surrogate children or years

[139] See, e.g., BNG Legal, 'Can Expats Adopt Cambodian Children? Dispelling the Myths' *Cambodian Law Blog: Legal updates from the Kingdom of Wonder*, 9 June 2011, available at cambodianlaw.wordpress.com/2011/06/09/can-expats-adopt-cambodian-children-dispelling-the-myths (accessed 10 December 2024).

[140] AGRAL, Art 31(2).

[141] ibid, Art 34(2).

[142] Y Sineat and D Keeton-Olsen, 'A Surrogate Family and the Law That Criminalized Them' *VOD*, 2 November 2020, available at vodenglish.news/a-surrogate-family-and-the-law-that-criminalized-them (accessed 9 February 2025).

[143] E Handley, 'Surrogacy Ban Lacks Force of Law' *The Phnom Penh Post*, 4 November 2016, available at www.phnompenhpost.com/national/surrogacy-ban-lacks-force-law (accessed 9 February 2025).

[144] At first, some legal experts claimed that the legal status of the directive was discrete, lacking endorsement by any specific laws: N Hyder-Rahman, 'Commercial Gestational Surrogacy: Unravelling the Threads between Reproductive Tourism and Child Trafficking' (2021) *Anti-Trafficking Review* 123, 125. See also Handley (n 143) (referring to a local legal expert Sok Sam Oeun, who commented that the prohibition of a certain action must be done by the law, not by *prakas*).

[145] A Barker, 'Australian Woman Charged with Running Illegal Surrogacy Clinic in Cambodia' *ABC News*, 21 November 2016, available at www.abc.net.au/news/2016-11-21/australian-woman-charged-over-illegal-surrogacy-clinic-cambodia/8042708 (accessed 10 December 2024). The Australian lady and her Cambodian associates were later found guilty and sent to prison: K Sovuthy, 'Australian Surrogacy Nurse Released From Jail' *Khmer Times*, 15 November 2018, available at www.khmertimeskh.com/550676/australian-surrogacy-nurse-released-from-jail (accessed 10 December 2024).

in prison for human trafficking.[146] The directive therefore effectively prohibited most forms of involvement in commercial surrogacy.

Despite the criminalisation, the Cambodian judiciary may well need to develop PIL rules on international child surrogacy. First, the UN Committee on Elimination of Discrimination against Women has urged Cambodia several times to repeal the 2016 *prakas* and has denounced the practice of releasing surrogate mothers from imprisonment only if they promise to raise the surrogate children on their own.[147] The Committee claimed that such practice created an additional financial obligation and emotional burden on women who had been forced to be surrogate mothers due to their vulnerability.[148] It further suggested that the criminalisation of surrogacy by the 2016 *prakas* led those vulnerable women to 'face discrimination and stigmatisation by their families and communities for having acted as surrogates'.[149] The Government of Cambodia did not respond to the recommendation favourably,[150] but its attitude might change over time. Second, banning commercial surrogacy will not by itself eradicate child surrogacy from Cambodia. For instance, a draft surrogacy law is expected to permit altruistic surrogacy in which the surrogate agrees not to receive monetary compensation.[151] Moreover, ever since the 2016 *prakas* was issued, commercial surrogacy has been practiced beyond the radar of the Cambodian police.[152] The Government is probably unable to crackdown on such illegal surrogacy completely as long as international demand for surrogate mothers exists, and a supply of financially pressured Cambodian women who opt to be surrogate mothers to earn a living continues.[153] Cambodian judges may therefore not fully avoid the possibility of facing PIL issues related to child surrogacy, such as the determination of applicable law to define cross-border relationships among a surrogate child, his or her

[146] E Handley, 'Cambodian Surrogates Face an Impossible Choice – Forced Motherhood, or Years in Prison' *ABC News*, 12 May 2019, available at www.abc.net.au/news/2019-05-12/cambodian-surrogates-forced-to-be-mothers-or-face-prison-time/11086640 (accessed 10 December 2024); H Beech, 'They Were Surrogates. Now They Must Raise the Children' *The New York Times*, 26 November 2022, available at https://www.nytimes.com/2022/11/26/world/asia/surrogacy-cambodia.html (10 December 2024).

[147] L Kijewski, 'UN Reiterates Call to Abolish Criminalization of Surrogates' *VOA News*, 14 November 2019, available at www.voacambodia.com/a/UN-reiterates-call-to-abolish-criminalization-of-surrogates/5164651.html (accessed 10 December 2024).

[148] UN Committee on the Elimination of Discrimination against Women, 'Concluding Observations on the 6th Periodic Report of Cambodia: Committee on the Elimination of Discrimination against Women (74th sess, 2019, Geneva)' (2019) 14, available at digitallibrary.un.org/record/3838743?ln=en#record-files-collapse-header (accessed 10 December 2024).

[149] ibid.

[150] Kijewski (n 147).

[151] K Meta, 'Kingdom Surrogacy Law Set to Lift Burden from "Victims"' *The Phnom Penh Post*, 19 January 2018, available at www.phnompenhpost.com/national/kingdom-surrogacy-law-set-lift-burden-victims (accessed 10 December 2024). The draft surrogacy law has long been overdue, and its text is not publicly available as of May 2023: M Lamy and V Sonyka, 'Surrogacy Law in the Kingdom Long Overdue' *Khmer Times*, 10 April 2020, available at www.khmertimeskh.com/711396/surrogacy-law-in-the-kingdom-long-overdue (accessed 10 December 2024); T Sokhavuth, 'Ministry to Review Draft Surrogacy Law with Legal Experts' *Khmer Times*, 11 April 2022, available at www.khmertimeskh.com/501056334/ministry-to-review-draft-surrogacy-law-with-legal-experts/ (accessed 10 December 2024).

[152] K Sarom, 'Chinese Surrogacy Father has Appeal Heard in Court' *The Phnom Penh Post*, 10 January 2020, available at www.phnompenhpost.com/national/chinese-surrogacy-father-has-appeal-heard-court (accessed 10 December 2024); BR Kongkea, '14 People Jailed for Involvement in Surrogacy and Human Trafficking' *Khmer Times*, 30 July 2020, available at www.khmertimeskh.com/50750358/14-people-jailed-for-involvement-in-surrogacy-and-human-trafficking (accessed 10 December 2024).

[153] RM Soco, 'Many Cambodian Women Still Victims of Poverty' *Khmer Times*, 3 March 2021, available at www.khmertimeskh.com/50819981/many-cambodian-women-still-victims-of-poverty/ (accessed 10 December 2024); ASEAN Secretariat and UN Women Regional Office for Asia and the Pacific, 'ASEAN Gender Outlook: Achieving the SDGs for All and Leaving No Woman or Girl Behind' (2021), available at data.unwomen.org/sites/default/files/documents/Publications/ASEAN/ASEAN%20Gender%20Outlook_final.pdf (accessed 10 December 2024).

surrogate mother and his or her biological mother. Unfortunately, Japanese law also lacks clear PIL rules on international child surrogacy.[154]

vi. Wrongful Removal of Children (Child Abduction)

There is a paucity of rules governing parental abduction in Cambodia. Parental abduction is not directly referred to in any legislation,[155] and Cambodia has yet to ratify the 1980 Hague Abduction Convention as of February 2025. Nonetheless, the general view among Cambodian citizens is that parental abduction does not constitute a criminal offence.[156] This is despite the fact that Cambodian law does not recognise divorced parents as having equal rights over the custody of their children.[157] The law requires such parents to have mutual consultation to decide who is to become the parental authority holder of their minor child.[158] If the consultation fails, the court will designate the parental authority holder, taking into account the interests of the child.[159]

The parental authority holder will have the right and duty to maintain the custody of the minor child and manage his or her property.[160] In contrast, the non-parental authority holder will merely obtain the right to meet and socialise with the child, although he or she owes the obligation to share the costs of caring the child with the parental authority holder.[161] Such imbalance between the parental authority holder and non-holder may exacerbate tensions between divorced parents and may trigger attempts at child abduction.[162] No outstanding number of international child abductions has been reported in Cambodia. However, there is a risk that this may change over time. Thus, the Government of the Kingdom should seriously start considering adoption of the Hague Abduction Convention.

Other types of child kidnapping and abduction are illegal under Cambodian law. For example, Article 327 of the Criminal Code 2009 prohibits 'taking away a minor from the person who has legal custody', imposing the offender imprisonment from one month to one year and a fine from 100,000 to 2,000,000 Riels (25–493 USD).[163] Furthermore, if the minor is kept outside the territory of Cambodia, the offender is to be punished with imprisonment from one year to three years and a fine from 2,000,000 to 6,000,000 Riels (493–1,479 USD). The Criminal Code therefore treats cross-border child abduction as a more serious offence than intra-country child kidnapping.

[154] See, e.g., T Minami, 'Issues Concerning Surrogacy Legislation: A Case Analysis of Australia [in Japanese]' (2018) 2 *Social Security Research* 578 (suggesting that Japan has no legislation regulating child surrogacy).

[155] International Centre for Missing & Exploited Children, 'Global Missing Children Research Initiative: Country-Specific Findings (Cambodia)' (2016), available at www.icmec.org/wp-content/uploads/2017/05/Cambodia-July-2016.pdf (accessed 10 December 2024).

[156] ibid.

[157] D van der Keur, 'Legal and Gender Issues of Marriage and Divorce in Cambodia' (2014) 3 *Cambodia Law and Policy Journal* 1 (noting that '[t]here is no option for joint custody after divorce in Cambodia').

[158] CC, Art 1037(1).

[159] ibid, Art 1037(3).

[160] ibid, Art 1034.

[161] ibid, Art 1040(1). Moreover, the non-parental authority holder may request the parental authority holder to report him/her the condition of the child: CC, Art 1041(1).

[162] J Chiancone, 'Parental Abduction: A Review of the Literature', available at www.ojp.gov/pdffiles1/ojjdp/190074.pdf (accessed 10 December 2024). However, international child abduction may take place without any explicit sign of conflict between the parents over the custody of the child: MA Kucinski, 'Creating a Successful Structure to Mediate International Parental Child Abduction Cases' (2012) 26 *American Journal of Family Law* 81.

[163] ngocedaw.org/wp-content/uploads/2015/05/Criminal_Code_EN-KH_Jan_2014.pdf (accessed 10 May 2025).

III. Conclusions

The Cambodian legal system contains rules on choice of law and recognition that regulate PIL issues on international family law partially and somewhat disproportionally. For example, the Marriage and Family Law contains a handful of PIL rules governing choice of law in marriage and matrimonial causes. However, it falls short of norms dealing with conflict of laws pertaining to the presumption of death. Cambodian law has left several child-related choice of law matters untouched. As discussed in section II.C, the Marriage and Family Law, the CC and other statutory norms do not provide explicit conflict of law rules on parental responsibility, guardianship, legitimacy and child abduction. In addition, there are no statutory texts on choice of law rules for child surrogacy, probably because commercial surrogacy is illegal under Cambodian law. Indeed, the 1993 Hague Adoption Convention and the Law on Inter-country Adoption govern various dimensions of international child adoption, including PIL aspects. Nonetheless, no rules guide how Cambodian judges shall decide issues on choice of law in the context of intra-country child adoption involving foreign elements. There are therefore salient legal vacuums in the field of choice of law, especially in child-related matters, in the international family law of Cambodia.

A straightforward option to fill the legal vacuum would be to establish specific legislation on choice of law.[164] It is also possible to address the ambiguity in Cambodian law by referring to Japan's AGRAL, as suggested by some commentators and as demonstrated elsewhere in this chapter.[165] However, the reference to Japan's choice of law principles may be no more than the second-best choice because not many legal experts are fully aware of Japanese legal influence in Cambodian law,[166] and because the Cambodian legal system is not the Japanese legal system in the end. Hence, Cambodian lawyers will ultimately have to decide on their set of choice of law norms to cover various conflict of laws issues in family law matters.

The new choice of law legislation may be based on Japan's AGRAL. Adopting an AGRAL model will hopefully improve legal consistency within Cambodian civil law.[167] Nonetheless, it will not be advisable for a wholesale transplant of the Japanese legal model into Cambodian PIL. The drafters of the new legislation should take into account other legal models, as in the cases of the drafting processes of the CC, CCP and other codes and laws.[168] Reviewing international legal instruments such as conventions and protocols prepared by the HCCH will also provide the drafters with international perspectives and insights on choice of law rules that reflect international trends of PIL, which will be useful to fill gaps in the current conflict of law rules of Cambodia.[169] In any event, promulgating a modern PIL legislation which covers transnational family affairs will advance legal certainty and transparency in the Kingdom, and enhance the welfare of children living in and outside the country.

[164] JICA (n 22) 9–11.

[165] Menzel (n 25) 490–91. See also section II.C above.

[166] Teramura 'Japan as a Source of Legal Ideas' (n 14) 27; C Forsaith, 'Cambodia' in L Malintoppi and C Tan (eds), *Investment Protection in Southeast Asia: A Country-by-Country Guide on Arbitration Laws and Bilateral Investment Treaties* (Leiden, Brill, 2016) 73.

[167] Menzel (n 25) 490–91.

[168] Teramura 'Japan as a Source of Legal Ideas' (n 14) 27.

[169] As discussed elsewhere in this chapter, Cambodian jurists appear to be reluctant to discuss the Kingdom's potential to adopt HCCH's instruments and doctrines. The 1993 Hague Adoption Convention is probably exceptional because the ratification by Cambodia of the Convention resulted from international attention to the Cambodian practice of intercountry child adoption.

9

Law of Corporations, Insolvency, Antitrust and Unfair Competition

I. Introduction

In an increasingly mobile and interconnected world, cross-border corporate activities and transnational company law issues related to such activities keep increasing. Accordingly, this chapter considers Cambodia's choice of law rules for questions of corporate affairs, corporate insolvency and competition. Legal questions that are 'external' to the management and structure of corporations – relationships with third parties – are out of the reach of this chapter, apart from those related to corporate insolvency and competition. The reason for this is that, since incorporation confers a company with the status of a legal person, a corporation's relationships with external third parties are governed by the same terms as any natural person's relationships with third parties, in accordance with the choice of law rules on contracts, torts and properties that are set out in Chapters 5, 6 and 7 respectively. In principle, the questions of corporate affairs dealt with in this chapter are those that are 'internal' to the corporation – its capacities, powers, the rights and obligations of its members and the authority, liability and duties of its officers (including aspects related to its internal management and governance). Exceptionally, the chapter also considers corporate affairs involving external relationships, such as insolvency and liquidation (i.e., 'winding-up') of corporations and unfair competition.

These issues of conflict of law are becoming more important for Cambodia. For instance, foreign direct investment (FDI) into the country has increased enormously since the conclusion of the Paris Peace Agreements in 1991. Between 1992 and 2023, the FDI net inflows into Cambodia saw a hundredfold growth from USD 0.033 to 3.96 billion,[1] while experiencing temporal slumps triggered by the COVID-19 pandemic.[2] The strong FDI growth in Cambodia is probably thanks to the government's structural reform in transiting from a centrally oriented economy to a market economy and its active promotion among foreign companies of investment into Cambodia.[3] Despite the country's poor performance in the

[1] World Bank, 'Foreign Direct Investment, Net Inflows (BoP, Current US$) – Cambodia' (2024), available at https://data.worldbank.org/indicator/BX.KLT.DINV.CD.WD?locations=KH (accessed 10 December 2024).

[2] P Jha, 'FDI Flow in Cambodia Steady, but for Corona Bump', *Khmer Times*, 25 October 2022, available at www.khmertimeskh.com/501173025/fdi-flow-in-cambodia-steady-but-for-corona-bump/ (accessed 10 December 2024).

[3] For example, see Article 1 of the Law on Investment (Effective 15 October 2021), stating that '[t]his Law aims to establish an open, transparent, predictable and favourable legal framework to attract and promote quality, effective and efficient investments by Cambodian nationals or foreigners for socio-economic development in the Kingdom of Cambodia'.

World Bank's Ease of Doing Business Rankings,[4] it maintains a liberal investment regime for foreign investors, which permits the full ownership by foreign individuals or companies of a corporate shareholding,[5] allows foreign investors to transfer their profits to overseas without strict restrictions,[6] and treats foreign and domestic investors equally in any industry sectors.[7] Thanks to these advantages, foreign business investment can be found in several key sectors across the country, especially the garment sector in special economic zones.[8] Moreover, the economic turbulence brought about by the COVID-19 pandemic prompted Cambodian jurists to reassess the desirability of Cambodian insolvency and restructuring frameworks that had rarely been used by companies in financial distress.[9] In addition, the Law on Competition was promulgated and came into force in 2021, which ignited a public debate on the guarantee of fair competition between domestic and foreign businesses in the country.[10]

Given the current landscape, it is striking that no literature has yet examined how domestic and foreign laws apply to the complex realm of corporate affairs with foreign elements under Cambodian private international law (PIL). Equally significant is the fact that certain areas of Cambodian PIL pertaining to corporate affairs are still in need of development, leading to substantial legal vacuums. This chapter aims to provide a comprehensive analysis that fills these crucial gaps, referring to relevant discussions on conflict of law rules under Japanese law where applicable, especially discussions on the Act on General Rules for Application of Laws (AGRAL),[11] as recommended by Menzel and suggested elsewhere in this volume.[12] Section II considers Cambodian choice of law rules on internal

[4] Cambodia was ranked 144th among 190 countries in the 2020 Ease of Doing Business Rankings, followed only by Laos (154th), Myanmar (165th) and Timor-Leste (181st) in Southeast Asia: World Bank, 'Ease of Doing Business Rankings' (2020), available at https://archive.doingbusiness.org/en/rankings?region=east-asia-and-pacific (accessed 10 December 2024). On how the World Bank utilised the Rankings to implement its policy and legislative proposals in the governments of transition economies, see N Teramura, 'JICA's Legal Technical Assistance Projects in Vietnam, Cambodia and Laos since the 1990s' in LC Kelly and G Sasges (eds), *Vietnam Over the Long Twentieth Century* (Singapore, Springer, 2024) 198–99.

[5] S Siphana, 'Legal Framework for Doing Business' (n.d.) 1, available at https://mfaic.gov.kh/files/uploads/PDFDoingBussinessForCambodia/2_Legal_Framework_for_Doing_B.pdf (accessed 10 December 2024).

[6] US Department of Commerce, 'Cambodia Country Commercial Guide: Cambodia – Foreign Exchange Controls' (n.d.), available at www.privacyshield.gov/ps/article?id=Cambodia-foreign-exchange-controls#:~:text=Cambodia%20%2D%20Foreign%20Exchange%20ControlsCambodia%20%2D%20Foreign%20Exchange%20Controls&text=Under%20the%201997%20Foreign%20Exchange,all%20types%20of%20international%20settlements (accessed 10 December 2024).

[7] See Law on Investment, Art 15.

[8] SM Thangavelu and others, 'Investment Facilitation and Promotion in Cambodia: Impact of Provincial-level Characteristics on Multinational Activities' (2023) *ERIA Discussion Paper Series*.

[9] L Tayseng, 'Bankruptcy Law: Role, Inefficiencies and Social Drama', *The Phnom Penh Post*, 25 May 2020, available at www.phnompenhpost.com/opinion/bankruptcy-law-role-inefficiencies-and-social-drama; H Haider, 'GFX Filing for Insolvency?', *Khmer Times*, 16 July 2021, available at www.khmertimeskh.com/50894896/gfx-filing-for-insolvency/ (accessed 10 December 2024). See also A Gurrea-Martínez, 'The Future of Insolvency Law in a Post-Pandemic World' (2022) 31 *International Insolvency Review* 385.

[10] S Ravindran, 'Competition Law Framework Grew Steadily in Last Two Years', *Khmer Times*, 10 July 2023, available at www.khmertimeskh.com/501321303/competition-law-framework-grew-steadily-in-last-two-years/ (accessed 10 December 2024); V Prum, 'Competition Law Up for Love', *The Phnom Penh Post*, 18 October 2021, available at www.phnompenhpost.com/opinion/competition-law-love (accessed 10 December 2024).

[11] (Act No 78 of 2006).

[12] J Menzel, 'Cambodian Law: Some Comparative and International Perspectives' in H Peng, K Phallack and J Menzel (eds), *Introduction to Cambodian Law* (Phnom Penh, Konrad-Adenauer-Stiftung Cambodia, 2012) 490–91. See also Chapters 2, 5, 6 and 7 in this volume.

corporate affairs, examining whether Cambodian PIL is amenable to the incorporation theory that suggests the company law applicable to a corporate entity is that of the entity's place of incorporation or registration. Section III delves into choice of law rules on corporate insolvency and conflict of laws questions on cross-border insolvency. Section IV provides a Cambodian perspective on choice of laws issues in antitrust and unfair competition law. Section V concludes.

II. Corporations and Other Entities

The choice of law rules for questions for company law may differ depending on whether Cambodia follows the real seat theory or the incorporation theory to determine the *lex societatis* – the law regulating the internal affairs of a company. The real seat theory, which was developed in Belgium and France in the 19th century, suggests that '[a] company's legal status follows the place where the fundamental decisions of the company's management are actually executed into management acts'.[13] Following the objective proper law test, the real seat theory seeks to identify the law to which the company is deemed to be most closely connected. Thus, this theory relies on a company's real seat (i.e., real place of management or control centre) as the connecting factor to decide the legal status of that company, presupposing that the company has been incorporated at its real seat. Accordingly, the company's existence is admitted only if it has its real seat in the state under whose law it has been incorporated. In other words, it does not recognise a company's existence if it has been incorporated under a law other than that of its real seat.[14] In contrast, the incorporation theory developed in England in the 19th century[15] states that 'the legal status of a company is defined by the company law of the state under whose jurisdiction it was founded'.[16] This theory regards the company's statutory seat (or place of registration) as the decisive connecting factor as it is generally connected to the place of incorporation. The theory is in line with the doctrine of party autonomy in that it enables the company's founders and shareholders to choose the company's law by selecting the place of incorporation.

It is evident that Cambodia follows the incorporation theory because its company law recognises the incorporation of foreign companies and bodies outside Cambodia, even if the company operates in the country. Article 1 of the Law on Commercial Enterprises – the law governing company incorporation and registration in Cambodia[17] – defines its scope of application as partnerships and companies carrying on businesses in Cambodia. Such

[13] M-P Weller and C Thomale, 'Companies' in J Basedow and others (eds), *Encyclopedia of Private International Law* (Cheltenham, Edward Elgar Publishing, 2017) 405.

[14] It is highly unlikely that a failed incorporation under the law of the place of incorporation is turned into a valid incorporation under the law of the real seat because it is impossible to recognise the incorporation of a company that does not exist.

[15] H Eidenmüller, 'Shell Shock: In Defence of the 'Real Seat Theory' in International Company Law', *Oxford Business Blog*, 25 March 2022, available at https://blogs.law.ox.ac.uk/business-law-blog/blog/2022/03/shell-shock-defence-real-seat-theory-international-company-law (accessed 10 December 2024).

[16] Weller and Thomale (n 13) 405.

[17] This Law regulates most corporate governance issues, including corporate form, governing bodies, transactions with related parties and basic shareholder rights: OECD, *Corporate Governance Frameworks in Cambodia, Lao PDR, Myanmar and Viet Nam* (Paris, OECD, 2019).

partnerships and companies include a foreign business, which the law defines as '*a legal person formed under the laws of a foreign country* having a place of business in and doing business in the Kingdom of Cambodia'.[18] Subject to the laws and jurisdictions of the courts in Cambodia,[19] such a foreign legal person may conduct business in the country through its commercial representative or relations office, branch or subsidiary.[20] The Law sets out the rules on the authority and management of the representative office and branch.[21] It also provides the rules on the incorporation and registration by a foreign company of its subsidiary in Cambodia, whose legal personality is deemed to be separate from the foreign company's personality.[22] The fact that the Law does not have any provisions on the internal corporate affairs of the foreign company may imply Cambodia's support for the incorporation theory in that the purpose of excluding such rules is to leave the matter to be regulated by the law of the place of incorporation.[23] Moreover, Article 48 of the Civil Code defines the foreign juristic persons under the Code as 'juristic persons incorporated under foreign law', also following the incorporation theory. These legislative decisions are likely to be advantageous for the Cambodian judiciary because they can ascertain a company's capacity relatively easily by looking at the law of the company's place of registration, which is normally resistant to change or manipulation.[24] However, the incorporation doctrine can be abused by foreign shell companies – companies without active business operations – for tax evasion and money laundering, or to hide and shield assets from creditors or government agencies,[25] which is reportedly happening in Cambodia.[26]

A. The Validity of Incorporation

As the scope of the *lex societatis* covers all matters on a corporation from its incorporation to dissolution, the courts in Cambodia are required to determine the validity of a company's incorporation based on the law of the place where it was incorporated, in accordance with the incorporation doctrine. A potential legal issue is whether the courts in Cambodia

[18] Law on Commercial Enterprises, Art 270 (emphasis added).

[19] ibid, Art 273.

[20] ibid, Article 271.

[21] ibid, Arts 274–82.

[22] ibid, Arts 283–86.

[23] Japanese private international law does not have any explicit choice of law rules as to legal persons in either statutes or Supreme Court, but a majority of practitioners and commentators agree to follow the incorporation theory to fill that gap in Japanese private international law: T Kanzaki, 'Lex Societatis' in M Dogauchi and Y Nakanishi (eds), *Leading Cases in Private International Law* (Tokyo, Yuhikaku Publishing, 2021) 41; T Kono, 'Japan' in J Basedow and others (eds), *Encyclopedia of Private International Law* (Cheltenham, Edward Elgar Publishing, 2017) 2223; K Nishioka and Y Nishitani, *Japanese Private International Law* (Oxford, Hart Publishing, 2021) 103 (suggesting that the drafters of the AGRAL did not include provisions on legal persons in the AGRAL because academic discussion on the scope of the *lex societatis* was still underdeveloped, no clear rules for international company law were not yet developed in the EU or elsewhere, and the Japanese judiciary and legal practice had not experienced any outstanding difficulties without written conflict rules on the *lex societatis*).

[24] Y Sakurada, *Private International Law [in Japanese]*, 7th edn, (Tokyo, Yuhikaku Publishing, 2020) 85; Nishioka and Nishitani (n 23) 103.

[25] Eidenmüller (n 15).

[26] JA Davies, 'Red Flags Abound in Prince Group's Offshore Dealings', *Radio Free Asia*, 8 February 2024, available at www.rfa.org/english/news/cambodia/prince-group-investigation-02082024130529.html (accessed 10 December 2024).

recognise the validity of a company's incorporation abroad if the law of the place of incorporation is significantly different from that of Cambodia.

This issue does not appear to have caught much attention from Japanese jurists. However, it has been discussed by the English judiciary, which also follows the incorporation theory.[27] In *Bumper Development Corporation v Commissioner of Police of the Metropolis and Others*,[28] the English Court of Appeal recognised the legal personality of an Indian temple that Lord Justice Purchas described as 'little more than a pile of stone' despite the fact that English law's definition of corporations or the like is the 'personified groups or series of individuals'.[29] Invoking the comity of nations, the Appeal Court held that it is unreasonable for the Court to dismiss a claim by a foreign Catholic cathedral having legal personality where it is situated simply on the ground that English law would not recognise a similarly established entity as a legal person.[30] The Court then held that:

> Arguing from the example of a Roman Catholic cathedral and in the belief that no distinction between institutions of the Christian church and those of other major religions would now be generally acceptable, we cannot see that in the circumstances of this case there is any offence to English public policy in allowing a Hindu religious institution to sue in our courts for the recovery of property which it is entitled to recover by the law of its own country.[31]

Accordingly, the key factor for the Court to recognise the Hindu temple's legal personality was essentially international comity – the fact that the law of India recognised the temple as a legal person and the Court did not believe that recognition of such circumstance would be offensive to public policy.

In contrast, Cambodian law's stringent requirement of reciprocity in the recognition and enforcement of foreign judgments has limited (if any) bearing on choice of law.[32] This is because the strict reciprocity requirement may be perceived as Cambodian jurists' limited respect for foreign sovereigns and their legal systems. The fundamental theory of PIL developed by Friedrich Carl von Savigny and practiced in civil law countries like Cambodia (through Japan) does not entirely free choice of law from international comity.[33] Savigny's concept of choice of law is based on the law of nations and also an idea of comity, 'insofar as he expected cooperation among sovereign nations to form the basis of a functioning and effective conflicts system'.[34] But, as Dutta points out, the application of foreign law in the *Savigny* tradition is in principle rooted in the implementation of the best private interest of the individuals concerned, such as their autonomy and their expectation that the law most closely connected to them governs their legal relations through the mechanical application of choice of law rules.[35] Accordingly, the doctrine of comity has only a limited relevance on

[27] R Mortensen, R Garnett and M Keyes, *Private International Law in Australia*, 5th edn, (Chatswood, LexisNexis, 2023) 629.

[28] [1991] 1 WLR 1362.

[29] ibid 1371.

[30] ibid 1373.

[31] ibid.

[32] See Chapter 10 in this volume.

[33] TW Dornis, 'Comity' in Jürgen Basedow and others (eds), *Encyclopedia of Private International Law* (Cheltenham, Edward Elgar Publishing, 2017) 384.

[34] ibid.

[35] A Dutta, 'Reciprocity' in Jürgen Basedow and others (eds), *Encyclopedia of Private International Law* (Cheltenham, Edward Elgar Publishing, 2017) 1467. See also generally M Sonnentag, 'Savigny, Friedrich Carl

choice of law in Cambodia, unlike the position of common law demonstrated by the English Court of Appeal above.

Accordingly, without significantly relying on the doctrine of comity, Cambodian Law maintains a system whereby a foreign law whose conception of company is significantly divergent from Cambodian law may be recognised in Cambodia. The Law on Commercial Enterprises and relevant laws explicitly recognise the legal personalities of foreign corporations under Cambodian law,[36] posing limits on their activities by requiring them to register their business activities and to comply with the legal and judicial systems of Cambodia in doing such activities.[37] This is a balanced approach in compliance with Savigny's theory because, on the one hand, it respects the autonomy of company stakeholders to choose the law governing their entities' incorporation (and other internal matters), and, on the other hand, it values foreign companies' and their business partners' expectation that their business activities within the Kingdom are to be governed by the law that is most closely connected to those activities – the law of Cambodia.

Some Cambodian jurists might nevertheless argue that foreign incorporation should be recognised within the framework for recognising and enforcing foreign judgments instead of the method of choice of law. They might rely for this on Article 48(2) of the Civil Code. The latter provides that foreign juristic persons – except nation states, administrative divisions of nation states and commercial companies – shall not be recognised as juristic persons, unless otherwise provided by Cambodian law or a treaty. The Article corresponds to Article 36(1) of the Civil Code of Japan, which some Japanese commentators invoke as a basis for imposing the conditions of judgment recognition and enforcement – indirect jurisdiction, guarantee of due process before the court of origin and compliance with the public policy of Japan[38] – on the recognition of the legal personality of foreign commercial corporations under Japanese law.[39] They claim that Article 36(1) is a provision for recognising foreign incorporation as an act of another state along the lines of Article 118 of the Civil Procedure Code of Japan, which sets out the grounds for recognising and enforcing foreign judgments. However, importing this thesis into Cambodian PIL may bring more inefficiency than efficiency by creating cumbersome proceedings to recognise foreign incorporation. Suppose a court in Cambodia interprets Article 48(2) of the Civil Code in line with Article 199 of the Civil Procedure Code (which is based on Article 118 of the Civil Procedure Code of Japan). In that case, the parties will be able to request the court to refuse the recognition of foreign incorporation based on the reciprocity requirement under Article 199(d). Then, the recognition of foreign incorporation will become virtually impossible because the Cambodian courts have thus far never admitted the existence of reciprocity between Cambodian and any state other than Vietnam.[40]

von' in Jürgen Basedow and others (eds), *Encyclopedia of Private International Law* (Cheltenham, Edward Elgar Publishing, 2017).

[36] Law on Commercial Enterprises, Art 270.

[37] ibid, Arts 271, 283–86. In addition, only natural persons or legal entities of Cambodian nationality are entitled to own land in the Kingdom of Cambodia: Land Law 2001, Art 8, and Constitution of Cambodia, Art 44.

[38] See Civil Procedure Code of Japan, Art 118.

[39] Kanzaki (n 23) 41; D Yokomizo, 'Reflections on Legal Persons and Conflict of Laws: Lex Societatis or Recognition of Foreign Corporate Personality? [in Japanese]' (2007) 135 *Journal of Civil and Commercial Law* 1045, 1070ff.

[40] See Chapter 10 in this volume.

B. Capacity and Powers

Under the incorporation theory, a company's capacity and powers are subject to the law of its place of incorporation. Thus, if the law of the place of incorporation restricts the company's capacity to enter into contracts, the restrictions are likely to be maintained under Cambodian law. If there are no such restrictions, and that law confers the company all the powers of an individual with full legal capacity, the company should be able to enjoy the same powers in Cambodia. However, this thesis can be challenged by a traditional and prevailing view on Japan's AGRAL – an inspiration for the choice of law rules in Cambodia.[41] It suggests that Article 4 of the AGRAL on persons' capacity to act is, by analogy, applicable to determine legal persons' capacity.[42] Article 4(1) of the AGRAL states that a person's capacity to act is governed by his/her national law, and thus the application of this rule to a legal person by analogy merely confirms the role of the *lex societatis* in the incorporation theory. However, Article 4(2) of the AGRAL provides that '[n]otwithstanding the preceding paragraph, a person shall be deemed to have the capacity to act, when [s/he] has the capacity to act under the law of the place of the act and all the parties of the juristic act are located in the same jurisdiction at the time of the act, even if [s/he] is a person with limited capacity under his/her … national law'. Applying this rule by analogy to a foreign company will limit the scope of application of the company's *lex societatis* to protect a third party in Cambodia.

It is submitted that Cambodian jurists should not import this legal principle into Cambodian law. First, those who argue for the analogous application of Article 4(2) of the AGRAL to legal entities suggest that the foreign companies which have completed a registration to carry out continuous transactions in Japan are exempted from that analogous application as the registration mandates those companies to comply with Japanese law (i.e., the law of the place of the act) in any event.[43] However, foreign companies are unable to undertake any business in Cambodia (whether continuously or temporarily) without complying with the Law on Commercial Enterprises[44] and without entering into the commercial register as required by the Law on Commercial Rules and Commercial Register.[45] The third-party protection advocated by those commentators in Japan is therefore already ensured by Cambodian law. Second, not a few Japanese commentators criticise the analogous application of Article 4(2) of the AGRAL to foreign companies for its complex choice of law construct. They suggest that, for the protection of third parties, it will suffice to have recourse to the public policy ground under Article 42 of the AGRAL.[46] As discussed

[41] Menzel (n 12) 490–91.

[42] Nishioka and Nishitani (n 23) 104; Y Tameike, *Lecture on Private International Law [in Japanese]* (Tokyo, Yuhikaku Publishing, 2005) 299; R Yamada, *Lectures on Private International Law [in Japanese]*, 3rd edn, (Tokyo, Yuhikaku Publishing, 2004) 235; Sakurada (n 24) 184.

[43] Nishioka and Nishitani (n 23) 104. See also the Companies Act (Act No 86 of 26 July 2005) of Japan, Arts 817 and 818.

[44] Art 272 of the Law on Commercial Enterprises provides that: 'A foreign business shall be considered to be "doing business" if the foreign business performs any of the following acts in the Kingdom of Cambodia: (a) Rent office or any other space for manufacturing, or processing, or performing services for more than one month; (b) Employs any person to work for it for more than one month; (3) *Performs any other act that laws of the Kingdom of Cambodia authorised for foreign natural and legal persons*' (emphasis added). See also Art 273 of the Law on Commercial Enterprises.

[45] (amended in 2022). See, for example, Art 17.

[46] Nishioka and Nishitani (n 23) 104.

in Chapter 2 in this volume, it is debatable whether the public policy exception for choice of law is maintainable under Cambodian law. However, in any event, Cambodian jurists will not find that the doctrine in Article 4 of the AGRAL makes any significant differences for foreign companies and their business partners in Cambodia, thanks to the Law on Commercial Enterprises and the Law on Commercial Rules and Commercial Register.

C. Members' Rights and Liabilities

Following the incorporation theory, any questions about the rights and liabilities of a company's members are also determined by the law of the place of incorporation. However, complexities may arise where several laws of incorporation are involved in relation to members' rights and liabilities.[47] For instance, if a subsidiary company purchased shares of its parent company, and these companies had been established in different jurisdictions, the court would be required to determine whether the subsidiary company was allowed to buy such stocks. If this stock purchase is permitted, the court would have to consider, among other issues, whether the subsidiary company has a voting right at general shareholder meetings, and whether the parent company's auditor may investigate the subsidiary company. The law governing these corporate issues is likely to be chosen from the law of the subsidiary company's incorporation and that of the parent company's incorporation,[48] considering whether these issues are closely related to parent companies (and their shareholders and creditors) or subsidiary companies (and their shareholders and creditors).[49]

D. Internal Management

As per the incorporation theory, questions of a company's internal management are also referred to the law of its incorporation. These include, among other matters, the validity of the appointment of the company's officers, the power of the officers to act on behalf of the company, and the nature of the officers' duties to the company.[50] In some Commonwealth countries (for example, Australia), corporate officers' duties, especially directors' duties, have been regarded as questions for the *lex fori* because the nature of such duties is often considered fiduciary and 'the law of the cause in questions that arise in equitable jurisdiction is often the law of the forum'.[51] However, this is unlikely to be the case in civil law countries where equitable jurisdiction does not exist in the courts,[52] and where the distinction

[47] Kanzaki (n 23) 40–41.

[48] ibid 41.

[49] Y Nishitani, 'Rules on Juristic Persons and Foreign Persons [in Japanese]' in Y Sakurada and M Dogauchi (eds), *Private International Law Annotated, Vol 1* (Tokyo, Yuhikaku Publishing, 2011) 168.

[50] Sakurada (n 24) 183.

[51] Mortensen, Garnett and Keyes (n 27) 631. See also *Paramasivam v Flynn* [1998] Federal Court Reports 90, 489. The English courts of equity settled the basic principles of fiduciary duties in the mid-nineteenth century. See J Getzler, 'Fiduciary Principles in English Common Law' in EJ Criddle, PB Miller and RH Sitkoff (eds), *The Oxford Handbook of Fiduciary Law* (Oxford, Oxford Univerity Press, 2019) 473–75.

[52] The origin of equitable jurisdiction in Australian courts is an old English system of jurisprudence in which judges make decisions based on general principles of fairness where strict application of common-law rules would lead to injustice.

between fiduciary law and contract law remains blurred.[53] For instance, Japanese company law incorporates the framework of agency law to define the fiduciary duties of corporate directors.[54] Accordingly, questions of a director's fiduciary duties are covered by the law governing the agency relationship between the director and his/her company. This law shall be the law of the place of incorporation because it is doubtful that the governing law of the director's service agreement will be one other than the *lex societatis*. In Cambodia, the Law on Commercial Enterprises does not offer rules providing the fiduciary duties of corporate officers. Such duties are provided by the Prakas on Corporate Governance of Listed Companies (the Listed Companies Prakas) and the Prakas on Corporate Governance of Listed Public Enterprises (the Listed Public Enterprises Prakas),[55] although these official proclamations (i.e., ministerial decisions) do not clarify whether the fiduciary duties of corporate officers derive from their agency relationship with the companies. However, as the heart of the corporate fiduciary duties is to require corporate managers – directors and officers – to pursue the interests of their company and shareholders continuously,[56] the law most closely connected to the duties shall be the law of the company's place of incorporation. Applying the *lex fori* to the fiduciary duties will lead to the application of the law of the company's main place of business to those duties. This may bring about inconvenience to Cambodian courts in handling the case of a foreign company doing business in Cambodia, because the country's company law does not have rules governing internal corporate affairs of foreign companies, including corporate officers' duties to the companies.[57]

III. Corporate Insolvency

It is generally accepted by most nations, including Japan, that cross-border insolvency proceedings and their effects (either procedural or substantive) are subject to the *lex concursus* – the law of the place where the insolvency proceedings have been opened.[58] No literature discusses whether Cambodia follows this PIL rule, and there is a paucity of cases that address the issues of insolvency, such as the questions of cross-border insolvency

[53] See, e.g., M Gelter and G Helleringer, 'Fiduciary Principles in European Civil Law Systems' in EJ Criddle, PB Miller and RH Sitkoff (eds), *The Oxford Handbook of Fiduciary Law* (Oxford, Oxford University Press, 2019) 583–602.

[54] JM Ramseyer and M Tamaruya, 'Fiduciary Principles in Japanese Law' in EJ Criddle, PB Miller and RH Sitkoff (eds), *The Oxford Handbook of Fiduciary Law* (Oxford, Oxford University Press, 2019) 646. See also Civil Code of Japan, Art 643, and Companies Act of Japan, Art 330.

[55] For example, the Listed Companies Prakas provides in Art 18 that 'The board of directors shall carry out their roles with the duty of care and loyalty to promote long-term success and sustain competitiveness of the listed companies, and act in the ultimate interests for the listed companies and shareholders. … The board of directors shall be liable for any damage incurred as a result of acting illegally, dishonestly or contrarily to the interests of the listed companies and shareholders'. See also Listed Public Enterprises Prakas, Art 19.

[56] J Velasco, 'Fiduciary Principles in Corporate Law' in EJ Criddle, PB Miller and RH Sitkoff (eds), *The Oxford Handbook of Fiduciary Law* (Oxford, Oxford University Press, 2019) 78.

[57] See Section II.D above.

[58] A Leandro, 'Insolvency, Applicable Law' in J Basedow and others (eds), *Encyclopedia of Private International Law* (Cheltenham, Edward Elgar Publishing, 2017) 931; Nishioka and Nishitani (n 23) 200.

and PIL.[59] However, Cambodia's Law on Insolvency (the Insolvency Law, enacted in 2007),[60] which has both substantive and procedural rules for insolvency proceedings,[61] provides in Article 6(1) that insolvency proceedings under the Law may be opened against a debtor that is a Cambodian partnership or legal entity, a natural person having a domicile and assets in Cambodia, a foreign partnership or legal person having assets in Cambodia, or a foreign natural person domiciled outside Cambodia but who holds assets in the country. Accordingly, the Insolvency Law covers both procedural and substantive issues of cross-border insolvency proceedings opened in Cambodia for Cambodian or foreign debtors having assets in the country, along the lines of the doctrine of the *lex concursus*.

Moreover, the following justifications of the *lex concursus* rule shall be applicable to international insolvency in Cambodia. (1) Insolvency proceedings inevitably involve procedural issues, so they shall be subject to a well-established choice of law principle that requires the unilateral application of the *lex fori* to international legal proceedings.[62] (2) The goals of insolvency proceedings are set out in the *lex fori*. Accordingly, from a functional point of view, those goals can be better achieved through the interplay between the respective roles conferred to competent national institutions and applicable national substantive rules of the forum.[63] (3) Insolvency proceedings are closely knit with the public interests of the forum, and thus the provisions governing insolvency shall be considered as the overriding mandatory rules of the forum.[64] On (1), Article 1 of the Insolvency Law states that the objective of the legal instrument is 'to establish the rules, conditions, procedures, and proceedings governing the insolvency in the Kingdom of Cambodia'. The Law, as the *lex fori*, therefore governs both procedural and substantive insolvency issues taking place in the Kingdom. On (2), the goals of insolvency proceedings listed up by the Insolvency Law are the collective, orderly and fair satisfaction of creditors' claims and the rehabilitation of the debtor's business for all businessmen and legal entities owning assets in Cambodia.[65] As the Law recognises,[66] the civil courts in Cambodia are better positioned to handle insolvency cases in the country because of their close proximity to the cases and their expertise in Cambodian law.[67] On (3), the public nature of insolvency proceedings opened in Cambodia

[59] J Cohen, 'Cambodia' in Asian Business Law Institute (ed), *Corporate Restructuring and Insolvency in Asia 2020* (Singapore, Asian Business Law Institute, 2020) 105.

[60] An unofficial English translation of the Insolvency Law prepared by the Council for the Development of Cambodia is available at https://cdc.gov.kh/wp-content/uploads/2022/04/Law-on-Insolvency_full-text_071016.pdf (accessed 10 May 2025).

[61] The Insolvency Law of Cambodia is inspired by diverse insolvency rules from civil and common law jurisdictions, such as Germany, Bulgaria, the United States, the Netherlands and Thailand. See Royal Government of Cambodia Ministry of Commerce, *Insolvency Law: Draft – June 2001*, www.wto.org/english/thewto_e/acc_e/khm_e/wtacckhm5_leg_4.pdf (accessed 10 May 2025). Many provisions in the Draft are maintained in the Insolvency Law of Cambodia effective today.

[62] Leandro (n 58) 931.

[63] ibid.

[64] ibid.

[65] Insolvency Law, Arts 2 and 3.

[66] ibid, Art 82.

[67] Note, however, that, according to Art 82(1) of the Insolvency Law, the civil courts are to transfer their jurisdiction over all insolvency cases to the Commercial Court upon its establishment. It is reported that the plan for the Ministry of Justice is to establish the Commercial Court as early as 2024, and the draft law on the establishment and operation of the Commercial Court and commercial procedures was finalised in November 2023, with support from the Asian Development Bank (ADB): O Bunthoeurn, 'Commercial Court Could Function 'As Early As 2024': Justice Ministry Officials', *The Phnom Penh Post*, 3 February 2023, available at www.phnompenhpost.

is confirmed by Article 8(1) of the Insolvency Law that allows the public prosecutor to file insolvency proceedings if a debtor fails to do so.[68] Both procedural and substantive aspects of international insolvency are therefore subject to Cambodian law before the courts in Cambodia following the *lex concursus* rule.

However, some provisions of the Insolvency Law require certain types of insolvency proceedings to be regulated by other legal instruments. Article 6(3) of the Law prohibits filings of insolvency proceedings against a debtor or creditor that is a covered entity under the Law on Banking and Financial Institutions (Banking Law),[69] the Law on Insurance (Insurance Law),[70] or the Law on the Issuance and Trading of Non-Governmental Securities (Securities Law),[71] unless otherwise provided by these Laws. Accordingly, insolvency proceedings for banks,[72] insurance companies[73] and securities businesses and firms[74] are subject to the special rules under their industry specific legislation.[75] The ensuing subsections consider the effect of those special rules and the Insolvency Law on substantive issues of insolvency, focusing on the assignment of property and discharge of debts.

com/business/commercial-court-could-function-early-2024-justice-ministry-officials (accessed 10 December 2024); BR Kongkea, 'Commercial Court Law Ready for Approval', *Khmer Times*, 9 November 2023, available at www.khmertimeskh.com/501389436/commercial-court-law-ready-for-approval/ (accessed 10 December 2024). However, the plan to establish the Commercial Court existed in as early as 1995, in the Law on Commercial Rules and Register: Council of ASEAN Chief Justices, 'Overview of Cambodian Judiciary' (n.d.), available at https://cacj-ajp.org/cambodia/judiciary/overview-of-cambodian-judiciary/ (accessed 10 December 2024).

[68] Although a Cambodia-based foreign legal consultant argues that the Minister of the Ministry of Commerce may file public interest applications for insolvency, such power of the Minister is not discernible from the text of the Insolvency Law: Cohen (n 59) 112; J Cohen, *Regional Guide to Bankruptcy Law: Cambodia* (Phnom Penh, Tilleke & Gibbins International 2020) 2. In fact, Article 8(1) of the Insolvency Law states that '[a] petition to open insolvency proceedings may be filed by a debtor, one or more creditors, the Director of Companies or the public prosecutor'. At the time of drafting the Insolvency Law, there appeared to be a plan to confer the Minister of Commerce with the authority to open insolvency proceedings: see Art 6(a) of the June 2001 Draft of the Insolvency Law, available at www.wto.org/english/thewto_e/acc_e/khm_e/wtacckhm5_leg_4.pdf (accessed 10 December 2024).

[69] (Effective 18 November 1999); an unofficial English translation of this legislation is available at: National Bank of Cambodia, 'Laws Applicable to Banks and Financial Institutions' (2015), available at www.nbc.gov.kh/english/legislation/laws_applicable_to_banks_and_financial_institutions.php (accessed 10 December 2024).

[70] (Effective 4 August 2014); an unofficial English translation of this legislation prepared by the Insurance Regulator of Cambodia (IRC) is available at https://irc.gov.kh/en/article?post=7c09d33b-1992-4954-8653-c099663ba779 (accessed 10 December 2024).

[71] (Effective 19 October 2007); an unofficial English translation of this legislation can be found in Acleda Securities, 'Law & Regulation' (n.d.), available at www.acledasecurities.com.kh/as/eng/md_law_regulation (accessed 10 December 2024).

[72] According to the Banking Law, 'banks' are legal entities licensed by the Central Bank of Cambodia to carry out banking operations as their regular business (Arts 1, 14 and 40) and incorporated locally in Cambodia or established as branches of foreign banks (Art 12).

[73] 'Insurance companies' refer to the public limited companies that have insurance licences issued by the Ministry of Finance and Economy of Cambodia: Insurance Law, Arts 41 and 47.

[74] According to Article 31 of the Securities Law, '[n]o person, except an exempt securities dealer or in respect of an exempt securities transaction as prescribed by sub-decree[s], shall conduct a securities business or hold himself out as conducting a securities business in the form of a securities firm unless the person has been licensed by the director general of [Cambodia Securities and Exchange Commission]'.

[75] Rules on insolvency proceedings for banks, insurance companies and security businesses or firms are set out respectively in Chapter XX of the Banking Law, Chapter 8 of the Insurance Law and Art 45(2) of the Securities Law. See also Sub-Decree No 24 ANKr.BK dated 26 February 2018 on Rehabilitation and Liquidation in the Securities Sector; Legal Affairs Department Securities and Exchange Regulator of Cambodia, 'Rehabilitation in the Securities Sector in the Event of Critical Financial Crisis' 28 January 2024, available at www.phnompenhpost.com/financial/rehabilitation-in-the-securities-sector-in-the-event-of-critical-financial-crisis (accessed 10 December 2024).

A. Effect of Insolvency on Assignments of Property

As per the *lex concursus* rule, and thus the insolvency regime of Cambodia, a bankruptcy estate shall be created upon the opening of the insolvency proceedings before the competent court.[76] This estate, which is under the control of the administrator,[77] consists of 'all assets, rights and claims of any kind in which the debtor has an ownership interest or to which the debtor is otherwise entitled on the date of opening of the insolvency proceedings or after that date'.[78] For the sake of forming the bankruptcy estate, any actions, such as legal proceedings or execution process by or on behalf of a creditor shall be suspended until the termination of the insolvency proceedings.[79] However, the administrator may allow a secured creditor 'to foreclose his mortgage, repossess and sell an encumbered asset (collateral), or in any other way avail himself of his security right and make himself paid by individual action'.[80]

These requirements may cause choice of law issues if the debtor and the creditor have concluded a contract on the assignment of the debtor's property containing a choice of law clause designating a law other than Cambodian law.[81] As those requirements not only impose insolvency issues but also limit the debtor's contractual rights on property assignment against the debtor, the creditor might attempt to invoke both insolvency and contract rules under the foreign law chosen by that contract. However, the creditor's attempt is unlikely to be successful. Cambodian PIL recognises the parties' freedom to choose the governing law of the contract but this freedom may not supersede the provisions of the Insolvency Law that are overriding mandatory rules linked to Cambodia's public interests as discussed above.

Choice of law issues related to property assignment may also arise from insolvency proceedings for banks, insurance companies and securities firms. Concerning the provisional administration of banks under financial distress, the Banking Law provides in Article 59 that the provisional administrator shall immediately 'make an assessment of whether or not the [bank] is solvent … and administer the current activities [of the bank] in order to preserve *as far as possible* the [bank's] solvency and maintain the rights of depositors and creditors'.[82] In other words, this law gives the provisional administrator authority to limit the creditor's rights over the bank's assets, against which the creditor may claim the protection of rights based on the law governing its contract with the bank. Note, however, that the creditor's claim is unlikely to be successful because the provisions of administration proceedings (and liquidation proceedings that potentially follow) reflect the public interest of Cambodia as the power to launch such proceedings is bestowed on the National Bank of Cambodia,[83] and because the provisions of the Banking Law prevail over those of the Insolvency Law.[84] Similarly, administration proceedings for insurance companies also have

[76] Insolvency Law, Art 20(1).
[77] ibid, Article 21.
[78] ibid, Article 20(2).
[79] ibid, Article 19(1).
[80] ibid, Article 19(2).
[81] JL Westbrook, 'Comity and Choice of Law in Global Insolvencies' (2019) 54 *Texas International Law Journal* 259, 265.
[82] (emphasis added).
[83] Banking Law, Arts 40 and 57.
[84] ibid, Art 10.

a public nature and thus supersede any provisions of the law designated by the contract between the insurers and their creditors. This is because the authority to commence the provisional administration of insolvent insurance companies, as well as the power to file a suit to the competent court for the liquidation of those companies, rests in the Ministry of Economy and Finance.[85] In addition, the Securities Law confirms its overriding mandatory nature, by providing that Cambodia Securities and Exchange Commission (CSEC) may commence the provisional administration of financially stressed securities firms under the Insolvency Law and other rules and regulations, subject to the provisions of the Securities Law.[86]

B. Effect of Insolvency on Discharge of Debts

The Insolvency Law, the Banking Law, the Insurance Law and the Securities Law recognise the discharge of debts as an effect of insolvency proceedings, albeit indirectly.[87] Such an effect of insolvency proceedings may conflict with the provisions of the proper law of the contract between the debtor and the creditor because the applicable law of the contract is expected to govern generally all aspects of the contract, including its validity, interpretation, breach, discharge and remedies.[88] However, as far as the Cambodian legal system observes the *lex concursus* rule and regards its rules on insolvency as overriding mandatory provisions of Cambodian law, the creditor is restrained from challenging the discharge of debts in insolvency proceedings by relying on the proper law of the contract.

The *Gibbs* rule developed in England states that the discharge of a debt may only be determined by the governing law of the debt, i.e., the law governing the contract stipulating about the debt, and by the courts of that jurisdiction alone.[89] It suggests that English courts shall not enforce a foreign insolvency decision discharging or modifying the terms of the debt governed by English law.[90] Whilst the English judiciary and several scholars and practitioners still defend the 120-year-old rule for the choice of law and the recognition of foreign insolvency proceedings,[91] the past Judicial Commissioner of Singapore called for the

[85] Insurance Law, Arts 73 and 81.

[86] Securities Law, Art 45.2.

[87] Art 62 of the Insolvency Law provides that the debtor shall restore the right to dispose remaining assets in the insolvency estate upon the termination of the insolvency proceedings following liquidation. Furthermore, Article 63 of the Law states that '[i]n the case of a debtor which is a company, the debtor shall be deemed dissolved upon the issuance of the court ruling terminating the insolvency proceedings upon liquidation, unless the termination of insolvency proceedings resulted from the satisfaction of all claims against the debtor'. Thus, upon the completion of the insolvency proceedings, the corporate debtor is to be released from its debt as a result of its dissolution. This rule applies to liquidation under the Baking Law (Art 62), the Insurance Law (Art 83) and the Securities Law (Art 45.2). See also Article 70 of the Insurance Law, for the dissolution of an insurance company following its voluntary liquidation.

[88] See Chapter 5 in this volume.

[89] *Antony Gibbs & Sons v Société Industrielle et Commerciale des* Métaux (1890) 25 QBD 399; N Srivastava, 'Heritage and Vitality: Whether the Rule in Antony Gibbs Is a Presumption' (2021) 29 *Insolvency Law Journal* 61, 61–63.

[90] I Mevorach, 'Overlapping International Instruments for Enforcement of Insolvency Judgments: Undermining or Strengthening Universalism?' (2021) 22 *European Business Organization Law Review* 283, 291.

[91] *Bakhshiyeva v Sberbank of Russia* [2018] EWCA Civ 2802; N Srivastava, 'Defending the Rule in Antony Gibbs', *Conflict of Lawsnet*, 18 August 2021, available at https://conflictoflaws.net/2021/defending-the-rule-in-antony-gibbs/#_ftn1 (accessed 10 December 2024); Srivastava (n 89); Financial Markets Law Committee, 'The Rule in

abolition of the *Gibbs* principle,[92] and it has met with a mixed reception amongst national courts in other common law jurisdictions.[93] Moreover, as Justice Reyes observed in *Hong Kong Institute of Education v Aoki Group (No 2)*,[94] many leading scholars of international insolvency and conflict of laws question the scope and utility of the *Gibbs* principle.[95] In light of the principle's limited acceptance in common law jurisdictions and the fact that Cambodia is under the civil law tradition, the country is not encouraged to import the *Gibbs* rule to limit its general observance to the *lex concursus* rule.

C. International Legal Instruments on Cross-border Insolvency

Several international legal instruments provide procedural and substantive rules on cross-border insolvency. These instruments may serve as tools for the courts in Cambodia to deal with cross-border insolvency matters beyond the reach of the Insolvency Law – e.g., foreign insolvency proceedings in which a Cambodian citizen is involved. Nevertheless, Cambodia appears to have little interest in adopting those instruments. For instance, the UNCITRAL Model Law on Cross-Border Insolvency was established by the Secretariat of the United Commission on International Trade Law (UNCITRAL) in 1997 to assist states to harmonise and modernise their insolvency laws to more effectively deal with cross-border insolvency proceedings for debtors experiencing severe financial distress or insolvency.[96] Sixty-three states and jurisdictions have legislation based on or influenced by the Model Law.[97] Nevertheless, nothing suggests that Cambodia plans to adopt the model legislation, although its provisions on the debtor's centre of main interests would help the Cambodian judiciary deal with concurrent and conflicting cross-border insolvency proceedings.[98]

Gibbs: Exploring Its Value and Practical Use in the Financial Markets as a Guarantor of Legal Predictability' (2024), available at https://fmlc.org/wp-content/uploads/2024/02/Paper-The-Rule-in-Gibbs-Exploring-its-value-and-practical-use-in-the-financial-markets-as-a-guarantor-of-legal-predictability-29-February-2024.pdf (accessed 10 December 2024); S Madaus, 'The Rule in Gibbs, or How to Protect Local Debt from a Foreign Discharge', *Oxford Business Law Blog*, 19 December 2018, available at https://blogs.law.ox.ac.uk/business-law-blog/blog/2018/12/rule-gibbs-or-how-protect-local-debt-foreign-discharge (accessed 10 December 2024).

[92] K Ramesh, 'The Gibbs Principle: A Tether on the Feet of Good Forum Shopping' (2017) 29 *Singapore Academy of Law Journal* 42.

[93] ibid 46–48.

[94] [2004] 2 HKC 397, [121]–[124].

[95] On criticisms on the Gibbs rule, see also V Sachdev, 'Choice of Law in Insolvency Proceedings: How English Courts' Continued Reliance on the Gibbs Principle Threatens Universalism' (2019) 93 *American Bankruptcy Law Journal* 343; M Verma and S Jain, 'Recognition of Insolvency Related Judgments: An Undetermined Sphere of International Insolvency', *KSLR Commercial & Financial Law Blog*, 18 September 2020, available at https://blogs.kcl.ac.uk/kslrcommerciallawblog/2020/09/18/recognition-of-insolvency-related-judgments-an-undetermined-sphere-of-international-insolvency-medhashree-verma-and-siddharth-jain/ (accessed 10 December 2024).

[96] UNCITRAL, 'UNCITRAL Model Law on Cross-Border Insolvency (1997)' (n.d.), available at https://uncitral.un.org/en/texts/insolvency/modellaw/cross-border_insolvency (accessed 10 December 2024).

[97] UNCITRAL, 'Status: UNCITRAL Model Law on Cross-Border Insolvency (1997)' (n.d.), available at https://uncitral.un.org/en/texts/insolvency/modellaw/cross-border_insolvency/status (accessed 10 December 2024).

[98] N Panha, 'Introducing the Center of Main Interests in International Insolvency Cases to Cambodian Law: A Comparative Analysis of the Model Law, the EU, US and Japan' (2015) 263 *Nagoya University Journal of Law and Politics* 465. The Model Law does not define the concept 'centre of main interests', but the interpretation of the term is elaborated in the Model Law's guide to enactment and interpretation: UNCITRAL, *UNCITRAL Model Law on Cross-Border Insolvency with Guide to Enactment and Interpretation* (Vienna, United Nations Publication, 2014) 70ff.

Apart from the UNCITRAL Model Law on Cross-Border Insolvency, there appear to be no international legal instruments on insolvency that Cambodia might consider adopting in the foreseeable future. It is not verified yet whether any state or jurisdiction has enacted or implemented the UNCITRAL Model Law on Recognition and Enforcement of Insolvency-Related Judgments.[99] The common ASEAN insolvency framework is still at a very early stage of development.[100] The Hague Conference on Private International Law (HCCH) has not published any legal instruments dealing with international insolvency proceedings.[101]

IV. Antitrust and Unfair Competition

Competition law is often called antitrust law and deals with any private restrictions that intend to lower competition intensity, such as mergers and acquisitions, abuses of dominant positions, horizontal and vertical agreements and concerted practices.[102] Unfair competition law refers to rules that address certain kinds of unfair business conduct exploiting competitors and clients (including consumers).[103] This section considers issues of choice of law in antitrust and unfair competition laws.

A. Competition (Antitrust) Law

No materials, not even the Competition Law (promulgated in 2021),[104] propose special choice of law rules for antitrust issues in Cambodia. Accordingly, which choice of law rules govern a competition law issue will depend on the nature of the relationship between the parties.[105] For instance, if a party seeks a declaration from the court on the nullity of anti-competitive contractual terms which s/he was forced by the other party to accept, the validity of the terms is to be examined in light of the law governing the contract. The governing law is to be determined based on choice of law rules for contracts.[106] If a party seeks

[99] UNCITRAL, 'UNCITRAL Model Law on Recognition and Enforcement of Insolvency-Related Judgments (2018)' (n.d.), available at https://uncitral.un.org/en/texts/insolvency/modellaw/mlij (accessed 10 December 2024).

[100] MN Imanullah, E Latifah and PDK Ratri, 'Aspects of International and Domestic Law Pertaining to the Establishment of ASEAN Cross-Border Insolvency Regulations: An Indonesian Perspective' (2018) 8 *Indonesian Law Review* 190; N Spuling, 'Cross-Border Insolvencies in Southeast Asia: Regional Insolvency Framework for ASEAN' (2021) *Doctoral Thesis, Tilburg University*, available at https://research.tilburguniversity.edu/en/publications/cross-border-insolvencies-in-southeast-asia-regional-insolvency-f (accessed 10 December 2024); R Anggriawan, 'Insolvency Proceedings: ASEAN and EU Comparison on the Rules of Foreign Court Jurisdiction' (2020) 3 *Indonesian Comparative Law Review* 35.

[101] HCCH, 'Conventions and Other Instruments' (2024), available at www.hcch.net/en/instruments/conventions (accessed 10 December 2024).

[102] J Basedow, 'Competition Law (Antitrust)' in J Basedow and others (eds), *Encyclopedia of Private International Law* (Cheltenham, Edward Elgar Publishing, 2017) 425–26.

[103] ibid.

[104] An unofficial translation of the Law on Competition prepared by the Consumer Protection Competition and Fraud Repression Directorate-General (CCF) is available at www.ccfdg.gov.kh/en/pdf-view/?filename=https://www.ccfdg.gov.kh/wp-content/uploads/2021/11/Final-08112021ENG_CAM_Law-on-Competition.pdf (accessed 10 December 2024).

[105] Nishioka and Nishitani (n 23) 201.

[106] See Chapter 5 in this volume.

compensation for damages or injunctive relief based on the violation of competition law, such as the formation of a cartel by the other party or an abuse by the other party of its dominant market position, the general choice of law rules for torts shall apply.[107] Then, the place where the damage occurs shall correspond to the place of a market that is or likely to be affected by the anti-competitive act. This is because of the strict territoriality of competition law,[108] and because it is simply difficult to conceive that the victim sustained damages in a place other than an affected marketplace. Moreover, the place of the affected market must be foreseeable to the tortfeasor (for instance, the place that the cartel deliberately targeted).

B. Unfair Competition Law

Examples of unfair business conduct include business defamation, false advertising, bait-and-switch, corporate spying, labour piracy and know-how infringement.[109] Many civil law countries, including Japan, have integrated unfair competition law with their tort regimes for the purposes of dealing with PIL issues.[110] Following the practice in these civil law countries, and because no material – e.g., the Law Concerning Marks, Trade Names and Acts of Unfair Competition[111] – suggests that Cambodia has special choice of law rules for unfair competition acts, the courts in Cambodia are likely to generally refer choice of law issues of unfair business conduct to Cambodian conflict of law rules on torts.[112]

In the context of Japanese PIL, Nishioka and Nishitani argue that unfair competition acts may have different natures, purposes and interests and, therefore, can be divided into market-based unfair competition acts and individual-based unfair competition acts.[113] The former refers to unfair competition practices that may distort targeted market orders, such as false advertising and passing off, whereas the latter refers to acts of unfair competition aimed at specific competitors, including corporate spying, labour piracy and know-how infringement. Nishioka and Nishitani suggest that 'market-based unfair competition should be governed by the law of the market that is or is likely to be affected, while the law applicable to individual-based unfair competition should be determined [by] the general choice of law rules for tort[s] in AGRAL'.[114] Cambodian jurists will probably be able to deal with the market-based unfair competition acts by considering the nature of the victims – the defendant's competitors or consumers – and the place(s) where those victims' interests were damaged because 'acts of unfair competition are considered to affect competitors and consumers at the place of market impact'.[115] If an unfair competition act affects several markets, and the victim is the wrongdoer's competitor with interests in those markets, the

[107] See Chapter 6 in this volume.
[108] Basedow (n 102) 427.
[109] Nishioka and Nishitani (n 23) 132.
[110] TW Dornis, 'Competition, Unfair' in J Basedow and others (eds), *Encyclopedia of Private International Law* (Cheltenham, Edward Elgar Publishing, 2017) 433; Nishioka and Nishitani (n 23) 132.
[111] An unofficial English translation of this legislation can be found in WIPO, 'Cambodia KH001: Law Concerning Marks, Trade Names and Acts of Unfair Competition' (n.d.), available at www.wipo.int/wipolex/en/text/567456 (accessed 10 December 2024).
[112] See Chapter 6 in this volume.
[113] Nishioka and Nishitani (n 23) 132.
[114] ibid 132.
[115] Dornis (n 110) 437–38.

laws of the affected markets would cumulatively or distributively (following the mosaic approach[116]) apply to the act of unfair competition.

V. Conclusions

The choice of law rules for dealing with questions of cross-border corporate affairs are only beginning to evolve in Cambodia. The evolution may be accelerated by obtaining inspiration from the substantive law of Cambodia and Japanese PIL, as demonstrated in this chapter. Cambodia's adoption of the incorporation theory is evident from the provisions of the Law on Commercial Enterprises.[117] Accordingly, the law of the place of incorporation is the primary law governing questions of company law, including the validity of incorporation, a company's capacity and powers, rights and liabilities of corporate members and the internal management of a company. The Insolvency Law reveals Cambodia's support for the *lex concursus* rule as the key principle for international insolvency cases.[118] Thus, the law of the place where an insolvency petition was filed for a company regulates the effect of insolvency on assignments of property and that of insolvency on discharge of debts. The Competition Law and the Law Concerning Marks, Trade Names and Acts of Unfair Competition are both silent on choice of law issues pertaining to antitrust and unfair competition, which is unlikely to trigger practical inconvenience because those issues will largely fall within the scope of choice of law rules for contractual obligations and non-contractual obligations. There is therefore likely to be no significant legal vacuum in the rules of Cambodian PIL for internal and external corporate affairs.

[116] ibid 437–39.
[117] See Section II.
[118] See Section III.

PART IV

Recognition and Enforcement

10

Recognition and Enforcement of Foreign Judgments

I. Introduction

Under Cambodian law, recognition is the acknowledgement by the court in Cambodia of the (binding) effects of foreign decisions in the Kingdom.[1] It may take place either automatically or through court decisions, such as a declaratory relief and a specific performance order, provided the conditions listed by Article 199 of the Code of Civil Procedure (CCP) are satisfied.[2] Enforcement, on the other hand, means the implementation or execution by the court of a foreign judgment in Cambodia upon the request by a party.[3] Recognition and enforcement are not mutually exclusive in that the latter is not plausible without implementing the former.[4] The court may not enforce a foreign judgment without recognising its effect in Cambodia, while recognition of the judgment is not always followed by enforcement by the court unless otherwise requested by the party.[5] In any event, recognition and enforcement are closely related under Cambodian law, as under the legal systems of other civil and common law countries.[6]

Several legal frameworks are applicable to the recognition and enforcement of foreign judgments in Cambodia, although the key legislation is the CCP. At the international law level,[7] the Kingdom has ratified some bilateral and multilateral treaties, such as the Agreement on Mutual Judicial Assistance in Civil Matters between the Kingdom of Cambodia and the Socialist Republic of Vietnam (Cambodia–Vietnam Judicial Assistance Treaty) of 2013,[8] and the International Convention on Civil Liability for Oil Pollution

[1] JICA, 'Commentary on Cambodian Code of Civil Procedure: Compulsory Execution and Provisional Remedies [in Japanese]' (n.d.) 25, available at www.moj.go.jp/content/000122393.pdf (accessed 10 December 2024).

[2] ibid.

[3] ibid. Recognition and enforcement are distinguished under Japanese law either: K Nishioka and Y Nishitani, *Japanese Private International Law* (Oxford, Hart Publishing, 2021) 205; J Yokoyama, *Private International Law in Japan* (Alphen aan den Rijn, Wolters Kluwer, 2019) 146ff.

[4] CCP, Art 352(3).

[5] JICA (n 1) 25.

[6] T Domej, 'Recognition and Enforcement of Judgments (Civil Law)' in F Ferrari and others (eds), *Encyclopedia of Private International Law* (Cheltenham, Edward Elgar Publishing, 2017); A Briggs, 'Recognition and Enforcement of Judgments (Common Law)' in F Ferrari and others (eds), *Encyclopedia of Private International Law* (Cheltenham, Edward Elgar Publishing, 2017).

[7] On the hierarchy of laws in Cambodia, see Chapter 2 in this volume.

[8] Cambodia ratified the Judicial Assistance Treaty by establishing the Law Approving the Agreement on Mutual Judicial Assistance in Civil Matters between the Kingdom of Cambodia and the Socialist Republic of Vietnam in 2014: Y Bun, 'Country Report: Cambodia' in A Chong (ed), *Recognition and Enforcement of Foreign Judgments in Asia* (Singapore, Asian Business Law Institute, 2017) 41.

Damage of 1969 (Brussels, 29 November 1969; the CLC Convention) by the International Maritime Organisation (IMO).[9] However, these international legal instruments are limited in their scope of application. Thus, as a leading Cambodian lawyer rightly suggests, the CCP is the primary law governing the recognition and enforcement of foreign judgments in the country.[10] The core provisions for the court to recognise and enforce foreign judgments are contained in the CCP.

Gaps in these core provisions may be filled by adopting relevant court decisions and literature on Japanese law, as those provisions mostly derive from Japanese legal principles. For instance, Article 199 of the CCP on the effect of foreign final judgments in Cambodia closely follows Article 118 of Japan's Code of Civil Procedure. Article 352 of the CCP sets out the rules for the court in Cambodia to execute foreign judgments, modelling after Article 24 of the Civil Execution Act of Japan (Act No 4 of 30 March 1979). Past court decisions by Cambodian courts are not particularly helpful due to the paucity of foreign judgments enforced by the court in Cambodia and the lack of support among Cambodian jurists for the doctrine of precedent.[11] This chapter therefore considers how Cambodian courts may recognise and enforce a foreign judgment by adopting Japanese legal thinking where appliable.

II. Recognition

Although both international law and domestic legislation are related to judgment recognition, Cambodia has not concluded any noticeable international legal instruments for the process apart from the Cambodia–Vietnam Judicial Assistance Treaty and the CLC Convention. It has not accepted the Convention of 2 July 2019 on the Recognition and Enforcement of Foreign Judgments in Civil or Commercial Matters (the 2019 Hague Judgments Convention) or the Convention of 30 June 2005 on Choice of Court Agreements (the 2005 Hague Choice of Court Convention).[12] No material suggests the country has any plan to adopt these international treaties soon.[13] Thus, foreign judgment recognition in Cambodia is largely governed by the CCP as discussed in the sub-sections that follow.

[9] https://treaties.un.org/pages/showDetails.aspx?objid=08000002801083db (accessed 10 December 2024).

[10] Bun (n 8) 38.

[11] Bun writes that 'we are unaware of any foreign judgment that has been recognised and enforced, or refused to be recognised and enforced by the Cambodian courts': ibid 38. See also A Larkin and P Yun, 'Cambodia' in A Reyes (ed), *Recognition and Enforcement of Judgments in Civil and Commercial Matters* (Oxford, Hart Publishing, 2019) 201 (suggesting '[d]espite the [Cambodia–Vietnam Judicial Assistance Treaty] having been in force more than a decade, to the author's knowledge, Cambodia has yet to see a Vietnamese court judgment brought to a local court for recognition and enforcement'). See also generally A Chong (ed) *Asian Principles for the Recognition and Enforcement of Foreign Judgments* (Singapore, Asian Business Law Institute, 2020). (Also, past court decisions are not sources of law under the Cambodian legal system: see Chapter 1 in this volume.)

[12] HCCH, 'Status Table: Convention of 2 July 2019 on the Recognition and Enforcement of Foreign Judgments in Civil or Commercial Matters' (2024), available at www.hcch.net/en/instruments/conventions/status-table/?cid=137 (accessed 10 December 2024); HCCH, 'Status Table: Convention of 30 June 2005 on Choice of Court Agreements' (2024), available at www.hcch.net/en/instruments/conventions/status-table/?cid=98 (accessed 10 December 2024).

[13] See generally Bun (n 8); Larkin and Yun (n 11).

A. Recognition under Bilateral, Multilateral Treaties and Conventions

The Cambodia–Vietnam Judicial Assistance Treaty covers, among other matters, the service of judicial documents, evidence transfer and the recognition and enforcement of court judgments and decisions. Article 21 of the Treaty sets out the conditions of the recognition and enforcement as follows:

1. the case does not fall into the exclusive jurisdiction of the courts of the Requested Party under the national laws of the Requested Party;
2. the litigants or their legal representatives have been duly summoned or declared absent in accordance with the national laws of the Requesting Party;
3. the court judgments or decisions have entered into legal effect and the statutes of limitation for execution of such judgments or decisions have not expired under the national law of the Requesting Party;
4. there has not been a legally effective civil court judgment or decision on the same case that has been made by the court of the Requested Party or there is no judgment or decisions by the court of a third country, which has been recognised for enforcement by the court of the Requested Party, or at the time of recognition of that judgment or decision, the court of the Requested Party has not registered or heard the same case;
5. the recognition and enforcement of the court judgments or decisions and consequences of the recognition and enforcement of such judgments or decisions shall not contradict the fundamental principles of law and public order of the Requested Party.[14]

These requirements are applicable to the recognition and enforcement in Cambodia of judgments issued by the courts in Vietnam, in addition to Articles 199 and 352 of the CCP.[15]

Moreover, Cambodia is a signatory to the CLC Convention and the 1992 Protocol that amended this Convention.[16] The aim of the CLC Convention is to provide adequate compensation for individuals 'who suffer oil pollution damage resulting from maritime casualties involving oil-carrying ships'.[17] Accordingly, the Convention applies exclusively to pollution damage caused in the territory (including the territorial sea) or exclusive economic zone of a Contracting State and includes preventive measures for such damage.[18] By extension, Article IX of the Convention provides that actions for compensation for such damage and

[14] Art 21 of the Cambodia–Vietnam Judicial Assistance Treaty quoted in Bun (n 8) 45. On the conditions for the recognition and enforcement of Cambodian judgments in Vietnam, see NB Du, 'Country Report: Socialist Republic of Vietnam' in A Chong (ed), *Recognition and Enforcement of Foreign Judgments in Asia* (Singapore, Asian Business Law Institute, 2017) 214–15. On the recognition and enforcement of foreign judgments in Vietnam generally, see NN Minh, TH Han and NTT Trang, 'Vietnam' in A Reyes (ed), *Recognition and Enforcement of Judgments in Civil and Commercial Matters* (Oxford, Hart Publishing, 2019).

[15] See Section II.B. below.

[16] IMO, 'Status of Conventions: Ratifications by State' (n.d.), available at https://wwwcdn.imo.org/localresources/en/About/Conventions/StatusOfConventions/x-Status.xlsx (accessed 10 December 2024). On amendments to the Convention, see generally NAM Gutiérrez, *Limitation of Liability in International Maritime Conventions: The Relationship between Global Limitation Conventions and Particular Liability Regimes* (Abingdon, Routledge, 2010).

[17] IMO, 'International Convention on Civil Liability for Oil Pollution Damage (CLC)' (n.d.), available at www.imo.org/en/About/Conventions/Pages/International-Convention-on-Civil-Liability-for-Oil-Pollution-Damage-(CLC).aspx (accessed 10 December 2024).

[18] CLC Convention, Art II.

preventive measures may only be raised before the courts of a Contracting State or States, mandating each contracting state to 'ensure that its Courts possess the necessary jurisdiction to entertain such actions for compensation'.[19]

Rules on the recognition of foreign judgments on oil pollution damage are set out in Article X.1 of the CLC Convention. The Article provides that '[a]ny judgment given by a Court with jurisdiction in accordance with Article IX which is enforceable in the State of origin where it is no longer subject to ordinary forms of review, shall be recognised in any Contracting State, except: (a) where the judgment was obtained by fraud; or (b) where the defendant was not given reasonable notice and a fair opportunity to present his case'. Thus, for a Contracting State's judgment on oil pollution damage to be recognised in another Contracting State, that judgment shall be (1) final and (2) free from fraud. Moreover, (3) it must have been issued by the Court without due process violations. The CLC Convention is silent on the implications of these requirements,[20] but this silence may not pose a serious practical challenge to judgment creditors. The reason for this is that, under the CLC Convention, the owner of the ship that has caused the pollution is allowed to invoke the benefit of limitation of liability by setting up a limitation fund, which represents the limits of that owner's compensation liability.[21] Once the fund has been constituted, the courts of the state where the fund is established shall have exclusive jurisdiction to decide all matters relating to the apportionment and distribution of the fund.[22] 'Situations in which there would be the need for a judgment given by a court in a Contracting State to be enforced in another Contracting State appear to be limited' because the owner of the ship who has caused the pollution would be keen to limit his/her liability and to take advantage of the benefit of limitation proceedings within the period specified under the domestic law of the Contracting State where the fund was constituted (if any).[23]

B. General Principles under Domestic Legislation

Article 199 of the CCP is a key provision for the recognition and enforcement of foreign judgments in Cambodia. It provides as follows.

> A final judgment of a foreign court shall be valid only where all of the following conditions are fulfilled: (a) jurisdiction is properly conferred on the foreign court by law or by treaty; (b) the losing defendant received service of summons or any other order necessary to commence the action, or responded without receiving such summons or order; (c) the contents of the judgment and the procedures followed in the action do not violate the public order or morals of Cambodia; and (d) there is a guarantee of reciprocity between Cambodia and the foreign country in which the court is based.

[19] CLC Convention, Art IX.

[20] As Cambodia is not a party to the Vienna Convention on the Law of Treaties, judgment creditors may not rely on it to interpret the provisions of the CLC Convention: United Nations, 'United Nations Treaty Collection: Vienna Convention on the Law of Treaties' (2024), available at https://treaties.un.org/pages/ViewDetailsIII.aspx?src=TREATY&mtdsg_no=XXIII-1&chapter=23&Temp=mtdsg3&clang=_en (accessed 10 December 2024).

[21] CLC Convention, Art V.3.

[22] ibid, Art IX.3.

[23] F Berlingieri, *International Maritime Conventions (Volume 3): Protection of the Marine Environment* (Abingdon, Routledge 2015) 154. See also CLC Convention, Art III.4; UNCTAD, *Liability and Compensation for Ship-Source Oil Pollution: An Overview of the International Legal Framework for Oil Pollution Damage from Tankers* (New York and Geneva, United Nations, 2012) 48.

Thus, for a foreign judgment to be effective in Cambodia, it must be final and satisfy requirements (a)–(d). The following subsections consider these five requirements based on relevant discussion of Japanese law because Article 199 of the CCP mirrors Article 118 of Japan's Code of Civil Procedure.

i. Final Judgments

The CCP does not elaborate on the meaning of 'a final judgment of a foreign court', and no accessible judgments of the Cambodian courts address that topic. However, Japanese jurists and commentators almost unanimously agree that a foreign court judgment is final under Japanese law if it is no longer subject to ordinary forms of review or appeal in the rendering state.[24] They suggest that foreign interlocutory judgments, provisional measures and judicial settlements are not final judgments that are recognisable and enforceable in Japan.[25] This definition of finality is likely to be accepted under Cambodian law. According to Article 180(1) of the CCP, a court may render a final judgment when it deems that no further trial is required for determining a legal claim based on the results of arguments and evidentiary investigation. The final judgment under Cambodian law is therefore one that concludes legal proceedings in whole or part,[26] which does not appear to contradict the definition of finality for foreign judgments under Japanese law.

However, it is uncertain how the courts in Cambodia should construe the notion of 'the judgment of a foreign court' under the CCP. In the context of Japanese law, the Supreme Court of Japan defines the judgment of a foreign court as '[a] final judgment rendered by a foreign court on private law relations by providing procedural guarantee to both parties, *regardless of the name, procedure, or form of judgment*'.[27] The Court further continues that '[e]ven if the judgment is called a decision or order, insofar as it possesses the characteristics of the above, it should be regarded as a judgment of a foreign court'.[28] Based on this statement by the Supreme Court, Kono suggests that the judgment of a foreign court means 'any judgment, decision, order or decree rendered by a foreign court in a dispute on private law matters'.[29] In fact, the courts in Japan have recognised and enforced various decisions rendered by a foreign court, including monetary and non-monetary judgments, summary judgments issued in adversarial proceedings, costs orders, default judgments, and permanent injunction orders.[30] However, what turns a foreign decision into a foreign judgment under Japanese law is not always clear. For instance, several commentators claim that admissions or waivers of claims and judicial settlements are not foreign judgments under Japanese law even if they have the same effect as final judgments in the rendering state.[31] Nevertheless, a few scholars opine that a foreign judgment based on a settlement agreement,

[24] Nishioka and Nishitani (n 3) 208; Yokoyama (n 3) 146; T Kono, 'Country Report: Japan' in A Chong (ed), *Recognition and Enforcement of Foreign Judgments in Asia* (Singapore, Asian Business Law Institute, 2017) 107.

[25] Kono (n 24) 107; Nishioka and Nishitani, *Japanese Private International Law* 208; Yokoyama, (n 3) 146.

[26] CCP, Art 180(2).

[27] *Gabindram Naraindas Sadhwani, et al v Kishinchando Naraindas Sadhwani, et al* [1998] Supreme Court 1994(O)1838, Judgments of the Supreme Court, available at www.courts.go.jp/app/hanrei_en/detail?id=392 (accessed 10 December 2024).

[28] ibid.

[29] Kono (n 24) 106. See also Yokoyama (n 3) 147.

[30] Kono (n 24) 106.

[31] Nishioka and Nishitani (n 3) 207; Kono (n 24) 107.

or consent order, may be recognised and enforced as a foreign judgment in Japan.[32] It is unclear which notion of a foreign judgment the courts in Cambodia would employ because they have so far never recognised or enforced any foreign judgment.[33] In addition, the official commentary of the CCP is silent on the definition of a foreign judgment.[34] However, the courts are likely to be encouraged to adopt a flexible notion of the term 'foreign judgment' if necessary, in light of the purposes of the recognition and enforcement of foreign judgments in Cambodia – (1) to avoid reopening and relitigating matters which have been adjudicated by the judge abroad, (2) to refrain from causing judicial inefficiency by having duplicative legal proceedings, (3) to forestall the issuing of conflicting foreign and domestic judgments, and (4) to increase the stability of international transactions in general.[35]

ii. Indirect Jurisdiction

Following Article 199(a) of the CCP, the courts in Cambodia will review the jurisdiction of the court of origin in recognising and enforcing a foreign judgment. However, there is no provision setting out grounds for indirect jurisdiction under Cambodian law, and this legal lacuna derives from Article 118 of Japan's Civil Procedure Code, on which Article 199 of the CCP is based. Under Japanese law, the lacuna is filled by a Supreme Court judgment in 2014 as follows:

> It is appropriate to construe that whether … a foreign country has indirect jurisdiction over an action other than an action concerning personal status should be determined in light of the rule of reason [i.e., naturalis ratio or *jôri*], … basically complying with the provisions on international jurisdiction under the Code of Civil Procedure of Japan and considering whether … it is appropriate for Japan to recognise a judgment rendered by the foreign court, in the context of the specific circumstances of the case.[36]

However, the fact that Article 199 of the CCP is based on Article 118 of the Civil Procedure Code of Japan does not justify Cambodian jurists adopting the above framework of indirect jurisdiction established by the Supreme Court of Japan. This is because the framework was established on the new version of the Japanese Civil Procedure Code, whereas the CCP is built upon the old version of the Code that contained no written rules on international jurisdiction.[37] Accordingly, the courts in Cambodia may rather find that previous legal practice in Japan on indirect jurisdiction surrounding the old edition of the Code is compatible with the CCP. In 1998, the Supreme Court of Japan held in respect of such practice as follows:

> Since there is no provision of law or ordinance which directly indicates on what grounds the country of judgment has international jurisdiction, nor are there treaties or established clear rules of international law, it should be decided by reason [i.e., naturalis ratio or *jôri*] in accordance with

[32] Nishioka and Nishitani (n 3) 207.

[33] Bun (n 8) 38; Larkin and Yun (n 11) 201.

[34] JICA, 'Commentary on Cambodian Code of Civil Procedure: Judgment Procedure [in Japanese]' (n.d.) available at www.moj.go.jp/content/000122394.pdf (accessed 10 December 2024); JICA (n 1) 25.

[35] See the accompanying commentary note on Article 199 of the CCP.

[36] *Company X v Individuals Y1, Y2, Y4, Y5 and Y 6, and Company Y3* [2014] Supreme Court of Japan 2011 (Ju)1781, Judgments of the Supreme Court, available at www.courts.go.jp/app/hanrei_en/detail?id=1232 (accessed 10 December 2024).

[37] See generally Chapter 4 in this volume.

> the idea of ensuring equal treatment of the parties and just and speedy trial. More specifically, whether … the country of judgment has international jurisdiction should be determined in the light of reason, basically in accordance with the provisions of the Code of Civil Procedure on the territorial jurisdiction of the courts from the viewpoint of whether it is appropriate to recognise the given foreign judgment, taking into consideration specific circumstances of each case.[38]

This approach is likely to conform to the current legal practice surrounding the CCP of Cambodia. As discussed in Chapter 4 of this volume, *naturalis ratio* or *jôri* has not been explicitly imported from Japanese law to the Cambodian legal system, although the CCP is based on Japan's Civil Procedure Code. Nevertheless, corresponding legal principles are effective under Cambodian law because Article 4 of the CCP, like *jôri*, mandates the courts in Cambodia to conduct civil actions fairly and speedily, obliging parties to take part in such actions honestly and in good faith. Thus, Cambodian jurists may rely on the Article to decide the international jurisdiction of the court of origin in accordance with the provisions of the CCP on the territorial jurisdiction of the courts in Cambodia.

Accordingly, the courts in Cambodia would acknowledge the jurisdiction of the court of origin if they found that one of the grounds of territorial jurisdiction under the CCP had been met. These grounds are, depending on the types of actions brought into the court, the defendant's domicile/residence/last known domicile, the place of performance of (contractual) obligations, the location of the defendant's property or security interest that may be seized, the place of tort, the location of the deceased's estate, and designation by the parties and voluntary submission by the defendant, among others.[39] However, Cambodian jurists should not apply these grounds too strictly because they are, in principle, grounds for domestic jurisdiction for the Cambodian courts. They should instead apply those grounds flexibly from the viewpoint of whether it is appropriate to recognise the foreign judgment under the specific circumstances of the relevant case.

iii. Proper Service of Process

Article 199(b) of the CCP requires Cambodian courts to examine whether a proper service of process has been made to the defendant by the court of origin or whether the defendant voluntarily appeared before the court without receiving such a process, to confirm that the defendant's right to be heard had been observed in the judgment's country of origin. Nevertheless, the Article does not elaborate on what rules or laws the courts in Cambodia may apply to decide the properness of the service of process. In the context of the recognition and enforcement of foreign judgments in Japan, the Supreme Court of Japan has held that the service of process by the court of origin does not have to comply with the laws and rules of Japanese civil procedure (i.e., the law of the forum) as long as the service of process has provided the defendant with sufficient notice to realise the commencement of the proceedings and exercise his/her right to be heard in the country of origin.[40] This approach is likely to be maintainable under Cambodian law as the courts in Cambodia may not force foreign courts to follow the rules and laws of Cambodian civil procedure.

[38] *Gabindram Naraindas Sadhwani, et al v Kishinchando Naraindas Sadhwani, et al.*

[39] See CCP, Arts 7ff. For details of the grounds of territorial jurisdiction under the CCP, see Chapter 4 in this volume.

[40] *Gabindram Naraindas Sadhwani, et al v Kishinchando Naraindas Sadhwani, et al.*

It is impractical to require a foreign court to make its service of process fully compatible with the law of the country of judgment enforcement because, at the time of issuing the service of process, the foreign court may not anticipate whether the final judgment of its proceedings will be enforced abroad. Even if the foreign court is aware of the possibility, it is unlikely to be able to decide at the beginning of the proceedings in which country that judgment will be enforced.[41] Therefore, as Bun points out, the threshold of the proper service of process by a foreign court is likely to be the general principle of '*la contradiction*' under Article 3 of the CCP, which requires a court to summon all the parties to allow them to plead and respond to each other.[42] Cambodian courts will therefore likely refuse to recognise and enforce a foreign judgment that has been issued as a result of service by public notice even if such service of process by such notice is admissible under the law of the country of origin.[43]

iv. Public Order or Morals

The courts in Cambodia may refuse the recognition and enforcement of a foreign judgment that contradicts the public order or morals of the country. 'The public order' and 'morals' allude to legal principles considered to be fundamental to Cambodia that may be generally encapsulated by the umbrella concept of public policy.[44] However, the interpretation of public policy in Cambodian courts is a complex and nuanced process, as neither Cambodian statutes nor court decisions define public policy,[45] leaving it subject to case-by-case interpretation by Cambodian courts.[46] This complexity underscores the need for further research and understanding. Since Cambodian law does not provide any guidance for the courts to interpret public policy, Cambodian jurists may find relevant discussion on the corresponding provision in Japanese law – Article 118(3) of the Code of Civil Procedure – useful.

Under Japanese law (and also other legal systems following the common law and civil law traditions), the public policy ground for judgment recognition and enforcement is twofold – procedural public policy and substantive public policy.[47] This twofold public policy ground, which is also potentially applicable under Cambodian law, is a key aspect to consider in the recognition and enforcement of foreign judgments in Cambodia. Procedural public policy concerns whether the foreign court's litigation proceedings are compatible with the enforcing state's fundamental principles of procedural law, while substantive public policy requires the enforcing court to review the foreign judgment's substance and contents based on the enforcing country's foundational legal order. According to Bun, the twofold public policy

[41] See also Domej (n 6) 1477 (suggesting that the requirement that service of process has taken place in a formally correct manner may create considerable room for abuse by the court of enforcement).

[42] Bun (n 8) 40.

[43] Commentary notes on Art 199 of the CCP and Nishioka and Nishitani (n 3) 210.

[44] YU Oppusunggu, 'Principle 9: Public Policy' in A Chong (ed), *Asian Principles for the Recognition and Enforcement of Foreign Judgements* (Singapore, Asian Business Law Institute, 2020) 118.

[45] The lack of definition of public policy under Cambodian law is inevitable because '[t]he content of the public policy defence is notoriously difficult to define': F Garcimartín and G Saumier, *Explanatory Report on the Convention of 2 July 2019 on the Recognition and Enforcement of Foreign Judgments in Civil or Commercial Matters* (The Hague, The Hague Conference on Private International Law – HCCH – Permanent Bureau, 2020) 120.

[46] Bun (n 8) 40; Larkin and Yun (n 11) 219.

[47] Yokoyama (n 3) 148; Nishioka and Nishitani (n 3) 212; Kono (n 24) 111; Domej (n 6) 1476; Briggs (n 6) 1479–80; I Thoma, 'Public Policy (*Ordre Public*)' in J Basedow and others (eds), *Encyclopedia of Private International Law* (Cheltenham, Edward Elgar Publishing, 2017) 1457.

ground at the recognition and enforcement stage may be maintained under Cambodian law,[48] although legal research on that ground (and other topics) is still at the beginning of development in the country.[49]

Japanese law commentators suggest that the purpose of procedural public policy is to safeguard fair trials and the party's right to be heard before the court of origin, albeit indirectly through examination by the enforcing court.[50] According to Kono, the ground of procedural public policy would be triggered by the enforcing court if it found out that: (1) the foreign judgment had been obtained by fraudulent means such as falsification of deeds or certificates, (2) the court of origin had acted unfairly in the proceedings or had violated principles of due process, (3) the defendant had not been given timely notice about significant procedural matters, or (4) there had been other (serious) procedural defects.[51] The connotation of these examples is likely to be that the enforcing court is not to interpret the ground of procedural public policy expansively. For instance, the Supreme Court of Japan held in 2019 that a failure to serve a judgment document in foreign proceedings should not immediately be deemed as a violation of procedural public policy by the enforcing country, because different countries and jurisdictions have different procedural rules on the service of a judgment document.[52] The Court further held that:

> Even if the litigation proceedings of a foreign judgment include elements … based on a system that is not adopted in Japan, such mere inclusion cannot immediately lead to a conclusion that the [judgment is contrary to the procedural public policy of Japan]. However, if such elements are found to be incompatible with the fundamental principle or fundamental idea of the legal order in Japan, the litigation proceedings [for obtaining the] foreign judgment should be found to be contrary to the [procedural] public policy [of Japan].[53]

Accordingly, only egregious procedural breaches or breaches of fundamental principles of procedural fairness at the court of origin may be deemed as a violation of procedural public policy at the enforcement stage under Japanese law.[54]

The courts in Cambodia may follow suit, because refusing to recognise or enforce a foreign judgment based on inevitable minor differences between the procedural law of the country of origin and that of Cambodia may further exclude the Kingdom from the global circulation of judgments in civil and commercial matters.[55] Such exclusion may bring about significant risks to international businesses engaging in cross-border activities with Cambodian parties, such as the ultimate deprivation by Cambodian courts of rights and remedies conferred by successful litigation before the court of origin. Therefore, as Bun points out, the requirement of the violation of the procedural policy would be met only where the enforcing court found serious procedural irregularities in the proceedings before

[48] Bun (n 8) 41.

[49] See generally C Seavmey, 'Challenges of Legal Education in Cambodia [in Japanese]' (2020) 85 *ICD News* 16.

[50] Nishioka and Nishitani (n 3) 213.

[51] Kono (n 24) 112.

[52] *XX v YY* [2019] Second Petty Bench of the Supreme Court of Japan 2017 (Ju)2177, Judgments of the Supreme Court, https://www.courts.go.jp/app/hanrei_en/detail?id=1628 (accessed 10 December 2024) para 4(2).

[53] ibid, para 4(1).

[54] M Haga, 'Public Policy (3): Procedural Public Policy' in M Dogauchi and Y Nakanishi (eds), *Leading Cases in Private International Law* (Tokyo, Yuhikaku Publishing, 2021) 197.

[55] See Asian Business Law Institute, *Enforcement of Foreign Judgments in ASEAN: Ranking the Portability of ASEAN Judgments within ASEAN* (Singapore, Asian Business Law Institute 2022) 7 (suggesting Cambodia has 'a comparatively illiberal regimes' for the enforcement of foreign judgments).

the court of origin, such as fraud in obtaining the judgment and the lack of a reasonable opportunity for the losing party to present his/her case.[56] Bun also suggests that the enforcing court may rely on the (procedural) public policy ground in refusing the recognition of a foreign judgment that conflicts with a judgment issued by a Cambodian court involving the same parties and same subject matter.[57]

Likewise, the ground of substantive public policy should be interpreted strictly to limit recourse to that ground to exceptional situations involving the infringements of national security or sovereignty of the country of recognition. A well-settled example of such situations under Japanese law is where recognition or enforcement is sought for a foreign judgment ordering the unsuccessful party to pay punitive damages in addition to compensation and litigation costs.[58] According to the Supreme Court of Japan, such damages are contrary to the basic principles and basic ideas of compensation for tort claims under Japanese law because:

> [T]he system of punitive damages … is designed to impose sanctions on the culprit and prevent similar acts in the future …, [and] is [thus] similar to criminal sanctions such as fines in Japan. In contrast, the system of damages based upon tort in Japan assesses the actual loss in a pecuniary manner, forces the culprit to compensate this amount, and thus enables the recovery of the disadvantage suffered by the victim and restores the status quo ante ….[59]

The system of damages under Cambodian tort law is not too distinct from that of Japan. Article 757 of the Civil Code (CC) provides monetary compensation as the primary remedy for tort damages. Article 758(1) states that the amount of monetary compensation is calculated by comparing the victim's economic situation that s/he would have been in if the tort had not occurred and his/her actual economic situation after the tortious act has been committed, as much as possible, based on statistics and other objective materials. As the CC does not recognise punitive damages as a valid remedy for tortious conduct, the courts in Cambodia are unlikely to recognise or enforce foreign judgments ordering the payment of punitive compensation. Nevertheless, they may not refuse recognition or enforcement of foreign punitive damage judgments altogether, because the purposes underlying punitive damages are diverse and sometimes can include the mitigation of the victim's psychological loss and litigation costs.[60] Cambodian judges may therefore consider recognising or enforcing a foreign punitive damages judgment partially, to the extent that the final damage awarded does not surpass the amount of the victim's actual loss.

Another potential ground for violating substantive public policy under Cambodian law that may be worth examining is the payment of gambling debts. Kono suggests that the recognition and enforcement of a foreign judgment on the payment of gambling debts may

[56] Bun (n 8) 41.

[57] ibid 44.

[58] Kono (n 24) 111; Yokoyama (n 3) 148; Nishioka and Nishitani (n 3) 212.

[59] *Northcon I, Oregon Partnership v Mansei Kogyo Co Ltd, et al* [1997] Third Petty Bench of the Supreme Court of Japan 1993 (O)1762, https://www.courts.go.jp/app/hanrei_en/detail?id=316 (accessed 10 December 2024). See also *X v Hondaya Incorporated and others* [2021] Third Petty Bench of the Supreme Court of Japan 2020 (Ju)170, Judgments of the Supreme Court, https://www.courts.go.jp/app/hanrei_en/detail?id=1830 (confirming that punitive compensation for loss or damage goes against public policy referred to in Art 118(3) of the Code of Civil Procedure of Japan (accessed 10 December 2024)).

[60] B Elbalti, 'Public Policy (2): Punitive Damages [in Japanese]' in M Dogauchi and Y Nakanishi (eds), *Leading Cases in Private International Law* (Tokyo, Yuhikaku Publishing, 2021) 195.

be against the substantive public policy of Japan because the Penal Code of Japan generally bans most forms of gambling, albeit with some exceptions.[61] Likewise, Cambodia's Law on the Suppression of Gambling provides in Article 1 that '[g]ambling of all kinds, in all places throughout the whole Kingdom of Cambodia shall be strictly prohibited, *except those permitted by the Royal government*'.[62] The Law on Management of Commercial Gaming (LMCG) states that commercial gambling activities, such as casino games, luck-based games (like lotteries) and betting games are permitted in certain commercial gaming zones under licences issued by the Commercial Gambling Management Commission of Cambodia (CGMC).[63] However, the LMCG reportedly restricts the following persons from playing such gambling activities: individuals who are mentally or financially incompetent, armed individuals, minors and employees of the gaming establishments conducing the gaming activities, as well as Cambodian citizens (including armed forces, public officials and elected citizens).[64] Thus, if a foreign judgment orders a person falling under one of these categories to pay gambling debts, the competent court in Cambodia will likely refuse the enforcement of that judgment by invoking the ground of substantive public policy.

v. *Reciprocity*

Cambodia maintains a stringent requirement of reciprocity for judgment recognition and enforcement.[65] According to Bun, 'a guarantee of reciprocity' requirement is most difficult to meet among the threshold requirements for judgment enforcement under Article 199 of the CCP because it allegedly requires the country of origin to have a mechanism to guarantee recognition and enforcement of judgments issued by Cambodian courts, and because such a mechanism is arguably found only in a treaty or convention concluded between the country of origin and Cambodia.[66] Cambodia has only one international agreement in force on reciprocal recognition and enforcement of foreign judgments – the Cambodia–Vietnam Judicial Assistance Treaty. As a result, the courts in Cambodia are unlikely to enforce foreign judgments other than those issued by Vietnamese courts.

However, Cambodian jurists may have to reconsider this strict approach for two reasons.

[61] Kono (n 24) 112. See generally Articles 185–187 of the Penal Code. However, Art 185 of the Penal Code provides that '[a] person who gambles is punished by a fine of not more than 500,000 yen or a petty fine; provided, however, that the same does not apply to a person who gambles occasionally provided for recreational amusement'. Thus, the gambling prohibition is subject to exceptions. On legal gambling in Japan, see generally E Johnston, 'How Japan Ensures You Gamble Exactly When and Where It Wants You to', *The Japan Times*, 8 June 2023, available at www.japantimes.co.jp/news/2023/06/08/national/gambling-pachinko-sports/ (accessed 10 December 2024).

[62] (Emphasis added).

[63] C Heng and S Tiv, 'Casino & Gaming: Promulgation of Law on Management of Commercial Gaming', *Client Update: Cambodia*, December 2020, available at https://kh.rajahtannasia.com/media/4383/2020-12-promulgation-of-law.pdf (accessed 10 December 2024).

[64] ibid.

[65] 'Broadly speaking, reciprocity [in the context of judgment recognition and enforcement] means that the courts of one country will enforce judgments rendered by the courts of another country, provided that the courts of that other country will reciprocate in the same way. That is, "I will enforce your judgments, if you will enforce mine"': Asian Business Law Institute (n 55) 3. See also Y Guo, 'Reciprocity' in A Chong (ed), *Asian Principles for the Recognition and Enforcement of Foreign Judgments* (Singapore, Asian Business Law Institute, 2020) 58.

[66] Bun (n 8) 41. See also Larkin and Yun (n 11) 205; Asian Business Law Institute (n 55) 7 (noting that 'Cambodia … will only recognise and enforce judgments from countries with which [it has] a bilateral agreement to do so').

First, the courts in Japan are inclined to construe 'a guarantee of reciprocity' more leniently than their counterparts in Cambodia. Corresponding to Article 199(d) of the CCP, Article 118(vi) of the Civil Procedure Code of Japan requires, as a condition of judgment recognition and enforcement, that a guarantee of reciprocity is in place between the rendering state and Japan. According to the Supreme Court of Japan, this reciprocity requirement would be satisfied 'if in the country where the foreign court rendering the judgment in issue is situated ..., the same type of the judgment as that rendered by a Japanese court would have effect under the conditions which are not different in the important points from those ... prescribed in [Article 118 of the CCP]'.[67] The justifications for this liberal approach are as follows. First, the country of origin may hardly provide the conditions for recognition and enforcement of foreign judgments that are exactly same as those in Japan, unless there exists a bilateral treaty between the two countries to such effect. Second, from the perspective of judicial economy, there is the growing need to prevent the issuing of inconsistent judgments between the same parties, especially in internationalised society today where the number of individuals crossing national borders is constantly increasing.[68] These justifications are likely to be applicable to Cambodia because of the globalisation of Cambodian economy and the integration of Cambodian workers into the international job market.[69]

Japanese courts generally support the liberal approach and have recognised and enforced judgments from various European, North American and Asian jurisdictions.[70] Certainly, they have refused to recognise judgments from Belgian and Mainland China. However, the rejection by the Tokyo District Court of the Belgian judgment in 1960 was triggered by the fact that Belgian courts at that time practised *révision au fond* (review of the merits) for the recognition and enforcement of foreign judgments.[71] As Belgian law relinquished this practice in 2004, Japanese judges today are likely to regard Belgian judgments as satisfying the reciprocity requirement under Japanese law.[72]

Several courts in Japan have refused the recognition and enforcement of judgments on civil and commercial matters from Mainland China because Chinese courts had denied the existence of a reciprocal relationship between China and Japan for judgment recognition and

[67] *Tae-Yong Chung v Burroughs Corporation* [1983] Third Petty Bench of the Supreme Court of Japan 1982 (O)826, 27 Japanese Annual of International Law 119.

[68] ibid.

[69] V Chheang, 'Cambodia Prioritises Economic Diplomacy', *East Asia Forum: Economics, Politics and Public Policy in East Asia and the Pacific*, 20 March 2021, available at www.eastasiaforum.org/2021/03/20/cambodia-prioritises-economic-diplomacy/ (accessed 10 December 2024); P Charadine, *Cambodia Within ASEAN: Twenty-Years in the Making* (Phnom Penh, Konrad-Adenauer Stiftung and Cambodian Institute for Cooperation and Peace, 2020) 16 (noting that foreign direct investment has been the main source of Cambodia's market expansion). See also T Kongnov, 'More Than One Million Cambodians Work Abroad and Sent about $3 Billion Every Year to Their Families', *Khmer Times*, 25 February 2022, available at www.khmertimeskh.com/501032136/more-than-one-million-cambodians-work-abroad-and-sent-about-3-billion-every-year-to-their-families/ (accessed 10 December 2024).

[70] H Ebisawa, 'Japan' in Louis Garb and Julian D.M Lew (eds), *Enforcement of Foreign Judgments* (Alphen aan den Rijn, Wolters Kluwer, 2023) 5–6. For the details of the foreign judgments enforced in Japan, see generally M Haga, 'Reciprocity as a Condition for the Recognition and Enforcement of Foreign Judgments (2): Its Contemporary Significance [in Japanese]' (2017) 90 *Journal of Law, Politics and Sociology* 25.

[71] *Saruma Co Ltd v Nozawa-gumi Co Ltd* [1960] Tokyo District Court 1956 (Wa) 5138, 8 Japanese Annual of International Law 181.

[72] B Elbalti, 'Foreign Judgments Recognition and Enforcement in Civil and Commercial Matters in Japan' (2019) *Osaka University Law Review* 1, 29; Nishioka and Nishitani (n 3) 216.

enforcement,[73] and because 'there [had reportedly] been no single case in which a foreign judgment [*in rem*] was recognised and enforced [in Mainland China] on the basis of the existence of reciprocity'.[74] This outcome has been criticised by some Japanese commentators who suggest that the reciprocity requirement has brought the reciprocal recognition and enforcement judgments between Japan and China to a stalemate. For instance, Okuda casts doubt on the constitutionality of that requirement under Japanese law.[75] Invoking Article 29 of the Constitution of Japan that guarantees the protection of property rights based on the public welfare of Japan,[76] he claims that restricting one's property claim by refusing the recognition or enforcement of foreign judgments is unconstitutional. According to him, 'the reciprocity requirement aims to retaliate for the refusal of recognition of Japanese judgments, with which the parties of the foreign judgment have no concern', and the applicant of judgment recognition and enforcement is not liable for the lack of reciprocity in the rendering state.[77] Moreover, some scholars point out that the reciprocity requirement under Chinese law has been relaxed (at least for some countries) since Chinese courts have recognised and enforced judgments from Germany, Singapore and the United States.[78] In 2023, it was reported that Shanghai Third Intermediate People's Court had confirmed reciprocity in recognition of Japanese bankruptcy decisions in China for the first time, holding that the lack of Japan–China reciprocity in the recognition and enforcement of civil and commercial

[73] *XX v YY* [2004] Osaka High Court 2003 (Ne) 2481 Japanese Annual of International Law 48, 171; Y Murakami, 'Reciprocity: Judgments from Mainland China [in Japanese]' in M Dogauchi and Y Nakanishi (eds), *Leading Cases in Private International Law* (Tokyo, Yuhikaku Publishing, 2021) 201. Note, however, Tokyo Family Court and Tokyo High Court have recognised Chinese divorce judgments because the 2004 Supreme People's Court Judicial Interpretation on the Recognition of Divorce has omitted the reciprocity requirement for the recognition of foreign divorce decrees involving a Chinese spouse: Y Nishitani, 'Coordination of Legal Systems by the Recognition of Foreign Judgments – Rethinking Reciprocity in Sino-Japanese Relationships' (2019) 14 *Frontiers of Law in China* 193, 227.

[74] *X v Y1 and Y2* [2015] Tokyo High Court, LEX/DB 25541803, 61 Japanese Yearbook of International Law 407, 410. According to Elbalti, the fact that any foreign judgments were unlikely to be recognised and enforced in China, was the decisive factor for the courts in Japan to refuse the recognition of the Chinese judgments: Elbalti (n 72) 27.

[75] Y Okuda, 'Unconstitutionality of Reciprocity Requirement for Recognition and Enforcement of Foreign Judgments in Japan' (2018) 13 *Frontiers of Law in China* 159.

[76] Art 29 of the Constitution provides that '[t]he right to own or to hold property is inviolable. Property rights shall be defined by law, in conformity with the public welfare'.

[77] Okuda (n 75) 169–70. Some German scholars have developed corresponding arguments in examining the compatibility of a guarantee of reciprocity with the Constitution of Germany. However, German courts and most German legal scholars are reportedly unsupportive of those arguments: M Haga, 'Reciprocity as a Condition for the Recognition and Enforcement of Foreign Judgments (1): Its Contemporary Signifiance' (2017) 90 *Journal of Law, Politics and Sociology* 1, 13–14.

[78] WS Dodge and W Zhang, 'Reciprocity in China-US Judgments Recognition' (2020) 53 *Vanderbilt Journal of Transnational Law* 1541; W Zhang, 'Sino–Foreign Recognition and Enforcement of Judgments: A Promising "Follow-Suit" Model?' (2017) 16 *Chinese Journal of International Law* 515; B Sun, 'The Future of Cross-Border Litigation in China: Enforcement of Foreign Commercial Judgments Based on Reciprocity' (2018) 50 *New York University Journal of International Law & Politics* 1135. However, Elbalti claims that 'these recent developments are unlikely to influence the attitude of Japanese courts. … Chinese courts affirmed reciprocity only with countries where it was shown that Chinese judgments had already been enforced there. … where it is shown that no Chinese judgements have been recognized in the rendering [s]tate, Chinese courts would continue to deny reciprocity with respect to those countries. In other words, the change of attitude of Chinese courts concerns only a very limited number of countries and does not show the likelihood or the high probability of recognizing foreign judgments in China where precedents of refusal to enforce Chinese judgments exist': Elbalti (n 72) 28. Some Chinese commentators concur with this argument: KF Tsang, 'Bilateral Treaty on Mutual Enforcement of Judgments between Japan and China: A Discussion on Legal Structure' (2019) 47 *Hitotsubashi Journal of Law and Politics* 31, 36.

judgments is 'not automatically applicable' to the recognition of bankruptcy proceedings.[79] The relaxation of reciprocity requirement might prompt Japanese courts to reconsider their approach to the reciprocity requirement for Chinese judgments,[80] although some Chinese commentators not only point out persistent inconsistencies in Chinese courts' judicial practice for reciprocity,[81] but also claim that Chinese courts have not necessarily moderated the reciprocity requirement and are unlikely to do so soon.[82] It therefore remains to be seen whether Japanese courts will adopt a more liberal interpretation of the reciprocity requirement for recognition and enforcement of judgments from Mainland China. However, the high threshold for Chinese judgments is exceptional under the liberal Japanese regime for judgment recognition and enforcement, and not a few Japanese commentators challenge that threshold for Chinese judgments.

As discussed elsewhere, Cambodia imported the reciprocity requirements for judgment recognition and enforcement from Article 118(vi) of the Civil Procedure Code of Japan. However, the courts in Japan have been interpreting the reciprocity requirements in the Article liberally. Thus, Japanese law and practice may not justify, despite being the source of Cambodia's reciprocity requirements, the rigid reciprocity requirement in Cambodia.

Second, the number of jurisdictions that have abolished the reciprocity requirement has been increasing due to a growing international concern over reciprocity for recognising and enforcing foreign judgments.[83] One of the basic roles of reciprocity in the recognition and enforcement of foreign decisions is to serve as a basis for increasing the prospects of judgment recognition and enforcement, and in enhancing mutual judicial cooperation between states.[84] However, as the above discussion on the lack of reciprocal relationship between Japan and China demonstrates, 'reciprocity regarding the recognition of foreign decisions appears to be no more than a last "*pièce de resistance*"' for the free movement of civil and commercial judgments.[85] This is somewhat unsurprising because the experience of the last decades, especially in the United States, suggests that the maintenance of reciprocity requirements in a legal system does not change the behaviour of other legal systems towards international judicial cooperation.[86] Moreover, the original idea of reciprocity was to encourage sovereign states to eliminate any element of inequality by virtue of guaranteeing the equality in the limitations placed by equal duties on their sovereign

[79] G Du and M Yu, 'Turning Point: China First Recognizes Japanese Bankruptcy Decision', *Conflict of Laws.net*, 11 March 2024, available at https://conflictoflaws.net/2024/turning-point-china-first-recognizes-japanese-bankruptcy-decision/ (accessed 10 December 2024).

[80] M Kawai, '"Reciprocity" between Japan and China in Recognition of Foreign Judgments [in Japanese]' (2020) *Keio Law Journal* 39, 82 (claiming that Japanese courts should enforce a judgment from China first, to help Chinese courts affirm a guarantee of reciprocity between Japan and China). See also Nishitani (n 73) 225ff.

[81] L Zhu, 'The Kolmar v Sutex Case on Reciprocity in Foreign Judgments Enforcement in China: A Welcome Development or Still on the Wrong Track?' (2018) 13 *Frontiers of Law in China* 202.

[82] KF Tsang, 'Enforcement of Foreign Commercial Judgments in China' (2018) 14 *Journal of Private International Law* 262; Z Tang, 'International Judicial Cooperation in Game Theory' (2020) 11 *Journal of International Dispute Settlement* 522.

[83] A Dutta, 'Reciprocity' in J Basedow and others (eds), *Encyclopedia of Private International Law* (Cheltenham, Edward Elgar Publishing, 2017) 1470. See also M Martinek, 'The Principle of Reciprocity in the Recognition and Enforcement of Foreign Judgments – History, Presence and No Future' (2017) 2017 *Journal of South African Law* 36.

[84] Dutta (n 83) 1470; D Stamboulakis, *Comparative Recognition and Enforcement: Foreign Judgments and Awards* (Cambridge, Cambridge University Press, 2022) 8–10.

[85] Dutta (n 83) 1470.

[86] JF Coyle, 'Rethinking Judgements Reciprocity' (2014) 92 *North Carolina Law Review* 1109, 1169; Dutta (n 83) 1470.

power.[87] States and jurisdictions may take advantage of reciprocity as a means of retaliation against the countries that have not enforced their judgments for parochial reasons. As a result of the inconveniences and challenges caused by reciprocity to the global circulation of judicial decisions,[88] states and territories have gradually relaxed reciprocity requirements for judgment recognition and enforcement.[89] Even the jurisdictions that still maintain such requirements have loosened their attitude towards reciprocity.[90] In the end, reciprocity is an archaic doctrine for the current practice surrounding the recognition and enforcement of foreign judgments. This point is well summarised by Elbalti in his comparative article as follows:

> [M]any jurisdictions have removed reciprocity from their judgment recognition requirements. … In other jurisdictions, reciprocity is either presumed or simply never applied. … [T]he judicial practice of many [s]tates that still require proof of reciprocity shows that the decisive factor in assessing whether reciprocity exists or not is the actual practice of the courts of the rendering [s]tate. These developments, coupled with the general trend towards the liberalization of the law and the practice of the recognition and enforcement of foreign judgments, make it possible to contend that in the overwhelming majority of cases, reciprocity will prove to be a requirement that can be easily satisfied. *Therefore, at the end of the day, the fate of reciprocity is to become a paper tiger with trimmed claws … a slogan with no real effects.*[91]

Therefore, rigid standards of reciprocity do not conform to today's liberal practice of the recognition and enforcement of foreign judgments around the world. A report on the portability of ASEAN judgments within ASEAN issued by the Asian Business Law Institute observes of Cambodia that '[t]he main hurdle [for the enforcement of judgments among the ASEAN member states] is that Cambodia and Laos have rigid standards of reciprocity. Cambodia and Laos will only enforce judgments from countries with which they have a bilateral agreement to do so'.[92] Maintaining such parochial rigidity is highly unlikely to improve Cambodia's investment attractiveness. The rigidity is also likely to undermine the international reputation of Cambodian judiciary and legal practice.

vi. Recognition for the Purposes of Establishing Res Judicata *and Issue Estoppel*

The basic principle of judgment recognition under Cambodian law is that foreign judgments satisfying the requirements provided in Article 199 of the CCP are automatically recognised in Cambodia.[93] No rules define the effect of judgment recognition. Nevertheless,

[87] A Lenhoff, 'Reciprocity and the Law of Foreign Judgments: A Historical – Critical Analysis' (1956) 16 *Louisiana Law Review* 465, 465–66.

[88] Guo (n 65) 58–59 (suggesting that the strict interpretation and application of reciprocity may encourage 'unnecessary protectionism and waste of judicial resources'). See also Asian Business Law Institute (n 55) 3ff (pointing out that the rigidity of the standard of reciprocity is the primary hurdle for the enforcement of foreign judgments).

[89] Dutta (n 83) 1470.

[90] See, for example, the case of Japan: Elbalti (n 72) 25–26; Kono (n 24) 113; Yokoyama (n 3) 150; Nishioka and Nishitani (n 3) 214–15.

[91] B Elbalti, 'Reciprocity and the Recognition and Enforcement of Foreign Judgments: A Lot of Bark but Not Much Bite' (2017) 13 *Journal of Private International Law* 184, 217–18 (emphasis added and footnote omitted).

[92] Asian Business Law Institute (n 55) 3.

[93] Automatic recognition of foreign judgments is the norm under Art 118 of the Code of Civil Procedure of Japan: Yokoyama (n 3) 146; Nishioka and Nishitani (n 3) 205.

the purpose of Article 199 of the CCP is to prevent Cambodian courts from conducting legal proceedings duplicating foreign litigation,[94] which means that the enforcing courts would likely confer *res judicata* effect on foreign judgments once they have met the requirements listed in Article 199. However, how the courts in Cambodia decide the substance of the *res judicata* effect is still being determined. Japanese commentators are divided on whether the effect is to be defined, in principle, by the law of the country of origin or that of the enforcing state.[95] The result of this academic discussion may affect how a foreign judgment gives rise to issue estoppel under Cambodian law.[96]

C. Special Rules under Domestic Legislation

Cambodian law does not have bespoke rules for recognising and enforcing foreign judgments on different categories of subject matters. The courts in Cambodia are therefore supposed to recognise and enforce foreign judgments within the requirements set out in Article 199 of the CCP, examining whether the foreign judgment at hand satisfies those criteria on a case-by-case basis, in light of the specific nature of that judgment. Among the requirements in Article 199, that of indirect jurisdiction is relevant to consider specific judgment recognition rules because Cambodian courts determine satisfaction of that requirement based on (but without strictly following) grounds of domestic jurisdiction of Cambodian courts under the CCP.[97] The courts may hear claims based on jurisdiction by agreement, jurisdiction by appearance,[98] or jurisdiction determined by the address of the defendant.[99] Some provisions in the CCP provide additional grounds of jurisdiction for specific subject matter, as discussed in the following subsections.[100]

i. Law of Obligations

Article 9 of the CCP sets out additional grounds of jurisdiction for contractual obligations. It allows parties to bring specific contract claims to certain first instance courts as follows. (1) A claim for performance of obligations can be brought to the court having territorial jurisdiction over the place where the obligations shall be performed.[101] (2) A payment of money claim for a bill or cheque can be brought to the court having territorial jurisdiction

[94] See Section II.B.i above.

[95] M Haga, 'Effect of Foreign Judgments: A General Observation [in Japanese]' (2010) 83 *Journal of Law, Politics and Sociology* 363, 386–89.

[96] Estoppel is rarely considered in the context of judgment recognition and enforcement under Cambodian law: Bun (n 8); Larkin and Yun (n 11). On estoppel and foreign judgments under common law, see R Mortensen, R Garnett and M Keyes, *Private International Law in Australia*, 5th edn, (Chatswood, LexisNexis, 2023) 134ff; A Bell, 'Country Report: Australia' in A Chong (ed), *Recognition and Enforcement of Foreign Judgments in Asia* (Singapore, Asian Business Law Institute, 2017).

[97] See Section II.B.ii above.

[98] CCP, Arts 13–14.

[99] ibid, Art 8.

[100] For the details of those special grounds and other grounds of jurisdiction, see Chapter 4 in this volume, which discusses the direct jurisdiction of Cambodian courts based on the grounds of territorial jurisdiction under the CCP.

[101] This ground may cover a claim of restitution for unjust enrichment arising from a contractual relationship, such as restitution after void sales contracts: see e.g., Nishioka and Nishitani (n 3) 221.

over the place where the money payment shall be made. (3) A claim for the performance of obligations against a person whose domicile is not in Cambodia or is unknown can be brought to the court having territorial jurisdiction over the location of that person's property, which is the subject of that claim, the claim's security or attachment by the court. (4) Performance of obligations against a juridical person whose administrative headquarters or business office is not in Cambodia or is unknown can be brought to the court having territorial jurisdiction over the location of that juridical person's property, which is the subject of that claim, the claim's security or attachment by the court.[102] Note, however, that these grounds are supplemental, in that they are not exclusive grounds for the courts to hear contractual claims.

Concerning tort claims, Article 9(f) of the CCP provides that actions based on tort may be brought before the court having jurisdiction over the location where the alleged tort occurred. Nevertheless, the location of a tort is not defined, so it may be the place where the alleged tort was committed, the place where the alleged damage from the tort occurred, or both. In addition, the CCP lacks the definition of the place of damage, which is problematic because damage from a tort, such as indirect or secondary damage, is omnipresent in some cases, especially in product liability cases and internet defamation cases. The courts in Cambodia may have to consider how they supplement the lack of those definitions in the CCP in determining the indirect jurisdiction of the court of origin. In any event, they will need to consider the laws of the country of origin and the forum.

The CCP does not contain special rules of jurisdiction for trust claims. Thus, as additional grounds of indirect jurisdiction for such claims, enforcing courts may rely on the grounds of jurisdiction for contractual obligations,[103] the place where the property subject to the trust agreement is located,[104] and the place where the tort related to the trust was arguably committed,[105] among others, depending on the nature of the trust and the claim involved.[106] The 2019 Trust Law and Prakas No 003 OSH/Prokor on Rules on the Management, Establishment and Functioning of Trust do not designate the court having jurisdiction over trust claims.

ii. Law of Property

In recognising and enforcing a foreign judgment on immovable property, a starting point for the enforcing court is to determine the indirect jurisdiction of the court of origin based on Article 9(g) of the CCP. This Article allows parties to bring actions related to an immovable to the court having territorial jurisdiction over the location of that immovable. Thus, the enforcing court in Cambodia is highly likely to endorse the indirect jurisdiction of the court of origin if the real property is located within the territorial limits of the court of origin.

Intellectual property (IP) rights protection is an area in need of significant improvement for Cambodian law. No specific Cambodian laws or regulations outline special rules of indirect jurisdiction for IP rights claims. This lack of additional grounds of indirect jurisdiction

[102] CCP, Arts 9(a)–(d).
[103] ibid, Arts 9(a)–(d).
[104] ibid, Art 9(g).
[105] ibid, Art 9(f).
[106] See Chapter 4 in this volume.

for foreign judgments on IP rights underscores the need for clarification and guidance in this area. Until new guidance is provided, Cambodian courts may continue to rely on Articles 8 and 9 of the CCP to determine the indirect jurisdiction for recognising foreign IP judgments.[107]

iii. Law of Succession to Property

To enforce a foreign judgment on succession to property, the enforcing court may have to consider several provisions in the CCP and the Annex of the Non-Suit Civil Case Procedural Law (Annex). Following Article 9(i) of the CCP, actions concerning a deceased's estate may be brought into the court having jurisdiction over (1) 'the location of the domicile of the deceased at the time the inheritance commences', (2) 'if such [a] person does not have a domicile in [the country of origin] or his/her domicile is unknown, the location of his/her residence', or (3) 'if such [a] person does not have a location of residence in [the country of origin] or his/her location of residence is unknown, the location of his/her last known domicile'. If the court of origin had territorial jurisdiction over one of these grounds, the enforcing court will likely endorse the indirect jurisdiction of that court. In addition, the Annex contains a comprehensive list of grounds of jurisdiction for non-contentious cases, and the courts in Cambodia may have to consult with the list when they examine the indirect jurisdiction of the court of origin pertaining to decisions on ritual objects and disqualification of a presumptive successor, among others.[108]

iv. Family Law[109]

a. Decrees of Marriage

According to the Marriage and Family Law, Cambodia recognises the validity of a marriage formally celebrated abroad between Cambodian citizens or between a Cambodian citizen and a foreign national.[110] However, the law only recognises such marriage to the extent that it does not violate Cambodian law.[111] Accordingly, Cambodian judges and legal officers are unlikely to enforce same-sex marriages, as the Constitution emphasises that marriage may take place 'between one husband and one wife'.[112] Indeed, one record showed that two women had held their wedding ceremony in 1995, and one of them acted as a husband.[113] Exceptionally, the local authority treated the relationship as a legal marriage and issued a marriage licence since one woman had three children from her previous heterosexual marriage.[114] However, the authority emphasised that it would not issue the marriage certificate if both women were single and had no child, as same-sex marriages could not produce

[107] See Chapter 4 in this volume.

[108] See generally Chapter 4 in this volume.

[109] Section II.C.iv is based on Section III of N Teramura, 'Cambodia' in A Reyes, W Lui and K Nishioka (eds), *Choice of Law and Recognition in Asian Family Law* (Oxford, Hart Publishing, 2023) 219–40.

[110] Marriage and Family Law, Art 79(1).

[111] ibid, Art 79(2).

[112] Constitution of Cambodia, Art 45.

[113] J Barber and HS Chheng, 'Husband and Wife with No Male Hassles', *The Phnom Penh Post*, 24 March 1995, available at www.phnompenhpost.com/national/husband-and-wife-no-male-hassles (accessed 10 December 2024).

[114] ibid.

babies.[115] This case appears to be an exception under the Cambodian legal system. In fact, when a French male and a Cambodian male tried to hold a wedding ceremony in 2018, the immigration police of their province stepped in.[116] The police justified the intervention, claiming that the marriage was illegal under Cambodian law.[117] It is therefore anticipated that the courts in Cambodia will be reluctant to enforce decrees of same-sex marriage issued by foreign institutions.[118]

On polygamous marriages, the CC explicitly prohibits bigamy, stating that '[a] person who has a spouse may not effect[uate] an additional marriage'.[119] Moreover, the Law on Monogamy criminalises bigamy with a term of imprisonment for six months to one year and/or a fine of between 200,000 to 1,000,000 Riels (49–245 USD).[120] These provisions are unsurprising as the Constitution defines marriage as a consensual relationship between a man and a woman.[121] Cambodia is home to around 300,000 Muslims.[122] However, no norms admit an exception for the minority population to have their traditional polygamous wedding as permitted by *shariah* law,[123] although the Constitution guarantees freedom of religion, albeit with some reservations.[124] Multiple marriages were practised among historical Cambodian figures, such as the late King Norodom Sihanouk, who was married to two or three wives, but the modern Cambodian law has not legalised bigamy.[125] Second marriages still occasionally take place in some parts of Cambodia – especially in rural areas – but they are practised informally without obtaining official marriage certificates.[126] Hence, the recognition of foreign decrees of polygamous marriage is likely to be rejected by Cambodian authorities.

b. Decrees of Nullity, Separation and Divorce

Foreign decisions on the annulment and termination of marriages are processed within the framework of the recognition of foreign judgments under Article 199 of the CCP because no rules are available in the Marriage and Family Law for Cambodian judges to handle

[115] ibid.

[116] BR Kongkea, 'Police Prevent Same-sex Wedding Ceremony', *Khmer Times*, 5 February 2018, available at www.khmertimeskh.com/106509/police-prevent-sex-wedding-ceremony/ (accessed 10 December 2024).

[117] ibid.

[118] On the Cambodian Government's unwillingness to legalise same-sex marriage, see P Sotheary, 'Kingdom Not Yet Ready for LGBT Laws: Hun Sen', *Khmer Times*, 21 February 2021, available at www.khmertimeskh.com/580112/kingdom-not-yet-ready-for-lgbt-laws-hun-sen/ (accessed 10 December 2024). Moreover, no discernible rules in the CC and other relevant legislation recognise civil partnerships and civil unions.

[119] CC, Art 949.

[120] Law on Monogamy, Art 9.

[121] Constitution of Cambodia, Art 45.

[122] worldpopulationreview.com/countries/cambodia-population (accessed 10 December 2024); F Sabeone, 'Islam in Cambodia: The Fate of the Cham Muslims' (2017) *European Institute for Asian Studies: EU-Asia at a Glance*, available at www.eias.org/wp-content/uploads/2016/03/EU_Asia_at_a_Glance_Sabeone_Cham_Cambodia_2017-1.pdf (accessed 10 May 2025).

[123] P Seangly and E Handley, 'To Have and to Hold: Polygamy in the Kingdom', *The Phnom Penh Post*, 10 February 2017, available at www.phnompenhpost.com/post-weekend/have-and-hold-polygamy-kingdom (accessed 10 December 2024).

[124] Constitution of Cambodia, Art 43. Note, however, that the Article guarantees the freedom of religion to the extent that it does not impact on other religious beliefs and does not contradict with public order and security. It also designates Buddhism as the national religion of Cambodia.

[125] Seangly and Handley (n 123).

[126] ibid.

the process. However, it is uncertain how the Cambodian courts will handle foreign judgments on nullity or termination of a marriage. The fact is that there has been no instance in which a Cambodian court has recognised and enforced or even refused to recognise and enforce, a foreign judgment. This is possibly due to the reciprocity requirement under Article 199(d).[127] It is submitted that the courts in Cambodia relax this requirement to enable the recognition of foreign decisions on nullity, separation and divorce. Otherwise, they would be required to conduct duplicative legal proceedings and those who have separated or been divorced from their partner abroad would have to file a new action to alter their marriage status in Cambodia.

c. Decrees Relating to the Well-being of the Child

Cambodia is a party to the Convention of 29 May 1993 on Protection of Children and Co-operation in Respect of Intercountry Adoption (the 1993 Hague Adoption Convention), which provides rules on the recognition and effects of international child adoptions roughly as follows. A contracting state of the Convention shall recognise by operation of law an international child adoption certified by the competent authority of another contracting state that has followed the provisions of the Convention.[128] What the Convention means by the recognition of an international child adoption includes the recognition of:

(a) 'the legal parent-child relationship between the child and his or her adoptive parents';
(b) 'parental responsibility of the adoptive parents for the child'; and
(c) 'the termination of a pre-existing legal relationship between the child and his or her mother and father, if the adoption has this effect in the Contracting State where it was made'.[129]

A contracting state may refuse the recognition of an adoption only where the adoption is manifestly contrary to its public policy, taking into consideration the best interests of the adopted child.[130] According to the HCCH's official guide on the Adoption Convention, '[n]on-recognition of the adoption would be an extreme sanction for very exceptional cases', such as where the adoption would violate fundamental rights of the adopted child's natural family.[131] This is indeed a rare instance because the Convention requires the competent authority of the state of adoption carefully to assess an international adoption's effect and impact on the child when judging his or her adoptability.[132] Cambodia therefore has a fundamental obligation to recognise international adoptions that have been certified by the Central Authorities of other member states of the Convention.[133]

[127] Bun (n 8) 38.
[128] 1993 Hague Child Adoption Convention, Art 23.
[129] ibid, Art 26(1).
[130] ibid, Art 24.
[131] HCCH, *The Implementation and Operation of the 1993 Hague Intercountry Adoption Convention: Guide to Good Practice* (Bristol, Family Law 2008) 116.
[132] 1993 Hague Child Adoption Convention, Art 4.
[133] Cambodia has not signed the 1996 Hague Convention on Parental Responsibility and Protection of Children and the 2007 Hague Child Support Convention. No noticeable materials suggest that the Cambodian authorities are keen to discuss the possibility of adopting the Conventions or some of their principles.

v. Laws of Corporations and Insolvency

The CCP does not set out special jurisdictional grounds for corporate cases. However, the Non-Suit Civil Case Procedural Law states that the following matters are under the exclusive jurisdiction of the court having territorial jurisdiction over the company's address: (1) appointment of a special director, (2) appointment of a special representative, (3) dissolution of the company, (4) appointment and removal of a capital contribution inspector, (5) permission for the company's stakeholders to convene an extraordinary general stakeholder meeting, and (6) amendments of articles of incorporation, among others.[134] Thus, the enforcing court in Cambodia would recognise the satisfaction of the ground of indirect jurisdiction if the foreign decision concerned one of these matters, provided that the decision was issued by the court having territorial jurisdiction over the address of the company disputed.

On insolvency proceedings, the 2007 Insolvency Law has jurisdiction provisions that the courts in Cambodia may adopt as bases for indirect jurisdiction. One may bring an insolvency action at a civil court against a debtor who is (1) a partnership or legal entity formed under the laws of Cambodia, (2) a natural person who is domiciled and owns assets in Cambodia, (3) a foreign partnership or legal person that owns assets in Cambodia, or (4) a foreign natural person who owns assets in Cambodia.[135] Insolvency proceedings against (3) and (4) are permissible in respect of their assets situated in Cambodia only, and such assets are either tangible assets located in the territory of Cambodia or assets or rights whose ownership or entitlement is registered under the authority of the Cambodian government.[136] The court in Cambodia would therefore be unlikely to enforce a foreign judgment on insolvency proceedings if the judgment was made solely against an asset situated outside the territory of the country of origin. It would recognise and enforce foreign insolvency proceedings against (1) a partnership or legal entity formed under the laws of the country of origin, (2) a natural person who is domiciled and owns assets in the country of origin, (3) a foreign partnership or legal person owning assets in the country of origin, or (4) a foreign natural person having assets in the country of origin.

vi. Competition Law

No rules in the CCP or other statutes confer Cambodian courts with exclusive jurisdiction over competition disputes.[137] Accordingly, indirect jurisdiction for competition law is likely to be determined by the enforcing court based on the general jurisdiction rules in the CCP on a case-by-case basis.[138] Competition law covers various areas of law, such as contractual disputes and tortious claims.[139] For example, disputes may arise from 'contracts which relate

[134] Non-Suit Civil Case Procedural Law, Art 4; Annex of the Non-Suit Civil Case Procedural Law, Art 1(11)–(22). (Available in Japanese at www.jica.go.jp/Resource/activities/issues/governance/portal/cambodia/ku57pq00002khh0b-att/non_suit_civil_case_procedural_law_ja_commentary.pdf; www.jica.go.jp/Resource/activities/issues/governance/portal/cambodia/ku57pq00002khh0b-att/non_suit_civil_case_procedural_law_ja.pdf respectively, accessed 10 May 2025).

[135] Insolvency Law, Arts 6(1) and 82.

[136] ibid, Art 6(2).

[137] See Chapter 4 in this volume.

[138] See Section II.B.ii. above.

[139] Nishioka and Nishitani (n 3) 226.

to a foreign target and contain anti-competitive clauses, e.g.,on exclusive dealership'.[140] The enforcing courts in Cambodia may discern indirect jurisdiction for foreign judgments on such competition-related contractual disputes in light of Articles 9(1)(a)–(d) of the CCP. If the victim of anti-competitive conduct has brought a compensation claim against members of a cartel in a foreign court,[141] and if the victim has requested a court in Cambodia to enforce the judgment issued by that court, the Cambodia court would consider the indirect jurisdiction of the foreign court based on Article 9(g) of the CCP, which recognises the place of tort as a ground for direct jurisdiction. However, even if the enforcing court accepts the indirect jurisdiction of the court of origin, the enforcing court may refuse to enforce the foreign judgment, invoking the Competition Law of Cambodia by way of the public policy ground in Article 199 of the CCP.[142]

III. Enforcement of Judgments

To enforce a foreign judgment in Cambodia, the prevailing party shall file an action for judgment enforcement to a competent court to obtain an execution judgment.[143] The competent court is the court having territorial jurisdiction over the debtor under Article 8 of the CCP, or, if the said Article cannot determine the jurisdiction, the court of first instance having territorial jurisdiction over the property that is the object of the foreign judgment.[144] In either case, the competent court is required to confirm the foreign judgment is final and binding in the country of origin and fulfils other conditions set out in Article 199 of the CCP.[145] If the foreign court does not satisfy these requirements for judgment recognition, the competent court shall dismiss the suit for foreign judgment enforcement. The competent court is not allowed to examine the merits of the foreign judgment.[146]

Once the prevailing party has obtained an execution judgment, s/he may proceed with enforcing the foreign judgment. The CCP allows the enforcement of monetary judgments against the debtor's tangible and intangible assets, such as (1) movables, (2) credit rights and other property rights, (3) immovables, and (4) vessels.[147] On (1), the request for execution against movables shall be filed to the bailiff at the first instance court having territorial jurisdiction over those movables.[148] On (2), enforcement against such rights falls under the jurisdiction of the court of first instance having territorial jurisdiction over the debtor (i.e., the defendant) determined by Article 8 of the CCP, or otherwise the court of first instance having territorial jurisdiction over the third party debtor prescribed by Article 8 of the CCP.[149] On (3), the following courts have the jurisdiction to enforce foreign judgments

[140] J Basedow, 'Competition Law (Antitrust)' in Jürgen Basedow and others (eds), *Encyclopedia of Private International Law* (Cheltenham, Edward Elgar Publishing, 2017) 430.

[141] ibid.

[142] See Nishioka and Nishitani (n 3) 226.

[143] CCP, Art 352(1). See also generally JICA (n 1) 25.

[144] CCP, Art 352(2).

[145] ibid, Art 352(2).

[146] ibid, Art 352(3). Moreover, Art 352(5) of the CCP requires the competent court to state in the execution judgment that it has permitted the execution of the foreign judgment.

[147] Bun (n 8) 46–47.

[148] CCP, Art 384(1).

[149] ibid, Art 402(3).

against immovables: (a) 'where the subject of the execution is land or registered building, the court of first instance having jurisdiction over the location of the immovable' and (b) 'where the subject of the execution is a jointly held share of land or registered building, a registered perpetual lease or usufruct, or a share in the foregoing rights, the court having jurisdiction over the place of registration of such rights'.[150] On (4), the execution against a vessel shall be conducted through auction by the execution court.[151] This is the first instance court having jurisdiction over the place where the vessel is located at the time of the commencement of the auction.[152] The CCP sets out different procedural rules for different subjects of enforcement of monetary judgments, and each execution court shall follow the rules tailored to its object's type of enforcement.[153]

In addition, the CCP allows the enforcement of non-monetary judgments, such as decisions on specific performance. Article 524(1) of the CCP provides that compulsory transfer of a real property (or a vessel) shall be effectuated by the bailiff at the execution court through transferring the possession of that property from the debtor to the creditor. Article 525(1) states that a compulsory transfer of movable property shall be made by the bailiff at the execution court by taking that movable from the debtor and delivering it to the creditor. The procedures for executing non-money decisions are prescribed in the Chapter Four of Book Six of the CCP.

IV. Conclusions

The CCP, other legislation and international legal instruments cover important issues of recognition and enforcement of foreign judgments in Cambodia. Article 199 of the CCP provides requirements for a foreign judgment to be recognised and enforced in Cambodia. Article 79 of the Marriage and Family Law comprises rules on recognising foreign marriage decrees in the country. Gaps in these frameworks can be addressed by referring to Japanese law commentators' research on corresponding provisions in Japan's Code of Civil Procedure, including but not limited to Article 118. In particular, the strict interpretation of reciprocity maintained by Cambodian courts should be reformed by referencing the liberal interpretation of the requirement under Japanese law, which will probably assist Cambodia in attracting greater foreign direct investment.[154] Referring to Japanese principles is a temporary gap-filling measure until the Cambodian judiciary publishes decisions on the recognition and enforcement of foreign judgments, emphasising the doctrine of *stare decisis* and the value of legal certainty.

Cambodia has adopted the Cambodia–Vietnam Judicial Assistance Treaty, the CLC Convention and the 1993 Hague Adoption Convention. Still, the number of matters likely referred to these treaties is not large due to their limited coverage. Cambodia should

[150] ibid, Art 418.
[151] ibid, Art 455(1).
[152] ibid, Art 456.
[153] See generally ibid, Chapter Two of Book Six.
[154] N Teramura, 'Recognition and Enforcement of Chinese Judgments in Cambodia: Uncertain Foundations of the Rigid Reciprocity Standards in Cambodian Law' in P Sooksripaisarnkit and SR Garimella (eds), *Legal Challenges of China's One Belt One Road Initiative: Private International Law Considerations*, (Abingdon, Routledge, 2025) [forthcoming].

therefore consider adopting more comprehensive frameworks on (1) foreign judgment recognition and enforcement (such as the 2019 Hague Judgments Convention and the 2005 Hague Choice of Court Convention), and (2) specific family law issues (such as the 1996 Hague Parental Responsibility and Protection of Children Convention and the 2007 Hague Child Support Convention). Overall, Cambodia has modern legal frameworks for recognising and enforcing foreign judgments, but they remain works in progress.

PART V

Arbitration

11

International Arbitration

I. Introduction

Merchants regard international commercial arbitration (ICA) as the norm for resolving cross-border disputes. They prefer this mode of alternative dispute resolution (ADR) to litigation because the former is neutral, efficient, flexible and confidential, and because, unlike court judgments, arbitral awards are enforceable virtually all over the world.[1] Being attracted to these alleged advantages,[2] Cambodian legal practitioners are now keen to promote ICA as the preferred method of dispute settlement for international business disputes.[3] For instance, the National Commercial Arbitration Centre (NCAC) – Cambodia's flagship arbitration institution – has organised seminars and workshops to raise the profile of ICA among business communities in the Kingdom.[4] It is hoped that the institution's efforts would lead to the increase of the Kingdom's modest ICA caseload in the near future.[5]

A notable barrier to promoting ICA in Cambodia is historic. The Kingdom adopted the United Nations Convention on the Recognition and Enforcement of Foreign Arbitral Awards (New York, 10 June 1958; the New York Convention) in 1960.[6] However, the next round of national discussion on ICA did not take place until the promulgation of the Law on the Approval and Implementation of the United Nations Convention on the Recognition and Enforcement of Foreign Arbitral Awards (by Royal Decree NS/RKM/0701/10) in 2001.[7]

[1] N Blackaby, C Partasides and A Redfern, *Redfern and Hunter on International Arbitration*, 7th edn, (Oxford, Oxford University Press, 2022) paras 1.122–28; GB Born, *International Commercial Arbitration*, 3rd edn, (Alphen aan den Rijn, Wolters Kluwer, 2020) 7–250; ML Moses, *The Principles and Practice of International Commercial Arbitration* (Cambridge, Cambridge University Press, 2017) 3–4.

[2] The advantages of ICA compared to international commercial litigation is being compromised due to the over-judicialisation of ICA: N Teramura, *Ex Aequo et Bono as a Response to the 'Over-Judicialisation' of International Commercial Arbitration* (Alphen aan den Rijn, Wolters Kluwer, 2020), Chapter 1; L Trakman and H Montgomery, 'The 'Judicialisation' of International Commercial Arbitration: Pitfall or Virtue?' (2017) 30 *Leiden Journal of International Law* 405.

[3] V Dara, 'Bun Youdy Reflects on Three Years at the National Commercial Arbitration Centre', *The Phnom Penh Post*, 24 March 2022, available at www.phnompenhpost.com/national-post-depth/bun-youdy-reflects-three-years-national-commercial-arbitration-centre (accessed 10 December 2024).

[4] V Dara, 'NCAC and Singapore's SIAC to Promote International Arbitration', *The Phnom Penh Post*, 24 March 2022, available at www.phnompenhpost.com/national/ncac-and-singapores-siac-promote-international-arbitration (accessed 10 December 2024); Post Staff, 'Cambodia Pushes Arbitration as an Alternative Commercial Dispute Resolution Mechanism', *The Phnom Penh Post*, 19 November 2019, available at www.phnompenhpost.com/post-focus/cambodia-pushes-arbitration-alternative-commercial-dispute-resolution-mechanism (accessed 10 December 2024).

[5] H Pisei, 'NCAC Trade Disputes Reach 27: Official', *The Phnom Penh Post*, 8 August 2021, available at www.phnompenhpost.com/business/ncac-trade-disputes-reach-27-official (accessed 10 December 2024).

[6] UNCITRAL, 'Status: Convention on the Recognition and Enforcement of Foreign Arbitral Awards (New York, 1958)' (n.d.), available at https://uncitral.un.org/en/texts/arbitration/conventions/foreign_arbitral_awards/status2 (accessed 10 December 2024).

[7] Y Bun and A Tamiya, 'Cambodian International Commercial Arbitration [in Japanese]' (2015) *Research Report for International Cooperation Department at the Ministry of Justice* 3, available at www.moj.go.jp/content/001148640.pdf (accessed 10 December 2024).

Then, as part of its accession to the WTO, the government of Cambodia committed itself in 2003 to implementing certain legal and judicial reforms,[8] including introducing a modern and reliable commercial dispute resolution system.[9] In 2006, the National Assembly of the Kingdom adopted the Law on Commercial Arbitration (the Arbitration Law) modelled after the 1985 UNCITRAL Model Law on International Commercial Arbitration (the Model Law),[10] requiring the establishment of an independent national arbitration centre in the country.[11] The government issued Sub-Decree No 124 ANKr.PK dated 12 August 2009 on the Organization and Operation of the National Commercial Arbitration Centre and Sub-decree No 182 ANKr.PK dated 31 December 2010 on the Amendments of the Sub-decree No 124 ANKr.PK, to enable the Arbitration Law to accommodate the creation of the NCAC.[12] These sub-decrees led to the establishment of NCAC in 2013.[13] The NCAC officially launched full operation in 2014.[14] ICA is therefore a relatively new development in Cambodia,[15] and many jurists and business persons in Cambodia have yet to familiar themselves with ICA.

Nonetheless, ICA has the potential to become the norm for resolving international business disputes in the Kingdom, whose judiciary has been criticised by international organisations for alleged corruption and weak support for the rule of law.[16] In fact, several Cambodian legal experts have been promoting arbitration as a way of bypassing inefficiencies of local court procedures.[17] ICA is therefore expected to be a significant mode of dispute resolution in Cambodia, and this chapter considers the legal environment surrounding that

[8] S Chea and H Sok, 'Cambodia's Accession to the WTO: 'Fast Track' Accession by a Least Developed Country' (2005) Managing the Challenges of WTO Participation: 45 Case Studies, available at www.wto.org/english/res_e/booksp_e/casestudies_e/case8_e.htm (accessed 10 December 2024).

[9] Bun and Tamiya (n 7) 3.

[10] UNCITRAL, 'Status: UNCITRAL Model Law on International Commercial Arbitration (1985), with amendments as adopted in 2006' (n.d.), available at https://uncitral.un.org/en/texts/arbitration/modellaw/commercial_arbitration/status (accessed 11 December 2024). Note, however, that the Arbitration Law adopted the Model Law without the 2006 amendments: RJW Haw and BJ Slott, 'Cambodia' in MJ Moser and J Choong (eds), *Asia Arbitration Handbook* (Oxford, Oxford University Press, 2011) 536.

[11] Arts 10–17 of the Arbitration Law.

[12] NCAC, 'About Us: Establishment' (2024), available at https://ncac.org.kh/establishment/ (accessed 11 December 2024); O Boltenko, 'Cambodia's Arbitration Centre Sets Off on Its First Flight', *Kluwer Arbitration Blog*, 10 June 2015, available at http://arbitrationblog.kluwerarbitration.com/2015/06/10/cambodias-arbitration-centre-sets-off-on-its-first-flight/ (accessed 11 December 2024).

[13] C Muyhong, 'Arbitrator Ready to Hear Cases', *The Phnom Penh Post*, 14 July 2014, available at www.phnompenhpost.com/business/arbitrator-ready-hear-cases (accessed 11 December 2024).

[14] ibid.

[15] K Phallack, 'Overview of the Cambodian Legal and Judicial System and Recent Efforts at Legal and Judicial Reform' in H Peng, K Phallack and J Menzel (eds), *Introduction to Cambodian Law* (Phnom Penh, Konrad-Adenauer-Stiftung Cambodia, 2012) 14.

[16] Transparency International, 'Corruption Perceptions Index 2023' (2024), available at www.transparency.org/en/cpi/2023?gad_source=1&gclid=Cj0KCQjwncWvBhD_ARIsAEb2HW8duSXLuItQiYOCFteUBFHBTSnXfSqT699mD3B6EiXzvD0EjVX_hT4aAt-KEALw_wcB (accessed 10 December 2024) (ranked Cambodia 158th out of 180 countries); Transparency International, 'CPI 2021 for Asia Pacific: Grand Corruption and Lack of Freedoms Holding Back Progress', *The Latest Updates on the Fight Against Corruption in Cambodia*, 25 January 2022, available at www.transparency.org/en/news/cpi-2021-for-asia-pacific-grand-corruption-holding-back-progress (noting that Cambodia was awarded by the Index one of the bottom scores in the Asia-Pacific region in 2021); World Justice Project, 'WJP Rule of Law Index®' (2024), available at https://worldjusticeproject.org/rule-of-law-index/global (accessed 10 December 2024) (ranked Cambodia 141st out of 142 countries).

[17] A Baliga, 'Corrupt Judiciary Putting off Investment, Businesses Say', *The Phnom Penh Post*, 10 October 2015, available at www.phnompenhpost.com/business/corrupt-judiciary-putting-investment-businesses-say (accessed 11 December 2024); S Chan, 'Firms Urged to Opt for Arbitration, Not Courts, to Settle Disputes', *Khmer Times*, 17 January 2016, available at www.khmertimeskh.com/34646/firms-urged-to-opt-for-arbitration-not-courts-to-settle-disputes/ (accessed 11 December 2024).

method of ADR. It also explores the intersection between private international law (PIL) and investment treaty arbitration – a transnational procedure to resolve investment disputes between a foreign investor and a host state.

Section II discusses the legal framework for ICA in Cambodia, focusing on the Arbitration Law. Section III examines arbitration institutions and organisations operating in the Kingdom. Section IV addresses selected PIL issues in ICA in Cambodia, such as the jurisdiction of the arbitral tribunal, choice of law and the recognition/enforcement of foreign arbitral awards. Section V considers PIL issues in investment arbitration, focusing on jurisdiction, applicable law and judgment recognition and enforcement. Section VI concludes the chapter.

II. The Legal Framework for International Commercial Arbitration in Cambodia

The key applicable law of arbitration proceedings in Cambodia is the Arbitration Law, which is based on the Model Law and comprises nine chapters. It applies to commercial arbitration regardless of its internationality,[18] although the Model Law explicitly states that it applies to ICA only.[19] Diverging from Article 1(2) of the Model Law,[20] the Arbitration Law relinquishes the principle of territoriality. However, not many parties are likely to contemplate applying the Arbitration Law to arbitral proceedings held outside the Kingdom because such a selection may leave them without sufficient access to court assistance to pursue the proceedings.[21] Moreover, the Arbitration Law sets out rules for the establishment of a national arbitration centre that cannot be found in the Model Law.[22] Thus, the Arbitration Law is built upon but still deviates from the Model Law.[23]

A. The Role of Courts

Following the Model Law,[24] the Arbitration Law provides in Article 5 that no court shall intervene in arbitral proceedings unless otherwise provided for in this Law. Court intervention is allowed under Article 6 for the appointment of an arbitrator (Articles 19(3)–19(5)),

[18] Arbitration Law, Arts 1 and 2.

[19] Model Law, Art 1(1). Nonetheless, Art 2(h) of the Arbitration Law defines when an arbitration becomes international, following Art 1(3) of the Model Law.

[20] It provides that '[t]he provisions of this Law … apply only if the place of arbitration is in the territory of this State'.

[21] T Nakamura and L Nottage, 'Arbitration in Japan' (2012) *Sydney Law School Legal Studies Research Paper* 8, available at http://ssrn.com/abstract=2070447 (suggesting that it is not advisable to select a foreign arbitration law to govern arbitral proceedings whose seat shall be in Japan because such a selection may leave the parties without access to court during the arbitral proceedings (accessed 11 December 2024)); Born (n 1), §11.01[c] (noting that '[i]n virtually all cases, in addition to creating serious uncertainties and risks, the selection of a foreign procedural law produces no benefits: commercial parties therefore virtually never make, or should be held to have made, such a choice').

[22] Arbitration Law, Arts 10–17.

[23] For a detailed comparison between the Arbitration Law and the Model Law, see C Forsaith, 'Cambodia' in L Malintoppi and C Tan (eds), *Investment Protection in Southeast Asia: A Country-by-Country Guide on Arbitration Laws and Bilateral Investment Treaties* (Leiden, Brill, 2016) 76–80.

[24] Model Law, Art 5.

the challenge of an arbitrator (Article 21(3)), the removal of an arbitrator (Article 22) and determination on the jurisdiction of the arbitral tribunal (Article 24(3)). Moreover, parties may request: a court in Cambodia for an interim measure of protection (Article 9); the Commercial/ Appeal/Supreme Court of the Kingdom for assistance in taking evidence (Article 35);[25] the Appellate Court for setting aside an arbitral award (Articles 42 and 44); and the Appellate Court for the (non-)recognition/enforcement of an arbitral award (Articles 45-46).[26] These rules for court intervention in the Arbitration Law largely correspond to those in the Model Law.[27]

It is difficult to predict what Cambodian courts' attitude will be towards ICA. This is because little is known about their decisions on arbitration as these are generally not available in the public domain.[28] Until 2014, there had reportedly been no successful application for the enforcement of a foreign arbitral award in Cambodia.[29] In March 2014, the Supreme Court reportedly confirmed the Court of Appeal's ruling in favour of the recognition and enforcement of an award issued in Seoul by the Korean Commercial Arbitration Board (KCAB).[30] However, this judgment does not by itself imply that the courts in Cambodia are pro-arbitration. In 2006, on the request of the President of the National Assembly, the Constitutional Council of Cambodia examined the constitutionality of the Arbitration Law.[31] The Council found that the Law was not contrary to the Constitution but stated that 'Article 5 of the [Arbitration Law] shall be interpreted that the court can intervene upon the request from the parties and that the judicial power shall not be limited'.[32] This statement can serve as evidence demonstrating the Cambodian courts' reluctance to relinquish their jurisdiction over commercial disputes. In fact, in several unpublished cases after the enactment of the Arbitration Law, the courts refused to refer matters to arbitration although the parties had included a valid arbitration clause in their contract,[33] and Article 8 of the Law

[25] Note that the Commercial Court is planned to be established in 2024: O Bunthoeurn, 'Commercial Court Could Function "As Early As 2024": Justice Ministry Officials', *The Phnom Penh Post*, 3 February 2023, available at www.phnompenhpost.com/business/commercial-court-could-function-early-2024-justice-ministry-officials (accessed 11 December 2024). Thus, the court the parties may normally request for such assistance in dealing with commercial cases is the Appeal Court in Phnom Penh: S Austermiller, 'Cambodian Alternative Dispute Resolution' in H Peng, K Phallack and J Menzel (eds), *Introduction to Cambodian Law* (Phnom Penh, Konrad-Adenauer-Stiftung Cambodia, 2012) 192.

[26] The Supreme Court has the conclusive jurisdiction to hear a challenge to the decision of the Appellate Court on recourse, recognition and enforcement of the arbitral award: Arbitration Law, Art 42.

[27] See Model Law, Arts 6 and 36; Forsaith (n 23) 76–80.

[28] R Weeramantry, 'International Investment Law and Practice in the Kingdom of Cambodia: An Evolving 'Rule Taker'?' in J Chaisse and L Nottage (eds), *International Investment Treaties and Arbitration across Asia* (Leiden, Brill, 2018) 306.

[29] A Larkin and L Sambo, 'Recent Developments in Commercial Arbitration in Cambodia' (2015) 17 *Asian Dispute Review* 12, 14; A Henderson, 'Enforcement of Arbitral Awards in Indochina: Law, Practice, and Alternatives' (2009) 26 *Journal of International Arbitration* 841, 853 (claiming with respect to the pre-2010s Cambodian judiciary that 'the lack of practical experience in [arbitration] and the presumed judicial unfamiliarity with relevant laws, together with lingering concerns about the reliability and independence of judicial systems, all suggest that it would be brave and pioneering move to try to enforce an award (domestic or foreign) through the courts [in Cambodia]; all the more so if the local counterparty is government-related or otherwise influential').

[30] Larkin and Sambo (n 29) 14. See also Section IV.C below.

[31] Decision N° 075/002/2006 CC.D of April 07, 2006, available at https://ccc.gov.kh/detail_info_en.php?_txtID=437 (accessed 11 December 2024).

[32] ibid.

[33] R Haw, BJ Slott and M Khieu, 'Cambodia' in Michael J Moser (ed), *Arbitration in Asia*, 2nd edn, (Huntington, Juris Publishing, 2008) CAM-10.

obliged the courts to refer such cases to arbitration. Such judgments cemented a general consensus among local and international commentators that the courts in the Kingdom will not stay or terminate court proceedings in favour of arbitration and will not hesitate to seek to revisit the merits of disputes and arbitral awards.[34] Thus, Cambodian courts are not as arbitration-friendly as the drafters of the Arbitration Law likely contemplated.

B. Form and Scope of Arbitration Agreements

Like the 1985 version of the Model Law, the Arbitration Law requires the form of an arbitration agreement to be in writing. This requirement is satisfied if an arbitration clause or a separate submission agreement is contained in (1) a document signed by the parties, (2) an exchange of letters or other means of electronic telecommunication that provide a record of the agreement, or (3) 'an exchange of statements of claim and defence in which the existence of an [arbitration] agreement is alleged by one party and not denied by another [party]'.[35] The written form requirement is also fulfilled if a contract in writing refers as its part a document containing an arbitration clause.[36] These rules correspond to Article 7(2) of the Model Law prior to its amendment in 2006.

On the scope of an arbitration agreement, Article 2(d) of the Arbitration Law provides that the parties may submit to arbitration 'all or certain disputes which have arisen or … may arise between them in respect of a defined legal relationship, whether contractual or not'. The parties may therefore not conclude an arbitration agreement that refers to all their future disputes without regard to a defined legal relationship.[37] Since the aim of this limitation is to safeguard the parties from a limitless and unpredictable submission to arbitration, a defined legal relationship can be assumed where a framework agreement contains an arbitration clause spanning disputes arising out of the additional contracts concluded within that framework. This would also be the position where an arbitration clause covers disputes between the parties within a given sphere, such as in disputes on the membership of an association, disputes arising out of a commodity consignment, and disputes over joint stock exchange activities.[38] Therefore, the scope of arbitration agreements is broad under the Arbitration Law.[39]

[34] Forsaith (n 23) 84.
[35] Arbitration Law, Art 7.
[36] ibid.
[37] Nakamura and Nottage (n 21) 10.
[38] R Wolff, 'Article II [Recognition of Arbitration Agreements]' in R Wolff (ed), *New York Convention: Article-by-Article Commentary*, 2nd edn, (London, Bloomsbury Publishing, 2019) 112. Note that the Arbitration Law does not clarify what may constitute a defined legal relationship. However, Art 2(d) of the Law is based on Art 7 of the Model Law that is modelled after Art II(1) of the New York Convention: UNCITRAL, *UNCITRAL 2012 Digest of Case Law on the Model Law on International Commercial Arbitration* (Vienna, Publishing and Library Section, United Nations Office, 2012) 25. Thus, in examining the implication of 'a defined legal relationship' under the Arbitration Law, one may take advantage of the interpretation of the terminology provided by commentators for the Convention.
[39] See also UNCITRAL, *UNCITRAL Secretariat Guide on the Convention on the Recognition and Enforcement of Foreign Arbitral Awards (New York, 1958)* (Vienna, Publishing and Library Section, United Nations Office, 2016) 49 (noting that 'a defined legal relationship' in Art II(1) of the New York Convention is 'very broad and seldom disputed in case law').

C. Arbitrability

Article 1 of the Arbitration Law limits arbitrable disputes to commercial ones.[40] Article 2(i) of the Law describes the commerciality requirement as follows:

> The term "commercial" should be given a wide interpretation so as to cover matters arising from all relationships of a commercial nature, whether contractual or not. Relationships of a commercial nature include, but are not limited to, the following transactions: any trade transaction for the supply or exchange of good or services; distribution agreement; commercial representation or agency; factoring; leasing; construction of works; consulting; engineering; licensing; investment; financing; banking; insurance; exploitation agreement or concession; joint venture and other forms of industrial or business co-operation; and carriage of goods or passenger by air, sea, rail or road.[41]

Since Article 2(i) permits the arbitrability of non-contractual disputes, some commentators claim that tort claims may also be arbitrable under the Arbitration Law,[42] in addition to those subject matters in the non-exhaustive list. Thus, the Article requires the courts in Cambodia to be flexible on the arbitrability of commercial disputes.

However, the concept of 'commercial' is not without limits. This has been discussed by commentators in the context of the footnote of Article 1 of the Model Law – the original of Article 2(i) of the Arbitration Law.[43] For instance, the UN Secretary-General suggested that the concept of commercial law does not cover 'labour or employment disputes and ordinary consumer claims, despite their relation to business'.[44] Born nevertheless opposes this view, arguing that the non-exclusive list in the footnote of Article 1 of the Model Law makes it difficult to exclude particular types of transactions from commercial disputes.[45] He further states that:

> [T]he Model Law's footnote extends expressly to "carriage of … passengers" and "consulting," which very arguably include at least certain consumer or employment relations – raising the question why other types of consumer and employment relations are any less "commercial" or more appropriately excluded entirely from the Model Law's coverage. The better view, …, is that the Model Law includes within its coverage both consumer and employment matters, subject to any specific non-arbitrability rules adopted in particular states pursuant to Article 1(5) of the Law.[46]

Born's point is valid, but one must not overlook the fact that the drafters of the Model Law intentionally excluded consumer and employment disputes in general from the

[40] Haw and Slott (n 10) 541.

[41] This provision was obviously imported from the footnote of Art 1 of the Model Law.

[42] Haw and Slott (n 10) 541.

[43] Note that the term 'commercial' under the Model Law is not bound by municipal laws, so courts and tribunals in Cambodia are not encouraged to interpret Art 2(i) of the Arbitration Law as per provisions of Cambodian legislation: P Binder, *International Commercial Arbitration and Mediation in UNCITRAL Model Law Jurisdictions* (Alphen aan den Rijn, Wolters Kluwer, 2019) 33–34.

[44] UN Secretary General, *Analytical Commentary on Draft Text of a Model Law on International Commercial Arbitration: Report of the Secretary-General (A/CN.9/264)* (Vienna, United Nations 1985) 10.

[45] Born (n 1) *International Commercial Arbitration*, §2.03[B][2][a].

[46] ibid, §2.03[B][2][a]. Art 1(5) of the Model Law provides that '[t]his Law shall not affect any other law of this State by virtue of which certain disputes may not be submitted to arbitration or may be submitted to arbitration only according to provisions other than those of this Law'. This provision was adopted by Art 1 of the Arbitration Law.

non-exhaustive list of commercial matters.[47] A plausible view would therefore be that the concept of 'commercial' encompasses activities with consumer or employment elements, but excludes wholly consumer or employment-related activities per se.[48] In addition, the concept is unlikely to cover matrimonial relationships, family affairs and matters requiring the application of criminal law, whereas whether it may comprise intellectual property rights and antitrust matters are left for interpretation.[49] Therefore, the boundary of the term 'commercial' is less obvious than it seems, although the concept has seldom been disputed in practice.[50] These limitations of the commerciality requirement under the Model Law are likely to apply to Cambodia's Arbitration Law.

D. Appointment of and Challenge of Arbitrators

The Arbitration Law sets out rules for arbitrator appointment/challenge in Articles 18–23. These provisions follow Articles 10–15 of the Model Law, enabling the parties to exercise their liberty in selecting and replacing arbitrators. Courts and the NCAC are basically not allowed to intervene in the liberty, as discussed in the following subsections.

i. Appointment of Arbitrators

With respect to the appointment of arbitrators, the Arbitration Law follows the principle of party autonomy. For example, the parties are free to agree to the number of arbitrators, provided that it is an odd number (Article 18). However, failing such agreement, the number shall be three regardless of whether the arbitral proceedings involve two or more parties. In addition, the parties have the liberty to agree on a procedure for appointing the arbitrators (Article 19(2)). If there is no such agreement, and if the parties have agreed to have one arbitrator, the sole arbitrator shall be appointed by a competent court (i.e., the Commercial, Appellate or Supreme Court of Cambodia) or the NCAC (Article 19(3)(b)). If there is no agreement on a procedure for arbitrator appointment, and if the parties have agreed to have three arbitrators, each party shall appoint one arbitrator, and the two appointed arbitrators shall appoint the third arbitrator (Article 19(3)(a)). However, if a party has failed to appoint one arbitrator within 30 days from the receipt of the other party's request to do so, or if the two appointed arbitrators have failed to choose the third arbitrator within 30 days of their appointment, the appointment of that third arbitrator shall be made by a competent court or the NCAC as per the request of a party (Article 19(3)(a)). Thus, arbitrator appointments by

[47] M Polkinghorne, T Timonen and N Larkimo, 'Article 1 – Scope of Application' in I Bantekas and others (eds), *UNCITRAL Model Law on International Commercial Arbitration: A Commentary* (Cambridge, Cambridge University Press, 2020) 9.

[48] ibid. See also *Patel v Kanbay International Inc* [2008] ONCA 867 CanLII, https://canlii.ca/t/220b1 (accessed 11 December 2024) [1]ff (in which the Ontario Court of Appeal did not recognise the commerciality of a dispute concerning the wrongful dismissal of an employee and negligent misrepresentation about the employee's value of shares he expected to acquire from the employment); *Uber Technologies Inc v Heller* [2020] SCC 16 (in which the Supreme Court of Canada denied the commerciality of an employment dispute and a dispute over one's status as an employee).

[49] Polkinghorne, Timonen and Larkimo (n 47) 8.

[50] ibid 9.

a competent court and the NCAC may only occur where the parties have failed to exercise their freedom to choose their adjudicators.

The parties under the Arbitration Law may also determine the qualifications of arbitrators. Unless they agree otherwise, no person shall be precluded from arbitrator appointment by reason of his/her nationality (Article 19(1)). Moreover, a court or the NCAC making an arbitrator appointment 'shall have due regard to any qualifications required of the arbitrator by the parties' agreement and to such considerations as are likely to secure the appointment of an independent and impartial arbitrator' (Article 19(5)). Then, the court or the NCAC is encouraged to appoint an arbitrator of a nationality other than those of the parties, to ensure arbitrator independence and impartiality. This requirement is unlikely to violate the principle of party autonomy as the parties opt for arbitration to refer their controversy to a neutral forum for dispute resolution.

ii. Challenge of Arbitrators

The Arbitration Law regards the principle of party autonomy as an integral part of arbitrator challenge. For instance, the parties may challenge an arbitrator only where: (1) 'circumstances exist that give rise to justifiable doubts as to his impartiality or independence' or (2) 'he does not possess qualifications agreed to by the parties' (Article 20). Moreover, the parties are free to agree on procedures for arbitrator challenge (Article 21(1)). Failing such agreement, a party who intends to challenge an arbitrator shall, within 15 days after realising the constitution of the arbitral tribunal or new circumstances affecting the arbitrator's impartiality/independence, send a written statement of the reasons for the challenge to the tribunal and the other party/parties (Article 21(2)). The tribunal shall then decide on the challenge, unless the challenged arbitrator withdraws from his/her office voluntarily. If the tribunal rejects the challenge, the challenging party may, within 30 days of receiving the notice of the rejection, request a competent court or the NCAC to decide on the challenge (Article 21(3)). The parties may request a competent court or the NCAC to decide whether to terminate the mandate of an arbitrator who has become *de jure* or *de facto* unable to perform his/her office or has failed to act without undue delay for other reasons, unless that arbitrator has withdrawn from his/her office, or the parties have agreed on the termination of the mandate (Article 22). Thus, party autonomy is a core tenet of arbitrator challenge under the Arbitration Law.

E. Seat and Language of Arbitration

As per Articles 28 and 30 of the Arbitration Law, the parties have the liberty to agree on the place and language of arbitration. Without the parties' selection of the seat, the arbitral tribunal shall decide the place of arbitration, taking account of the circumstances of the case, such as the intention of the parties (Article 28). Then, the place of arbitration is not identical to the 'venue' of arbitration. Unless otherwise agreed by the parties, the arbitral tribunal may, at any place, consult its members, hear witnesses, experts or the parties, or inspect equipment, property or any documents. Moreover, if there is no agreement on the language to be used in the arbitration proceedings, the arbitral tribunal shall determine that language (Article 30). Whether the language was designated by the parties or the tribunal, the latter may order the former to translate any documentary evidence into that language.

F. Conduct of Proceedings

Like the Model Law,[51] the Arbitration Law enables the parties to agree on the rules of arbitral procedure, and the tribunal shall follow such rules in conducting the proceedings (Article 27). If there is no such agreement, the arbitral tribunal may conduct the arbitration as it considers appropriate, as long as the tribunal observes the provisions of the Arbitration Law. In either case, the tribunal is required by Article 26 to treat the parties equally, giving each party full opportunity to present his/her case. This subsection examines the conduct of arbitral proceedings stipulated in the Arbitration Law, focusing on (1) proceedings, (2) court assistance in taking evidence and (3) settlement.

First, unless otherwise agreed by the parties, the arbitral proceedings commence on the date when the claimant gives the respondent notice of referring the dispute to arbitration (Article 29). The claimant shall then submit a statement of claim within the period agreed by the parties or determined by the arbitral tribunal, and the respondent shall file a statement of defence in response to that claim (Article 31). The parties would be free to modify their statements during the arbitral proceedings, unless they agreed otherwise, and unless the tribunal determined that the amendment would cause undue delay. Moreover, subject to any agreement by the parties, the tribunal shall decide whether to hold oral hearings or conduct document-based proceedings (Article 32). In either case, the tribunal shall ensure that the parties are given sufficient advance notice of any hearing and meeting, and that '[a]ll statements, documents or other information supplied to the arbitral tribunal by one party shall be communicated to the other party' (Article 32). Further, the tribunal may appoint an expert or experts to examine specific issues in the arbitral proceedings, ordering the parties to cooperate with the expert(s) in that examination (Article 34). Overall, the provisions concerning arbitral proceedings are mostly the same as those in the Model Law.[52]

Second, the arbitral tribunal, or a party with the tribunal's approval, may ask a competent court (i.e., the Appeal or Supreme Court) for assistance in taking evidence as provided in the court's rules on evidence collection (Article 35). Such assistance would be needed where the tribunal had to order non-parties to provide evidence or if the parties to the arbitral proceedings refused to comply with the tribunal's evidentiary orders made against them.[53] According to the Code of Civil Procedure (CCP), the tribunal/party may request a competent court to issue a ruling on document submission (Article 151) and to preserve evidence (Article 163). However, no materials suggest that the courts in Cambodia, which seem reluctant to support arbitration,[54] are keen to provide the parties with assistance in taking evidence for the arbitral proceedings.

[51] See Model Law, Art 19.
[52] See ibid, Arts 21, 23–24 and 26.
[53] UNCITRAL (n 38) 118.
[54] See Section II.A.

Third, the Arbitration Law's rules on settlement diverge from the corresponding provisions in the Model Law. Whereas the Model Law presupposes settlement by the parties during arbitral proceedings,[55] the Arbitration Law allows the parties to settle the dispute not only during arbitral proceedings but also before the commencement of 'formal arbitral proceedings' (Article 38(2)). Further, the tribunal is allowed to initiate settlement of the dispute before the commencement of 'formal arbitral proceedings', upon request by both parties (Article 38), although the Model Law does not authorise the tribunal to perform such an active role in assisting settlement.[56] Since the Arbitration Law does not elaborate on the 'formal arbitral proceedings', it is controversial as arbitrators may also start acting as quasi-mediator under the Law.[57] Where settlement has been reached before or during the formal arbitration process, the tribunal under the Arbitration Law may record the settlement in the form on an award on agreed terms (Articles 38(2) and 38(3)).

G. Arbitral Awards

Chapter VII of the Arbitration Law sets out rules on the elements of an arbitral award. For example, unless the parties agree otherwise, the arbitral award (and any other decision of the tribunal) is made by a majority of the members of the tribunal (Article 37). The parties are free to agree on the rules of law to be applied by the tribunal to the merits of the dispute (Article 36(1)).[58] They may also authorise the tribunal to decide *ex aequo et bono* through an explicit agreement (Article 36(3)). Without any choice of law agreement and *ex aequo et bono* agreement, the tribunal is to apply the law that it considers appropriate (Article 36(2)). In any event, the tribunal shall take into account the provisions of the arbitration agreement and the usages of the trade and customs applicable to the transaction in dispute (Article 36(4)). The award shall be in writing and signed by the arbitrator(s) (Article 39(1)). In arbitral proceedings with more than one arbitrator, the signatures of the majority of the arbitrators are sufficient to effectuate the award, provided that the award states the reason for any omitted signature (Article 39(1)). Moreover, the award shall furnish the reasons on which it is based (Article 39(2)), but exceptions lie where there is a contrary agreement between the parties, or where the award is a consent award under Article 38. The award shall also state its date and the place of arbitration, and the latter is deemed to be the place where the award has been made (Article 39(4)). Once the award has been made, a copy of the award signed by the majority of the arbitrators shall be sent to the parties (Article 39(5)). In addition, the tribunal may correct any errors in the award upon request of a party or on its authority within 30 days after the issuance of the award (Articles 41(1)–(2)). Also, the tribunal may issue an additional award to address points presented in the proceedings but omitted from the arbitral award if a party so requests and unless otherwise agreed by the parties (Article 41(3)). Overall, those rules about arbitral awards in the Arbitration Law are compatible with those in the Model Law.[59]

[55] Model Law, Art 30.
[56] Forsaith (n 23) 77.
[57] ibid.
[58] See also Section IV.B below.
[59] See Model Law, Arts 28–33.

H. Foreign Lawyers' Involvement

Foreign lawyers may serve as arbitration counsel and arbitrators in international arbitration in Cambodia. According to the Law on the Bar,[60] a foreign lawyer may practice law in the Kingdom only with the authorisation of the Bar Council[61] – the governing board of the Bar Association of the Kingdom of Cambodia.[62] Whether the Bar Council grants the authorisation depends on the qualification of the foreign lawyer and the availability of similar opportunities to Cambodian lawyers in that foreign lawyer's country of origin.[63] Once authorised, the foreign lawyer may represent his/her clients in any adjudicatory bodies.[64] Even without authorisation, the foreign lawyer may practice law with a Cambodian lawyer before the courts or other institutions, provided that s/he is a qualified lawyer in his/her country of origin and does not represent his/her clients (and allows the Cambodian Lawyer to do so).[65] On arbitrator appointment, the Law on the Bar provides in Article 3 that (foreign) lawyers may be assigned as arbitrators only where permitted by the law,[66] and the Arbitration Law allows the parties to appoint any Cambodian/foreign natural persons as arbitrators.[67] Thus, foreign lawyers are not barred from participating in ICA proceedings in Cambodia.

III. Arbitration Institutions and Organisations in Cambodia

There are two national arbitration institutions in Cambodia – the NCAC and the Arbitration Council.[68] There are no regional arbitration bodies in the country. However, some foreign-based institutions/organisations have been operating in the Kingdom either individually or in cooperation with those national institutions.

A. NCAC

The NCAC was established in 2013 by the leadership of the Ministry of Commerce, with the support of the Asian Development Bank (ADB) and the International Finance Corporation (IFC) – a sister organisation of the World Bank.[69] The Arbitration Law defines in Article 10 the objectives of the NCAC as follows: (1) to promote arbitration as a means of

[60] English text of the Law on the Bar is available at https://www.wto.org/english/thewto_e/acc_e/khm_e/wtacckhm3a3_leg_50.pdf (accessed 11 December 2024). See also generally Phallack (n 15) 15–16.

[61] Law on the Bar, Art 6.

[62] ibid, Art 9.

[63] ibid, Art 6.

[64] ibid, Art 3. Note, however, that the foreign lawyer is not allowed to perform any activity for attracting clients: ibid, Art 7.

[65] ibid, Art 5.

[66] ibid, Art 3.

[67] Arbitration Law, Art 11.

[68] Council of ASEAN Chief Justices, 'Overview of Cambodian Alternative Dispute Resolution System' (n.d.), available at https://cacj-ajp.org/cambodia/legal-system/overview-of-cambodian-alternative-dispute-resolution-system/ (accessed 11 December 2024); Weeramantry (n 28) 305–06.

[69] Boltenko (n 12); S Kiri, 'Message From President' (2024), available at https://ncac.org.kh/message-from-president/ (accessed 11 December 2024). See also Section I above.

settling commercial disputes in Cambodia, (2) to establish infrastructure and rules for the administration of arbitral proceedings, and (3) to maintain high-quality standards of arbitral proceedings (including those for arbitrator qualifications) in Cambodia. In line with these aims, the NCAC has organised in-person and online events to promote arbitration among local businesses and legal practitioners,[70] as well as among civil servants.[71] The institution issued the NCAC Arbitration Rules in 2014 based on Arbitration Rules of the Singapore International Arbitration Centre (SIAC),[72] and it revised the NCAC Rules in 2021, providing parties with new procedural options, such as expedited procedure, documents-only procedure, virtual hearings and interim measures from an emergency arbitrator.[73] The NCAC has been offering the Arbitration Skill Training Course which includes introductory, intermediate and advanced level courses, to increase the number and quality of individual arbitrators in Cambodia.[74] Those who successfully complete the Training Course may proceed to the Arbitrator Exam organised by the NCAC's Examination Committee. A successful result allows a person to become a registered arbitrator at the NCAC.[75] As Cambodia's Justice Ministry and business sector have been supportive of those initiatives for the promotion of arbitration,[76] there has allegedly been a steady rise in the number of business disputes referred to the NCAC.[77]

B. Arbitration Council

The Arbitration Council is an independent national institution which was established in 2003 with the support of the Ministry of Labour and technical assistance from the International Labour Organisation (ILO).[78] The mission of the Council is to assist parties

[70] Dara (n 4); Post Staff (n 4).

[71] H Haider, 'Civil Servants Are to Receive Special Arbitration Training to Resolve Commercial Disputes', *Khmer Times*, 30 July 2021, available at www.khmertimeskh.com/50904570/civil-servants-are-to-receive-special-arbitration-training-to-resolve-commercial-disputes/ (accessed 11 December 2024).

[72] S Sarath, 'Arbitration Rules Under Review', *Khmer Times*, 28 July 2020, available at www.khmertimeskh.com/50749327/arbitration-rules-under-review/ (accessed 11 December 2024).

[73] H Haider, 'New Commercial Arbitration Rules Enter into Force', *Khmer Times*, 28 June 2021, available at www.khmertimeskh.com/50882539/new-commercial-arbitration-rules-enter-into-force/ (accessed 11 December 2024).

[74] NCAC, 'Services: Trainings' (2024), available at https://ncac.org.kh/en/services/training/ (accessed 11 December 2024).

[75] 2021 NCAC Internal Rules, Art 12, available at https://ncac.org.kh/wp-content/uploads/2022/09/NCAC-INTERNAL-RULES-EN-Final.pdf (accessed 11 December 2024) (noting that passing the Arbitrator Exam is not a mandatory requirement for becoming NCAC's registered arbitrator).

[76] S Sarath, 'Local Arbitration Centre Needs More Time to Build Confidence', *Khmer Times*, 21 May 2020, available at www.khmertimeskh.com/50725360/local-arbitration-centre-needs-more-time-to-build-confidence/ (accessed 11 December 2024) (in which the vice-president of the Cambodia Chamber of Commerce expressed the private sector's support for NCAC); Chan (n 17). However, some businesspersons are critical to NCAC's activities: K Makara, 'Concerns about Arbitration Centre', *The Phnom Penh Post*, 2 October 2009, available at www.phnompenhpost.com/business/concerns-about-arbitration-centre (accessed 11 December 2024).

[77] K Sothear, 'Demand for Arbitration Rises Among Businesses', *Khmer Times*, 25 May 2022, available at www.khmertimeskh.com/501081634/demand-for-arbitration-rises-among-businesses/ (accessed 11 December 2024).

[78] Arbitration Council, 'The Arbitration Council: Background' (n.d.), available at www.arbitrationcouncil.org/about-ac/the-arbitration-council/ (accessed 11 December 2024). Moreover, international donors such as the government of Sweden and USAID have provided the Council with financial aid: T Vida, 'Sweden Contributes to Arbitration Council', *Khmer Times*, 7 March 2019, available at www.khmertimeskh.com/50584566/sweden-contributes-to-arbitration-council/ (accessed 11 December 2024); T Vida, '$2 Million Grant to Aid Kingdom's Labour Relations and Dispute Resolution', *Khmer Times*, 28 February 2020, available at www.khmertimeskh.

in resolving collective labour disputes in accordance with the Labour Law of Cambodia.[79] The arbitration body is therefore specialised in domestic labour cases, and the success of the institution is evident from its 2000 published arbitral awards, many of which are in English.[80] It is nonetheless hoped that the institution will contribute to facilitating and demystifying recourse to (commercial) arbitration through providing first-hand training and experience for Cambodian legal practitioners.[81]

C. Other Arbitration-Related Organisations Operating in Cambodia

Several arbitration institutions and associations have been operating in the Kingdom. For instance, the SIAC signed in 2022 the Memorandum of Understanding with the NCAC to organise events and training programmes on international arbitration jointly in Cambodia.[82] The Singapore Institute of Arbitrators (SIArb), in cooperation with IFC, offered a series of training course on arbitration skills and commercial law to the first batch of NCAC accredited arbitrators.[83] The Japan Commercial Arbitration Association (JCAA) and the Japan International Dispute Resolution Centre (JIDRC), along with the Royal University of Law and Economics (RULE) in Phnom Penh and Nagoya University in Japan, co-hosted a joint webinar on 'Recent Trends in Arbitration in Cambodia and Japan' in 2021.[84] The International Chamber of Commerce (ICC) administered four arbitration cases involving Cambodian parties in 2020.[85] Thus, not a few foreign organisations conduct arbitration-related activities in the Kingdom.

IV. Selected Private International Law Issues in International Commercial Arbitration in Cambodia

PIL plays an important role in ICA. Indeed, Berman stated in a lecture at the Hague Academy of Private International Law that 'given [international commercial] arbitration's international character and its core mission of resolving disputes between private parties [of different jurisdictions], arbitration may fairly be regarded as the quintessential [PIL]

com/696018/2-million-grant-to-aid-kingdoms-labour-relations-and-dispute-resolution/ (accessed 11 December 2024).

[79] Arbitration Council (n 78).

[80] Arbitration Council, 'Arbitral Awards' (n.d.), available at www.arbitrationcouncil.org/arbitral-decision/arbitral-award/ (accessed 11 December 2024).

[81] Weeramantry (n 28) 306.

[82] SIAC, 'SIAC Signs Memorandum of Understanding with the National Commercial Arbitration Centre in Cambodia', *SIAC Press Release*, 24 March 2022, available at https://siac.org.sg/wp-content/uploads/2022/07/Press-Release-SIAC-Signs-Memorandum-of-Understanding-with-the-National-Commercial-Arbitration-Centre-in-Cambodia.pdf (accessed 11 December 2024).

[83] H Chhay, 'National Commercial Arbitration Centre: Development and Challenges', *Arbitration Asia*, February 2021, available at https://arbitrationasia.rajahtannasia.com/national-commercial-arbitration-centre-development-and-challenges/ (accessed 11 December 2024).

[84] www.jcaa.or.jp/files/news/attach00000219.pdf (accessed 11 December 2024).

[85] ICC, *ICC Dispute Resolution 2020 Statistics* (Paris, ICC, 2021) 25.

endeavour'.[86] This section explores challenges to tribunals and courts under Cambodia's legal framework for ICA, focusing on PIL's principal dimensions: the exercise of jurisdiction, the choice of applicable law and the recognition and enforcement of (foreign) adjudicatory outcomes.[87]

A. Jurisdiction of the Arbitral Tribunal

The Arbitration Law sets out rules on the competence of an arbitral tribunal to determine its jurisdiction. According to Article 24(1), the arbitral tribunal may rule on its own jurisdiction to decide the dispute (including any objections to the existence/validity of the arbitration agreement). A plea that the tribunal lacks jurisdiction shall be raised not later than the submission of the statement of defence, whereas a plea that the tribunal exceeds the scope of its authority shall be raised promptly when grounds for the excessive jurisdiction arise in the course of the arbitral proceedings (Article 24(2)). In either case, the tribunal may admit a later plea if it finds the delay justified. Moreover, it may decide on a plea on jurisdiction as a preliminary issue or as part of the merits hearing (Article 24(3)). If the tribunal rules on the plea as a preliminary question, any party may request a competent court to finally decide the matter within 30 days after receipt of that ruling. If the tribunal instead decides on the plea as a matter of merits, a party who is dissatisfied with the upholding may challenge the final award by requesting a competent court to set aside the award as per Article 44.[88]

On the grounds for the tribunal's declining jurisdiction in arbitral proceedings in Cambodia, the first sentence of Article 24(1) states that the existence and validity of the arbitration agreement are jurisdictional issues.[89] This point is echoed in several cases concerning Article 16 of the Model Law – the original of Article 24 of the Arbitration Law.[90] The concept of jurisdiction can be extended to issues other than the existence/scope/validity of the arbitration agreement because the opening sentence of Article 24(1) provides that the tribunal may rule on its jurisdiction 'including' any objections to those issues on the arbitration agreement.[91] The Arbitration Law does not clarify the implication of this opening sentence, but the Model Law embraces a broader conception of the notion of jurisdiction. For example, under the Model Law, the tribunal is entitled to determine gateway issues such as 'waiver, delay … time limits, notice, laches, estoppels and other conditions precedent to an obligation to arbitrate',[92] as well as the binding effect of an arbitration agreement

[86] GA Bermann, 'International Arbitration and Private International Law: General Course on Private International Law' (2016) 381 *Collected Courses of the Hague Academy of International Law* 41, 53.

[87] GA Bermann, 'Private International Law in International Arbitration' in F Ferrari and DP Arroyo (eds), *Private International Law: Contemporary Challenges and Continuing Relevance* (Cheltenham, Edward Elgar Publishing, 2019) 464ff.

[88] In NCAC arbitration proceedings, where a party challenges the competence of the NCAC before the constitution of the tribunal, the Appointment and Proceedings Committee of the NCAC shall decide if it is *prima facie satisfied* with continuing the proceedings: NCAC Arbitration Rules 2021, Art 34.1.

[89] Similarly, the opening sentence of Art 34.2 of the NCAC Rules states that '[t]he [t]ribunal shall have the power to rule on its own jurisdiction, including on any objections with respect to the existence, validity or scope of the arbitration agreement'.

[90] UNCITRAL (n 38) 77.

[91] ibid 77–78.

[92] *BG Group Plc v Republic of Argentina* [2014] US Supreme Court 12–138, 134 Supreme Court Reporter 1198, 1202; M Polkinghorne and others, 'Article 16: Competence of Arbitral Tribunal to Rule on Its Own Jurisdiction'

on a third party, the arbitrability of a dispute and an arbitration agreement's compatibility with public policy.[93] Arbitrators are expected to treat these procedural matters as jurisdictional issues in arbitration proceedings under the Arbitration Law.

Article 24(1) (and Article 16 of the Model Law) is silent on the law the tribunal shall apply in deciding its jurisdiction. However, the Arbitration Law states which law governs issues of capacity, validity, and arbitrability in the context of the annulment of arbitral awards under Article 44 and the refusal of the recognition/enforcement of arbitral awards under Article 46. Both provisions require the Appeal Court to consider a challenge to (the recognition/enforcement of) an arbitral award, provided that the party making the request furnishes proof that 'a party to the arbitration agreement … was under some incapacity; or the said agreement is not valid *under the law to which the parties have subjected it or, failing, any indication by the parties, under the law of the Kingdom of Cambodia*' (Articles 44(2)(a)(i) and 46 (1)(a) (emphasis added)). These provisions primarily govern the parties' recourse to a competent court, but an arbitral tribunal seated in Cambodia nonetheless must abide by those choice of law rules because the tribunal's decision on its competence is ultimately subject to court review (Article 24(3)),[94] and because the tribunal has a professional moral duty to issue an enforceable arbitral award.[95] The tribunal is therefore likely to decline its jurisdiction if the parties request arbitration on matters that are non-arbitrable under the Arbitration Law and the Model Law, such as family, consumer and employment disputes and other controversies involving criminal issues.

B. Choice of Law

Arbitral choice of law is generally thought of as the determination of the law applicable to substantive law issues – the merits of a dispute.[96] The Arbitration Law sets out in Article 36 choice of law rules for ICA in Cambodia as follows. First, the arbitral tribunal is mandated to apply the rules of law chosen by the parties (Article 36(1)). 'Rules of law' may comprise any instruments mutually accepted by the parties and in compliance with the public policy of the forum, including but not limited to state law, the *lex mercatoria*, equitable principles (i.e., *ex aequo et bono*), religious law (e.g., Islamic law), international and regional treaties, and public international law.[97] Thus, the parties are free to designate the UNIDROIT Principles of International Commercial Contracts 2016 (UNIDROIT Principles) and/or the United Nations Convention on Contracts for the International Sale of Goods (Vienna,

in I Bantekas and others (eds), *UNCITRAL Model Law on International Commercial Arbitration: A Commentary* (Cambridge, Cambridge University Press, 2020) 299.

[93] Bermann (n 87) 475.

[94] Polkinghorne and others (n 92) 299.

[95] M Platte, 'An Arbitrator's Duty to Render Enforceable Awards' (2003) 20 *Journal of International Arbitration* 307; Blackaby, Partasides and Redfern (n 1) para 9.141(suggesting that 'the arbitral tribunal will want to do its best, as a matter of professional pride, to ensure that the award is enforceable: having been entrusted with the duty of determining a dispute for the parties, it will naturally wish to ensure that its duty is properly and effectively discharged'); C Boog and B Moss, 'The Lazy Myth of the Arbitral Tribunal's Duty to Render an Enforceable Award', *Kluwer Arbitration Blog*, 28 January 2013, available at http://arbitrationblog.kluwerarbitration.com/2013/01/28/the-lazy-myth-of-the-arbitral-tribunals-duty-to-render-an-enforceable-award/ (accessed 11 December 2024).

[96] Bermann (n 87) 477.

[97] I Bantekas, 'Article 28: Rules Applicable to Substance of Dispute' in I Bantekas and others (eds), *UNCITRAL Model Law on International Commercial Arbitration: A Commentary* (Cambridge, Cambridge University Press, 2020) 739–40.

1980; CISG) as the law governing the merits of their dispute,[98] although Cambodia is not a member of the CISG.[99] In making the designation, the parties may adopt a combination of different rules of law,[100] as long as they make the choice unambiguously, either in the arbitration agreement or in a separate agreement.[101] If the parties then choose the law or legal system of a given state, the tribunal is required to treat the designation as a direct reference to the substantive law of that state and not to its conflict of laws rules.

Second, failing such an agreement to the rules of law, the arbitral tribunal shall apply the law it considers appropriate (Article 36(2)). 'The appropriate law' is the national law determined by the conflict of laws rules that the tribunal considers applicable.[102] However, neither the Arbitration Law nor the Model Law offers a threshold for the applicable conflict of laws rules. Accordingly, the tribunal may 'employ its own criteria (or common sense) in deciphering the law, rules, legal system or combinations thereof that are closest to the parties' shared intention',[103] provided that it observes the mandatory provisions of the *lex arbitri* as the violation of such rules may lead to the annulment of the arbitral award.[104] This choice of law approach is in compliance with Article 36(4) requiring the tribunal to decide all cases in accordance with the provisions of the arbitration agreement.

Third, the tribunal may decide *ex aequo et bono* or as *amiable compositeur* if the parties have conferred it the power to do so (Article 36(4)). There is no outstanding distinction between the situations where the tribunal decides *ex aequo et bono* and where it acts as *amiable compositeur*.[105] In either scenario, the tribunal 'decide[s] a dispute in accordance with their sense of fairness and good conscience, instead of rigorously applying terms of a specific body of law'.[106] However, that sense of fairness may not be arbitrary or subjective. In fact, the arbitrators who have the power of *ex aequo et bono* need to render arbitral awards following the specifications of a contract in a way that conforms with the contextual interpretation of contract terms under applicable substantive law.[107] If they deem the consequences of the interpretation unfair or unjust based on the circumstances of the case, the arbitrators may deviate from that interpretation in accordance with the applicable usages of trade.[108] Only in situations in which they realise the application of the contract terms and/or relevant trade usages do not lead to a fair and just arbitral decision, may they rely more on their views of fairness and good conscience.[109] But this reliance shall abide by the

[98] UNCITRAL (n 38) 121; Bermann (n 87) 477.

[99] UNCITRAL, 'Status: United Nations Convention on Contracts for the International Sale of Goods (Vienna, 1980) (CISG)' (n.d.), available at https://uncitral.un.org/en/texts/salegoods/conventions/sale_of_goods/cisg/status (accessed 10 December 2024).

[100] Bantekas (n 97) 743–44.

[101] ibid.

[102] UNCITRAL (n 38) 121.

[103] Bantekas (n 97) 748. In contrast, Art 32.1 of the NCAC Rules does not require the tribunal to decide the applicable law by way of the appropriate conflict of laws rules.

[104] Bantekas (n 97) 748; Art 44(2)(b)(ii) of the Arbitration Law.

[105] N Teramura, 'The Strengths and Weaknesses of Arguments Pertaining to *Ex Aequo et Bono*' (2019) 15 *Asian International Arbitration Journal* 63.

[106] N Teramura, '*Ex Aequo et Bono*: An Overlooked and Undervalued Opportunity for International Commercial Arbitration', *Kluwer Arbitration Blog*, 25 November 2018, available at http://arbitrationblog.kluwerarbitration.com/2018/11/18/ex-aequo-et-bono-an-overlooked-and-undervalued-opportunity-for-international-commercial-arbitration/ (accessed 11 December 2024).

[107] Teramura (n 2) 183–84 (also referring to 'the prevailing trend of … contextual interpretations of contracts in most of the applicable substantive rules of law).

[108] ibid 184.

[109] ibid.

mandatory rules of the *lex arbitri* and the law of the obvious place(s) of award recognition/enforcement.[110] Thus, the arbitrators deciding *ex aequo et bono* may not exercise their discretion without restriction.[111] The decision-making process involves a succinct analysis of the legal norms, facts and trade usages that are relevant to the case at hand.

Whether it applies the rules of law or decides *ex aequo et bono*, the tribunal is required in all cases to take into account the usages of trade and customs applicable to the transaction in dispute. The Model Law does not provide any statutory definition for the usages of trade and customs. The aim of the legal instrument is to harmonise international arbitration law in the face of divergent national legal systems,[112] and Sanders points out that the idea of trade usages under UNCITRAL instruments consists of various concepts of such usages in different jurisdictions.[113] According to Schmitthoff, the uniformly accepted definition for trade usages is: '[a] method of dealing or a way of conduct generally observed in a particular line of business with such regularity that it is accepted as binding by those engaged in that line of business'.[114] This broad concept may include not only contractual practices normally followed in a particular trade or industry group,[115] but also the principles and rules of law observed in international instruments, arbitral awards and comparative law.[116] The tribunal deciding *ex aequo et bono* is not encouraged by the Model Law to determine whether a practice constitutes usages of trade because '[u]sage is a factual issue that exists independent of the law and receives its legitimacy from observance by the mercantile community itself'.[117] Since ICA is a legal process of resolving private disputes, it is not an ideal forum for defining trade usages.[118] The arbitrators may therefore only determine the applicability of alleged trade usages to the disputed transaction, on the basis of 'trade practices that are adduced in arbitral hearings, the knowledge the arbitrators have of such usages and published materials on those usages, such as in trade association journals'.[119]

C. Recognition and Enforcement of Arbitral Awards

The recognition and enforcement of arbitral awards are governed by several legal instruments, including the Arbitration Law, the New York Convention and the Law on the Approval and Implementation of the United Nations Convention on the Recognition and

[110] ibid. On the mechanisms of the narrowly-tailored subjective perspective of arbitrators, see N Teramura, '*Ex Aequo et Bono* and Arbitration Theories: An Arbitrator's Subjective Perspective of Fairness as the Final 'Gap-Filler'' (2020) 38 *ASA Bulletin* 350.

[111] N Teramura, 'Challenging the Arbitrariness Perception of Ex Aequo et Bono to (Re-)discover Procedural Diversity' in SF Ali and others (eds), *Diversity in International Arbitration: Why It Matters and How to Sustain It* (Cheltenham and Camberley, Edward Elgar Publishing, 2022).

[112] Teramura (n 2) Chapter 2.

[113] P Sanders, 'Notes on Article 33(4)' (n.d.), 1, available at www.arbitration-icca.org/media/0/12741828662200/021.pdf (accessed 11 December 2024). On diverse definitions of trade usages by different commentators, see HE Erdem, 'The Role of Trade Usages in ICC Arbitration' in L Lévy and Y Derains (eds), *Liber Amicorum en l'Honneur de Serge Lazareff* (Paris, Editions A Pedone, 2011) 248–49.

[114] CM Schmitthoff, *International Trade Usages* (Paris, ICC Publishing 1987) 14–15.

[115] F Gélinas, 'Trade Usages as Transnational Law' in F Gélinas (ed), *Trade Usages and Implied Terms in the Age of Arbitration* (Oxford, Oxford University Press, 2016) 258–65.

[116] ibid 258.

[117] J Coetzee, 'The Role and Function of Trade Usage in Modern International Sales Law' (2015) 20 *Unform Law Review* 243, 253.

[118] Teramura (n 2) 104.

[119] ibid 102.

Enforcement of Foreign Arbitral Awards (New York Convention Implementation Law).[120] These instruments may overlap because the Arbitration Law has rules on award recognition/enforcement that apply to both domestic and foreign arbitral awards,[121] In contrast, the New York Convention governs the recognition/enforcement of foreign arbitral awards, which the New York Convention Implementation Law defines as awards made in countries other than Cambodia or those made in Cambodia in accordance with the procedural laws of countries other than Cambodia.[122] It is accepted practice among Cambodian practitioners that the New York Convention is the primary legal source for the recognition/enforcement of foreign arbitral awards.[123] There is only likely to be minimal conflict between the New York Convention and the Arbitration Law because the latter's recognition and enforcement rules are modelled after those in the Model Law,[124] which closely follow the relevant provisions of the New York Convention.[125]

As per Article III of the New York Convention, Cambodia is obliged to recognise foreign arbitral awards as binding and enforce them in accordance with its rules of procedure, provided that the party applying for recognition/enforcement supplies the competent court (i.e., the Court of Appeal[126]) in Cambodia with the duly authenticated originals or duly certified copies of the arbitral award and agreement (Article IV.1).[127] The other party may challenge the recognition/enforcement of the award if s/he furnishes to the competent court proof that one of the grounds for award non-recognition/enforcement in Article V.1 is satisfied.[128] These grounds are: (a) invalidity of the arbitration agreement, (b) violation of due process, (c) excess of the tribunal's authority, (d) irregularity in the composition of the tribunal or arbitral procedure, and (e) the award non-binding/annulled/suspended. Moreover, Article V.2 confers the competent court power to refuse award recognition/enforcement where the subject matter of the dispute is not arbitrable under the law of Cambodia or where the recognition/enforcement would be contrary to the public policy of Cambodia.

Because of the pro-enforcement policy of the New York Convention,[129] judges in Cambodia are encouraged to construe the grounds of award non-recognition under Article V narrowly.[130] The Convention expects the judges to accept the existence of those grounds in serious or extreme cases only.[131] However, the attitude of the Cambodian judiciary

[120] Bun and Tamiya (n 7) 11. In addition, the CCP contains rules on the execution by the court of arbitral awards (Art 353).

[121] Arbitration Law, Art 45.

[122] New York Convention Implementation Law, Art 2(1); Bun and Tamiya (n 7) 11.

[123] Bun & Associates, 'Introductory Guide: Commercial Arbitration in Cambodia' (2014) 10, available at www.bun-associates.com/wp-content/uploads/2019/01/Introductory-Guide-Commercial-Arbitration-in-Cambodia.pdf (accessed 11 December 2024); D Hem and B Chankoulika, 'Commercial Arbitration in Cambodia', *BNG Legal Newsletter*, February 2017, available at https://bnglegal.com/cn/wp-content/uploads/2017/02/170206-Commercial-arbitration-in-Cambodia.pdf-February.pdf (accessed 11 December 2024).

[124] Compare Arts 45–46 of the Arbitration Law with Arts 35–36 of the Model Law.

[125] UNCITRAL (n 38) 168ff.

[126] New York Convention Implementation Law, Arts 2 and 17.

[127] See also Art V.2 of the New York Convention that requires the party applying for recognition/enforcement to produce a certified translation of the award or agreement if these documents were not in an official language of the country in which the award is relied upon.

[128] See also New York Convention Implementation Law, Art 15.

[129] New York Convention, Art III; UNCITRAL (n 39) 77.

[130] UNCITRAL (n 39) 124ff.

[131] AJ van den Berg, 'The New York Convention of 1958: An Overview' (n.d.), 13, available at https://cdn.arbitration-icca.org/s3fs-public/document/media_document/media012125884227980new_york_convention_of_1958_overview.pdf (accessed 11 December 2024).

towards the pro-enforcement bias is unlikely to be discernible from past judgments, whose details are not always accessible to the public.[132] In 2014, the Supreme Court reportedly upheld a pro-enforcement decision by the Court of Appeal.[133] Larkin and Sambo summarise the case as follows:

> The [Korean Commercial Arbitration Board (KCAB)] award resolved a commercial dispute between multiple Korean parties who had entered into contractual agreements in relation to the financing and development of a large-scale commercial and residential project in Phnom Penh. In May 2012, in accordance with art 353 of the [CCP] and arts 6 and 7 of the Law on the Approval and Implementation of [New York Convention] (2001), the prevailing party in the KCAB arbitration proceedings sought enforcement of the award in Cambodia by filing a motion in the Court of Appeal of Cambodia. The Court of Appeal issued its decision recognising and enforcing the award in April 2013. … One of the non-prevailing parties subsequently filed an appeal motion with the Supreme Court of Cambodia seeking annulment of the Court of Appeal's decision. That motion was ultimately rejected by the Supreme Court, on the ground that the appeal had been brought out of time.[134]

The Supreme Court indeed ruled in favour of the recognition and enforcement of the foreign arbitral award. However, it is unclear whether and how the Court addressed the grounds of Article V of the Convention.[135]

V. Investment Treaty Arbitration

Investment treaty arbitration is a procedure for solving investment disputes between a foreign investor and a host state before an arbitral tribunal established pursuant to an arbitration agreement contained in appliable investment treaties, such as a bilateral investment treaty (BIT), a free trade agreement (FTA) or a treaty with investment provisions (TIPs).[136] To guarantee foreign investors with (at least some) protection for their investment in host states, typical investment treaties afford them protection from expropriation, fair and equitable treatment,[137] national treatment, most-favoured-nation treatment, full protection, and security and dispute settlement by a neutral third party – mediation and/or arbitration,[138]

[132] Forsaith (n 23) 103.

[133] Weeramantry (n 28) 306; Forsaith (n 23) 103.

[134] Larkin and Sambo (n 29) 14.

[135] Forsaith (n 23) 85–86.

[136] Investment treaty arbitration is a subcategory of investment arbitration (or investor-state arbitration). In investment arbitration, a tribunal is established by an investment treaty or an arbitration agreement included in any investment contract between an investor and a host state: A von Walter, 'State Contracts and the Relevance of Investment Contract Arbitration: I. Investor-State Contracts in the Context of International Investment Law' in M Bungenberg and others (eds), *International Investment Law: A Handbook* (London, Bloomsbury T&T Clark, 2015) 85, 99ff.

[137] Among 2538 BITs signed between 1959 and 2016, 2418 (95%) have a fair and equitable treatment clause: UNCTAD, 'Investment Policy Hub: Mapping of IIA Clauses' (n.d.), available at https://investmentpolicy.unctad.org/pages/1031/mapping-of-iia-clauses (accessed 11 December 2024).

[138] S Hobe, 'The Law Relating to Aliens, the International Minimum Standard and State Responsibility: I. The Development of the Law of Aliens and the Emergence of General Principles of Protection under Public International Law' in M Bungenberg and others (eds), *International Investment Law* (London, Bloomsbury T&T Clark, 2015) 13; T Meshel, 'The Use and Misuse of the Corruption Defence in International Investment Arbitration' (2013) 30 *Journal of International Arbitration* 267, 270–71.

which is often called investor-state dispute settlement (ISDS). Cambodia signed 27 BITs from 1994 to 2018 (of which 11 are not in force) and 20 TIPs[139] between 1980 and 2023.[140] These treaties typically contain ISDS provisions that aim at providing a remedy to foreign investors for alleged breaches of their legal protection prescribed in the treaty through arbitrations administered by the International Centre for Settlement of Investment Disputes (ICSID)[141] or ad-hoc arbitrations following the UNCITRAL Arbitration Rules (2021).[142] Whether an arbitration proceeds under the ICSID Convention (and the ICSID Arbitration Rules (2022)) or the UNCITRAL Arbitration Rules, it will not be immune from issues of PIL as discussed in the ensuing subsections.[143]

A. Jurisdiction of the Arbitral Tribunal

In investment treaty arbitration, the jurisdiction of a tribunal generally derives from an offer of consent to arbitration expressed by states in their investment treaty and an acceptance of that offer by a foreign investor's filing of arbitration proceedings under the treaty.[144] Under the ICSID Rules and the UNCITAL Arbitration Rules adopted by the investment treaty, the foreign investor and the host state are subject to the doctrine of competence-competence,[145] which gives the tribunal the authority to rule on its jurisdiction. The primary rules governing the tribunal's jurisdictional ruling are the rules of the investment treaty.[146] Thus, the tribunal is required to determine the issues of jurisdiction based on these rules.

For instance, under the Cambodia–Hungary BIT (signed in 2016), '[a]ny dispute which may arise between an investor of one Contracting Party and the other Contracting Party in connection with an investment in the territory of that other Contracting Party' that cannot be settled through amicable negotiations within six months, may be referred by the investor

[139] TIPs refer to various types of investment treaties that are not BITs, including but not limited to broad economic treaties, such as investment-related obligations commonly found in BITs, treaties with limited investment-related provisions and treaties only containing 'framework' clauses for enhancing cooperation and negotiation in the area of investment: UNCTAD, 'International Investment Agreements Navigator' (n.d.), available at https://investmentpolicy.unctad.org/international-investment-agreements (accessed 11 December 2024).

[140] UNCTAD, 'International Investment Agreements Navigator: Cambodia' (n.d.), available at https://investmentpolicy.unctad.org/international-investment-agreements/countries/33/cambodia (accessed 11 December 2024). Note that 20 TIPs include the ASEAN Investment Agreement signed in 1987 but terminated later.

[141] Convention on the Settlement of Investment Disputes between States and Nationals of Other States (Washington, 18 March 1965; the ICSID Convention) came into force in Cambodia in 2005: ICSID, 'About ICSID: Database of ICSID Member States' (2024), available at https://icsid.worldbank.org/about/member-states/database-of-member-states (accessed 11 December 2024).

[142] See, e.g., Art 8 of the Cambodia–Hungary BIT (signed in 2016), Art 17.4 of the Cambodia–Japan BIT (signed in 2007) and Art 33.1 of the ASEAN Comprehensive Investment Agreement (signed in 2009). Exceptionally, Art 10.2 of the Cambodia–Croatia BIT (signed in 2001) recognises ISDS by 'by arbitration in accordance with the Rules of Arbitration of the International Chamber of Commerce'.

[143] JA Bischoff, 'Arbitration, Investment' in J Basedow and others (eds), *Encyclopedia of Private International Law* (Cheltenham, Edward Elgar Publishing, 2018) 101–05.

[144] C Schreuer, 'Jurisdiction and Applicable Law in Investment Treaty Arbitration' (2014) 1 *McGill Journal of Dispute Resolution* 1, 2; F Balcerzak, 'Jurisdiction of Tribunals in Investor–State Arbitration and the Issue of Human Rights' (2014) 29 *ICSID Review – Foreign Investment Law Journal* 216, 219–20.

[145] ICSID Convention, Art 41(1); UNCITRAL Arbitration Rules, Art 23.1.

[146] Schreuer (n 144) 2.

to the ICSID in light of the applicable provisions of the ICSID Convention.[147] Article 25(1) of the Convention provides:

> The jurisdiction of the [ICSID] shall extend to any legal dispute arising directly out of an investment, between a Contracting State (or any constituent subdivision or agency of a Contracting State designated to the [ICSID] by that State) and a national of another Contracting State, which the parties to the dispute consent in writing to submit to the Centre.

What constitutes an 'investment' is determined based on the definition of investment in the applicable investment treaty. Many BITs and TIPs, including the Cambodia–Hungary BIT, define 'investment' broadly, requiring it to be legal under the law of the host state.[148] On 'any constituent subdivision or agency of a Contracting State designated to the Centre by that State', the tribunal in *Cambodia Power Company v Kingdom of Cambodia and Electricité du Cambodge* held that designation in conformity with Article 25(1) is a written designation that is communicated directly or indirectly (through a treaty or legislation) to the ICSID.[149] Moreover, the ICSID Convention states 'national of another contracting state' as any natural person or juridical person 'who had the nationality of a Contracting State other than the State party to the dispute'.[150] The jurisdiction of the tribunal in investment arbitration shall therefore be determined primarily in accordance with the applicable investment treaty and, secondarily, other rules adopted by the treaty, such as the provisions of the ICSID Convention or the UNCITRAL Arbitration Rules.[151]

[147] Cambodia–Hungary BIT, Art 8.

[148] Art 1.1 of the Cambodia–Hungary BIT provides: 'The term "investment" shall comprise every kind of asset invested in connection with economic activities by an investor of one Contracting Party in the territory of the other Contracting Party in accordance with the laws and regulations of the latter and shall include, in particular, though not exclusively: a) movable and immovable property as well as any other rights *in rem* such as mortgages, liens, pledges and similar rights; b) shares, stocks and debentures of companies or any other form of participation in a company; c) claims to money or to any performance having an economic value associated with an investment; d) intellectual and industrial property rights, including copyrights, trademarks, patents, designs, rights of breeders, technical processes, know-how, trade secrets, geographical indications, trade names and goodwill associated with an investment; e) any right conferred by law or under contract and any licenses and permits pursuant to law, including the concessions to search for, extract, cultivate or exploit natural resources'. Regarding the tribunal's jurisdiction and the legality requirement, see generally N Teramura, L Nottage and B Jetin (eds), *Corruption and Illegality in Asian Investment Arbitration* (Singapore, Springer, 2024).

[149] ICSID Case No. ARB/09/18, Decision on Jurisdiction dated 22 March 2011 [217]–[246].

[150] ICSID Convention, Art 25(2).

[151] For example, an investment tribunal typically declines jurisdiction over an investor's claim if they find that the investment project has violated the host state's law by involving corruption and other serious illegal misconduct: N Teramura, L Nottage and B Jetin, 'Bribery and Other Serious Investor Misconduct in Asian Investment Arbitration' in N Teramura, L Nottage and B Jetin (eds), *Corruption and Illegality in Asian Investment Arbitration* (Singapore, Springer, 2024). Moreover, according to Hwang and Chan, '[t]he jurisdiction of an investment treaty tribunal generally depends on whether the claimant-investor satisfies four necessary jurisdictional requirements that establish the existence of adjudicative power: (i) *ratione voluntaris* (whether there was unqualified consent to arbitrate the claim in question); (ii) *ratione personae* (whether the claimant is a covered investor under the treaty); (iii) *ratione materiae* (whether the subject matter of the claim is within the scope of the treaty, i.e., whether there is a covered investment); and (iv) *ratione temporis* (whether the treaty was in force when the dispute arose): M Hwang and A Chang, 'Corruption in International Investment Arbitration' in N Teramura, L Nottage and B Jetin (eds), *Corruption and Illegality in Asian Investment Arbitration* (Singapore, Springer, 2024) 161. See also A Newcombe, 'Investor Misconduct: Jurisdiction, Admissibility or Merits?' in C Brown and K Miles (eds), *Evolution in Investment Treaty Law and Arbitration*, vol Cambridge (Cambridge, Cambridge University Press, 2011) 192–93.

B. Choice of Law

The inquiry into the law 'applicable' to the substance of an investor-state dispute is not as simple as it seems. Most treaties do not contain any choice of law provisions for investment arbitration,[152] while some contain applicable law clauses that indicate several sources of law without elaborating on their hierarchy.[153] The Cambodia–Czech Republic BIT (signed in 2008) exceptionally contains a sequential list of applicable rules of law comprising the applicable provisions of the BIT, relevant agreements between the two countries, the law of the host state, among others. However, the list is neither binding nor exclusive.[154] Further complicating these issues of choice of law is Article 42(1) of the ICSID Convention, which provides that:

> The Tribunal shall decide a dispute in accordance with such rules of law as may be agreed by the parties. In the absence of such agreement, the Tribunal shall apply the law of the Contracting State party to the dispute (including its rules on the conflict of laws) and such rules of international law as may be applicable.

This provision does not offer guidance for a tribunal on how to deal with conflicting sources of law specified in the applicable investment treaty. However, the lack of guidance is unlikely to cause major challenges because most investment treaties do not contain a choice of law clause. If the investment treaty does not have an applicable law provision, the second sentence of Article 42(1) becomes relevant. The sentence calls for the mandatory application of the law of the host state and the 'rules of international law as may be applicable', without clarifying when the rules of international law 'may be applicable'. This ambiguity in Article 42(1) has been the focus of a vigorous debate among jurists and legal scholars.[155]

Four approaches are available to interpret the second sentence of Article 42(1), concerning the applicability of municipal law and international law to the substance of the dispute.

(1) In *Klöckner v Cameroon*[156] and *Amco Asia Corp. v Indonesia*,[157] the ICSID Ad-hoc Committees stated that the application of international law shall be complementary and corrective in that international law would only play a role where there is a lacuna in

[152] See, for example, the Cambodia–Hungary BIT, the Cambodia–Russian Federation BIT (signed in 2015), the Belarus–Cambodia BIT (signed in 2014), the Cambodia–Netherlands BIT (signed in 2003) and the Cambodia–Vietnam BIT (signed in 2001). See also Y Banifatemi, 'The Law Applicable in Investment Treaty Arbitration' in K Yannaca-Small (ed), *Arbitration Under International Investment Agreements: A Guide to the Key Issues* (Oxford, Oxford University Press, 2010) 200 (stating, '[p]ractice shows that in the majority of cases, there was no choice of law provision in the arbitrations initiated on the basis of a bilateral investment treaty).

[153] Art 17.14 of the Cambodia–Japan BIT (signed in 2007) provides that '[a]n arbitral tribunal [established by the ICSID Convention or the UNCITRAL Arbitration Rules] shall decide the issues in [investment] dispute in accordance with this Agreement and applicable rules of international law.

[154] Art 8.3 of the Cambodia–Czech Republic BIT (signed in 2008) mandates the arbitral tribunal to decide on the basis of law, '*taking into account* the sources of law in the following sequence' (emphasis added): (1) 'the provisions of this Agreement, and other relevant Agreements between the Contracting Parties'; (2) 'the law in force of the Contracting Party concerned'; (3) 'the provisions of special agreements relating to the investment'; and (4) 'the general principles of international law'.

[155] M Sasson, *Substantive Law in Investment Treaty Arbitration: The Unsettled Relationship between International Law and Municipal Law*, 2nd edn, (Alphen aan den Rijn, Wolters Kluwer, 2017) 47.

[156] *Klöckner Industrie-Anlagen GmbH and others v United Republic of Cameroon and Société Camerounaise des Engrais*, ICSID Case No. ARB/81/2, Decision of the Ad Hoc Committee (Unofficial English Translation) [69].

[157] *Amco Asia Corporation and others v Republic of Indonesia*, ICSID Case No. ARB/81/1, Ad hoc Committee Decision on the Application for Annulment (English) [21]–[22].

domestic law, or where there is an inconsistency between domestic law and international law. This view is based on the *travaux préparatoires* of the ICSID Convention and the delegates' vote on Article 42(1) during the negotiations of the Convention.[158]

(2) Reisman and Arsanjani distinguish investment contract disputes from investment treaty disputes. In Resiman's view, national law primarily governs investment contract cases, and the application of national law to such cases would be precluded by international law only in exceptional cases where there exist 'genuine' *lacunae* in the applicable municipal law or where there are inconsistencies between national and international laws that host state law does not offer a method of fulfilment or adjustment on, such as a violation of a fundamental international law principle, like *pacta sunt servanda* and a peremptory international human rights norm.[159] On investment treaty disputes, in their review article on *Klöckner v Cameroon* and *Amco Asia Corp. v Indonesia*, Reisman and Arsanjani suggest that a BIT, a treaty, shall be interpreted in accordance with international law even if it does not have an explicit choice of law clause because it 'constitutes the *eo ipso* applicable law to claims for the breaches of the protections contained therein'.[160] In other words, they claim that the second sentence of Article 42(1) does not apply to any investment treaty disputes because an investment treaty is, by itself, the parties' agreement on applicable law.

(3) Gaillard and Banifatemi opine that an investment tribunal under Article 42(1) has complete discretion to adopt both domestic and international rules of law as it deems appropriate.[161] Based on the ICSID Ad-hoc Committee's decision in *Wena v Egypt*,[162] they claim that 'and' in the second sentence of Article 42(1) confers each ICSID tribunal authority to decide the applicability of any rules of international law, without any initial requirement of identifying either a *lacuna* or an inadequacy of the domestic law of the host state.[163]

(4) Sasson argues that none of these approaches are satisfactory. According to her, an approach proposed by Aron Broches – the first Secretary General of the ICSID – most effectively resolves the uncertainties in Article 42(1) as it is (arguably) closest to the intent of the Contracting Parties to the ICSID Convention.[164] She summarises the Broches' approach as follows: '[A] tribunal should apply international law only when (a) national law provides for the application of international law, (b) where the subject matter is regulated directly by

[158] According to Sasson, '[t]he Committee's research into the Convention's travaux, however, was flawed': Sasson (n 155) 64. Moreover, Reisman and Arsanjani state that the legislative history of Art 42(1) is 'evidence of the clashing views about the role of international and domestic law': WM Reisman and MH Arsanjani, 'Applicable Law under the ICSID Convention: The Tortured History of the Interpretation of Article 42' in M Kinnear and others (eds), *Building International Investment Law: The First 50 Years of ICSID* (Alphen aan den Rijn, Wolters Kluwer, 2015) 12.

[159] WM Reisman, 'The Regime for Lacunae in the ICSID Choice of Law Provision and the Question of Its Threshold' (2000) 15 *ICSID Review – Foreign Investment Law Journal* 362, 368, 374–80.

[160] Reisman and Arsanjani (n 158) 11.

[161] E Gaillard and Y Banifatemi, 'The Meaning of "and" in Article 42(1), Second Sentence, of the Washington Convention: The Role of International Law in the ICSID Choice of Law Process' (2003) 18 *ICSID Review – Foreign Investment Law Journal* 375.

[162] *Wena Hotels Ltd. v Arab Republic of Egypt*, ICSID Case No. ARB/98/4, Decision (Annulment Proceeding). The ad-hoc Committee concluded in paragraph 40 that '[w]hat is clear is that the sense and meaning of the negotiations leading to the second sentence of Article 42(1) allowed for both legal orders to have a role. The law of the host State can indeed be applied in conjunction with international law if this is justified. So too international law can be applied by itself if the appropriate rule is found in this other ambit'.

[163] Gaillard and Banifatemi (n 161) 399, 403ff.

[164] Sasson (n 155) 49.

international law, and (c) when national law violates international law'.[165] Sasson insists that this is the intended meaning of the Article which 'makes sense as a matter of international law'.[166]

Accordingly, there are different views on the approaches to the interpretation of Article 42(1) of the ICSID Convention. Thus, the discussion on the law governing the substance of investment arbitration does not seem to have settled yet.[167] There is no material on Cambodia's experience in dealing with questions of the law governing the merits of an investor-state dispute under Article 42 of the Convention.[168] It remains to be seen what approach to the interpretation of the Article will be taken for resolving the choice of law issue in investment arbitration involving Cambodia. The role of Cambodian PIL in the choice of law in investment arbitration depends on the interpretative approach adopted by the tribunal.

C. Recognition and Enforcement of Arbitral Awards

Rules on the recognition and enforcement of investment arbitral awards can be found in Article 54(1) of the ICSID Convention. The Article provides:

> Each Contracting State shall recognize an award rendered pursuant to this Convention as binding and enforce the pecuniary obligations imposed by that award within its territories as if it were a final judgment of a court in that State. A Contracting State with a federal constitution may enforce such an award in or through its federal courts and may provide that such courts shall treat the award as if it were a final judgment of the courts of a constituent state.

Accordingly, the ICSID regime does not provide grounds for the refusal of recognition and enforcement of ICSID awards, although the award recognition and enforcement may be limited by the law of state immunity enforced in the host state.[169] Such grounds for refusal are available for non-ICSID arbitration awards under the New York Convention,[170] unless otherwise provided in an applicable investment treaty.[171]

[165] ibid. See also A Broches, 'The Convention on the Settlement of Investment Disputes Between States and Nationals of Other States: Applicable Law and Default Procedure' in P Sanders (ed), *International Arbitration: Liber Amicorum for Martin Domke* (Leiden, Martinus Nijhoff, 1967).

[166] Sasson (n 155) 49.

[167] See M Benedettelli, 'Determining the Applicable Law in Commercial and Investment Arbitration: Two Intertwined Road Maps for Conflicts-Solving' (2022) 37 *ICSID Review – Foreign Investment Law Journal* 687, 692–96; JA Bischoff, 'Conflict of Laws and International Investment Arbitration' (2018) 7 *European International Arbitration Review* 143; U Kriebaum, 'Article 42' in SW Schill and others (eds), *Schreuer's Commentary on the ICSID Convention: A Commentary on the Convention on the Settlement of Investment Disputes between States and Nationals of Other States* (Cambridge, Cambridge University Press, 2022) 882–96; AK Bjorklund and L Vanhonnaeker, 'Article 42' in J Fouret, R Gerbay and GM Alvarez (eds), *The ICSID Convention, Regulations and Rules: A Practical Commentary* (Cheltenham, Edward Elgar Publishing, 2019) 360–68.

[168] See, for example, *Cambodia Power Company v. Kingdom of Cambodia*, ICSID Case No. ARB/09/18 (of which available documents can be found at www.italaw.com/cases/3445 (accessed 11 December 2024)) and *Qiong Ye and Jianping Yang v Kingdom of Cambodia*, ICSID Case No. ARB/21/42 (of which limited data is available at https://investmentpolicy.unctad.org/investment-dispute-settlement/cases/1186/qiong-ye-and-jianping-yang-v-cambodia (accessed 11 December 2024)).

[169] ICSID Convention, Art 55.

[170] See, for example, Art 8.4 of the Belarus–Cambodia BIT and Art 17.13 of the Cambodia–Japan BIT.

[171] For instance, without referring to the applicability of the grounds for refusal to enforce arbitral awards under Art V of the New York Convention, the Cambodia-Hungary BIT provides in Art 8.7 that '*[t]he award shall be final*

VI. Conclusions

This chapter has examined the legal environment surrounding ICA in Cambodia, focusing on: (1) the applicable law of arbitral proceedings, (2) arbitration institutions and organisations, and (3) the main PIL issues in ICA. On (1), the Arbitration Law is modern, but its deviation from the Model Law might undermine the growing popularity of ICA in the Kingdom. The statute is based on the original 1985 version of the UNCITRAL Model Law, and does not take into account amendments to the Model Law adopted in 2006. This is not against the international trend of ICA because many Model Law jurisdictions have yet to adopt the provisions introduced by the 2006 amendments.[172] However, the 2006 decision of the Constitutional Council turned Article 5 of the Arbitration Law into a potential ground for judicial intervention to arbitral proceedings. This might lead foreign investors and legal practitioners to raise their eyebrows towards ICA in Cambodia. On (2), the NCAC, as Cambodia's only commercial arbitration institution, is eager to promote ICA and its services in and outside the Kingdom. Its efforts have brought about the gradual but steady rise of their caseload. Several foreign arbitration organisations and institutions, including but not limited to SIAC, SIArb, JCAA, JIDRC and ICC, have engaged in arbitration-related activities in the Kingdom. On (3), the Arbitration Law sets out rules for the arbitral tribunal's jurisdiction and choice of law, which are modelled after the corresponding provisions of the UNCITRAL Model Law. Nothing suggests that the courts in Cambodia will interpret those rules in a way that contradicts international practice under the Model Law. The Appeal Court of Cambodia should recognise or enforce foreign arbitral awards in accordance with the pro-enforcement scheme of the New York Convention, but whether the Court maintains a pro-enforcement bias is unclear from the Supreme Court's judgment in 2014 that has yet to be published. Overall, it would take some time for Cambodia to catch up with regional competitors, such as Singapore and Hong Kong, in the development of ICA.

This chapter has also considered the key PIL issues in investment arbitration related to Cambodia, such as the jurisdiction of the arbitral tribunal, choice of law and the recognition and enforcement of arbitral awards. Many of Cambodia's BITs and TIPs comprise ISDS clauses that enable investors to bring claims against host states in arbitration proceedings under the ICSID Convention, the UNCITRAL Arbitration Rules or institutional rules. These legal instruments contain foundational conflict of laws rules for investment arbitration. However, the second sentence of Article 42(1) of the ICSID Convention poses complex issues of applicable rules of law in investment arbitration, as discussed in Section V.B above. These issues are subjects of controversy among legal experts, so the government of Cambodia should monitor closely how ICSID tribunals apply Article 42(1) to determine the law governing the substance of the dispute in the absence of parties' agreement on applicable law.

and binding on the parties to the dispute and shall be executed in accordance with the law of the Contracting Party in the territory of which the investment has been made and the award is relied upon' (emphasis added).

[172] In fact, not many countries and territories have adopted the text of 2006 amendments: UNCITRAL (n 10).

12

The Harmonisation of Private International Law

I. Cambodia's Role in the Work of the Hague Conference, UNCITRAL, UNIDROIT and Other Organisations

Cambodia's interest in the harmonisation of private international law (PIL) is likely to be passive at best and weak at worst.[1] For many years, efforts towards the global harmonisation of PIL, especially in the field of transnational commercial law, have been carried out by international institutions and organisations of public and private natures. However, Cambodia has not actively joined or supported the works of those bodies. Since its first session in 1893, the Hague Conference on Private International Law (HCCH) has published various international conventions, protocols and soft law instruments to enhance the progressive unification of the rules of PIL.[2] Cambodia is not a member of this international organisation.[3] It has adopted only one convention of the HCCH to date – the Convention on Protection of Children and Co-operation in Respect of Intercountry Adoption (the Hague Adoption Convention),[4] and the ratification by the country of this legal instrument was the result of strong international pressure for reforming the practice of intercountry adoption in Cambodia, which was undermining the rights of children and their families.[5] In other words, the international community pressured Cambodia to adopt the legal framework to crack down on illegal intercountry adoption targeting Cambodian children.

The United Nations Commission on International Trade Law (UNCITRAL) has been playing a pivotal role in developing and maintaining robust cross-border legal frameworks for the progressive harmonisation and modernisation of the law of international

[1] The aim of legal harmonisation is to reduce existing differences between legal systems, not to eliminate them (unlike legal unification): F Ferrari, 'Uniform Substantive Law and Private International Law' in J Basedow and others (eds), *Encyclopedia of Private International Law* (Cheltenham, Edward Elgar Publishing, 2017) 1772.

[2] M Pertegás, 'Hague Conference on Private International Law' in J Basedow and others (eds), *Encyclopedia of Private International Law* (Cheltenham, Edward Elgar Publishing, 2017) 870.

[3] HCCH, 'HCCH Members' (2024), available at www.hcch.net/en/states/hcch-members (accessed 11 December 2024); Pertegás (n 2) 870.

[4] HCCH, 'Hague Conventions: Signatures, Ratifications, Approvals and Accessions: Status on 21 November 2024' (2024), available at https://assets.hcch.net/docs/ccf77ba4-af95-4e9c-84a3-e94dc8a3c4ec.pdf (accessed 11 December 2024), 'HCCH NON-MEMBER PARTIES (66)' section.

[5] K Meta and E Handley, 'Report Gives Voice to Mothers Deceived by Cambodia's Orphanage Racket', *The Phnom Penh Post*, 30 March 2018, available at www.phnompenhpost.com/national-post-depth/report-gives-voice-mothers-deceived-cambodias-orphanage-racket (accessed 11 December 2024); See also Chapter 8 in this volume.

trade, commerce and investment.[6] UNCITRAL is composed of 70 member states of the United Nations (UN) that are elected by the General Assembly of the UN for terms of six years, reflecting the world's diverse geographic regions and its principal economic and legal systems.[7] However, the General Assembly has never elected Cambodia to be a member of this core legal body of the UN system in international trade law,[8] possibly due to its reserved attitude towards UNCITRAL's legal harmonisation initiatives. For instance, Cambodia has adopted only a few UNCITRAL Conventions and Model Laws: The United Nations Convention on the Recognition and Enforcement of Foreign Arbitral Awards (New York, 1958; the New York Convention), the UNCITRAL Model Law on International Commercial Arbitration (1985) (with amendments adopted in 2006) and the UNCITRAL Model Law on Electronic Commerce (1996).[9] It has yet to ratify UNCITRAL's key international legal instruments for legal harmonisation, such as the United Nations Convention on Contracts for the International Sale of Goods (Vienna, 1980; CISG) and the Singapore Convention on Mediation (the Singapore Mediation Convention).[10] The country's passivity in UNCITRAL's activities is also evident from its non-participation in Working Groups. For example, Working Group II (Dispute Settlement), which is composed of all state members of the UNCITRAL, considered draft model provisions on technology-related dispute resolution and adjudication at its 79th session in February 2024.[11] However, Cambodia did not attend or send any observers to the meeting, despite the participation of delegates from several Southeast Asian countries.[12] Likewise, Working Group IV (Electronic Commerce), which consists of all state members of UNCITRAL, held its 66th session to discuss the use of artificial intelligence (AI) and automation in contracting and data provision contracts in Vienna from 16 to 20 October 2023.[13] Cambodia did not send a representative to the event, apart from some observers, unlike its neighbouring countries of Singapore, Thailand and Vietnam.[14] Thus, Cambodia's overall commitment to UNCITRAL's legal harmonisation activities does not appear to be outstanding.

Founded in 1926 as one of six specialised agencies of the League of Nations, the International Institute for the Unification of Private Law (UNIDROIT) is an independent intergovernmental organisation that aims to formulate uniform law instruments, principles and rules to achieve the harmonisation, modernisation and coordination of private

[6] UNCITRAL, 'Homepage' (2024), available at https://uncitral.un.org/en/content/homepage (accessed 11 December 2024); F Ferrari, 'UNCITRAL' in Jürgen Basedow and others (eds), *Encyclopedia of Private International Law* (Cheltenham, Edward Elgar Publishing, 2017) 1759.

[7] UNCITRAL, 'Origin, Mandate and Composition of UNCITRAL' (2024), available at https://uncitral.un.org/en/about/faq/mandate_composition (accessed 11 December 2024).

[8] UNCITRAL, 'Member States History' (2024), available at https://uncitral.un.org/en/about/faq/mandate_composition/memberhistory (accessed 11 December 2024).

[9] UNCITRAL, 'Overview of the Status of UNCITRAL Conventions and Model Laws' (2024), available at https://uncitral.un.org/sites/uncitral.un.org/files/media-documents/uncitral/en/overview-status-table.pdf (accessed 11 December 2024).

[10] ibid.

[11] UNCITRAL, 'A/CN.9/1166 – Report of Working Group II (Dispute Settlement) on the Work of Its Seventy-Ninth Session (New York, 12–16 February 2024)' (2024) 2, available at https://docs.un.org/en/A/CN.9/1166 (accessed 11 December 2024).

[12] ibid 3 (noting that Malaysia, Singapore, Vietnam and observers from the Philippines attended the session).

[13] UNCITRAL, 'A/CN.9/1162 – Report of Working Group IV (Electronic Commerce) on the Work of Its Sixty-Sixth Session (Vienna, 16–20 October 2023)' (2024) 2, available at https://docs.un.org/en/A/CN.9/1162 (accessed 11 December 2024).

[14] ibid.

law between states and groups of states.[15] As Cambodia has not acceded to the UNIDROIT Statute, it has yet to obtain the membership status of the institution.[16] Among many UNIDROIT instruments in the fields of civil procedure, commercial contracts, international sales, among others, the only legal instrument that the country has adopted expressly is the UNIDROIT Convention on Stolen or Illegally Exported Cultural Objects.[17] Cambodian legislation does not clearly disallow the use of UNIDROIT Principles of International Commercial Contracts as the rules of law governing a contract in international litigation and arbitration.[18] But otherwise, Cambodia has played little part (if any) in UNIDROIT's legal harmonisation initiatives.

Cambodia's limited involvement in legal harmonisation projects by these international organisations indicates that the country lacks strong interest in the global harmonisation of PIL. However, the Cambodian judiciary appears to be interested in legal harmonisation at a regional level, albeit in some areas of PIL, as follows.

In 2017, the Second China-ASEAN Justices Forum was held in Nanning, China. The participants and special guests of the event exchanged their views on '"justice and regional judicial cooperation in the Internet era", especially, coordination and integration of commercial laws of various countries in the region, the establishment of a cross-border dispute resolution mechanism and the development of international judicial assistance within the area'.[19] The Forum culminated in a statement in which the participating countries agreed to explore coordination and integration of national commercial laws and consider the appropriate promotion of mutual recognition and enforcement of civil and commercial judgments among states.[20] Justice You Ottara, the Deputy President of the Supreme Court of the Kingdom of Cambodia, joined this statement. The statement does not have legally binding force over participating countries. However, the fact that commentators regard it as a key achievement for mutual judgment recognition and enforcement among China and ASEAN states,[21] and the fact that the Deputy President signed the statement confirming the need for commercial law integration, indicates the Cambodian judiciary's readiness to cooperate with legal harmonisation in the region, even though the willingness might probably be underpinned by China's economic influence over Cambodia through the Belt and Road Initiative.[22]

[15] H Kronke, 'UNIDROIT' in J Basedow and others (eds), *Encyclopedia of Private International Law* (Cheltenham, Edward Elgar Publishing, 2017) 1766; UNIDROIT, 'About UNIDROIT' (2021), available at www.unidroit.org/about-unidroit/ (accessed 11 December 2024).

[16] UNIDROIT, 'Membership' (2021), available at www.unidroit.org/about-unidroit/members-states-2/ (accessed 11 December 2024).

[17] UNIDROIT, 'Instruments' (2021), available at www.unidroit.org/instruments/ (accessed 11 December 2024).

[18] See Chapters 5 (on contracts) and 11 (on arbitration) in this volume.

[19] 'Nanning Statement of the 2nd China-ASEAN Justice Forum' (2017), available at www.chinajusticeobserver.com/p/nanning-statement-of-the-2nd-china-asean-justice-forum (accessed 19 December 2024).

[20] ibid.

[21] W Gu, 'China' in A Reyes (ed), *Recognition and Enforcement of Judgments in Civil and Commercial Matters* (Oxford, Hart Publishing, 2019) 45; RH Huang and W Gu, 'China's Recognition and Enforcement of Foreign Securities Judgments against Overseas-listed Chinese Companies' (2023) 26 *Journal of International Economic Law* 577, 581; J Huang, 'Reciprocal Recognition and Enforcement of Foreign Judgments in China: Promising Developments, Prospective Challenges and Proposed Solutions' (2019) 88 *Nordic Journal of International Law* 250, 260.

[22] M Mit, 'China's Continuing Influence over Cambodia's Economy', *East Asia Forum*, 1 May 2024, available at https://eastasiaforum.org/2024/05/01/chinas-continuing-influence-over-cambodias-economy/ (accessed

Some leading Cambodian legal experts, on a personal level, have participated in various projects for the harmonisation of PIL in ASEAN, such as the Asian Principles for the Recognition and Enforcement of Foreign Judgments project by the Asian Business Law Institute (ABLI).[23] However, it remains to be seen whether such personal interest in the regional convergence of PIL may extend beyond specific areas of the law, and whether the interest is generally shared among jurists and commentators in Cambodia.[24] Cambodia is therefore generally not very involved in the regional and international harmonisation of private international law.

II. The Future of Private International Law

Given Cambodia's current stage of development in conflict of laws rules, it may not be ready to contribute to the global harmonisation of private international just yet. This section proposes three crucial steps for developing Cambodian PIL, with the primary aim of assisting the country in becoming more actively involved in the regional and global harmonisation movements.

First, the Cambodian judiciary is encouraged to introduce greater transparency and accountability. As mentioned elsewhere in this volume and pointed out by many commentators, it is not the norm for the courts in Cambodia to publish past judicial decisions because lawyers in Cambodia do not consider precedent to be important or persuasive.[25] Some might argue that this lack of transparency is inevitable because judgments in Cambodia are not considered as the primary source of law, are not widely published, and lack adequate judicial reasoning.[26] The circumstances surrounding judgment publication in Cambodia have been slow to improve. In 2017, the Japan International Cooperation Agency (JICA), the Ministry of Justice of Cambodia (MOJ), the Ministry of Land Management Urban Planning and Construction of Cambodia (MLMUPCC) and the Cambodian Supreme Court, Court of Appeal and First Instance Courts launched the Legal and Judicial Development Project (Phase V) to establish a streamlined process of judgment publication and commence the publication of court decisions.[27] As a result, the MOJ published

11 December 2024); H Yu, *Understanding China's Belt and Road Initiative* (Singapore, Springer 2024), Table 6.1 Chinese BRI-affiliated investments and construction in Cambodia, 2013–2022.

[23] Y Bun, 'Country Report: Cambodia' in Adeline Chong (ed), *Recognition and Enforcement of Foreign Judgments in Asia* (Singapore, Asian Business Law Institute, 2017) 37. According to its website, ABLI aims at removing 'unnecessary or undesirable differences between Asian legal systems that pose obstacles to free and seamless trade' and 'has been assigned an Asian-centric focus, a polycentric and practice-oriented identity, and a projects-based strategy for promoting convergence': ABLI, 'About Us' (2024), available at https://abli.asia/about-us/ (accessed 11 December 2024).

[24] In fact, other ABLI's legal convergence projects do not appear to have been joined by experts in Cambodian law: ABLI, 'Projects' (2024), available at https://abli.asia/projects/ (accessed 11 December 2024).

[25] See Chapter 2 in this volume; N Teramura, 'Japan as a Source of Legal Ideas: A View from the Mekong Subregion of ASEAN' (2021) 13 *New Voices in Japanese Studies* 19, 34.

[26] Y Shinoda, 'Report on the Investigation of Cambodian Court Judgments (1) [in Japanese]' (2019) 79 *ICD News* 60; A Kamiki, 'Report on the Investigation of Cambodian Court Judgements [in Japanese]' (2011) 48 *ICD News* 25; N Teramura, 'Cambodia' in A Reyes and W Lui (eds), *Direct Jurisdiction: Asian Perspectives* (Oxford, Hart Publishing, 2021) 201–03. See also Chapter 4 in this volume.

[27] JICA, 'Outline of the Project: The Legal and Judicial Development Project (Phase V)' (2024), available at www.jica.go.jp/Resource/project/english/cambodia/025/outline/index.html (accessed 11 December 2024).

44 civil verdicts on 31 December 2020.[28] The number has not increased dramatically since then – only 104 decisions are now publicly available.[29] However, more judgments should be published in the field of PIL to increase judicial transparency and to assist in generating conflict of law rules in Cambodian law. Other civil law countries, like France and Japan, do not also treat court decisions as binding sources of law. However, their courts publish judicial decisions as a persuasive source of law to guarantee legal certainty and fill gaps in legislation,[30] and some branches of PIL have been created out of decisions by their courts.[31] Thus, the fact of Cambodia being a civil law country cannot justify its courts refraining from publishing their decisions.

Second, Cambodia should be more open to following international legal instruments on PIL. As mentioned in the last section, the number of such instruments adopted by Cambodia is not great: (1) the Hague Adoption Convention, (2) the New York Convention, (3) the UNCITRAL Model Law on International Commercial Arbitration, (4) the UNCITRAL Model Law on Electronic Commerce, and (5) the UNIDROIT Convention on Stolen Cultural Objects. In contrast, Japan – an inspiration of Cambodian PIL – has ratified seven HCCH conventions[32] and two UNCITRAL treaties,[33] maintaining memberships in the HCCH and UNCITRAL from 1957 and 1968 (respectively).[34] It has not expressly adopted any legal instruments of UNIDROIT.[35] However, the country has been a member of the body since 1954,[36] and its Justice Ministry has been investing into the promotion of the UNIDROIT Principles of International Commercial Contracts among law students and beyond in Japan for some time.[37] As Japan's example demonstrates, international treaties and non-binding legal instruments have been instrumental for states to develop and harmonise PIL rules for the past decades.[38] Cambodia should not underestimate international

[28] N Chheng, 'Courts' Decisions Now Published as Reference Source', *The Phnom Penh Post*, 4 January 2021, available at www.phnompenhpost.com/national/courts-decisions-now-published-reference-source (accessed 11 December 2024).

[29] MOJ, 'Court Decisions on Actual Civil Cases' (n.d.), available at www.moj.gov.kh/kh/actual-civil-judgments (accessed 10 December 2024).

[30] E Steiner, *French Law: A Comparative Approach*, 2nd edn, (Oxford, Oxford University Press 2018) 71–74; H Oda, *Japanese Law*, 4th edn, (Oxford, Oxford University Press, 2021) 41–44.

[31] Steiner (n 30) 64; T Kono, 'Japan' in Jürgen Basedow and others (eds), *Encyclopedia of Private International Law* (Cheltenham, Edward Elgar Publishing, 2017) 2220; N Teramura, 'Cambodia' in K Nishioka (ed), *Treatment of Foreign Law in Asia* (Oxford, Hart Publishing, 2023) 182; Chapter 4 in this volume.

[32] These conventions are Convention of 1 March 1954 on Civil Procedure, Convention of 24 October 1956 on the Law Applicable to Maintenance Obligations towards Children, Convention of 5 October 1961 on the Conflicts of Laws Relating to the Form of Testamentary Dispositions, Convention of 5 October 1961 Abolishing the Requirement of Legalisation for Foreign Public Documents, Convention of 15 November 1965 on the Service Abroad of Judicial and Extrajudicial Documents in Civil or Commercial Matters, Convention of 2 October 1973 on the Law Applicable to Maintenance Obligations and Convention of 25 October 1980 on the Civil Aspects of International Child Abduction: HCCH (n 4).

[33] These treaties are the New York Convention and CISG: UNCITRAL (n 9). Also, Japan has ratified the Singapore Mediation Convention.

[34] HCCH, 'Member: Japan' (2024), available at www.hcch.net/en/states/hcch-members/details1/?sid=47 (accessed 11 December 2024); UNCITRAL (n 8).

[35] UNIDROIT (n 17).

[36] UNIDROIT (n 16).

[37] Intercollegeate Negotiation Competition, 'Outline' (2024), available at www.negocom.jp/eng/what/ (accessed 11 December 2024); L Nottage, 'Symposium Paper: Afterthoughts – International Commercial Contracts and Arbitration' (2010) 17 *Australian International Law Journal* 197, 204.

[38] M Pertegás, 'Treaties in Private International Law' in J Basedow and others (eds), *Encyclopedia of Private International Law* (Cheltenham, Edward Elgar Publishing, 2017) 1743–47.

organisations' efforts in the global development of PIL. Cambodian legal experts are acquiring capacity and expertise to commit more to such efforts by international legal bodies, thanks to long-term support from international donors.[39]

Third, Cambodia should consider updating its legislation on PIL. Because the Civil Procedure Code of Cambodia is based on an old version of Japan's Civil Procedure Code, it does not contain explicit rules on the international jurisdiction of Cambodian courts.[40] Jurists in Cambodia are encouraged to establish clear rules on direct jurisdiction. They may take advantage of Articles 3.2–3.12 of the current version of the Civil Procedure Code of Japan as sources of inspiration for the reform. Cambodian law does not appear to have enough rules for choice of law.[41] There are several conflict of laws rules in the Civil Code,[42] the Marriage and Family Law[43] and the Arbitration Law.[44] However, Cambodia needs comprehensive legislation, such as Japan's Act on the General Rules of Application of Laws (AGRAL), that comprises various choice of law rules to deal with diverse conflicts of laws issues arising from the globalised Cambodian economy.[45]

This book has demonstrated how Japan's Civil Procedure Code, the AGRAL and Japanese legal principles may serve as bases for Cambodia to reform its legislation on private international law, addressing international jurisdiction, conflict of laws, the recognition and enforcement of foreign judgments and international arbitration. It will take time to reform law codes and establish new legal rules in Cambodia because drafting them from scratch is not an easy task, and the legislative process of the country often requires official and unofficial steps and negotiations.[46] A practical approach to law reform could start by the issuing of relevant low-level legal instruments, such as Proclamations (Prakas) and Sub-Decrees (Anu-Kret), by ministries.[47] The author hopes that the discussion in this book can serve as a starting point for a dialogue among legal experts in Cambodian law for considering the next reform of Cambodian private international law, regardless of whether the experts agree or disagree with the suggestions made here.

[39] Nobumichi Teramura, 'JICA's Legal Technical Assistance Projects in Vietnam, Cambodia and Laos since the 1990s' in LC Kelly and G Sasges (eds), *Vietnam Over the Long Twentieth Century* (Singapore, Springer, 2024); Teramura (n 25) 21.

[40] See Chapter 4 in this volume.

[41] See Chapter 2 in this volume.

[42] See Chapter 5 in this volume.

[43] See Chapter 8 in this volume.

[44] See Chapter 11 in this volume.

[45] J Menzel, 'Cambodian Law: Some Comparative and International Perspectives' in H Peng, K Phallack and J Menzel (eds), *Introduction to Cambodian Law* (Phnom Penh, Konrad-Adenauer-Stiftung Cambodia, 2012) 490–91.

[46] See generally B Lawrence, 'The National Assembly and Senate of the Kingdom of Cambodia' in PJ Yap and R Abeyratne (eds), *Routledge Handbook of Asian Parliaments* (Abingdon, Routledge, 2023) 125–38.

[47] K Phallack, 'Overview of the Cambodian Legal and Judicial System and Recent Efforts at Legal and Judicial Reform' in H Peng, K Phallack and J Menzel (eds), *Introduction to Cambodian Law* (Phnom Penh, Konrad-Adenauer-Stiftung Cambodia, 2012) 9.

BIBLIOGRAPHY

Books

ASEAN Secretariat, *Handbook on ASEAN Consumer Protection Laws and Regulation* (Jakarta, ASEAN Secretariat, 2018)

Asian Business Law Institute, *Enforcement of Foreign Judgments in ASEAN: Ranking the Portability of ASEAN Judgments within ASEAN* (Singapore, Asian Business Law Institute, 2022)

Beever, A, *The Law of Private Nuisance* (Oxford, Hart Publishing, 2013)

Berlingieri, F, *International Maritime Conventions (Volume 3): Protection of the Marine Environment* (Abingdon, Routledge, 2015)

Binder, P, *International Commercial Arbitration and Mediation in UNCITRAL Model Law Jurisdictions* (Alphen aan den Rijn, Wolters Kluwer, 2019)

Blackaby, N, Partasides C and Redfern, A, *Redfern and Hunter on International Arbitration*, 7th edn, (Oxford, Oxford University Press, 2022)

Born, GB, *International Commercial Arbitration*, 3rd edn, (Alphen aan den Rijn, Wolters Kluwer, 2020)

Charadine, P, *Cambodia Within ASEAN: Twenty-Years in the Making* (Phnom Penh, Konrad-Adenauer Stiftung and Cambodian Institute for Cooperation and Peace, 2020)

Cohen, J, *Regional Guide to Bankruptcy Law: Cambodia* (Phnom Penh, Tilleke & Gibbins International, 2020)

Dirwan, P and Peeyushi, D, *Private International Law: Indian and English*, 4th edn, (Delhi, Deep & Deep Publications, 1998)

First Asia Division at JICA, *Evaluation Report on Japanese Cooperation to Support the Formulation of Key Government Policies on the Legal and Judicial System in the Kingdom of Cambodia [in Japanese]* (JICA, 2002)

Fox, H and Webb, P, *The Law of State Immunity* revised and updated 3rd edn (Oxford, Oxford University Press, 2015)

Gaillard, E, *Legal Theory of International Arbitration* (Leiden, Martinus Nijhoff Publishers, 2010)

Garcimartín, F and Saumier, G, *Explanatory Report on the Convention of 2 July 2019 on the Recognition and Enforcement of Foreign Judgments in Civil or Commercial Matters* (The Hague, The Hague Conference on Private International Law – HCCH – Permanent Bureau, 2020)

Geertz, C, *Local Knowledge: Further Essays in Interpretive Anthropology* (New York, Basic Books, 2000)

Gutiérrez, NAM, *Limitation of Liability in International Maritime Conventions: The Relationship between Global Limitation Conventions and Particular Liability Regimes* (Abingdon, Routledge, 2010)

HCCH, *Note on Habitual Residence and Scope of the 1993 Hague Convention on Protection of Children and Co-operation in Respect of Intercountry Adoption* (HCCH – Permanent Bureau, 2018)

HCCH, *The Implementation and Operation of the 1993 Hague Intercountry Adoption Convention: Guide to Good Practice* (Bristol, Family Law, 2008)

Huber, P, *Rome II Regulation: Pocket Commentary* (Munich, Sellier European Law Publishers, 2011)

ICC, *ICC Dispute Resolution 2020 Statistics* (Paris, ICC, 2021)

Ikehara, S, Egawa, H and Yamada, R, *The General Theory of Private International Law and Nationality Law [in Japanese]* (Tokyo, Yuhikaku Publishing, 1973)

Industrial Development and Public Policy Department at JICA, *Legal Technical Assistance for Cambodia: The History and Methodology of the Assistance of JICA in Drafting the Civil Code and the Civil Procedure Code [in Japanese]* (2012)

Industry Development and Public Policy Department at JICA, *The Final Evaluation Report on the Project for the Improvement of the Training on Civil Matters at the Royal School for Judges and Prosecutors of the Royal Academy for Judicial Professions (Phase 2) [in Japanese]* (2012)

J Yokoyama, *Private International Law in Japan* (Alphen aan den Rijn, Wolters Kluwer, 2019)

JICA, *Commentary on the Civil Code of the Kingdom of Cambodia [in Japanese]* (JICA, 2011)

Jolly, S and Khanderia, S, *Indian Private International Law* (Oxford, Hart Publishing, 2021)
Koide, K, *Commentary on the Act on General Rules for Application of Laws [in Japanese]* (Tokyo, Shojihomu Publishing, 2014)
Law, J (ed), *A Dictionary of Law* (Oxford, Oxford University Press, 2018)
Low, SF, *Colonial Law Making* (Singapore, NUS Press, 2024)
Matsuo, H, *Politics, Economy and Law in Developing Asia: A Reflection on Law and Development* (Tokyo, Keio University Press, 2022)
Ministry of Land Management Urban Planning and Construction and United Nations Cambodia, *Cambodia Urban Forum: Smart, Sustainable and Inclusive Urban Development* (Ministry of Land Management, Urban Planning and Construction and United Nations Cambodia, 2019)
Mortensen, R, Garnett, R and Keyes, M, *Private International Law in Australia*, 5th edn, (Chatswood, LexisNexis, 2023)
Moses, ML, *The Principles and Practice of International Commercial Arbitration* (Cambridge, Cambridge University Press, 2017)
Nishioka K and Nishitani, Y, *Japanese Private International Law* (Oxford, Hart Publishing, 2021)
Nottage, L and others, *ASEAN Consumer Law Harmonisation and Cooperation: Achievements and Challenges* (Cambridge, Cambridge University Press, 2019)
Oda, H, *Japanese Law*, 4th edn, (Oxford, Oxford University Press, 2021)
Public Policy Department at JICA, *The Ex-ante Evaluation Report on the Project for the Improvement of the Training on Civil Matters at the Royal School for Judges and Prosecutors of the Royal Academy for Judicial Professions (Phase 2) [in Japanese]* (2009)
Public Policy Department at JICA, *The Mid-term Review Report on the Project for the Improvement of the Training on Civil Matters at the Royal School for Judges and Prosecutors of the Royal Academy for Judicial Professions (Phase 2) [in Japanese]* (2010)
Ricketson, S and Ginsburg, J, *International Copyright and Neighbouring Rights: The Berne Convention and Beyond*, 3rd edn, (Oxford, Oxford University Press, 2023)
Sakurada, Y, *Private International Law [in Japanese]*, 7th edn, (Tokyo, Yuhikaku Publishing, 2020)
Sasson, M, *Substantive Law in Investment Treaty Arbitration: The Unsettled Relationship between International Law and Municipal Law*, 2nd edn, (Alphen aan den Rijn, Wolters Kluwer, 2017)
Sawaki, T and Dogauchi, M, *Introduction to Private International Law [in Japanese]* (Tokyo, Yuhikaku Publishing, 2018)
Schaafsma, SJ, *Intellectual Property in the Conflict of Laws: The Hidden Conflict-of-law Rule in the Principle of National Treatment* (Cheltenham and Camberley, Edward Elgar Publishing, 2022)
Schmitthoff, CM, *International Trade Usages* (Paris, ICC Publishing, 1987)
Social Development Department at JICA, *The Final Evaluation Report on the Project for the Improvement of Training on Civil Matters at the Royal School for Judges and Prosecutors of the Royal Academy for Judicial Professions [in Japanese]* (2008)
Stamboulakis, D, *Comparative Recognition and Enforcement: Foreign Judgments and Awards* (Cambridge, Cambridge University Press, 2022)
Steiner, E, *French Law: A Comparative Approach*, 2nd edn, (Oxford, Oxford University Press, 2018)
Tameike, Y, *Lecture on Private International Law [in Japanese]* (Tokyo, Yuhikaku Publishing, 2005)
Teramura, N, *Ex Aequo et Bono as a Response to the 'Over-Judicialisation'of International Commercial Arbitration* (Alphen aan den Rijn, Wolters Kluwer, 2020)
Teramura, N, Nottage, L and Jetin, B (eds), *Corruption and Illegality in Asian Investment Arbitration* (Singapore, Springer, 2024)
UN Secretary General, *Analytical Commentary on Draft Text of a Model Law on International Commercial Arbitration: Report of the Secretary-General (A/CN.9/264)* (Vienna, United Nations, 1985)
UNCITRAL, *UNCITRAL 2012 Digest of Case Law on the Model Law on International Commercial Arbitration* (Vienna, Publishing and Library Section, United Nations Office, 2012)
UNCITRAL, *UNCITRAL Model Law on Cross-Border Insolvency with Guide to Enactment and Interpretation* (Vienna, United Nations Publication, 2014)
UNCITRAL, *UNCITRAL Secretariat Guide on the Convention on the Recognition and Enforcement of Foreign Arbitral Awards (New York, 1958)* (Vienna, Publishing and Library Section, United Nations Office, 2016)
UNCITRAL, *UNCITRAL, HCCH and UNIDROIT Legal Guide to Uniform Instruments in the Area of International Commercial Contracts, with a Focus on Sales* (Vienna, United Nations Publishing and Library Section, 2021)

UNCTAD, *Liability and Compensation for Ship-Source Oil Pollution: An Overview of the International Legal Framework for Oil Pollution Damage from Tankers* (New York and Geneva, United Nations, 2012)

UNIDROIT, *UNIDROIT Principles of International Commercial Contracts 2016* (Rome, UNIDROIT, 2016)

United Nations Development Programme, *A Transparent and Accountable Judiciary to Deliver Justice for All* (Bangkok, United Nations Development Programme, 2016)

Vickery, M, *Kampuchea: Politics, Economy and Society* (London, Frances Pinter (Publishers), 1986)

von Savigny, FC, *A Treatise on the Conflict of Laws and the Limits of their Operation in Respect of Place and Time* (William Guthrie tr, Edinburgh, T & T Clark Law Publishers, 1869)

WIPO, *Guide to the Berne Convention for the Protection of Literary and Artistic Works (Paris Act, 1971)* (Paris, WIPO, 1978)

World Intelligence Partners Japan Co Ltd, *Research Report on Personal Status Law in the Kingdom of Cambodia [in Japanese]* (Tokyo, Ministry of Justice of Japan, 2018)

Yamada, R, *Lectures on Private International Law [in Japanese]*, 3rd edn, (Tokyo, Yuhikaku Publishing, 2004)

Yu, H, *Understanding China's Belt and Road Initiative* (Singapore, Springer, 2024)

Book Chapters

Audit, B, 'Private International Law' in GA Bermann and E Picard (eds), *Introduction to French Law* (Alphen aan den Rijn, Wolters Kluwer, 2008) 453–74

Austermiller, S, 'Cambodian Alternative Dispute Resolution' in H Peng, K Phallack and J Menzel (eds), *Introduction to Cambodian Law* (Phnom Penh, Konrad-Adenauer-Stiftung Cambodia, 2012) 181–95

Banifatemi, Y, 'The Law Applicable in Investment Treaty Arbitration' in K Yannaca-Small (ed), *Arbitration Under International Investment Agreements: A Guide to the Key Issues* (Oxford, Oxford University Press, 2010) 191–210

Bantekas, I, 'Article 28: Rules Applicable to Substance of Dispute' in I Bantekas and others (eds), *UNCITRAL Model Law on International Commercial Arbitration: A Commentary* (Cambridge, Cambridge University Press, 2020) 732–57

Basedow, J, 'Choice of Law' in J Basedow and others (eds), *Encyclopedia of Private International Law* (Cheltenham, Edward Elgar Publishing, 2017) 311–20

Basedow, J, 'Competition Law (Antitrust)' in J Basedow and others (eds), *Encyclopedia of Private International Law* (Cheltenham, Edward Elgar Publishing, 2017) 425–32

Basedow, J, 'Escape Clauses' in J Basedow and others (eds), *Encyclopedia of Private International Law* (Cheltenham, Edward Elgar Publishing, 2017) 668–74

Basedow, J, 'Foundations of Private International Law in Intellectual Property' in J Basedow, T Kono and A Metzger (eds), *Intellectual Property in the Global Arena: Jurisdiction, Applicable Law, and the Recognition of Judgments in Europe, Japan and the US* (Heidelberg, Mohr Siebeck GmbH & Co. KG, 2010) 3–29

Bell, A, 'Country Report: Australia' in A Chong (ed), *Recognition and Enforcement of Foreign Judgments in Asia* (Singapore, Asian Business Law Institute, 2017) 6–18

Bermann, GA, 'Private International Law in International Arbitration' in F Ferrari and DP Arroyo (eds), *Private International Law: Contemporary Challenges and Continuing Relevance* (Cheltenham, Edward Elgar Publishing, 2019) 464–83

Biel, Ł, 'Linguistic Approaches' in M Siems and PJ Yap (eds), *The Cambridge Handbook of Comparative Law* (Cambridge, Cambridge University Press, 2024) 91–112

Bischoff, JA, 'Arbitration, Investment' in J Basedow and others (eds), *Encyclopedia of Private International Law* (Cheltenham, Edward Elgar Publishing, 2018) 97–106

Bjorklund, AK, and Vanhonnaeker, L, 'Article 42' in J Fouret, R Gerbay and GM Alvarez (eds), *The ICSID Convention, Regulations and Rules: A Practical Commentary* (Cheltenham, Edward Elgar Publishing, 2019) 347–68

Bonomi, A, 'Succession' in J Basedow and others (eds), *Encyclopedia of Private International Law* (Cheltenham, Edward Elgar Publishing, 2017) 1682–91

Boren, K, 'Cambodian Private Law: A Snapshot' in H Peng, K Phallack and J Menzel (eds), *Introduction to Cambodian Law* (Phnom Penh, Konrad-Adenauer-Stiftung Cambodia, 2012) 73–96

Bosman, L, 'Note General Editor Cambodia (2017): Supplement No. 93' in L Bosman (ed), *ICCA International Handbook on Commercial Arbitration* (Alphen aan den Rijn, Wolters Kluwer, 2020) i

Brand, O, 'Language as a Barrier to Comparative Law' in F Olsen, A Lorz and D Stein (eds), *Translation Issues in Language and Law* (Cham, Springer, 2009) 18–34

Briggs, A, 'Recognition and Enforcement of Judgments (Common Law)' in F Ferrari and others (eds), *Encyclopedia of Private International Law* (Cheltenham, Edward Elgar Publishing, 2017) 1479–85

Broches, A, 'The Convention on the Settlement of Investment Disputes Between States and Nationals of Other States: Applicable Law and Default Procedure' in P Sanders (ed), *International Arbitration: Liber Amicorum for Martin Domke* (Leiden, Martinus Nijhoff, 1967) 12–22

Bun, Y, 'Country Report: Cambodia' in A Chong (ed), *Recognition and Enforcement of Foreign Judgments in Asia* (Singapore, Asian Business Law Institute, 2017) 37–48

Cohen, J, 'Cambodia' in Asian Business Law Institute (ed), *Corporate Restructuring and Insolvency in Asia 2020* (Singapore, Asian Business Law Institute, 2020) 104–46

Corneloup, S, 'France – The Evolving Balance Between the Judge and the Parties in France' in Y Nishitani (ed), *Treatment of Foreign Law – Dynamics towards Convergence?* (Cham, Springer, 2017) 157–83

Cuniberti, G, 'France' in J Basedow and others (eds), *Encyclopedia of Private International Law* (Cheltenham, Edward Elgar Publishing, 2017) 2079–90

d'Avout, L, 'Property and Proprietary Rights' in Jürgen Basedow and others (eds), *Encyclopedia of Private International Law* (Cheltenham, Edward Elgar Publishing, 2017) 1428–36

Damar, D, 'Flag' in Jürgen Basedow and others (eds), *Encyclopedia of Private International Law* (Cheltenham, Edward Elgar Publishing, 2017) 755–65

Dickinson, A, 'Rome II Regulation (Non-contractual Obligations)' in J Basedow and others (eds), *Encyclopedia of Private International Law* (Cheltenham, Edward Elgar Publishing, 2017) 1563–74

Docquier, F and Marfouk, A, 'International Migration by Education Attainment, 1990-2000' in C Ozden and M Schiff (eds), *International Migration, Remittances and the Brain Drain* (London, Palgrave Macmillan, 2006) 151–200

Dogauchi, M, 'Incidental Questions [in Japanese]' in M Dogauchi and Y Nakanishi (eds), *Leading Cases in Private International Law* (Tokyo, Yuhikaku Publishing, 2021) 6–7

Domej, T, 'Recognition and Enforcement of Judgments (Civil Law)' in F Ferrari and others (eds), *Encyclopedia of Private International Law* (Cheltenham, Edward Elgar Publishing, 2017) 1471–79

Dornis, TW, 'Competition, Unfair' in J Basedow and others (eds), *Encyclopedia of Private International Law* (Cheltenham, Edward Elgar Publishing, 2017) 432–41

Du, NB, 'Country Report: Socialist Republic of Vietnam' in A Chong (ed), *Recognition and Enforcement of Foreign Judgments in Asia* (Singapore, Asian Business Law Institute, 2017) 211–29

Dutta, A, 'Reciprocity' in J Basedow and others (eds), *Encyclopedia of Private International Law* (Cheltenham, Edward Elgar Publishing, 2017) 1466–71

Dutta, A, 'Trust' in Jürgen Basedow and others (eds), *Encyclopedia of Private International Law* (Cheltenham, Edward Elgar Publishing, 2017) 1752–58

Ebisawa, H, 'Japan' in Louis Garb and Julian D.M Lew (eds), *Enforcement of Foreign Judgments* (Alphen aan den Rijn, Wolters Kluwer, 2023) 1–16

Elbalti, B, 'Public Policy (2): Punitive Damages [in Japanese]' in M Dogauchi and Y Nakanishi (eds), *Leading Cases in Private International Law* (Tokyo, Yuhikaku Publishing, 2021) 194–95

Erdem, HE, 'The Role of Trade Usages in ICC Arbitration' in L Lévy and Y Derains (eds), *Liber Amicorum en l'Honneur de Serge Lazareff* (Paris, Editions A Pedone, 2011) 247–65

Ferrari, F, 'UNCITRAL' in Jürgen Basedow and others (eds), *Encyclopedia of Private International Law* (Cheltenham, Edward Elgar Publishing, 2017) 1758–66

Ferrari, F, 'Uniform Substantive Law and Private International Law' in J Basedow and others (eds), *Encyclopedia of Private International Law* (Cheltenham, Edward Elgar Publishing, 2017) 1772–79

Forsaith, C, 'Cambodia' in L Malintoppi and C Tan (eds), *Investment Protection in Southeast Asia: A Country-by-Country Guide on Arbitration Laws and Bilateral Investment Treaties* (Leiden, Brill, 2016) 73–108

Garnett, R, 'Substance and Procedure' in J Basedow and others (eds), *Encyclopedia of Private International Law* (Cheltenham, Edward Elgar Publishing, 2017) 1668–75

Gélinas, F, 'Trade Usages as Transnational Law' in F Gélinas (ed), *Trade Usages and Implied Terms in the Age of Arbitration* (Oxford, Oxford University Press, 2016) 253–78

Gelter M and Helleringer, G, 'Fiduciary Principles in European Civil Law Systems' in EJ Criddle, PB Miller and RH Sitkoff (eds), *The Oxford Handbook of Fiduciary Law* (Oxford, Oxford University Press, 2019) 583–602

Getzler, J, 'Fiduciary Principles in English Common Law' in EJ Criddle, PB Miller and RH Sitkoff (eds), *The Oxford Handbook of Fiduciary Law* (Oxford, Oxford University Press, 2019) 470–89

Graziano, TK, 'Products liability' in J Basedow and others (eds), *Encyclopedia of Private International Law* (Cheltenham, Edward Elgar Publishing, 2017) 1414–22

Graziano, TK, 'Traffic Accidents' in Jürgen Basedow and others (eds), *Encyclopedia of Private International Law* (Cheltenham, Edward Elgar Publishing, 2017) 1718–26

Gu, W, 'China' in A Reyes (ed), *Recognition and Enforcement of Judgments in Civil and Commercial Matters* (Oxford, Hart Publishing, 2019) 31–50

Guo, Y, 'Reciprocity' in A Chong (ed), *Asian Principles for the Recognition and Enforcement of Foreign Judgments* (Singapore, Asian Business Law Institute, 2020) 57–76

Haga, M, 'Public Policy (3): Procedural Public Policy' in M Dogauchi and Y Nakanishi (eds), *Leading Cases in Private International Law* (Tokyo, Yuhikaku Publishing, 2021) 196–97

Haw, R, Slott, BJ and Khieu, M, 'Cambodia' in Michael J Moser (ed), *Arbitration in Asia*, 2nd edn, (Huntington, Juris Publishing, 2008) CAM-3-CAM-12

Haw, RJW and Slott, BJ, 'Cambodia' in MJ Moser and J Choong (eds), *Asia Arbitration Handbook* (Oxford, Oxford University Press, 2011) 534–58

Hayakawa, S, 'Public Policy (4): South Korean Law Not Recognising the Division of Property in Divorce' in M Dogauchi and Y Nakanishi (eds), *Leading Cases in Private International Law* (Tokyo, Yuhikaku Publishing, 2021) 28–29

Hobe, S, 'The Law Relating to Aliens, the International Minimum Standard and State Responsibility: I. The Development of the Law of Aliens and the Emergence of General Principles of Protection under Public International Law' in M Bungenberg and others (eds), *International Investment Law* (London, Bloomsbury T&T Clark, 2015) 6–22

Hwang, M and Chang, A, 'Corruption in International Investment Arbitration' in N Teramura, L Nottage and B Jetin (eds), *Corruption and Illegality in Asian Investment Arbitration* (Singapore, Springer, 2024) 149–84

Kaneko, Y, 'Japan's Civil Code Drafting Support for Socialist Reform Countries: Diversity of Normative Choice' in Y Kaneko (ed), *Civil Law Reforms in Post-Colonial Asia: Beyond Western Capitalism* (Cham, Springer, 2019) 155–76

Kanzaki, T, 'Lex Societatis' in M Dogauchi and Y Nakanishi (eds), *Leading Cases in Private International Law* (Tokyo, Yuhikaku Publishing, 2021) 40–41

Kanzaki, T, 'Limitation on Torts by Public Policy [in Japanese]' in Y Sakurada and M Dogauchi (eds), *Private International Law Annotated, Vol 1* (Tokyo, Yuhikaku Publishing, 2011) 526–39

Kanzaki, T, 'Rights in Rem in Vehicles [in Japanese]' in M Dogauchi and Y Nakanishi (eds), *Leading Cases in Private International Law*, 3rd edn, (Tokyo, Yuhikaku Publishing, 2021) 48–49

Kieninger, E-M, 'Expropriation' in J Basedow and others (eds), *Encyclopedia of Private International Law* (Cheltenham, Edward Elgar Publishing, 2017) 726–31

Kitazawa, A, 'Article 41' in M Dogauchi and Y Sakurada (eds), *Private International Law Annotated [in Japanese]*, vol 2 (Tokyo, Yuhikaku Publishing, 2011) 309–31

Kiyohara, H, 'Civil Code' in H Peng, K Phallack and J Menzel (eds), *Introduction to Cambodian Law* (Phnom Penh, Konrad-Adenauer-Stiftung Cambodia, 2012) 99–134

Kleinschmidt, J, 'Agency and Authority of Agents' in Jürgen Basedow and others (eds), *Encyclopedia of Private International Law* (Cheltenham, Edward Elgar Publishing, 2017) 29–39

Kono, T, 'Country Report: Japan' in A Chong (ed), *Recognition and Enforcement of Foreign Judgments in Asia* (Singapore, Asian Business Law Institute, 2017) 101–16

Kono, T, 'Japan' in J Basedow and others (eds), *Encyclopedia of Private International Law* (Cheltenham, Edward Elgar Publishing, 2017) 2219–29

Kono, T, 'Public Policy [in Japanese]' in Y Sakurada and M Dogauchi (eds), *Private International Law Annoted, Vol 2* (Tokyo, Yuhikaku Publishing, 2011) 332–43

Kono, T, 'Territoriality' in J Basedow and others (eds), *Encyclopedia of Private International Law* (Cheltenham, Edward Elgar Publishing, 2017) 1702–09

Kriebaum, U, 'Article 42' in SW Schill and others (eds), *Schreuer's Commentary on the ICSID Convention: A Commentary on the Convention on the Settlement of Investment Disputes between States and Nationals of Other States* (Cambridge, Cambridge University Press, 2022) 797–906

Kronke, H, 'UNIDROIT' in J Basedow and others (eds), *Encyclopedia of Private International Law* (Cheltenham, Edward Elgar Publishing, 2017) 1766–71

Larkin, A and Yun, P, 'Cambodia' in A Reyes (ed), *Recognition and Enforcement of Judgments in Civil and Commercial Matters* (Oxford, Hart Publishing, 2019) 201–07

Layton, A and Dinelli, A, 'Proper Law (Doctrine)' in J Basedow and others (eds), *Encyclopedia of Private International Law* (Cheltenham, Edward Elgar Publishing, 2017) 1422–28

Lawrence, B, 'The National Assembly and Senate of the Kingdom of Cambodia' in PJ Yap and R Abeyratne (eds), *Routledge Handbook of Asian Parliaments* (Abingdon, Routledge, 2023) 125–42

Leandro, A, 'Insolvency, Applicable Law' in J Basedow and others (eds), *Encyclopedia of Private International Law* (Cheltenham, Edward Elgar Publishing, 2017) 931–39

Mankowski, P, 'Dépeçage' in J Basedow and others (eds), *Encyclopedia of Private International Law* (Cheltenham, Edward Elgar Publishing, 2017) 526–28

Mansel, H-P, 'Connecting Factor' in J Basedow and others (eds), *Encyclopedia of Private International Law* (Cheltenham, Edward Elgar Publishing, 2017) 441–52

Mansel, H-P, 'Nationality' in J Basedow and others (eds), *Encyclopedia of Private International Law* (Cheltenham, Edward Elgar Publishing, 2017) 1289–301

Masuda, F, 'Depeçage' in M Dogauchi and Y Nakanishi (eds), *Leading Cases in Private International Law* (Tokyo, Yuhikaku Publishing, 2021) 56–57

Menzel, J, 'Cambodian Law: Some Comparative and International Perspectives' in H Peng, K Phallack and J Menzel (eds), *Introduction to Cambodian Law* (Phnom Penh, Konrad-Adenauer-Stiftung Cambodia, 2012) 477–93

Michaels, R, 'Jurisdiction, Foundations' in Jürgen Basedow and others (eds), *Encyclopedia of Private International Law* (Cheltenham, Edward Elgar Publishing, 2017) 1042–51

Mikazuki, A, 'The Application of Foreign Law and the Court [in Japanese]' in T Sawaki and Y Aoyama (eds), *Theories of International Civil Procedure Law* (Tokyo, Yuhikaku Publishing, 1987) 239–83

Minh, NN, Han, TH and Trang, NTT, 'Vietnam' in A Reyes (ed), *Recognition and Enforcement of Judgments in Civil and Commercial Matters* (Oxford, Hart Publishing, 2019) 179–200

Mohan, M, 'Cambodia' in S Chesterman, H Owada and B Saul (eds), *The Oxford Handbook of International Law in Asia and the Pacific* (Oxford, Oxford University Press, 2019) 497–524

Monzonís, CA, 'Spain: The Application of Foreign Laws in Spain – Critical Analysis of the Legal Novelties of 2015' in Y Nishitani (ed), *Treatment of Foreign Law – Dynamics towards Convergence?* (Cham, Springer, 2017) 329–46

Morishita, T, 'Dealing with Unascertainlable Foreign Law [in Japanese]' in M Dogauchi and Y Nakanishi (eds), *Leading Cases in Private International Law* (Tokyo, Yuhikaku Publishing, 3rd edn, 2021) 210–11

Morris, C, 'Justice Inverted' in K Brickell and S Springer (eds), *The Handbook of Contemporary Cambodia* (Abingdon, Routledge, 2016) 29–41

Murakami, Y, 'Reciprocity: Judgments from Mainland China [in Japanese]' in M Dogauchi and Y Nakanishi (eds), *Leading Cases in Private International Law* (Tokyo, Yuhikaku Publishing, 2021) 200–01

Nakano, S, 'Japan: Proof of and Information about Foreign Law in Japan' in Y Nishitani (ed), *Treatment of Foreign Law – Dynamics towards Convergence?* (Cham, Springer, 2017) 529–40

Narasaki, M, 'Rights in Rem in Ships [in Japanese]' in M Dogauchi and Y Nakanishi (eds), *Leading Cases in Private International Law*, 3rd edn, (Tokyo, Yuhikaku Publishing, 2021) 50–51

Newcombe, A, 'Investor Misconduct: Jurisdiction, Admissibility or Merits?' in C Brown and K Miles (eds), *Evolution in Investment Treaty Law and Arbitration*, vol Cambridge (Cambridge, Cambridge University Press, 2011) 187–200

Nishitani, Y, 'Rules on Juristic Persons and Foreign Persons [in Japanese]' in Y Sakurada and M Dogauchi (eds), *Private International Law Annotated, Vol 1* (Tokyo, Yuhikaku Publishing, 2011) 139–78

Nishitani, Y, 'Treatment of Foreign Law: Dynamics Towards Convergence? – General Report' in Y Nishitani (ed), *Treatment of Foreign Law – Dynamics towards Convergence?* (Cham, Springer, 2017) 3–60

Nottage, L and others, 'Chapter 4 – Regulating Consumer Contracts in ASEAN: Variation and Change' in L Nottage and others (eds), *ASEAN Consumer Law Harmonisation and Cooperation: Achievements and Challenges* (Cambridge, Cambridge University Press, 2019) 205–60

Oppusunggu, YU, 'Principle 9: Public Policy' in A Chong (ed), *Asian Principles for the Recognition and Enforcement of Foreign Judgements* (Singapore, Asian Business Law Institute, 2020) 112–29

Peng, H, 'The Modern Era of Cambodian Constitutionalism: Constitutional Analysis of Historical and Contemporary Development' in H Peng, K Phallack and J Menzel (eds), *Introduction to Cambodian Law* (Phnom Penh, Konrad-Adenauer-Stiftung Cambodia, 2012) 25–69

Pertegás, M, 'Hague Conference on Private International Law' in J Basedow and others (eds), *Encyclopedia of Private International Law* (Cheltenham, Edward Elgar Publishing, 2017) 870–75

Pertegás, M, 'Treaties in Private International Law' in J Basedow and others (eds), *Encyclopedia of Private International Law* (Cheltenham, Edward Elgar Publishing, 2017) 1743–48

Phallack, K, 'Cambodian Labour and Employment Law' in H Peng, K Phallack and J Menzel (eds), *Introduction to Cambodian Law* (Phnom Penh, Konrad-Adenauer-Stiftung Cambodia, 2012) 287–311

Phallack, K, 'Overview of Contemporary Civil Procedures of Cambodia' in H Peng, K Phallack and J Menzel (eds), *Introduction to Cambodian Law* (Phnom Penh, Konrad-Adenauer-Stiftung Cambodia, 2012) 155–80

Phallack, K, 'Overview of the Cambodian Legal and Judicial System and Recent Efforts at Legal and Judicial Reform' in H Peng, K Phallack and J Menzel (eds), *Introduction to Cambodian Law* (Phnom Penh, Konrad-Adenauer-Stiftung Cambodia, 2012) 5–22

Phun, V, 'Country Factsheet 2: Judicial Training in Cambodia' in A Nababan et al (eds), *Judicial Training in ASEAN: A Comparative Overview of Systems and Programs* (Phnom Penh, Konrad-Adenauer-Stiftung Cambodia, 2014) 31–34

Polkinghorne, M and others, 'Article 16: Competence of Arbitral Tribunal to Rule on Its Own Jurisdiction' in I Bantekas and others (eds), *UNCITRAL Model Law on International Commercial Arbitration: A Commentary* (Cambridge, Cambridge University Press, 2020) 292–313

Polkinghorne, M, Timonen, T and Larkimo, N, 'Article 1 – Scope of Application' in I Bantekas and others (eds), *UNCITRAL Model Law on International Commercial Arbitration: A Commentary* (Cambridge, Cambridge University Press, 2020) 1–24

Pozzo, B, 'Comparative Law and Language' in M Bussani and U Mattei (eds), *The Cambridge Companion to Comparative Law* (Cambridge, Cambridge University Press, 2012) 88–113

Ramseyer, JM and Tamaruya, M, 'Fiduciary Principles in Japanese Law' in EJ Criddle, PB Miller and RH Sitkoff (eds), *The Oxford Handbook of Fiduciary Law* (Oxford, Oxford University Press, 2019) 643–63

Reisman, WM and Arsanjani, MH, 'Applicable Law under the ICSID Convention: The Tortured History of the Interpretation of Article 42' in M Kinnear and others (eds), *Building International Investment Law: The First 50 Years of ICSID* (Alphen aan den Rijn, Wolters Kluwer, 2015) 3–12

Remien, O, 'Germany: Proof of and Information about Foreign Law – Duty to Investigate, Expert Opinions and a Proposal for Europe' in Y Nishitani (ed), *Treatment of Foreign Law – Dynamics towards Convergence?* (Cham, Springer, 2017) 183–220

Rendak, N and Eastman, D, 'Legal and Judicial Reform: Recent Developments and Prospects' in DT Coe and others (eds), *Cambodia: Rebuilding for a Challenging Future* (Washington DC, IMF, 2006) 99–109

Ricketson, S, 'The Trademark Provisions in the Paris Convention for the Protection of Industrial Property' in I Calboli and JC Ginsburg (eds), *The Cambridge Handbook of International and Comparative Trademark Law* (Cambridge, Cambridge University Press, 2020) 3–26

Rühl, G, 'Private International Law, Foundations' in J Basedow and others (eds), *Encyclopedia of Private International Law* (Cheltenham, Edward Elgar Publishing, 2017) 1381–90

Sakano, I, 'Registration of Land-Ownership in Cambodia: Protection of Private Rights in Development' in Y Kaneko, N Kadomatsu and BZ Tamanaha (eds), *Land Law and Disputes in Asia In Search of an Alternative for Development* (Abingdon, Routledge, 2021) 57–63

Sano, H, 'Special Rule for Product Liability [in Japanese]' in Y Sakurada and M Dogauchi (eds), *Private International Law Annotated, Vol 1* (Tokyo, Yuhikaku Publishing, 2011) 460–78

Serena, S, 'Cambodian Family Law: Development and Challenges Ahead' in H Peng, K Phallack and J Menzel (eds), *Introduction to Cambodian Law* (Phnom Penh, Konrad-Adenauer-Stiftung Cambodia, 2012) 137–51

Shimanami, R, 'Patent Right Infringement [in Japanese]' in M Dogauchi and Y Nakanishi (eds), *Leading Cases in Private International Law*, 3rd edn, (Tokyo, Yuhikaku Publishing, 2021) 84–85

Siehr, K, 'Evasion of laws (fraus legis)' in J Basedow and others (eds), *Encyclopedia of Private International Law* (Cheltenham, Edward Elgar Publishing, 2017) 698–709

Sonnentag, M, 'Renvoi' in Jürgen Basedow and others (eds), *Encyclopedia of Private International Law* (Cheltenham, Edward Elgar Publishing, 2017) 1538–45

Sonnentag, M, 'Savigny, Friedrich Carl von' in Jürgen Basedow and others (eds), *Encyclopedia of Private International Law* (Cheltenham, Edward Elgar Publishing, 2017) 1609–15

Sovath, P, 'Economic Law: Intellectual Property Rights' in H Peng, K Phallack and J Menzel (eds), *Introduction to Cambodian Law* (Phnom Penh, Konrad-Adenauer-Stiftung Cambodia, 2012) 267–84

Takahashi, H, 'The Formation of Central and Local Administrative Systems of the Modern Cambodia and the Political Bodies behind the Reform [in Japanese]' in N Amakawa (ed), *Reconstruction and Development of Cambodia* (Chiba, Institute of Developing Economies, Japan External Trade Organization (IDE-JETRO), 2001) 73ff

Takeshita, K, 'Change of Governing Law by the Parties [in Japanese]' in Y Sakurada and M Dogauchi (eds), *Private International Law Annotated, Vol 1* (Tokyo, Yuhikaku Publishing, 2011) 510–25

Tayseng, L, 'Formation of Contract and Third Parties in Cambodia' in M Chen-Wishart, A Loke and S Vogenauer (eds), *Formation and Third Party Beneficiaries* (Oxford, Oxford University Press, 2018) 343–64

Teramura, N, 'Cambodia' in A Reyes and W Lui (eds), *Direct Jurisdiction: Asian Perspectives* (Oxford, Hart Publishing, 2021) 201–19

Teramura, N, 'Cambodia' in A Reyes, W Lui and K Nishioka (eds), *Choice of Law and Recognition in Asian Family Law* (Oxford, Hart Publishing, 2023) 219–40

Teramura, N, 'Cambodia' in K Nishioka (ed), *Treatment of Foreign Law in Asia* (Oxford, Hart Publishing, 2023) 171–91

Teramura, N, 'Challenging the Arbitrariness Perception of Ex Aequo et Bono to (Re-)discover Procedural Diversity' in SF Ali and others (eds), *Diversity in International Arbitration: Why It Matters and How to Sustain It* (Cheltenham and Camberley, Edward Elgar Publishing, 2022) 229–41

Teramura, N, 'JICA's Legal Technical Assistance Projects in Vietnam, Cambodia and Laos since the 1990s' in LC Kelly and G Sasges (eds), *Vietnam Over the Long Twentieth Century* (Singapore, Springer, 2024) 185–204

Teramura, N, 'Recognition and Enforcement of Chinese Judgments in Cambodia: Uncertain Foundations of the Rigid Reciprocity Standards in Cambodian Law' in P Sooksripaisarnkit and SR Garimella (eds), *Legal Challenges of China's One Belt One Road Initiative: Private International Law Considerations* (Abingdon, Routledge, 2025) [forthcoming]

Teramura, N, Nottage, L, and Jetin, B, 'Bribery and Other Serious Investor Misconduct in Asian Investment Arbitration' in N Teramura, L Nottage and B Jetin (eds), *Corruption and Illegality in Asian Investment Arbitration* (Singapore, Springer, 2024) 1–36

Thoma, I, 'Public Policy (*Ordre Public*)' in J Basedow and others (eds), *Encyclopedia of Private International Law* (Cheltenham, Edward Elgar Publishing, 2017) 1453–60

Tu, G, 'Macau: Proof and Information About Foreign Law in Macau' in Y Nishitani (ed), *Treatment of Foreign Law – Dynamics towards Convergence?* (Cham, Springer, 2017) 541–48

TW Dornis, 'Comity' in Jürgen Basedow and others (eds), *Encyclopedia of Private International Law* (Cheltenham, Edward Elgar Publishing, 2017) 382–91

UNCITRAL, 'Explanatory Note by the UNCITRAL Secretariat on the United Nations Convention on Contracts for the International Sale of Goods' in UNCITRAL (ed), *United Nations Convention on Contracts for the International Sale of Goods* (Vienna, Publishing and Library Section of United Nations Office, 2010) 33–41

van Dam, C, 'Transnational Tort Law' in P Zumbansen (ed), *The Oxford Handbook of Transnational Law* (Oxford, Oxford University Press, 2021) 555–74

Vanrath, P, 'The Basics of Substantial Cambodian Criminal Law' in H Peng, K Phallack and J Menzel (eds), *Introduction to Cambodian Law* (Phnom Penh, Konrad-Adenauer-Stiftung Cambodia, 2012) 199–225

Velasco, J, 'Fiduciary Principles in Corporate Law' in EJ Criddle, PB Miller and RH Sitkoff (eds), *The Oxford Handbook of Fiduciary Law* (Oxford, Oxford University Press, 2019) 61–78

Vicente, DM, 'Intellectual Property, Applicable Law' in J Basedow and others (eds), *Encyclopedia of Private International Law* (Cheltenham, Edward Elgar Publishing, 2017) 961–69

von Walter, A, 'State Contracts and the Relevance of Investment Contract Arbitration: I. Investor-State Contracts in the Context of International Investment Law' in M Bungenberg and others (eds), *International Investment Law: A Handbook* (London, Bloomsbury T&T Clark, 2015) 80–152

Watt, HM, 'Party Autonomy' in J Basedow and others (eds), *Encyclopedia of Private International Law* (Cheltenham, Edward Elgar Publishing, 2017) 1336–41

Weeramantry, R, 'International Investment Law and Practice in the Kingdom of Cambodia: An Evolving 'Rule Taker'?' in J Chaisse and L Nottage (eds), *International Investment Treaties and Arbitration across Asia* (Leiden, Brill, 2018) 303–34

Weller, M-P and Thomale, C, 'Companies' in J Basedow and others (eds), *Encyclopedia of Private International Law* (Cheltenham, Edward Elgar Publishing, 2017) 404–11

Wilderspin, M, 'Contractual Obligations' in Jürgen Basedow and others (eds), *Encyclopedia of Private International Law* (Cheltenham, Edward Elgar Publishing, 2017) 473–79

Wilderspin, M, 'Overriding Mandatory Provisions' in J Basedow and others (eds), *Encyclopedia of Private International Law* (Cheltenham, Edward Elgar Publishing, 2017) 1330–36

Wolff, R, 'Article II [Recognition of Arbitration Agreements]' in R Wolff (ed), *New York Convention: Article-by-Article Commentary*, 2nd edn, (London, Bloomsbury Publishing, 2019) 91–158

Yamamoto, K, 'Application of Foreign Law [in Japanese]' in Y Sakurada and M Dogauchi (eds), *Private International Law Annotated, Vol 2* (Tokyo, Yuhikaku Publishing, 2011) 350–67

Yokomizo, D, 'Japan' in T Kono (ed), *Intellectual Property and Private International Law: Comparative Perspectives* (Oxford, Hart Publishing, 2012) 763–91

Yokoyama, H, 'The Employee's Invention for Patent [in Japanese]' in M Dogauchi and Y Nakanishi (eds), *Leading Cases in Private International Law*, 3rd edn, (Tokyo, Yuhikaku Publishing, 2021) 86–87

Journal Articles

Alberti, CP and Bigge, DM, 'Ascertaining the Content of the Applicable Law and Iura Novit Tribunus: Approaches in Commercial and Investment Arbitration' (2015) 70 *Dispute Resolution Journal* 1

Allarousse, V, 'A Comparative Approach to the Conflict of Characterization in Private International Law' (1991) 23 *Case Western Reserve Journal of International Law* 479

Anggriawan, R, 'Insolvency Proceedings: ASEAN and EU Comparison on the Rules of Foreign Court Jurisdiction' (2020) 3 *Indonesian Comparative Law Review* 35

Balcerzak, F, 'Jurisdiction of Tribunals in Investor–State Arbitration and the Issue of Human Rights' (2014) 29 *ICSID Review – Foreign Investment Law Journal* 216

Benedettelli, M, 'Determining the Applicable Law in Commercial and Investment Arbitration: Two Intertwined Road Maps for Conflicts-Solving' (2022) 37 *ICSID Review – Foreign Investment Law Journal* 687

Bermann, GA, 'International Arbitration and Private International Law: General Course on Private International Law' (2016) 381 *Collected Courses of the Hague Academy of International Law* 41

Bischoff, JA, 'Conflict of Laws and International Investment Arbitration' (2018) 7 *European International Arbitration Review* 143

Bonell, MJ, 'Soft Law and Party Autonomy: The Case of the UNIDROIT Principles' (2005) 51 *Loyola Law Review* 229

Bouwers, GJ, 'Tacit Choice of Law in International Commercial Contracts: An Analysis of Asian Jurisdictions and the Asian Principles of Private International Law' (2021) 26 *Uniform Law Review* 14

Brakman, S-V, 'The Principle of Subsidiarity in the Hague Convention on Intercountry Adoption: A Philosophical Analysis' (2019) 33 *Ethics & International Affairs* 207

Brilmayer, L, 'Rights, Fairness, and Choice of Law' (1989) 98 *The Yale Law Journal* 1277

Buckley, RP 'The 1993 Revision of the Uniform Customs and Practice for Document Credits' (1995) 28 *George Washington Journal of International Law and Economics* 265

Bun & Associates, 'Governing Law and Dispute Resolution [in Japanese]' (2017) *Bun & Associates Newsletter*

Chhina, RK, 'The Uniform Customs and Practice for Documentary Credit (the UCP): Are They Merely a Set of Contractual Terms?' (2015) 30 *Banking & Finance Law Review* 245

Coetzee, J, 'The Role and Function of Trade Usage in Modern International Sales Law' (2015) 20 *Unform Law Review* 243

Coyle, JF, 'Rethinking Judgements Reciprocity' (2014) 92 *North Carolina Law Review* 1109

Dickinson, A, 'Cross-Border Torts in EC Courts – A Response to the Proposed "Rome II" Regulation' (2002) 13 *European Business Law Review* 369

Dodge, WS and Zhang, W, 'Reciprocity in China-US Judgments Recognition' (2020) 53 *Vanderbilt Journal of Transnational Law* 1541

Donovan, DA, 'Cambodia: Building a Legal System from Scratch' (1993) 27 *The International Lawyer* 445

Elbalti, B, 'Foreign Judgments Recognition and Enforcement in Civil and Commercial Matters in Japan' (2019) *Osaka University Law Review* 1

Elbalti, B, 'Reciprocity and the Recognition and Enforcement of Foreign Judgments: A Lot of Bark but Not Much Bite' (2017) 13 *Journal of Private International Law* 184

Gabriel, HD, 'The Advantages of Soft Law in International Commercial Law: The Role of UNIDROIT, UNCITRAL, and the Hague Conference' (2009) 34 *Brooklyn Journal of International Law* 655

Gaillard, E and Banifatemi, Y, 'The Meaning of "and" in Article 42(1), Second Sentence, of the Washington Convention: The Role of International Law in the ICSID Choice of Law Process' (2003) 18 *ICSID Review – Foreign Investment Law Journal* 375

Gurrea-Martínez, A, 'The Future of Insolvency Law in a Post-Pandemic World' (2022) 31 *International Insolvency Review* 385

Haga, M, 'Effect of Foreign Judgments: A General Observation [in Japanese]' (2010) 83 *Journal of Law, Politics and Sociology* 363

Haga, M, 'Reciprocity as a Condition for the Recognition and Enforcement of Foreign Judgments (2): Its Contemporary Significance [in Japanese]' (2017) 90 *Journal of Law, Politics and Sociology* 25

Haga, M, 'Reciprocity as a Condition for the Recognition and Enforcement of Foreign Judgments (1): Its Contemporary Signifiance' (2017) 90 *Journal of Law, Politics and Sociology* 1

Hayakawa, S, 'International Aspects of Succession [in Japanese]' (1999) 1 *Yearbook of Japanese Private International Law* 79

Henderson, A, 'Enforcement of Arbitral Awards in Indochina: Law, Practice, and Alternatives' (2009) 26 *Journal of International Arbitration* 841

Huang, J, 'Reciprocal Recognition and Enforcement of Foreign Judgments in China: Promising Developments, Prospective Challenges and Proposed Solutions' (2019) 88 *Nordic Journal of International Law* 250

Huang, RH and Gu, W, 'China's Recognition and Enforcement of Foreign Securities Judgments against Overseas-listed Chinese Companies' (2023) 26 *Journal of International Economic Law* 577

Hyder-Rahman, N, 'Commercial Gestational Surrogacy: Unravelling the Threads between Reproductive Tourism and Child Trafficking' (2021) *Anti-Trafficking Review* 123

Imanullah, MN, Latifah, E and Ratri, PDK, 'Aspects of International and Domestic Law Pertaining to the Establishment of ASEAN Cross-Border Insolvency Regulations: An Indonesian Perspective' (2018) 8 *Indonesian Law Review* 190

Isoi, M, 'Real Property Registration in Cambodia [in Japanese]' (2014) 60 *ICD News* 33

Ito, A, 'Legal Education and Professional Legal Training in Laos: Towards the Birth of Lao Jurisprudence [in Japanese]' (2020) 82 *ICD News* 40

Ito, M, 'Professional Legal Education at the Royal School for Judges and Prosecutors in Cambodia [in Japanese]' (2022) 90 *ICD News* 47

Ito, M, 'The History of JICA's Legal Technical Assistance in Cambodia [in Japanese]' (2021) 87 *ICD News* 47, 50

Kamiki, A, 'Report on the Investigation of Cambodian Court Judgements [in Japanese]' (2011) 48 *ICD News* 25

Kanetake, E, 'Real Property Registration in Cambodia [in Japanese]' (2017) 73 *ICD News* 41

Kasaya, Y, 'Codification of Law in the French Protectorate of Cambodia (1) [in Japanese]' (2019) 81 *ICD News* 29

Kasaya, Y, 'Codification of Law in the French Protectorate of Cambodia (2) [in Japanese]' (2020) 84 *ICD News* 246

Kasaya, Y, 'Honorary Titles and Job Titles of Ministers in French Colonial Cambodia: A Study Based on the Royal Ordinances Regulating Membership of the Council of Ministers [in Japanese]' (2016) 1 *Nagoya University Asian Law Bulletin* 58

Kaufmann-Kohler, G, 'The Arbitrator and the Law: Does He/She Know It? Apply It? How? And a Few More Questions' (2005) 21 *Arbitration International* 631

Kawai, M, '"Reciprocity" between Japan and China in Recognition of Foreign Judgments [in Japanese]', (2020) *Keio Law Journal* 39

Kidane, S, 'Private International Law Principles on Intellectual Property: Recent Development of Court Precedents in Japan and Current Characteristics' (2009) 52 *Japanese Yearbook of International Law* 454

Kim, C, 'The 1995 Private International Law of North Korea' (1998) 29 *California Western International Law Journal* 205

Kono, T, 'Comparative Analysis of Recent Developments in Private International Law in Japan and Europe from a Japanese Perspective' (2008) 51 *Japanese Yearbook of International Law* 217

Kucinski, MA, 'Creating a Successful Structure to Mediate International Parental Child Abduction Cases' (2012) 26 *American Journal of Family Law* 81

Kuong, T, 'Development of Legal Norms on Marriage and Divorce in Cambodia – The Civil Code Between Foreign Inputs and Local Growth (I)' (2016) 1 *Nagoya University Asian Law Bulletin* 69

Larkin A, and Sambo, L, 'Recent Developments in Commercial Arbitration in Cambodia' (2015) 17 *Asian Dispute Review* 12

Leng, S, 'Problems in Translating Cambodian Civil Code and Civil Procedure Code and Future Prospects [in Japanese]' (2016) 68 *ICD News*

Lenhoff, A, 'Reciprocity and the Law of Foreign Judgments: A Historical – Critical Analysis' (1956) 16 *Louisiana Law Review* 465

Leto, M, 'Whose Best Interest? International Child Abduction Under the Hague Convention' (2002) 3 *Chicago Journal of International Law* 247

Loizou, S, 'Revisiting the "Content-of-Laws" Enquiry in International Arbitration' (2018) 78 *Louisiana Law Review* 811

Loo, H, 'In the Child's Best Interests: Examining International Child Abduction, Adoption, and Asylum' (2016) 17 *Chicago Journal of International Law* 609

Ly, FD, Friedman, MW and di Brozolo, LGR, 'International Law Association International Commercial Arbitration Committee's Report and Recommendations on Ascertaining the Contents of the Applicable Law in International Commercial Arbitration' (2010) 26 *Arbitration International* 193

Mankowski, P, 'The New Japanese Private International Law Act from a European Perspective' (2008) 51 *Japanese Yearbook of International Law* 241

Marco, AD and others, 'Global Markets for Technology: Evidence from Patent Transactions' (2017) 46 *Research Policy* 1644

Martinek, M, 'The Principle of Reciprocity in the Recognition and Enforcement of Foreign Judgments – History, Presence and No Future' (2017) 2017 *Journal of South African Law* 36

Meier, FM, 'Unification of Choice-of-law Rules for Defamation' (2016) 12 *Journal of Private International Law* 492

Meshel, T, 'The Use and Misuse of the Corruption Defence in International Investment Arbitration' (2013) 30 *Journal of International Arbitration* 267

Mevorach, I, 'Overlapping International Instruments for Enforcement of Insolvency Judgments: Undermining or Strengthening Universalism?' (2021) 22 *European Business Organization Law Review* 283

Minami, T, 'Issues Concerning Surrogacy Legislation: A Case Analysis of Australia [in Japanese]' (2018) 2 *Social Security Research* 578

Misawa, A, 'Supporting the Training of Judges and Prosecutors in Cambodia [in Japanese]' (2004) 18 *ICD News* 1

Morishima, A, 'Reflection on the Legal and Judicial Development Project for Drafting the Civil Code of Cambodia [in Japanese]' (2003) 11 *ICD News* 4

Ng, EKH, 'Revisiting International Tort Actions in Hong Kong' (2019) 13 *Hong Kong Journal of Legal Studies* 19

Nicholson, P and Kuong, T, 'Japanese Legal Assistance: An East Asian Model of Legal Assistance and Rule of Law?' (2014) 6 *Hague Journal on the Rule of Law* 141

Nishitani, Y, 'Coordination of Legal Systems by the Recognition of Foreign Judgments -- Rethinking Reciprocity in Sino-Japanese Relationships' (2019) 14 *Frontiers of Law in China* 193

Nishitani, Y, 'Intellectual Property in Japanese Private International Law' (2005) 48 *Japanese Annual of nternational Law* 87

Nishitani, Y, 'International Jurisdiction of Japanese Courts in a Comparative Perspective' (2013) 60 *Netherlands International Law Review* 251

Nishitani, Y, 'Party Autonomy in Contemporary Private International Law: The Hague Principles on Choice of Law and East Asia' (2016) 59 *Japanese Yearbook of International Law* 300

Nishitani, Y, 'Treatment of and Access to Foreign Law in Japan' (2018) 23 *Journal of Japanese Law* 69

Nottage, L, 'Symposium Paper: Afterthoughts – International Commercial Contracts and Arbitration' (2010) 17 *Australian International Law Journal* 197

Nygh, PE, 'The Reasonable Expectations of the Parties as a Guide to the Choice of Law in Contract and in Tort' (1995) 251 *Collected Courses of the Hague Academy of International Law* 269

Okuda, Y, 'Reform of Japan's Private International Law: Act on the General Rules of the Application of Laws' (2006) 8 *Yearbook of Private International Law* 145

Okuda, Y, 'Unconstitutionality of Reciprocity Requirement for Recognition and Enforcement of Foreign Judgments in Japan' (2018) 13 *Frontiers of Law in China* 159

Panha, N, 'Introducing the Center of Main Interests in International Insolvency Cases to Cambodian Law: A Comparative Analysis of the Model Law, the EU, US and Japan' (2015) 263 *Nagoya University Journal of Law and Politics* 465

Papp, E and Teramura, N, 'Enforcing Singapore Judgments in Cambodia: Reciprocity under the Loupe' (2025) *Asian Journal of International Law*, First View, 1

Parker, S, 'The Best Interests of the Child – Principles and Problems' (1994) 8 *International Journal of Law, Policy and the Family* 26

Pejovic, C, 'Civil Law and Common Law: Two Different Paths Leading to the Same Goal' (2001) 32 *Victorian University of Wellington Law Review* 817

Phallack, K, 'Labour Arbitration in Cambodia: Law and Practice' (2010) 1 *Cambodian Yearbook of Comparative Legal Studies* 163

Piersanti, V and others, 'Surrogacy and "Procreative Tourism": What Does the Future Hold from the Ethical and Legal Perspectives?' (2021) 57 *Medicina (Kaunas)* 47

Platte, M, 'An Arbitrator's Duty to Render Enforceable Awards' (2003) 20 *Journal of International Arbitration* 307

Ramesh, K, 'The Gibbs Principle: A Tether on the Feet of Good Forum Shopping' (2017) 29 *Singapore Academy of Law Journal* 42

Reisman, WM, 'The Regime for Lacunae in the ICSID Choice of Law Provision and the Question of Its Threshold' (2000) 15 *ICSID Review – Foreign Investment Law Journal* 362

Ren, TM, 'Revisiting the Double Actionability Rule in Singapore: Time for a Change' (2021) 2021 *Singapore Journal of Legal Studies* 155

Robilant, AD, 'Genealogies of Soft Law' (2006) 54 *The American Journal of Comparative Law* 499

Sachdev, V, 'Choice of Law in Insolvency Proceedings: How English Courts' Continued Reliance on the Gibbs Principle Threatens Universalism' (2019) 93 *American Bankruptcy Law Journal* 343

Sakai, N and Kamata, S, 'The Doctrine of Precedent in Vietnam [in Japanese]' (2017) 73 *ICD News* 29

Sakano, I, 'Reflection on Diverse Issues in Legal Technical Assistance for Cambodia [in Japanese]' (2021) 87 *ICD News* 57

Sakano, I, 'Reflection on the Legal and Judicial Development Project for Drafting the Civil and Civil Procedure Codes of Cambodia [in Japanese]' (2003) 7 *ICD News* 91

Sakano, I, 'Various Challenges for Legal Technical Assistance in Cambodia [in Japanese]' (2021) 87 *ICD News* 57

Samnang, R, 'Succession in Cambodia: Background, Disqualification and Types' (2019) 2 *UC Working Paper Series* 74

Schreuer, C, 'Jurisdiction and Applicable Law in Investment Treaty Arbitration' (2014) 1 *McGill Journal of Dispute Resolution* 1

Seavmey, C, 'Challenges of Legal Education in Cambodia [in Japanese]' (2020) 85 *ICD News* 16

Sen, SH, 'Speech delivered by Samdech Hun Sen, Prime Minister of the Royal Government of Cambodia, at the Opening Ceremony' (2003) 7 *ICD News* 25

Shinoda, Y, 'Report on the Investigation of Cambodian Court Judgments (1) [in Japanese]' (2019) 79 *ICD News* 60

Skytioti, S, 'Comparative Law and Language with Reference to Case Law' (2021) 66 *Studies in Logic, Grammar and Rhetoric* 105

Smolin, DM, 'Child Laundering: How the Intercountry Adoption System Legitimizes and Incentivizes the Practices of Buying, Trafficking, Kidnapping, and Stealing Children' (2006) 52 *The Wayne Law Review* 113

Srivastava, N, 'Heritage and Vitality: Whether the Rule in Antony Gibbs Is a Presumption' (2021) 29 *Insolvency Law Journal* 61

Stewart, DP, 'The UN Convention on Jurisdictional Immunities of States and Their Property' (2005) 99 *American Journal of International Law* 194

Sun, B, 'The Future of Cross-Border Litigation in China: Enforcement of Foreign Commercial Judgments Based on Reciprocity' (2018) 50 *New York University Journal of International Law & Politics* 1135

Takahashi, K, 'A Major Reform of Japanese Private International Law' (2006) 2 *Journal of Private International Law* 311

Takahashi, K, 'Japan's Newly Enacted Rules on International Jurisdiction: with a Reflection on Some Issues of Interpretation' (2011) 13 *Japanese Yearbook of Private International Law* 146

Takahashi, K, 'The Jurisdiction of Japanese Courts in a Comparative Context' (2015) 11 *Journal of Private International Law* 103

Takeshita, M, 'Reflection on the Technical Assisting for Cambodia to Draft the Civil Procedure Code and Challenges for the Legal Technical Assistance Projects [in Japanese]' (2003) 9 *ICD News* 25

Tamagaki, S, 'The Arbitration Council in Cambodia: Impacts of the 2016 Law on Trade Unions and Prakas No. 303 by the Ministry of Labour and Vocational Training [in Japanese]' (2019) 80 *ICD News* 56

Tang, Z, 'International Judicial Cooperation in Game Theory' (2020) 11 *Journal of International Dispute Settlement* 522

Tang, Z, 'Law Applicable in the Absence of Choice – The New Article 4 of the Rome I Regulation' (2008) 71 *Modern Law Review* 785

Teramura, N, 'Ex Aequo et Bono and Arbitration Theories: An Arbitrator's Subjective Perspective of Fairness as the Final 'Gap-Filler'' (2020) 38 *ASA Bulletin* 350

Teramura, N, 'Japan as a Source of Legal Ideas: A View from the Mekong Subregion of ASEAN' (2021) 13 *New Voices in Japanese Studies* 19

Teramura, N, 'The Strengths and Weaknesses of Arguments Pertaining to *Ex Aequo et Bono*' (2019) 15 *Asian International Arbitration Journal* 63

Thangavelu, SM and others, 'Investment Facilitation and Promotion in Cambodia: Impact of Provincial-level Characteristics on Multinational Activities' (2023) *ERIA Discussion Paper Series*

Torii, J, 'The Response of Hague Child Protection Conventions to the Globalisation of Family Life [in Japanese]' (2011) 607 *International Issues* 1

Trakman L and Montgomery, H, 'The 'Judicialisation' of International Commercial Arbitration: Pitfall or Virtue?' (2017) 30 *Leiden Journal of International Law* 405

Tsang, KF, 'Bilateral Treaty on Mutual Enforcement of Judgments between Japan and China: A Discussion on Legal Structure' (2019) 47 *Hitotsubashi Journal of Law and Politics* 31

Tsang, KF, 'Double Actionability: An Outdated Rule in Modern Times?' (2017) 86 *UMKC Law Review* 73

Tsang, KF, 'Enforcement of Foreign Commercial Judgments in China' (2018) 14 *Journal of Private International Law* 262

Uchiyama, A, 'Cambodian Judiciary: The Court of First Instance [in Japanese]' (2017) 73 *ICD News* 48

van der Keur, D, 'Legal and Gender Issues of Marriage and Divorce in Cambodia' (2014) 3 *Cambodia Law and Policy Journal* 1

Vathana, AV, 'Keynote Speech: The Establishment of Cambodia's Civil Procedure Code and Japan's Legal Technical Assistance [in Japanese]' (2007) 31 *ICD News* 9

Waincymer, J, 'International Arbitration and the Duty to Know the Law' (2011) 28 *Journal of International Arbitration* 201

Warshaw, A, 'Uncertainty from Abroad: Rome II and the Choice of Law for Defamation Claims' (2006) 32 *Brooklyn Journal of International Law* 269

Westbrook, JL, 'Comity and Choice of Law in Global Insolvencies' (2019) 54 *Texas International Law Journal* 259

Yokomizo, D, 'Reflections on Legal Persons and Conflict of Laws: Lex Societatis or Recognition of Foreign Corporate Personality? [in Japanese]' (2007) 135 *Journal of Civil and Commercial Law* 1045

Zhang, W, 'Sino–Foreign Recognition and Enforcement of Judgments: A Promising "Follow-Suit" Model?' (2017) 16 *Chinese Journal of International Law* 515

Zhu, L, 'The Kolmar v Sutex Case on Reciprocity in Foreign Judgments Enforcement in China: A Welcome Development or Still on the Wrong Track?' (2018) 13 *Frontiers of Law in China* 202

Online Resources

'Adoption Scammer Gets 18 Months in Jail' *ABC News*, 8 January 2006, available at abcnews.go.com/WNT/story?id=267559&page=1

'Babies for Sale: No Warranty' *The Sydney Morning Herald*, 16 December 2003, available at www.smh.com.au/national/babies-for-sale-no-warranty-20031216-gdhzp5.html

'Nanning Statement of the 2nd China-ASEAN Justice Forum' (2017), available at www.chinajusticeobserver.com/p/nanning-statement-of-the-2nd-china-asean-justice-forum

ABLI, 'About Us' (2024), available at https://abli.asia/about-us/

ABLI, 'Projects' (2024), available at https://abli.asia/projects/

Acleda Securities, 'Law & Regulation' (n.d.), available at www.acledasecurities.com.kh/as/eng/md_law_regulation

Amarthalingam, S, 'Cambodia Eyes Key Role in Electronics, Auto Hubs in SEA', *The Phnom Penh Post*, 5 May 2022, available at www.phnompenhpost.com/special-reports/cambodia-eyes-key-role-electronics-auto-hubs-sea

Arbitration Council, 'Arbitral Awards' (n.d.), available at www.arbitrationcouncil.org/arbitral-decision/arbitral-award/

Arbitration Council, 'Arbitral Awards' (n.d.), available at www.arbitrationcouncil.org/arbitral-decision/arbitral-award/

Arbitration Council, 'Law' (n.d.), available at www.arbitrationcouncil.org/resources/laws-regulations/law/

Arbitration Council, 'The Arbitration Council: Background' (n.d.), available at www.arbitrationcouncil.org/about-ac/the-arbitration-council/

ASEAN Law Association, 'About ALA: Objectives' (n.d.), available at www.aseanlawassociation.org/about-ala/#1571425345512-313f5198-86e5

ASEAN Law Association, 'About ALA: Standing Committees' (n.d.), available at www.aseanlawassociation.org/about-ala/#1572932443790-bff759c2-d61d

ASEAN Secretariat and UN Women Regional Office for Asia and the Pacific, 'ASEAN Gender Outlook: Achieving the SDGs for All and Leaving No Woman or Girl Behind' (2021), available at data.unwomen.org/sites/default/files/documents/Publications/ASEAN/ASEAN%20Gender%20Outlook_final.pdf

ASEAN, 'ASEAN Intellectual Property Portal: Cambodia' (2024), available at www.aseanip.org/Resources/ASEAN-IP-Offices-Details/Cambodia

Asian Legal Information Institute, 'Constitutional Council of Cambodia' (n.d.), available at www.asianlii.org/kh/cases/KHCCl/

Bainbridge, B, 'US Adoption Agent Guilty of Visa Fraud' *The Phnom Penh Post*, 19 December 2003, available at www.phnompenhpost.com/national/us-adoption-agent-guilty-visa-fraud

Baliga, A, 'Corrupt Judiciary Putting off Investment, Businesses Say', *The Phnom Penh Post*, 10 October 2015, available at www.phnompenhpost.com/business/corrupt-judiciary-putting-investment-businesses-say

Barber, J and Chheng, HS, 'Husband and Wife with No Male Hassles', *The Phnom Penh Post*, 24 March 1995, available at www.phnompenhpost.com/national/husband-and-wife-no-male-hassles

Barker, A, 'Australian Woman Charged with Running Illegal Surrogacy Clinic in Cambodia' *ABC News*, 21 November 2016, available at www.abc.net.au/news/2016-11-21/australian-woman-charged-over-illegal-surrogacy-clinic-cambodia/8042708

Baysal, P and Atar, M, 'A Comparative Analysis of Content-of-Laws Inquiry and Its Importance for International Commercial Arbitration', *Kluwer Arbitration Blog*, 25 January 2020, available at http://arbitrationblog.kluwerarbitration.com/2020/01/25/a-comparative-analysis-of-content-of-laws-inquiry-and-its-importance-for-international-commercial-arbitration/

Beech, H, 'They Were Surrogates. Now They Must Raise the Children' *The New York Times*, 26 November 2022, available at https://www.nytimes.com/2022/11/26/world/asia/surrogacy-cambodia.html

Bhati, A, 'Choice of Law And Mandatory Provisions', *Lex Kambujadesa Blawg: A Commentary on Cambodian Law and Practice*, 15 December 2018.

Blomberg, M, 'Surrogate Mothers from Cambodia Given Suspended Jail Terms in Landmark Case' *Reuters*, 31 March 2020, available at www.reuters.com/article/us-cambodia-surrogacy-women-idUSKBN21I1NS

BNG Legal, 'Can Expats Adopt Cambodian Children? Dispelling the Myths' *Cambodian Law Blog: Legal updates from the Kingdom of Wonder*, 9 June 2011, available at cambodianlaw.wordpress.com/2011/06/09/can-expats-adopt-cambodian-children-dispelling-the-myths

BNG Legal, 'Ship Registration in Cambodia' (2021) *BNG Newsletter*, available at https://bnglegal.com/wp-content/uploads/2021/02/Newsletters_of_Ship-Registration-in-Cambodia.pdf

Boltenko, O, 'Cambodia's Arbitration Centre Sets Off on Its First Flight', *Kluwer Arbitration Blog*, 10 June 2015, available at http://arbitrationblog.kluwerarbitration.com/2015/06/10/cambodias-arbitration-centre-sets-off-on-its-first-flight/

Boog, C and Moss, B, 'The Lazy Myth of the Arbitral Tribunal's Duty to Render an Enforceable Award', *Kluwer Arbitration Blog*, 28 January 2013, available at http://arbitrationblog.kluwerarbitration.com/2013/01/28/the-lazy-myth-of-the-arbitral-tribunals-duty-to-render-an-enforceable-award/

Boskovic, O, 'Boskovic on Rome II and Defamation', *Conflict of Laws net*, 20 July 2010, available at http://conflictoflaws.net/2010/boskovic-on-rome-ii-and-defamation/

Brander, H, 'Fake or Fact? (1) Digital Docs Manipulation and How to Spot It', (*Counsel*, 15 January 2021), available at www.counselmagazine.co.uk/articles/fake-or-fact-digital-docs-manipulation-how-to-spot-it-(1)

Bun & Associates, 'Introductory Guide: Commercial Arbitration in Cambodia' (2014), available at www.bun-associates.com/wp-content/uploads/2019/01/Introductory-Guide-Commercial-Arbitration-in-Cambodia.pdf

Bun, Y and Tamiya, A, 'Cambodian International Commercial Arbitration [in Japanese]' (2015) *Research Report for International Cooperation Department at the Ministry of Justice* 3, available at www.moj.go.jp/content/001148640.pdf

Bunthoeurn, O, 'Commercial Court Could Function 'As Early As 2024': Justice Ministry Officials', *The Phnom Penh Post*, 3 February 2023, available at www.phnompenhpost.com/business/commercial-court-could-function-early-2024-justice-ministry-officials

Busssat, M, 'Ship Registration in Cambodia' (2021) *HBS Law: Legal Brief*, available at www.hbslaw.asia/images/Related-Publications/2021/Ship-Registration-in-Cambodia.pdf

Cambodian League for the Promotion and Defense of Human Rights (LICADHO), 'Cambodia's Stolen Children: Fraud and Corruption in the Inter-country Adoption System' (2018), available at www.licadho-cambodia.org/reports/files/226LICADHOAdoptionReport30March2018_ENG.pdf

CCF Director-General, 'Laws & Regulations: Laws, Regulations and Other Legal Documents Related to the Roles and Functions of the CCF Directorate-General' (2021), available at www.ccfdg.gov.kh/en/laws-regulations/

CDC, 'Laws and Regulations' (n.d.), available at http://cdc.gov.kh/laws-and-regulations/

Chan, S, 'Firms Urged to Opt for Arbitration, Not Courts, to Settle Disputes', *Khmer Times*, 17 January 2016, available at www.khmertimeskh.com/34646/firms-urged-to-opt-for-arbitration-not-courts-to-settle-disputes/

Chea, S and Sok, H, 'Cambodia's Accession to the WTO: 'Fast Track' Accession by a Least Developed Country' (2005) Managing the Challenges of WTO Participation: 45 Case Studies available at www.wto.org/english/res_e/booksp_e/casestudies_e/case8_e.htm

Chhay, H, 'National Commercial Arbitration Centre: Development and Challenges', *Arbitration Asia*, February 2021, available at https://arbitrationasia.rajahtannasia.com/national-commercial-arbitration-centre-development-and-challenges/

Chheang, V, 'Cambodia Prioritises Economic Diplomacy', *East Asia Forum: Economics, Politics and Public Policy in East Asia and the Pacific*, 20 March 2021, available at www.eastasiaforum.org/2021/03/20/cambodia-prioritises-economic-diplomacy/

Chheng, N, 'Courts' Decisions Now Published as Reference Source', *The Phnom Penh Post*, 4 January 2021, available at www.phnompenhpost.com/national/courts-decisions-now-published-reference-source

Chiancone, J, 'Parental Abduction: A Review of the Literature', available at www.ojp.gov/pdffiles1/ojjdp/190074.pdf

Chong, A, (ed) *Asian Principles for the Recognition and Enforcement of Foreign Judgments* (Asian Business Law Institute, 2020)

Corbett, S, 'Where Do Babies Come From?' *The New York Times Magazines*, 16 June 2002, available at www.nytimes.com/2002/06/16/magazine/where-do-babies-come-from.html

Council of ASEAN Chief Justice, 'About CACJ: Mission Statement' (n.d.), available at https://cacj-ajp.org/about-cacj/mission-statement/

Council of ASEAN Chief Justice, 'Sources of Laws in Cambodia' (n.d.), available at https://cacj-ajp.org/cambodia/legal-system/cambodian-laws/overview/sources-of-laws-in-cambodia/

Council of ASEAN Chief Justices, 'Cambodia' (n.d.), available at https://cacj-ajp.org/cambodia/

Council of ASEAN Chief Justices, 'Overview of Cambodian Alternative Dispute Resolution System' (n.d.), available at https://cacj-ajp.org/cambodia/legal-system/overview-of-cambodian-alternative-dispute-resolution-system/

Council of ASEAN Chief Justices, 'Overview of Cambodian Judiciary' (n.d.), available at https://cacj-ajp.org/cambodia/judiciary/overview-of-cambodian-judiciary/

Council of Europe, 'Treaty Office: Chart of Signatures and Ratifications of Treaty 062' (2024), available at www.coe.int/en/web/conventions/full-list?module=signatures-by-treaty&treatynum=062

Dara, V, 'Bun Youdy Reflects on Three Years at the National Commercial Arbitration Centre', *The Phnom Penh Post*, 24 March 2022, available at www.phnompenhpost.com/national-post-depth/bun-youdy-reflects-three-years-national-commercial-arbitration-centre

Dara, V,; NCAC and Singapore's SIAC to Promote International Arbitration', *The Phnom Penh Post*, 24 March 2022, available at www.phnompenhpost.com/national/ncac-and-singapores-siac-promote-international-arbitration

Darwin, H and Rithy, C, 'Ship Arrest in Cambodia', *BNG Legal*, June 2016, available at http://bnglegal.com/cn/wp-content/uploads/2016/08/160729-Ship-Arrest-In-Cambodia-June-2016.pdf

Davidson, H and Lin, CH, 'Hundreds of Taiwanese Trafficked to Cambodia and Held Captive by Telecom Scam Gangs', *The Guardian*, 23 August 2022, available at www.theguardian.com/world/2022/aug/23/hundreds-of-taiwanese-trafficked-to-cambodia-and-held-captive-by-telecom-scam-gangs

Davies, JA, 'Red Flags Abound in Prince Group's Offshore Dealings', *Radio Free Asia*, 8 February 2024, available at www.rfa.org/english/news/cambodia/prince-group-investigation-02082024130529.html

Du, G and Yu, M, 'Turning Point: China First Recognizes Japanese Bankruptcy Decision', *Conflict of Laws.net*, 11 March 2024, available at https://conflictoflaws.net/2024/turning-point-china-first-recognizes-japanese-bankruptcy-decision/

Eidenmüller, H, 'Shell Shock: In Defence of the 'Real Seat Theory' in International Company Law', *Oxford Business Blog*, 25 March 2022, available at https://blogs.law.ox.ac.uk/business-law-blog/blog/2022/03/shell-shock-defence-real-seat-theory-international-company-law

European Commission and Hague Conference on Private International Law, 'Access to Foreign Law in Civil and Commercial Matters: Conclusions and Recommendations' (2012), available at https://assets.hcch.net/docs/b093f152-a4b3-4530-949e-65c1bfc9cda1.pdf

Financial Markets Law Committee, 'The Rule in Gibbs: Exploring Its Value and Practical Use in the Financial Markets as a Guarantor of Legal Predictability' (2024), available at https://fmlc.org/wp-content/uploads/2024/02/Paper-The-Rule-in-Gibbs-Exploring-its-value-and-practical-use-in-the-financial-markets-as-a-guarantor-of-legal-predictability-29-February-2024.pdf

Fontaine, A, 'The Insurance and Reinsurance Law Review: Cambodia', *The Insurance and Reinsurance Law Reviews*, 24 April 2022, available at https://backend.bun-associates.com/attributes/publication/file_1666840442.pdf

Goldberg, AB and Apton, D, 'U.S. Families Learn Truth About Adopted Cambodian Children' *ABC News*, 12 January 2007, available at abcnews.go.com/2020/International/story?id=611826&page=1

GTZ-Cambodia Land Management Project and the World Bank Justice for the Poor Program, 'Towards Institutional Justice? A Review of the Work of Cambodia's Cadastral Commission in Relation to Land Dispute Resolution' (2006) *The World Bank Justice for the Poor Program*, available at http://documents.worldbank.org/curated/en/309161468222269820/pdf/408230Towards01nal0Justice01PUBLIC1.pdf

Haider, H, 'Civil Servants Are to Receive Special Arbitration Training to Resolve Commercial Disputes', *Khmer Times*, 30 July 2021, available at www.khmertimeskh.com/50904570/civil-servants-are-to-receive-special-arbitration-training-to-resolve-commercial-disputes/

Haider, H, 'GFX Filing for Insolvency?', *Khmer Times*, 16 July 2021, available at www.khmertimeskh.com/50894896/gfx-filing-for-insolvency/

Haider, H, 'New Commercial Arbitration Rules Enter into Force', *Khmer Times*, 28 June 2021, available at www.khmertimeskh.com/50882539/new-commercial-arbitration-rules-enter-into-force/

Handley, E and Meta, K, '"I Will Not Give Them the Baby": the Plight of Cambodia's Detained Surrogates', *The Guardian*, 2 October 2018, available at www.theguardian.com/global-development/2018/oct/02/i-will-not-give-them-the-baby-plight-cambodia-detained-surrogates

Handley, E, 'Surrogacy Ban Lacks Force of Law' *The Phnom Penh Post*, 4 November 2016, available at www.phnompenhpost.com/national/surrogacy-ban-lacks-force-law

Handley, K, 'Cambodian Surrogates Face an Impossible Choice – Forced Motherhood, or Years in Prison' *ABC News*, 12 May 2019, available at www.abc.net.au/news/2019-05-12/cambodian-surrogates-forced-to-be-mothers-or-face-prison-time/11086640

Hartley, T, 'Hartley on The Problem of "Libel Tourism"', *Conflict of Laws.net*, 19 July 2010, available at http://conflictoflaws.net/2010/hartley-on-the-problem-of-libel-tourism/

Haskel, D, 'Guest Article from Abacus IP – 20 Years of Patent Law in Cambodia: Milestones and Future Outlook', *European Commission IP Helpdesk: News Article*, 3 April 2023, available at https://intellectual-property-helpdesk.ec.europa.eu/news-events/news/guest-article-abacus-ip-20-years-patent-law-cambodia-milestones-and-future-outlook-2023-03-25_en

HCCH, 'Conventions and Other Instruments' (2024), available at www.hcch.net/en/instruments/conventions

HCCH, 'Country Profile 1993 Hague Intercountry Adoption Convention: State of Origin (the Kingdom of Cambodia)' (2021), available at assets.hcch.net/docs/cb910351-cb41-4832-8a9a-8fbd8e680122.pdf

HCCH, 'Hague Conventions: Signatures, Ratifications, Approvals and Accessions: Status on 21 November 2024' (2024), available at https://assets.hcch.net/docs/ccf77ba4-af95-4e9c-84a3-e94dc8a3c4ec.pdf

HCCH, 'HCCH Members' (2024), available at www.hcch.net/en/states/hcch-members

HCCH, 'International Hague Network of Judges (IHNJ)' (2022), available at https://assets.hcch.net/docs/665b2d56-6236-4125-9352-c22bb65bc375.pdf

HCCH, 'Member: Japan' (2024), available at www.hcch.net/en/states/hcch-members/details1/?sid=47

HCCH, 'Status Table: Convention of 1 August 1989 on the Law Applicable to Succession to the Estates of Deceased Persons' (2015), available at www.hcch.net/en/instruments/conventions/status-table/?cid=62

HCCH, 'Status Table: Convention of 1 July 1985 on the Law Applicable to Trusts and on their Recognition' (2024), available at www.hcch.net/en/instruments/conventions/status-table/?cid=59

HCCH, 'Status Table: Convention of 14 March 1978 on the Law Applicable to Agency' (2022), available at www.hcch.net/en/instruments/conventions/status-table/?cid=89

HCCH, 'Status Table: Convention of 18 March 1970 on the Taking of Evidence Abroad in Civil or Commercial Matters' (2023) www.hcch.net/en/instruments/conventions/status-table/?cid=82

HCCH, 'Status Table: Convention of 19 October 1996 on Jurisdiction, Applicable Law, Recognition, Enforcement and Co-operation in Respect of Parental Responsibility and Measures for the Protection of Children' (2024), available at www.hcch.net/en/instruments/conventions/status-table/?cid=70

HCCH, 'Status Table: Convention of 2 July 2019 on the Recognition and Enforcement of Foreign Judgments in Civil or Commercial Matters' (2024), available at www.hcch.net/en/instruments/conventions/status-table/?cid=137

HCCH, 'Status Table: Convention of 2 October 1973 Concerning the International Administration of the Estates of Deceased Persons' (2014), available at www.hcch.net/en/instruments/conventions/status-table/?cid=83

HCCH, 'Status Table: Convention of 2 October 1973 on the Law Applicable to Products Liability' (2012), available at www.hcch.net/en/instruments/conventions/status-table/?cid=84

HCCH, 'Status Table: Convention of 2 October 1973 on the Law Applicable to Maintenance Obligations' (2013), available at www.hcch.net/en/instruments/conventions/status-table/?cid=86

HCCH, 'Status Table: Convention of 23 November 2007 on the International Recovery of Child Support and Other Forms of Family Maintenance' (2024), available at www.hcch.net/en/instruments/conventions/status-table/?cid=131

HCCH, 'Status Table: Convention of 25 October 1980 on the Civil Aspects of International Child Abduction' (2022), available at www.hcch.net/en/instruments/conventions/status-table/?cid=24

HCCH, 'Status Table: Convention of 29 May 1993 on Protection of Children and Co-operation in Respect of Inter-country Adoption' (2024), available at www.hcch.net/en/instruments/conventions/status-table/?cid=69

HCCH, 'Status Table: Convention of 30 June 2005 on Choice of Court Agreements' (2024), available at www.hcch.net/en/instruments/conventions/status-table/?cid=98

HCCH, 'Status Table: Convention of 4 May 1971 on the Law Applicable to Traffic Accidents' (2014), available at www.hcch.net/en/instruments/conventions/status-table/?cid=81

HCCH, 'Status Table: Convention of 5 October 1961 Abolishing the Requirement of Legalisation for Foreign Public Documents' (2024), available at www.hcch.net/en/instruments/conventions/status-table/?cid=41

HCCH, 'Status Table: Convention of 5 October 1961 on the Conflicts of Laws Relating to the Form of Testamentary Dispositions' (2017), available at www.hcch.net/en/instruments/conventions/status-table/?cid=40

HCCH, 'Status Table: Protocol of 23 November 2007 on the Law Applicable to Maintenance Obligations' (2022), available at www.hcch.net/en/instruments/conventions/status-table/?cid=133

HCCH, 'Status Tables: Principles on Choice of Law in International Commercial Contracts' (2024), available at www.hcch.net/en/instruments/conventions/publications1/?dtid=41&cid=135

Hem, D, and Chankoulika, B, 'Commercial Arbitration in Cambodia', *BNG Legal Newsletter*, February 2017, available at https://bnglegal.com/cn/wp-content/uploads/2017/02/170206-Commercial-arbitration-in-Cambodia.pdf-February.pdf

Heng, C and Tiv, S, 'Casino & Gaming: Promulgation of Law on Management of Commercial Gaming', *Client Update: Cambodia*, December 2020, available at https://kh.rajahtannasia.com/media/4383/2020-12-promulgation-of-law.pdf

Hioe, B, 'Taiwan Grapples with Human Trafficking Spike', *The Diplomat*, 1 September 2022, available at https://thediplomat.com/2022/09/taiwan-grapples-with-human-trafficking-spike/

Holligan, J and others, 'UPDATE: Overview of the Cambodian History, Governance and Legal Sources' (2019) GlobaLex available at www.nyulawglobal.org/globalex/Cambodia1.html#_CPK/DK_period:_1975

Hunt, L, 'Taiwan Frets for 'Thousands' Trafficked Into Cambodia', *The Diplomat*, 16 August 2022, available at https://thediplomat.com/2022/08/taiwan-frets-for-thousands-trafficked-into-cambodia/

Huot, C and Rith, S, 'Hope of Justice Lies in School for Judges', *The Phnom Penh Post*, 21 November 2003, available at www.phnompenhpost.com/national/hope-justice-lies-school-judges

Hutt, D, 'Should Cambodia Ban Casinos?', *The Diplomat*, 30 August 2022, available at https://thediplomat.com/2022/08/should-cambodia-ban-casinos/

IAEA, 'Convention on Supplementary Compensation for Nuclear Damage: Latest Status' (2020), available at www.iaea.org/sites/default/files/22/06/supcomp_status.pdf

IAEA, 'Vienna Convention on Civil Liability for Nuclear Damage: Latest Status' (2024), available at www.iaea.org/sites/default/files/24/03/63_vc_status.pdf

ICAO, 'Contracting Parties to the Convention for the Unification of Certain Rules Relating to International Carriage by Air Signed at Warsaw On 12 October 1929 and the Protocol Modifying the Said Convention Signed at the Hague on 28 September 1955' (n.d.), available at www.icao.int/secretariat/legal/List%20of%20Parties/WC-HP_EN.pdf

ICAO, 'Convention for the Unification of Certain Rules For International Carriage by Air Done at Montreal on 28 May 1999' (n.d.), available at www.icao.int/secretariat/legal/List%20of%20Parties/Mtl99_EN.pdf

ICAO, 'Status of Cambodia with Regard to International Air Law Instruments' (n.d.), available at www.icao.int/secretariat/legal/Status%20of%20individual%20States/cambodia_en.pdf

ICC, 'Business Solutions' (n.d.), available at https://iccwbo.org/business-solutions/

ICC, 'Incoterms® 2020' (n.d.), available at https://iccwbo.org/resources-for-business/incoterms-rules/incoterms-2020/

ICSID, 'About ICSID: Database of ICSID Member States' (2024), available at https://icsid.worldbank.org/about/member-states/database-of-member-states

ILO, 'NORMLEX (Information System on International Labour Standards): Ratifications for Cambodia' (n.d.), available at www.ilo.org/dyn/normlex/en/f?p=NORMLEXPUB:11200:0::NO::p11200_country_id:103055

IMO, 'International Convention on Civil Liability for Oil Pollution Damage (CLC)' (n.d.), available at www.imo.org/en/About/Conventions/Pages/International-Convention-on-Civil-Liability-for-Oil-Pollution-Damage-(CLC).aspx

IMO, 'Status of Conventions: Ratifications by State' (n.d.), available at https://wwwcdn.imo.org/localresources/en/About/Conventions/StatusOfConventions/x-Status.xlsx

InforMARE, 'International Conventions: Membership List' (2022), available at www.informare.it/dbase/convuk.htm (not accessible as at 12 December 2024)

Intercollegeate Negotiation Competition, 'Outline' (2024), available at www.negocom.jp/eng/what/

International Centre for Missing & Exploited Children, 'Global Missing Children Research Initiative: Country-Specific Findings (Cambodia)' (2016), available at www.icmec.org/wp-content/uploads/2017/05/Cambodia-July-2016.pdf

Iriinafuku, S, 'Connecting Factors [in Japanese]' (n.d.), available at https://eu-info.jp/IPR/4.html

Iriinafuku, S, 'Lecture Note on Private International Law: Divorce' [in Japanese] (2021), available at eu-info.jp/IPR/dev.html

Iriinafuku, S, 'The Characterisation of Legal Relations [in Japanese]' (n.d.), available at https://eu-info.jp/IPR/3.html#_ftn3

Iriinafuku, S, 'The Preliminary Question [in Japanese]' (n.d.), available at https://eu-info.jp/IPR/8.html

JETRO, 'Enforcement of Intellectual Property Rights in Cambodia [in Japanese]' (2018), 15, available at www.jetro.go.jp/ext_images/world/asia/kh/ip/pdf/survey_201810_kh.pdf

Jha, P, 'FDI Flow in Cambodia Steady, but for Corona Bump', *Khmer Times*, 25 October 2022, available at www.khmertimeskh.com/501173025/fdi-flow-in-cambodia-steady-but-for-corona-bump/

JICA, 'Commentary on Cambodian Code of Civil Procedure: Compulsory Execution and Provisional Remedies [in Japanese]' (n.d.), available at www.moj.go.jp/content/000122393.pdf

JICA, 'Commentary on Cambodian Code of Civil Procedure: Judgment Procedure [in Japanese]' (n.d.) available at www.moj.go.jp/content/000122394.pdf

JICA, 'Outline of the Project: The Legal and Judicial Development Project (Phase V)' (2024), available at www.jica.go.jp/Resource/project/english/cambodia/025/outline/index.html

JICA, 'Portal Site for the Legal Technical Assistance Projects by JICA: Cambodia' (n.d.), available at www.jica.go.jp/activities/issues/governance/portal/index.html

JICA, 'The Legal and Judicial Development Project (Phase 3): Materials' (n.d.), available at www.jica.go.jp/project/english/cambodia/0701047/materials/index.html

JICA, 'The Legal and Judicial Development Project (Phase V): Outline of the Project' (2017), available at https://www.jica.go.jp/project/english/cambodia/025/outline/index.html

Johnston, E, 'How Japan Ensures You Gamble Exactly When and Where It Wants You to', *The Japan Times*, 8 June 2023, available at www.japantimes.co.jp/news/2023/06/08/national/gambling-pachinko-sports/

Kang, T, 'Are Cambodia and Laos Really Any Closer to Resolving Their Border Dispute?', *The Diplomat*, 21 May 2018, available at https://thediplomat.com/2018/05/are-cambodia-and-laos-really-any-closer-to-resolving-their-border-dispute/

Khmer Times Writer, 'Ministry of Commerce Urges Implementation of Consumer Protection Laws', *Khmer Times*, 13 July 2022, available at www.khmertimeskh.com/501111823/ministry-of-commerce-urges-implementation-of-consumer-protection-laws/

Khmer Times, 'Cambodia Property Growth Well Poised by the End of 2022', *Khmer Times*, 2 November 2022, available at www.khmertimeskh.com/501179287/cambodia-property-growth-well-poised-by-the-end-of-2022-2/

Kijewski, L, 'UN Reiterates Call to Abolish Criminalization of Surrogates' *VOA News*, 14 November 2019, available at www.voacambodia.com/a/UN-reiterates-call-to-abolish-criminalization-of-surrogates/5164651.html

Kiri, S, 'Message From President' (2024), available at https://ncac.org.kh/message-from-president/

Koemsoeun, S, 'Cambodia, Thailand Discuss Border Posts', *Khmer Times*, 23 January 2023, available at www.khmertimeskh.com/501224027/cambodiathailand-discuss-border-posts/

Kongkea, BR, '14 People Jailed for Involvement in Surrogacy and Human Trafficking' *Khmer Times*, 30 July 2020, available at www.khmertimeskh.com/50750358/14-people-jailed-for-involvement-in-surrogacy-and-human-trafficking

Kongkea, BR, 'Commercial Court Law Ready for Approval', *Khmer Times*, 9 November 2023, available at www.khmertimeskh.com/501389436/commercial-court-law-ready-for-approval/

Kongkea, BR, 'Commercial Courts in the Pipeline to Attract More Investors', *Khmer Times*, 25 January 2021, available at www.khmertimeskh.com/50806501/commercial-courts-in-the-pipeline-to-attract-more-investors/

Kongkea, BR, 'Police Prevent Same-sex Wedding Ceremony', *Khmer Times*, 5 February 2018, available at www.khmertimeskh.com/106509/police-prevent-sex-wedding-ceremony/

Kongnov, T, 'CCCC Handled 140 Cases of Counterfeit Products Last Year', *Khmer Times*, 24 January 2022, available at www.khmertimeskh.com/501011959/cccc-handled-140-cases-of-counterfeit-products-last-year/

Kongnov, T, 'More Than One Million Cambodians Work Abroad and Sent about $3 Billion Every Year to Their Families', *Khmer Times*, 25 February 2022, available at www.khmertimeskh.com/501032136/more-than-one-million-cambodians-work-abroad-and-sent-about-3-billion-every-year-to-their-families/

Kubo, AE, 'Cambodia to Lift Ban on International Adoptions: The Resumption of Intercountry Adoptions Comes Four Years after Reports of Child Abuse and Trafficking' *The Diplomat*, 10 December 2013, available at thediplomat.com/2013/12/cambodia-to-lift-ban-on-international-adoptions

Lamy, M and Sonyka, V, 'Surrogacy Law in the Kingdom Long Overdue' *Khmer Times*, 10 April 2020, available at www.khmertimeskh.com/711396/surrogacy-law-in-the-kingdom-long-overdue

Legal Affairs Department Securities and Exchange Regulator of Cambodia, 'Rehabilitation in the Securities Sector in the Event of Critical Financial Crisis' 28 January 2024, available at www.phnompenhpost.com/financial/rehabilitation-in-the-securities-sector-in-the-event-of-critical-financial-crisis

Lovgren, S, 'Southeast Asia's Most Critical River Is Entering Uncharted Waters', *National Geographic*, 31 January 2020, available at www.nationalgeographic.com/science/article/southeast-asia-most-critical-river-enters-uncharted-waters

M van Eechoud, 'The Position of Broadcasters and Other Media under 'Rome II' Proposed EC Regulation on the Law Applicable to Non-contractual Obligations' (2006) IRIS Plus (Supplement to IRIS – Legal Observations of the European Audiovisual Observatory), available at www.obs.coe.int/; https://papers.ssrn.com/sol3/papers.cfm?abstract_id=973774

Madaus, S, 'The Rule in Gibbs, or How to Protect Local Debt from a Foreign Discharge', *Oxford Business Law Blog*, 19 December 2018, available at https://blogs.law.ox.ac.uk/business-law-blog/blog/2018/12/rule-gibbs-or-how-protect-local-debt-foreign-discharge

Makara, K, 'Concerns about Arbitration Centre', *The Phnom Penh Post*, 2 October 2009, available at www.phnompenhpost.com/business/concerns-about-arbitration-centre

McDowell, R, 'Rush Is On To Adopt Cambodia Babies' *AP News*, 25 July 1998, available at apnews.com/article/b21178898d6e12e01469a9135ca3356a

Meta, K and Handley, E, 'Report Gives Voice to Mothers Deceived by Cambodia's Orphanage Racket', *The Phnom Penh Post*, 30 March 2018, available at www.phnompenhpost.com/national-post-depth/report-gives-voice-mothers-deceived-cambodias-orphanage-racket

Meta, K, 'Kingdom Surrogacy Law Set to Lift Burden from "Victims"' *The Phnom Penh Post*, 19 January 2018, available at www.phnompenhpost.com/national/kingdom-surrogacy-law-set-lift-burden-victims

Meynell, D, 'Documentary Credits: Rules, Guidelines & Terminology', *ICC Academy*, 17 December 2019, available at https://icc.academy/documentary-credits-rules-guidelines-terminology/

Ministry of Commerce, 'Business Registration' (n.d.), available at www.businessregistration.moc.gov.kh/starting-a-business-2/register/

Ministry of Foreign Affairs and International Cooperation, 'Clarification' (2017), available at https://pressocm.gov.kh/wp-content/uploads/2017/10/ENG-Ministry-of-Foreign-Affairs-and-International-Cooperation-201710-1-5.pdf

Ministry of Justice of Japan, 'Legal Technical Assistance Activities by the International Cooperation Department ~Contributing to the World is Japan's Strength!~: Cambodia' [in Japanese], available at www.moj.go.jp/housouken/houso_houkoku_cambo.html

Mit, M, 'China's Continuing Influence over Cambodia's Economy', *East Asia Forum*, 1 May 2024, available at https://eastasiaforum.org/2024/05/01/chinas-continuing-influence-over-cambodias-economy/

MOJ, 'Court Decisions on Actual Civil Cases' (n.d.), available at www.moj.gov.kh/kh/actual-civil-judgments

MOJJ, 'Cambodia [in Japanese]' (n.d.), available at www.moj.go.jp/housouken/houso_houkoku_cambo.html

Morning Studio Editors, 'Cambodia's Property Investment Market Well-Positioned for Post-Pandemic Recovery ahead of Next Year's Southeast Asian Games', *South China Morning Post*, 3 August 2022, available at www.scmp.com/presented/property/international/topics/cambodias-emerging-property-market/article/3186913/recovery

Murdoch, L, 'Australian Couples' Baby Plans in Limbo as Cambodia Bans Commercial Surrogacy' *The Sydney Morning Herald*, 2 February 2022, available at www.smh.com.au/world/australian-couples-baby-plans-in-limbo-as-cambodia-bans-commercial-surrogacy-20161104-gshx2x.html

Muyhong, C, 'Arbitrator Ready to Hear Cases', *The Phnom Penh Post*, 14 July 2014, available at www.phnompenhpost.com/business/arbitrator-ready-hear-cases

Nakamura, T and Nottage, L, 'Arbitration in Japan' (2012) *Sydney Law School Legal Studies Research Paper* 8, available at http://ssrn.com/abstract=2070447

National Bank of Cambodia, 'Laws Applicable to Banks and Financial Institutions' (2015), available at www.nbc.gov.kh/english/legislation/laws_applicable_to_banks_and_financial_institutions.php

National Committee for Sub-National Democratic Development, 'Gazetteer Database Online' (n.d.) http://db.ncdd.gov.kh/gazetteer/view/index.castle

NCAC, 'About Us: Establishment' (2024), available at https://ncac.org.kh/establishment/

NCAC, 'Services: Trainings' (2024), available at https://ncac.org.kh/en/services/training/

Neilson, KE, 'They Killed All the Lawyers: Rebuilding the Judicial System in Cambodia' (1996) Occasional Paper #13, 1, available at www.uvic.ca/research/centres/capi/research/home/researchpublications/papers/Neilson_Killed_Lawyers.pdf

Nop, K, 'Cambodia: What Should Be Included in a Contract?', *Nop Legal: Page of Business Law*, 14 May 2021, available at https://noplegal.com/2021/05/14/what-should-be-included-in-a-contract/

Nortajuddin, A, 'Cambodia's Fight Against Counterfeit Goods', *The ASEAN Post*, 25 September 2020, available at https://theaseanpost.com/article/cambodias-fight-against-counterfeit-goods

OAS: Department of International Law, 'Multilateral Treaties: Inter-American Convention on Proof of and Information on Foreign Law' (n.d.), available at www.oas.org/juridico/English/sigs/b-43.html

OECD, 'Paris Convention: Latest Status of Ratifications or Accessions' (2024), available at www.oecd-nea.org/jcms/pl_31798/paris-convention-latest-status-of-ratifications-or-accession

OECD, *Corporate Governance Frameworks in Cambodia, Lao PDR, Myanmar and Viet Nam* (Paris, OECD 2019)

Open Development Cambodia, 'Administration' (2015) https://opendevelopmentcambodia.net/topics/administration/#ref-79177-3

Parra-Aranguren, G, 'Explanatory Report on the Convention on Protection of Children and Co-Operation in Respect of Intercountry Adoption' (1994), available at assets.hcch.net/upload/expl33e.pdf

Phanet, H, 'Cambodian E-commerce Surges Nearly a Fifth in 2021', *The Phnom Penh Post*, 3 July 2022, available at www.phnompenhpost.com/business/cambodian-e-commerce-surges-nearly-fifth-2021

Phanet, H, 'Cambodia-US Trade Rises 32%', *The Phnom Penh Post*, 10 January 2022, available at www.phnompenhpost.com/business/cambodia-us-trade-rises-32

Phanet, H, 'Trade with Japan Extends Growth in 2021', *The Phnom Penh Post*, 13 January 2022, available at www.phnompenhpost.com/business/trade-japan-extends-growth-2021

Pisei, H, 'NCAC Trade Disputes Reach 27: Official', *The Phnom Penh Post*, 8 August 2021, available at www.phnompenhpost.com/business/ncac-trade-disputes-reach-27-official

Pisei, H, 'New Trust Law Stabilises Real Estate Sector', *The Phnom Penh Post*, 16 November 2023, available at www.phnompenhpost.com/business/new-trust-law-stabilises-real-estate-sector

Pisei, H, 'South Korea Trade Nearly $870M in Jan-Nov', *The Phnom Penh Post*, 20 December 2021, available at www.phnompenhpost.com/business/south-korea-trade-nearly-870m-jan-nov

Pisel, H, 'Cambodia's Q1 Trade Volume Hits over $13B', *The Phnom Penh Post*, 16 April 2022, available at www.phnompenhpost.com/business/cambodias-q1-trade-volume-hits-over-13b

Post Staff, 'Cambodia Pushes Arbitration as an Alternative Commercial Dispute Resolution Mechanism', *The Phnom Penh Post*, 19 November 2019, available at www.phnompenhpost.com/post-focus/cambodia-pushes-arbitration-alternative-commercial-dispute-resolution-mechanism

Prum, V, 'Competition Law Up for Love', *The Phnom Penh Post*, 18 October 2021, available at www.phnompenhpost.com/opinion/competition-law-love

Ravindran, S, 'Competition Law Framework Grew Steadily in Last Two Years', *Khmer Times*, 10 July 2023, available at www.khmertimeskh.com/501321303/competition-law-framework-grew-steadily-in-last-two-years/

Royal Government of Cambodia Ministry of Commerce, *Insolvency Law: Draft – June 2001*, www.wto.org/english/thewto_e/acc_e/khm_e/wtacckhm5_leg_4.pdf

Sabeone, F, 'Islam in Cambodia: The Fate of the Cham Muslims' (2017) *European Institute for Asian Studies: EU-Asia at a Glance*, available at www.eias.org/wp-content/uploads/2016/03/EU_Asia_at_a_Glance_Sabeone_Cham_Cambodia_2017-1.pdf

Sanders, P, 'Notes on Article 33(4)' (n.d.), available at www.arbitration-icca.org/media/0/12741828662200/021.pdf

Sarath, S, 'Arbitration Rules Under Review', *Khmer Times*, 28 July 2020, available at www.khmertimeskh.com/50749327/arbitration-rules-under-review/

Sarath, S, 'Local Arbitration Centre Needs More Time to Build Confidence', *Khmer Times*, 21 May 2020, available at www.khmertimeskh.com/50725360/local-arbitration-centre-needs-more-time-to-build-confidence/

Sarom, K, 'Chinese Surrogacy Father has Appeal Heard in Court' *The Phnom Penh Post*, 10 January 2020, available at www.phnompenhpost.com/national/chinese-surrogacy-father-has-appeal-heard-court

Sassoon, AM and Dara, M, 'Kingdom's Judiciary Perceived as Most Corrupt: UNDP', *The Phnom Penh Post*, 11 April 2016, available at www.phnompenhpost.com/national/kingdoms-judiciary-perceived-most-corrupt-undp

Seangly, P and Handley, E, 'To Have and to Hold: Polygamy in the Kingdom', *The Phnom Penh Post*, 10 February 2017, available at www.phnompenhpost.com/post-weekend/have-and-hold-polygamy-kingdom

SIAC, 'SIAC Signs Memorandum of Understanding with the National Commercial Arbitration Centre in Cambodia', *SIAC Press Release*, 24 March 2022, available at https://siac.org.sg/wp-content/uploads/2022/07/Press-Release-SIAC-Signs-Memorandum-of-Understanding-with-the-National-Commercial-Arbitration-Centre-in-Cambodia.pdf

Sineat, Y and Keeton-Olsen, D, 'A Surrogate Family and the Law That Criminalized Them' *VOD*, 2 November 2020, available at vodenglish.news/a-surrogate-family-and-the-law-that-criminalized-them

Singapore Courts: The Judiciary, 'Judgments' (2024), available at www.judiciary.gov.sg/judgments

Singapore International Dispute Resolution Academy (SIDRA), 'Singapore Convention on Mediation: Jurisdictions' (2021), available at www.singaporeconvention.org/jurisdictions

Siphana, S, 'Legal Framework for Doing Business' (n.d.), 1 available at https://mfaic.gov.kh/files/uploads/PDFDoingBussinessForCambodia/2_Legal_Framework_for_Doing_B.pdf

Sithika, S, 'CCF Holds Workshop on Consumer Protection Programmes', *Khmer Times*, 14 July 2022, available at www.khmertimeskh.com/501112262/ccf-holds-workshop-on-consumer-protection-programmes/

Smith, PJ and Tavsothaly, T, 'Cambodian Trust Law', *BNG Legal*, December 2019, available at http://bnglegal.com/wp-content/uploads/2019/12/191219-BNG-Newsletter-December-Trust-law.pdf

Sochan, R, 'Commerce Ministry Official Addresses Intellectual Property Conference', *The Phnom Penh Post*, 16 July 2022, available at www.phnompenhpost.com/business/commerce-ministry-official-addresses-intellectual-property-conference

Soco, RM, 'Many Cambodian Women Still Victims of Poverty' *Khmer Times*, 3 March 2021, available at www.khmertimeskh.com/50819981/many-cambodian-women-still-victims-of-poverty/#:~:text=A%20study%20published%20on%20Monday,104%20women%20live%20in%20poverty

Sokhavuth, T, 'Ministry to Review Draft Surrogacy Law with Legal Experts' *Khmer Times*, 11 April 2022, available at www.khmertimeskh.com/501056334/ministry-to-review-draft-surrogacy-law-with-legal-experts/

Sothear, K, 'Demand for Arbitration Rises Among Businesses', *Khmer Times*, 25 May 2022, available at www.khmertimeskh.com/501081634/demand-for-arbitration-rises-among-businesses/

Sotheary, P, 'Kingdom Not Yet Ready for LGBT Laws: Hun Sen', *Khmer Times*, 21 February 2021, available at www.khmertimeskh.com/580112/kingdom-not-yet-ready-for-lgbt-laws-hun-sen/

Sovuthy, K, 'Australian Surrogacy Nurse Released From Jail' *Khmer Times*, 15 November 2018, available at www.khmertimeskh.com/550676/australian-surrogacy-nurse-released-from-jail

Spiess, R, 'Investors, Government Talk Intellectual Property', *The Phnom Penh Post*, 12 February 2018, available at www.phnompenhpost.com/business/investors-government-talk-intellectual-property

Spuling, N, 'Cross-Border Insolvencies in Southeast Asia: Regional Insolvency Framework for ASEAN' (2021) *Doctoral Thesis, Tilburg University*, available at https://research.tilburguniversity.edu/en/publications/cross-border-insolvencies-in-southeast-asia-regional-insolvency-f

Sreypich, M and Dickinson, M, 'Fishing for Plastic', *VOD*, 17 September 2021, available at https://vodenglish.news/trash-on-the-surface-microplastics-below-hundreds-of-tons-of-plastic-carried-daily-by-phnom-penh-rivers-research-finds/

State Judiciary Department: Brunei Darussalam, 'Judgments Search' (n.d.) www.judiciary.gov.bn/SJD%20Site%20Pages/Judgment%20Search.aspx

Tayseng, L, 'Bankruptcy Law: Role, Inefficiencies and Social Drama', *The Phnom Penh Post*, 25 May 2020, available at www.phnompenhpost.com/opinion/bankruptcy-law-role-inefficiencies-and-social-drama

Tayseng, L, 'Importance of Publicity of Judicial Process and Publication of Judicial Decisions', *The Phnom Penh Post*, 12 April 2022, available at www.phnompenhpost.com/opinion/importance-publicity-judicial-process-and-publication-judicial-decisions

Teramura, N, '*Ex Aequo et Bono*: An Overlooked and Undervalued Opportunity for International Commercial Arbitration', *Kluwer Arbitration Blog*, 25 November 2018, available at http://arbitrationblog.kluwerarbitration.com/2018/11/18/ex-aequo-et-bono-an-overlooked-and-undervalued-opportunity-for-international-commercial-arbitration/

The Sydney Morning Herald Staff Writer, 'Babies for Sale: No Warranty', *The Sydney Morning Herald*, 16 December 2003, available at www.smh.com.au/national/babies-for-sale-no-warranty-20031216-gdhzp5.html

The University of Melbourne, 'Southeast Asian Region Countries Law: Cambodia – Courts and Cases' (n.d.), available at https://unimelb.libguides.com/c.php?g=930183&p=6721971

The World Bank Group, 'Land Management and Administration Project' (2024), available at https://projects.worldbank.org/en/projects-operations/project-detail/P070875

Transparency International, 'Corruption Perceptions Index 2023' (2024), available at www.transparency.org/en/cpi/2023?gad_source=1&gclid=Cj0KCQjwncWvBhD_ARIsAEb2HW8duSXLuItQiYOCFteUBFHBTSnXf-SqT699mD3B6EiXzvD0EjVX_hT4aAt-KEALw_wcB

Transparency International, 'CPI 2021 for Asia Pacific: Grand Corruption and Lack of Freedoms Holding Back Progress', *The Latest Updates on the Fight Against Corruption in Cambodia*, 25 January 2022, available at www.transparency.org/en/news/cpi-2021-for-asia-pacific-grand-corruption-holding-back-progress

Um, K, 'The Cambodian Diaspora: Community Building in America', *Asia Society*, n.d., available at https://asiasociety.org/cambodian-diaspora

Umeda, S, 'Cambodian Law – Global Legal Collection Highlights', *In Custodia Legis: Law Librarians of Congress*, 7 July 2014, available at https://blogs.loc.gov/law/2014/07/cambodian-law-global-legal-collection-highlights/

UN Committee on the Elimination of Discrimination against Women, 'Concluding Observations on the 6th Periodic Report of Cambodia: Committee on the Elimination of Discrimination against Women (74th sess, 2019, Geneva)' (2019) 14, available at digitallibrary.un.org/record/3838743?ln=en#record-files-collapse-header

UNCITRAL, 'A/CN.9/1162 – Report of Working Group IV (Electronic Commerce) on the Work of Its Sixty-Sixth Session (Vienna, 16–20 October 2023)' (2024), available at https://docs.un.org/en/A/CN.9/1162

UNCITRAL, 'A/CN.9/1166 – Report of Working Group II (Dispute Settlement) on the Work of Its Seventy-Ninth Session (New York, 12–16 February 2024)' (2024), available at https://docs.un.org/en/A/CN.9/1166

UNCITRAL, 'Homepage' (2024), available at https://uncitral.un.org/en/content/homepage

UNCITRAL, 'Member States History' (2024), available at https://uncitral.un.org/en/about/faq/mandate_composition/memberhistory

UNCITRAL, 'Origin, Mandate and Composition of UNCITRAL' (2024), available at https://uncitral.un.org/en/about/faq/mandate_composition

UNCITRAL, 'Overview of the Status of UNCITRAL Conventions and Model Laws' (2024), available at https://uncitral.un.org/sites/uncitral.un.org/files/media-documents/uncitral/en/overview-status-table.pdf

UNCITRAL, 'Status: Convention on the Recognition and Enforcement of Foreign Arbitral Awards (New York, 1958)' (n.d.), available at https://uncitral.un.org/en/texts/arbitration/conventions/foreign_arbitral_awards/status2

UNCITRAL, 'Status: UNCITRAL Model Law on Cross-Border Insolvency (1997)' (n.d.), available at https://uncitral.un.org/en/texts/insolvency/modellaw/cross-border_insolvency/status

UNCITRAL, 'Status: UNCITRAL Model Law on International Commercial Arbitration (1985), with amendments as adopted in 2006' (n.d.), available at https://uncitral.un.org/en/texts/arbitration/modellaw/commercial_arbitration/status

UNCITRAL, 'Status: United Nations Convention on Contracts for the International Carriage of Goods Wholly or Partly by Sea (New York, 2008) (the "Rotterdam Rules")' (n.d.), available at https://uncitral.un.org/en/texts/transportgoods/conventions/rotterdam_rules/status

UNCITRAL, 'Status: United Nations Convention on Contracts for the International Sale of Goods (Vienna, 1980) (CISG)' (n.d.), available at https://uncitral.un.org/en/texts/salegoods/conventions/sale_of_goods/cisg/status

UNCITRAL, 'Status: United Nations Convention on International Bills of Exchange and International Promissory Notes (New York, 1988)' (n.d.), available at https://uncitral.un.org/en/texts/payments/conventions/bills_of_exchange/status

UNCITRAL, 'Status: United Nations Convention on the Carriage of Goods by Sea (Hamburg, 1978) (the "Hamburg Rules")' (n.d.), available at https://uncitral.un.org/en/texts/transportgoods/conventions/hamburg_rules/status

UNCITRAL, 'UNCITRAL Model Law on Cross-Border Insolvency (1997)' (n.d.), available at https://uncitral.un.org/en/texts/insolvency/modellaw/cross-border_insolvency

UNCITRAL, 'UNCITRAL Model Law on Recognition and Enforcement of Insolvency-Related Judgments (2018)' (n.d.), available at https://uncitral.un.org/en/texts/insolvency/modellaw/mlij

UNCTAD, 'International Investment Agreements Navigator: Cambodia' (n.d.), available at https://investmentpolicy.unctad.org/international-investment-agreements/countries/33/cambodia

UNCTAD, 'International Investment Agreements Navigator' (n.d.), available at https://investmentpolicy.unctad.org/international-investment-agreements

UNCTAD, 'Investment Policy Hub: Mapping of IIA Clauses' (n.d.), available at https://investmentpolicy.unctad.org/pages/1031/mapping-of-iia-clauses

UNHCR, 'Convention on Legal Aid and Legal Relations in Civil, Family and Criminal Cases, Adopted in Minsk on 22 January 1993 (The Minsk Convention)' (n.d.), available at www.unhcr.org/protection/migration/4de4edc69/convention-legal-aid-legal-relations-civil-family-criminal-cases-adopted.html

UNHCR, 'States Parties to the 1951 Convention Relating to the Status of Refugees and the 1967 Protocol' (n.d.) available at www.unhcr.org/media/states-parties-1951-convention-and-its-1967-protocol

UNIDROIT, 'About UNIDROIT: Overview' (2021), available at www.unidroit.org/about-unidroit/overview/

UNIDROIT, 'About UNIDROIT' (2021), available at www.unidroit.org/about-unidroit/

UNIDROIT, 'Convention on International Interests in Mobile Equipment (Cape Town, 2001) – States Parties' (2021), available at www.unidroit.org/instruments/security-interests/cape-town-convention/states-parties/

UNIDROIT, 'Instruments' (2021), available at www.unidroit.org/instruments/

UNIDROIT, 'Membership' (2021), available at www.unidroit.org/about-unidroit/members-states-2/

UNIDROIT, 'Protocol to the Convention on International Interests in Mobile Equipment on Matters Specific to Aircraft Equipment – States Parties' (2021), available at www.unidroit.org/instruments/security-interests/aircraft-protocol/states-parties/

UNIDROIT, 'UNIDROIT Convention on Stolen or Illegally Exported Cultural Objects (Rome, 1995) – Status' (2021), available at www.unidroit.org/instruments/cultural-property/1995-convention/status/#

United Nations, 'Completed Peacekeeping Operations: UNTAC (February 1992 – September 1993)' (2003), available at https://peacekeeping.un.org/sites/default/files/past/untac.htm

United Nations, 'United Nations Convention on the Law of the Sea (Montego Bay, 10 December 1982): Status' (2024), available at https://treaties.un.org/Pages/ViewDetailsIII.aspx?src=TREATY&mtdsg_no=XXI-6&chapter=21&Temp=mtdsg3&clang=_en

United Nations, 'United Nations Treaty Collection: Convention for the Settlement of Certain Conflicts of Laws in Connection with Cheques (Geneva, 19 March 1931)' (n.d.), available at https://treaties.un.org/pages/LONViewDetails.aspx?src=LON&id=558&chapter=30&clang=_en

United Nations, 'United Nations Treaty Collection: Convention on the Contract for the International Carriage of Goods by Road (CMR)' (n.d.), available at https://treaties.un.org/Pages/ViewDetails.aspx?src=IND&mtdsg_no=XI-B-11&chapter=11&clang=_en

United Nations, 'United Nations Treaty Collection: Convention Providing a Uniform Law for Bills of Exchange and Promissory Notes (Geneva, 7 June 1930)' (n.d.), available at https://treaties.un.org/pages/LONViewDetails.aspx?src=LON&id=559&chapter=30&clang=_en

United Nations, 'United Nations Treaty Collection: Vienna Convention on the Law of Treaties' (2024), available at https://treaties.un.org/pages/ViewDetailsIII.aspx?src=TREATY&mtdsg_no=XXIII-1&chapter=23&Temp=mtdsg3&clang=_en

US Citizenship and Immigration Services, 'Adoption Information: Cambodia' (2013), available at www.uscis.gov/adoption/uscis-country-specific-processing/adoption-information-cambodia

US Department of Commerce, 'Cambodia Country Commercial Guide: Cambodia – Foreign Exchange Controls' (n.d.), available at www.privacyshield.gov/ps/article?id=Cambodia-foreign-exchange-controls#:~:text=Cambodia%20%2D%20Foreign%20Exchange%20ControlsCambodia%20%2D%20Foreign%20Exchange%20Controls&text=Under%20the%201997%20Foreign%20Exchange,all%20types%20of%20international%20settlements

US Department of State–Bureau of Consular Affairs, 'Intercountry Adoption News and Notices: Government of Cambodia Announcement on Intercountry Adoptions' (2021), available at travel.state.gov/content/travel/en/News/Intercountry-Adoption-News/government-of-cambodia-announcement-on-intercountry-adoptions-.html

van den Berg, AJ, 'The New York Convention of 1958: An Overview' (n.d.), 13, available at https://cdn.arbitration-icca.org/s3fs-public/document/media_document/media012125884227980new_york_convention_of_1958_overview.pdf

Vatsa, V, 'Rights of an Illegitimate Child' *Jus Corpus Law Journal* (24 June 2021), available at www.juscorpus.com/rights-of-an-illegitimate-child

Verma, M and Jain, S, 'Recognition of Insolvency Related Judgments: An Undetermined Sphere of International Insolvency', *KSLR Commercial & Financial Law Blog*, 18 September 2020, available at https://blogs.kcl.ac.uk/kslrcommerciallawblog/2020/09/18/recognition-of-insolvency-related-judgments-an-undetermined-sphere-of-international-insolvency-medhashree-verma-and-siddharth-jain/

Vida, T, '$2 Million Grant to Aid Kingdom's Labour Relations and Dispute Resolution', *Khmer Times*, 28 February 2020, available at www.khmertimeskh.com/696018/2-million-grant-to-aid-kingdoms-labour-relations-and-dispute-resolution/

Vida, T, 'Regional Appeal Courts Open on April 1', *Khmer Times*, 25 March 2020, available at www.khmertimeskh.com/50705314/regional-appeal-courts-open-on-april-1/

Vida, T, 'Sweden Contributes to Arbitration Council', *Khmer Times*, 7 March 2019, available at www.khmertimeskh.com/50584566/sweden-contributes-to-arbitration-council/

Vireak, T, 'Cambodia Continues Intellectual Property Cooperation with EU', *The Phnom Penh Post*, 28 January 2020, available at www.phnompenhpost.com/business/cambodia-continues-intellectual-property-cooperation-eu

von Hein, J, 'Von Hein on Rome II and Defamation', *Conflict of Laws.net*, 19 July 2010, available at https://conflictoflaws.net/2010/von-hein-on-rome-ii-and-defamation/

Welsh, J, 'Int'l Adoptions of Local Children Double in 2006' *The Cambodian Daily*, 5 March 2007, available at https://english.cambodiadaily.com/news/intl-adoptions-of-local-children-double-in-2006-73458/

Wilwohl, J, '40 Years After KR Victory, Has Cambodia Dealt With Its Past?', *The Cambodia Daily*, 18 April 2015, available at https://english.cambodiadaily.com/news/40-years-after-kr-victory-has-cambodia-dealt-with-its-past-82106/

WIPO, 'Cambodia Joins Berne Convention', *News*, 3 April 2023, available at www.wipo.int/about-wipo/en/dg_tang/news/2021/news_0069.html

WIPO, 'Cambodia KH001: Law Concerning Marks, Trade Names and Acts of Unfair Competition' (n.d.), available at www.wipo.int/wipolex/en/text/567456

WIPO, 'Contracting Parties: Paris Convention (Total Members: 180)' (n.d.), available at www.wipo.int/wipolex/en/treaties/ShowResults?search_what=C&treaty_id=2

WIPO, 'Lisbon Agreement for the Protection of Appellations of Origin and their International Registration: Status on July 11, 2024' (2024) available at www.wipo.int/export/sites/www/treaties/en/docs/pdf/lisbon.pdf

WIPO, 'Madrid Agreement Concerning the International Registration of Marks and Protocol Relating to the Madrid Agreement Concerning the International Registration of Marks: Status on May 3, 2024' (2024) available at www.wipo.int/export/sites/www/treaties/en/docs/pdf/madrid_marks.pdf

WIPO, 'Members: Cambodia' (n.d.), available at www.wipo.int/members/en/details.jsp?country_code=KH

WIPO, 'Cambodia Joins Berne Convention', *News*, 3 April 2023, available at www.wipo.int/about-wipo/en/dg_tang/news/2021/news_0069.html

Woodside, A and David, S, 'Gov't Looks to 2014 for Adoptions' *The Phnom Penh Post*, 5 December 2013, available at www.phnompenhpost.com/national/gov%E2%80%99t-looks-2014-adoptions

World Bank, 'Data: Foreign Direct Investment, Net Inflows (% of GDP) – Cambodia' (2024), available at https://data.worldbank.org/indicator/BX.KLT.DINV.WD.GD.ZS?locations=KH

World Bank, 'Foreign Direct Investment, Net Inflows (BoP, Current US$) – Cambodia' (2024), available at https://data.worldbank.org/indicator/BX.KLT.DINV.CD.WD?locations=KH

World Justice Project, 'WJP Rule of Law Index®' (2024), available at https://worldjusticeproject.org/rule-of-law-index/global

WTO, 'Member Information: Cambodia and the WTO' (n.d.), available at www.wto.org/english/thewto_e/countries_e/cambodia_e.htm

Zhang, L, 'Cambodia's Legal Education', *In Custodia Legis: Law Librarians of Congress*, 20 October 2021, available at https://blogs.loc.gov/law/2021/10/cambodias-legal-education/?loclr=bloglaw#:~:text=Currently%2C%20legal%20education%20in%20Cambodia,only%20a%20few%20public%20universities

INDEX